R. Carroll

Exploring Literature

by Ann Chatterton Klimas

PEARSON

AGS Globe

Shoreview, MN

About the Author

Ann Chatterton Klimas has spent more than 25 years developing educational materials for both traditional and electronic media. She received her Bachelor of Arts from Mary Washington College of the University of Virginia and Master of Arts from The John Hopkins University. As a teacher, Ms. Klimas has worked with students of all levels, teaching language arts and history, broadcast journalism, and screenwriting. She has written textbooks and instructional materials for a variety of media, including public and commercial broadcast television. In her current position with Maryland Public Television, Ms. Klimas is the chief information architect of content writer for an extensive series of interactive Internet experiences for students, teachers, and families. She has also written and guided other writers in the development of several award-winning educational television series.

Acknowledgments appear on pages 572–574, which constitutes an extension of this copyright page.

Literature Consultant

Jack Cassidy, Ph.D., Associate Dean, College of Education and Professor of Curriculum and Instruction, Texas A & M University—Corpus Christi, Corpus Christi, Texas

The publisher wishes to thank the following educators for their helpful comments during the review process for *Exploring Literature*. Their assistance has been invaluable.

Beth Christensen, English Teacher, Dakota Meadows Middle School, North Mankato, MN; **Victoria F. Dunn,** Special Education Director, Southwest High School, Houston, TX; **Kathy Ferguson,** Instructional Support Teacher, Secondary Campuses, San Antonio, TX; **Sandra M. Hammerbeck,** Language Arts Teacher, Centennial Middle School, Lino Lakes, MN; **Nora Kennedy,** Special Education Reading Teacher, Lakeside High School, Atlanta, GA; **Patrick Lowrey,** Special Education Teacher, Harrison High School, Lafayette, IN; **Wendy Mason,** Special Education Teacher, Magnolia High School, Anaheim, CA; **Shannan M. Matthews,** Special Education Literature/Composition Teacher, Columbia High School, Decatur, GA; **Frank S. Santa Maria,** Language Arts Department Chair, Murdock Middle School, Port Charlotte, FL; **Thomas G. Smith,** Teacher, Facilitator/Inter-Disciplinary Studies, Thomas Snell Weaver High School, Hartford, CT

Publisher's Project Staff

Vice President of Curriculum and Publisher: Sari Follansbee, Ed.D.; Director of Curriculum Development: Teri Mathews; Managing Editor: Patrick Keithahn; Editor: Karen Anderson; Development Assistant: Bev Johnson; Director of Creative Services: Nancy Condon; Project Coordinator/Designer: Jen Willman; Senior Buyer: Mary Kaye Kuzma; Product Manager—Curriculum: Brian Holl

ISBN 0-7854-4075-5

5 6 7 8 9   V051   14 13 12 11 10

1-800-328-2560
www.agsglobe.com

Contents

How to Use This Book: A Study Guide

This book is an anthology of literature. An anthology is a collection of literature written by different authors. The literature can be poems, plays, short stories, essays, parts of novels, folktales, legends, or myths. Sometimes an anthology contains selections from a certain country or continent. For example, you might have an anthology with great literature from America. Sometimes anthologies are organized around different genres, or types of literature. Then, you might have sections on poems, short stories, plays, essays, or folktales.

Reading a Literature Anthology

This anthology contains much enjoyable literature. An anthology helps you understand yourself and other people. Sometimes you will read about people from other countries. Sometimes you will read about people who lived in the past. Try to relate what the author is saying to your own life. Ask yourself: Have I ever felt this way? Have I known anyone like this person? Have I seen anything like this?

A literature anthology can also help you appreciate the beauty of language. As you read, find phrases or sentences that you particularly like. You may want to start a notebook of these phrases and sentences. You may also want to include words that are difficult.

This anthology is also important because it introduces you to great works of literature. Many times, you will find references to these works in everyday life. Sometimes you will hear a quotation on TV or read it in the newspaper. Great literature can come in many forms. On the next page are definitions of some kinds of literature genres in an anthology.

Genre Definitions

autobiography a person's life story, written by that person

biography a person's life story told by someone else (you will find biographies of many famous authors in this book)

diary a daily record of personal events, thoughts, or private feelings
- A diary is like a journal, but a diary often expresses more of the writer's feelings.

drama a story told through the words and actions of characters, written to be performed as well as read; a play

essay a written work that shows a writer's opinions on some basic or current issue

fable a short story or poem with a moral (lesson about life), often with animals who act like humans
- Aesop was a famous author of fables.

fiction writing that is imaginative and designed to entertain
- In fiction, the author creates the events and characters.
- Short stories, novels, folktales, myths, legends, and most plays are works of fiction.

folktale a story that has been handed down from one generation to another
- The characters are usually either good or bad.
- Folktales make use of rhyme and repetitive phrases.
- Sometimes they are called tall tales, particularly if they are humorous and exaggerated.
- Folktales are also called folklore.

journal writing that expresses an author's feelings or first impressions about a subject
- Students may keep journals that record thoughts about what they have read.
- People also keep travel journals to remind themselves of interesting places they have seen.

legend a traditional story that at one time was told orally and was handed down from one generation to another
- Legends are like myths, but they do not have as many supernatural forces.
- Legends usually feature characters who actually lived, or real places or events.

myth an important story, often part of a culture's religion, that explains how the world came to be or why natural events happen
- A myth usually includes gods, goddesses, or unusually powerful human beings.
- Myths were first oral stories, and most early cultures have myths.

nonfiction writing about real people and events
- Essays, speeches, diaries, journals, autobiographies, and biographies are all usually nonfiction.

novel fiction that is book-length and has more plot and character details than a short story

poem a short piece of literature that usually has rhythm and paints powerful or beautiful impressions with words
- Often, poems have sound patterns such as rhyme.
- Songs are poetry set to music.

prose all writing that is not poetry
- short stories, novels, autobiographies, biographies, diaries, journals, and essays are examples of prose.

science fiction fiction that is based on real or imagined facts of science
- Most stories are set in the future.
- Jules Verne was one of the first science fiction authors.

short story a brief work of prose fiction that includes plot, setting, characters, point of view, and theme
- Edgar Allan Poe was a great writer of short stories.

How to Read This Book

Different works of literature should be read in different ways. However, there are some basic methods you should use to read all works of literature.

Before Beginning a Unit

- Read the unit title and selection titles.
- Read the paragraphs that introduce the unit.
- Look at the pictures and other artwork in the unit.
- Think about what you already know about the unit.
- Think about what you might want to learn.
- Develop questions in your mind that you think will be answered in this unit.

Before Reading a Selection

- Read the selection's title.
- Look at the pictures and other artwork.
- Read the background material included in About the Author and About the Selection.
- Read the Objectives and think about what you will learn by reading the selection.

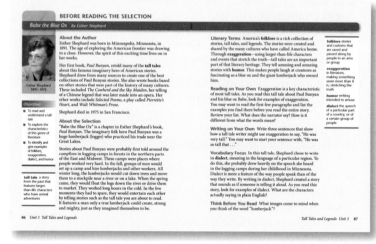

- Read the Literary Terms and their definitions.
- Complete the Before Reading the Selection activities. These activities will help you read the selection, understand vocabulary, and prepare for the reading.

As You Read a Selection

- Read the notes in the side margins. These will help you understand and think about the main ideas.

- Think of people or events in your own life that are similar to those described.

- Reread sentences or paragraphs that you do not understand.

- Predict what you think will happen next.

- Read the definitions at the bottom of the page for words that you do not know.

- Record words that you do not know. Also, write questions or comments you have about the text.

After Reading a Selection

- Reread interesting or difficult parts of the selection.

- Reflect on what you have learned by reading the selection.

- Complete the After Reading the Selection review questions and activities. The activities will help you develop your grammar, writing, speaking, listening, viewing, technology, media, and research skills.

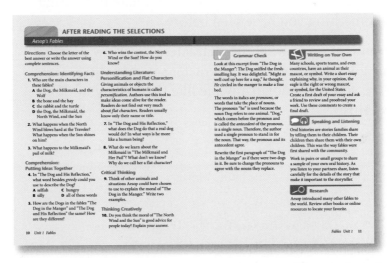

Reading Certain Types of Literature

The methods already described will help you understand all kinds of literature. You may need to use additional methods for specific types of literature.

Reading Poetry

- Read the poem aloud.

- Listen to the sounds of the words.

- Picture the images the author is describing.

- Reread poems over and over again to appreciate the author's use of language.

Reading Essays

- Review the questions in the After Reading the Selection before you begin reading.

- Use the questions to think about what you are reading.

- Remember that essays usually express an author's opinions. Try to understand why the author may have formed these opinions.

Reading Plays

- Picture the setting of the play. Since there usually is not much description given, try to relate the setting to something you have seen before.

- Pay attention to what the characters say. How does this give clues about the character's personality? Have you ever known anyone like this? Are you like this?

Tips for Better Reading

Literary Terms

Literary Terms are words or phrases that we use to study and discuss works of literature. These terms describe the ways an author helps to make us enjoy and understand what we are reading. Some of the terms also describe a genre, or specific type of literature. In this anthology, you will see white boxes on the side of the Before Reading the Selection pages. In these boxes are Literary Terms and their definitions. These terms are important in understanding and discussing the selection being read. By understanding these Literary Terms, readers can appreciate the author's craft. You can find the definitions for all of the Literary Terms used in this book in the Handbook of Literary Terms on page 539.

setting the place and time in a story

plot the series of events in a story

theme the main idea of a literary work

Using a Graphic Organizer

A graphic organizer is visual representation of information. It can help you see how ideas are related to each other. A graphic organizer can help you study for a test, organize information before writing an essay, or organize details in a literature selection. You will use graphic organizers for different activities throughout this textbook. There are 14 different graphic organizers listed below. You can read a description and see an example of each graphic organizer in Appendix A in the back of this textbook.

- Character Analysis Guide
- Story Map
- Main Idea Graphic (Umbrella)
- Main Idea Graphic (Table)
- Main Idea Graphic (Details)
- Venn Diagram
- Sequence Chain

- Concept Map
- Plot Mountain
- Structured Overview
- Semantic Table
- Prediction Guide
- Semantic Line
- KWL Chart

Taking Notes

You will read many selections in this literature anthology. As you read, you may want to take notes to help remember what you have read. You can use these notes to keep track of events and characters in a story. Your notes may also be helpful for recognizing common ideas among the selections in a unit. You can review your notes as you prepare to take a test. Here are some tips for taking notes:

■ Write down only the most important information.

■ Do not try to write every detail or every word.

■ Write notes in your own words.

■ Do not be concerned about writing in complete sentences. Use short phrases.

Using the Three-Column Chart

One good way to take notes is to use a three-column chart. Make your own three-column chart by dividing a sheet of notebook paper into three equal parts. In Column 1, write the topic you are reading about or studying. In Column 2, write what you learned about this topic as you read or listened to your teacher. In Column 3, write questions, observations, or opinions about the topic, or write a detail that will help you remember the topic. Here are some examples of different ways to take notes using the three-column chart.

The topic I am studying	What I learned from reading the text or class discussion	Questions, observations, or ideas I have about the topic
Fiction	• one genre of literature • many different types of fiction—science fiction, adventure, detective stories, romance, suspense	• The book I am reading right now is fiction. It is an adventure story. • I wonder if poetry is part of the fiction genre.

Vocabulary Word	Definition	Sentence with Vocabulary Word
Premises	a building or part of a building	Students are not allowed on the school **premises** during the weekend.

Literary Term	Definition	Example from Selection
Exaggeration	a use of words to make something seem more than it is; stretching the truth to a great extent	He was exactly five feet six inches in height, and six feet five inches in circumference. His head was a perfect sphere . . . . (Wouter Van Twiller)

Character	Character Traits Found in the Selection	Page Number
John Krakauer	Conflict, person against self—Krakauer wonders if he will run out of oxygen before returning to camp.	p. 355
	Determined—Krakauer is determined to make it back to camp even though his oxygen has run out and it is snowing on the mountain.	p. 358
	Thankful—After reaching camp, Krakauer is thankful that he is safe.	p. 360

Stage of Plot	Example from Text	Questions, Observations, and Ideas
Rising Action	"And how easy it would be to kill him. And he deserves it. Does he? No! What the devil!... I could cut his throat—*zip, zip!* I wouldn't give him time to resist. . . ." (p. 104)	This is a good example of rising action because it introduces the conflict of the story.

What to Do About Words You Do Not Know

- If the word is in **bold type,** look for the definition of the word at the bottom of the page.

- If the word is not in bold type, read to the end of the sentence and maybe the next sentence. Can you determine the meaning now?

- Look at the beginning sound of the unknown word. Ask yourself, "What word begins with this sound and would make sense here?"

- Sound out the syllables of the word.

- If you still cannot determine the meaning, see if you know any parts of the word: prefixes, suffixes, or roots.

- If this does not work, write the word on a note card or in a vocabulary notebook. Then look up the word in a dictionary after you have finished reading the selection. Reread the passage containing the unknown word after you have looked up its definition.

- If the word is necessary to understand the passage, look it up in a dictionary or glossary immediately.

Word Study Tips

- Start a vocabulary file with note cards to use for review.

- Write one word on the front of each card. Write the unit number, selection title, and the definition on the back.

- You can use these cards as flash cards by yourself or with a study partner to test your knowledge.

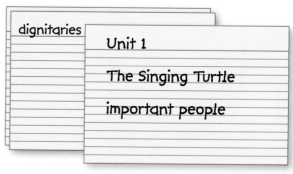

dignitaries

Unit 1

The Singing Turtle

important people

Before the Test Day

- Make sure you have read all of the selections assigned.

- Review the Literary Terms and definitions for each selection.

- Review your answers to the After Reading the Selection questions.

- Reread the Unit Summary and review your answers to the Unit Review.

- Review any notes that you have taken or graphic organizers you have developed.

- Ask your teacher what kinds of questions will be on the test.

- Try to predict what questions will be asked. Think of and write answers to those questions.

- Review the Test-Taking Tip at the bottom of each Unit Review page.

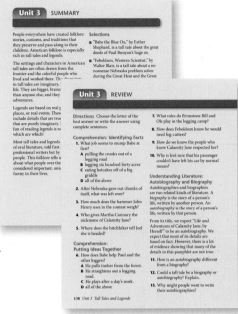

During the Test

- Come to the test with a positive attitude.

- Write your name on the paper.

- Preview the test and read the directions carefully.

- Plan your time.

- Answer the questions that you know first.

- Then go back and answer the more difficult questions.

- Allow time to reread all of the questions and your answers.

Water Baby and the Moon
Jessie Willcox Smith, 1916

Unit 1 | Fables

Fables are one of the oldest forms of stories. Since the time of Aesop, who probably lived between 600 and 500 B.C., people have told, written, and passed along fables. One reason fables have remained popular is that they teach truths about human life that never go out of style. They teach these truths using colorful characters and amusing events that people have always enjoyed.

In this unit, you will read fables from several cultures and from different periods in history.

"Storytelling is the oldest form of education."

—Terry Tempest Williams, *Pieces of White Shell*, 1984

Unit 1

About Fables

As long as there have been people, there have been stories. People create stories to entertain themselves, to pass the time, or to help them remember. They tell stories to explain the world around them.

Some stories, called fables, try to teach people something about life. Fables are one of the oldest *genres,* or types, of stories. Some of the fables we still read and tell each other today are more than 2,000 years old. Many of these come from the ancient Greek storyteller Aesop.

Fables are fictional stories. This means they are made up, or invented. However, fables usually tell truths that all people can recognize. This is one reason that people today still enjoy reading and hearing this genre of stories.

Fables share some other characteristics:

■ Many fables were not written down at first. They were told out loud. Long ago, most people did not know how to read and write. Instead, they handed stories down to their children and others by telling the stories over and over again.

■ Fables are usually short and simple. They tell an entire story in a few paragraphs. Fables have characters and plots, just as other, longer stories do.

In fables, though, the characters are not fully described. The plot—or what happens in the story—does not take long to unfold.

■ The characters in fables are often animals who act like people. They speak to each other as people would. They care about the things people value. For example, in the fable "The Fox and the Grapes," the fox decides that some grapes that are growing too high for him to reach are probably sour anyway. Even if he could reach them, he would not want to eat them. We know that a fox would not think this way. But we probably have heard people say, "Well, I didn't want it anyway," about something they really wanted very much. Giving animals or objects the characteristics of humans is called *personification.*

■ Fables do not spend much time describing what characters look like or how they behave. Instead, they depend on what we already know about such characters. For example, we know what an owl looks like. We usually think of owls as wise creatures. When we read about an owl in a fable, we expect the owl to behave wisely.

"The Fox and the Grapes,"
from Aesop's Fables.
Engraving by Herrick, 1879.

The characters in fables are called *flat characters*. We don't find out much about them. They do not change or develop the way characters do in other kinds of stories.

■ Fables usually teach a lesson about life. This lesson is called a *moral*. For example, in the fable "The Mouse and the Lion," the lion spares the mouse's life when the mouse pleads with him. She tells him that she will surely repay his kindness some day. Even though the lion doubts what the mouse says, he decides to let her go. Later, the mouse saves the lion by chewing away the nets in which he has become tangled. The moral of the story, or its message about life, is that both strong and weak creatures need each other.

Each fable in this unit has a moral. The first four are from Aesop: "The Dog in the Manger," "The Dog and His Reflection," "The North Wind and the Sun," and "The Milkmaid and Her Pail." The next three fables come from different cultures. "The King and the Shirt" is adapted from a fable written by the great Russian author Leo Tolstoy. "How the Fly Saved the River" is an Ojibwa fable. "The Singing Turtle" is a fable from Haiti.

BEFORE READING THE SELECTIONS

About the Author

Many people have heard the story about the famous race between the tortoise and the hare. The slower tortoise—or turtle—crosses the finish line before the hare—or rabbit—who is faster. The tortoise was slow but steady. This unexpected win shows us that, no matter what, we all have a chance to win the race.

This story is one of the **fables** introduced to the world by the Greek slave Aesop. A fable is a story that teaches a lesson about life. We know very little about Aesop, except that he was born between 600 and 500 B.C. Aesop himself never wrote down his fables, but he told them to many people. Hundreds of years after Aesop died, his fables were collected in books and translated into many languages.

Some people think that Aesop did not actually create these fables, but simply retold old stories he had heard. We may never know whether this is true.

About the Selections

"The Dog in the Manger" and "The Dog and His Reflection" are two of Aesop's fables. Each story has a dog that thinks, speaks, and behaves like a human being. Both dogs are greedy and lose something because of their selfishness.

"The North Wind and the Sun" and "The Milkmaid and Her Pail" are two more of Aesop's fables. Aesop uses people in these two fables—a traveler and a milkmaid. A milkmaid is a person who milks cows. Both the North Wind and the Sun behave like people who are having an argument.

Literary Terms **Characters** are the people or animals in a story. In fables, few details about the characters are presented. We know them only by their names or their titles. These characters are **flat characters**. These characters do not change, no matter what happens in the **plot** or the events in the fable. The author chooses them simply to illustrate the **moral** or lesson of the fable. By using **personification,** authors present animal characters in such a way that they seem to be human. Authors also choose animal characters that might have a deeper meaning to the people who read the fables. For example, people expect that a tortoise will be slow. People reading the fable know that the tortoise is a **symbol** of slowness.

Reading on Your Own As you read the first two fables, think about their plots. How are they similar? How are they different? Use a Venn Diagram, described in Appendix A, to help you track the plots as you read.

Writing on Your Own What are some lessons about life, or morals, that you think should be included in a modern-day fable? Write two paragraphs that explain why these lessons are important ones for people to learn today.

Vocabulary Focus **Idioms** are expressions that do not mean what the words say. For example, if people say "you can catch more flies with honey than with vinegar," they are not talking about flies. They are saying you can accomplish more by being nice. As you read the fables, look for these kinds of idioms. What do the words say? What does the expression actually mean?

Think Before You Read What is the difference between a fable and a news report? Think about the purpose for each and the way each is written.

character
a person or animal in a story, poem, or play

flat character
a character that is based on a single trait or quality and is not well developed

plot the series of events in a story

moral a lesson or message about life told in a story

personification giving characters such as animals or objects the characteristics or qualities of humans

symbol something that represents something else

idiom a phrase that has a different meaning than its words really mean

Birddog II, **Diana Ong**

The Dog in the Manger

The Farmer had just finished filling the manger with soft, dry hay when the Dog came by. The Dog sniffed the fresh-smelling hay. It was delightful. "Might as well curl up here for a nap," he thought. He circled in the manger to make a fine bed. Then he settled down, tucking his nose under his tail. Before long, he was asleep.

The Cattle came into the barn after working all day in the field. They were tired and hungry. When they smelled the new hay, they moved quickly toward the manger.

Their noise woke up the Dog. He sprang up and began to bark loudly. "How dare you lowly creatures try to eat my bed," he snarled. He would not let them come anywhere near the manger.

The Cattle looked at the Dog with disgust. "How selfish he is," said the oldest Cow. "Everyone knows that Cattle—not dogs—eat hay. A bone or some juicy meat is much more to his liking. But will he let us near the manger? Not him! How could such a thing happen?" The other Cattle lowed hungrily in agreement.

The Farmer heard the Cattle. He hurried into the barn. When he saw what the Dog was doing, he took a stick and chased him out. The Cattle then enjoyed their dinner of fresh hay for which they had worked so hard.

Do not keep others from enjoying something you cannot enjoy yourself.

As you read, look for the characters in this fable.

A *manger* is an open box that holds feed for farm animals.

What is another way to state the moral of this fable, in your own words?

The Dog and His Reflection

The Dog took his daily stroll through the town. As he passed the shops, the butcher threw him a bone. The Dog hurried off, holding his tasty prize firmly in his jaw.

As he crossed a narrow bridge over the river, he happened to look down. To his surprise, he saw another dog looking up at him from beneath the water. The dog in the water had an even bigger bone than he did. The Dog thought, "That dog down there is really not so big. Surely I can take that bone away from him. Then I will have two fine bones to enjoy tonight."

The Dog quickly dropped his bone into the water and jumped off the bridge. But suddenly, things seemed to go all wrong. The water was much deeper than it looked. There was no dog in the water. Worse than that, there was no bone.

The Dog was dismayed. He swam slowly to the shore and dragged himself out of the river. He never saw his bone again.

Being greedy is very foolish.

As you read, look for the characteristics that make this story a fable.

Here the Dog is thinking as a human being would. This is an example of personification.

Dog with Bone and its Reflection in a Pool,
artist unknown

Man Protecting Himself from the Weather, Kim LaFave

The North Wind and the Sun

The North Wind and the Sun were quarreling. Each one thought she was stronger than the other. The Sun said her warm rays were much more powerful than the North Wind's icy blasts. The North Wind said this was nonsense.

As the two argued, a Traveler came along, wearing a heavy, long, gray overcoat. As he passed, the North Wind and the Sun stopped for a moment.

"Our arguing is senseless. There is only one way to settle this—a contest," said the Sun.

"Fine with me," the North Wind blasted back. "What do you have in mind?"

"Do you see the Traveler over there, the one with the huge coat? The first one that can make him take it off is surely the strongest."

"Agreed," said the North Wind. "It will be simple." At once, she drew in her breath and aimed an icy blast of wind at the Traveler. The wind pushed at the edges of his coat and they fluttered wildly. The Traveler immediately buttoned up his coat and turned up the collar. The North Wind tried even harder. Her gusts became even colder and stronger. But, the colder the wind, the tighter the Traveler held onto the coat.

Then it was the Sun's turn. At first, her beams were very gentle. The Traveler looked up with relief. It was a pleasure to feel the Sun's warmth after the freezing gales of the North Wind. He turned down his collar. The Sun's rays grew warmer. The Traveler unbuttoned the coat. He was beginning to feel uncomfortably warm. Finally, he could not stand it any longer. He shed his coat and sat under a shady tree to cool off.

You can catch more flies with honey than with vinegar.

As you read, note the plot, or series of events, in the story.

Why might the North Wind be a symbol of anger and harshness?

Who wins the contest?

This moral is an *idiom*.

The Milkmaid and Her Pail

**Woman with Pitcher,
Rufino Tamayo**

The Milkmaid had just finished milking her cows. Her pail was full of fresh milk. She placed the heavy container carefully on her head, and began to walk back to her home. As she walked, she began to think to herself.

"This is fine, rich milk," she thought. "The cows must have been eating well. Their milk has plenty of cream in it. It will be easy to churn it into golden butter. People at the market will surely buy it all. With the money I get, I will buy many eggs to hatch. Won't the yard look pretty with all the little yellow chicks pecking at the ground? When the spring comes, the chicks will be big enough to sell. With the money I get from that, I will buy a lovely dress to wear to the fair. Everyone will see how beautiful I am. Every man there will want me to be his wife. But that is not how I want to live my life. I will just turn my head and tell them to go away."

When she thought this, she turned her head quickly—to show those men what she thought of them. The pail of milk toppled down. The rich milk quickly disappeared into the soil. With the spilt milk went her dreams of the butter and the chicks and the dress and the men—and the Milkmaid's pride.

Do not count your chickens before they hatch.

As you read, decide why the Milkmaid is a flat character.

In this paragraph, the Milkmaid dreams of her bright future. What is the first thing that must happen if her dreams are to come true?

Why does the Milkmaid's pride disappear with the milk?

The moral of this fable is an idiom. It means, "Don't count on things happening before they do."

Aesop's Fables

Directions Choose the letter of the best answer or write the answer using complete sentences.

Comprehension: Identifying Facts

1. Who are the main characters in these fables?
   A the Dog, the Milkmaid, and the Wolf
   B the bone and the hay
   C the rabbit and the turtle
   D the Dog, the Milkmaid, the North Wind, and the Sun

2. What happens when the North Wind blows hard at the Traveler? What happens when the Sun shines on him? He Puts his Coat an.

3. What happens to the Milkmaid's pail of milk? It Spiled

Comprehension: Putting Ideas Together

4. In "The Dog and His Reflection," what word besides *greedy* could you use to describe the Dog?
   A selfish   C hungry
   B silly   D all of these words

5. How are the Dogs in the fables "The Dog in the Manger" and "The Dog and His Reflection" the same? How are they different? They Both are selfish

6. Who wins the contest, the North Wind or the Sun? How do you know?

Understanding Literature: Personification and Flat Characters

Giving animals or objects the characteristics of humans is called *personification*. Authors use this tool to make ideas come alive for the reader. Readers do not find out very much about *flat characters*. Readers usually know only their name or title.

7. In "The Dog and His Reflection," what does the Dog do that a real dog would do? In what ways is he more like a human being?

8. What do we learn about the Milkmaid in "The Milkmaid and Her Pail"? What don't we know? Why do we call her a flat character? the milk maid wants a bress, she is only happy

Critical Thinking

9. Think of other animals and situations Aesop could have chosen to use to explain the moral of "The Dog in the Manger." Write two examples. A baby cow, monkey cat.

Thinking Creatively

10. Do you think the moral of "The North Wind and the Sun" is good advice for people today? Explain your answer. yes. Because it means you should stop

Grammar Check

Look at this excerpt from "The Dog in the Manger": The Dog sniffed the fresh-smelling hay. It was delightful. "Might as well curl up here for a nap," *he* thought. *He* circled in the manger to make a fine bed.

The words in italics are *pronouns*, or words that take the place of nouns. The pronoun "he" is used because the noun Dog refers to one animal. "Dog," which comes before the pronoun and is called the *antecedent* of the pronoun, is a single noun. Therefore, the author used a single pronoun to stand in for the noun. That way, the pronoun and its antecedent agree.

Rewrite the first paragraph of "The Dog in the Manger" as if there were two dogs in it. Be sure to change the pronouns to agree with the nouns they replace.

 ## Writing on Your Own

Many schools, sports teams, and even countries, have an animal as their mascot, or symbol. Write a short essay explaining why, in your opinion, the eagle is the right or wrong mascot, or symbol, for the United States. Create a first draft of your essay and ask a friend to review and proofread your work. Use these comments to create a final draft.

 ## Speaking and Listening

Oral histories are stories families share by telling them to their children. Their children then share them with their own children. This was the way fables were first shared with the community.

Work in pairs or small groups to share a sample of your own oral history. As you listen to your partners share, listen carefully for the details of the story that make it important to the storyteller.

 ## Research

Aesop introduced many other fables to the world. Review other books or online resources to locate your favorite.

More Fables   *by Leo Tolstoy and Ojibwa Fable*

Leo Tolstoy
1828–1910

About the Authors and Selections

Through the years, many well-known authors have created fables of their own. Leo Tolstoy, the famous Russian writer, is one of them. Tolstoy, who was born in 1828, is best known for his novels *Anna Karenina* and *War and Peace.*

Tolstoy decided that people could make their lives worthwhile only by living simply and serving others. By 1890, he had sold all his property and become a vegetarian. He decided to give up the copyrights on his writing. He continued to look for ways to lead a more pure and worthwhile life until he died in 1910.

"The King and the Shirt" is very much like the fables of Aesop. It has a simple plot, tells us a message about life, and features flat characters. The main characters in Tolstoy's fable are people, not animals. Tolstoy does not sum up the message of his fable by stating its moral, but the fable suggests a moral even so. This fable has a surprise ending.

Many cultures teach important lessons in their fables. The Ojibwa tale "How the Fly Saved the River" is one of these. The Ojibwa are native people who live mainly in southern Canada and northern states such as Michigan and Minnesota. The Ojibwa were originally hunters and fishers. Today, some Ojibwa continue to hunt and fish, but many have other jobs as well. They still continue to give their children important messages about life through fables such as "How the Fly Saved the River." This story tells that mental strength can be much more important than physical strength.

Literary Terms In literature, **irony** happens when the reader expects a certain event and a different, or opposite, event occurs. For example, in "The King and the Shirt," the king's messengers expect to find the shirt of a happy man, and so do the readers. The irony is that the only happy man they can find does not even own a shirt. When people talk about the **hero** of a story or novel, they are talking about the main character. The main character is the one that is most important to the story. Heroes in literature can be brave like the heroes in everyday life. However, they do not have to be.

Reading on Your Own Authors have a purpose, or reason, for creating their stories. They want to give their readers information, entertain them, or convince them to do something. Sometimes, they want do all three things. You can sometimes find a hint about the **author's purpose** in the title they have chosen for their work. Based on the titles they chose, what are the purposes for which these authors wrote their fables?

Writing on Your Own Based on what you have learned about the characteristics of fables, write two paragraphs about what you expect to see in these two fables.

Vocabulary Focus Verbs are action words that authors can use in a number of ways. Verbs can describe action ("All his wise men *gathered* together . . .") Verbs can also describe a state of being ("there *was* a beautiful river.") As you read these fables, look for verbs the author uses to create a particularly interesting picture.

Think Before You Read Based on their titles, which fable do you think you will like best?

irony the difference between what is expected to happen in a story and what does happen

hero the leading character in a story, novel, play, or film

author's purpose the reason(s) for which the author writes

The King and the Shirt

As you read, look for examples of irony.

A king once fell ill.

"I will give half my kingdom to the man who can cure me," he said.

All his wise men gathered together to decide how the king could be cured. But no one knew. Only one of the wise men said what he thought would cure the king.

"If you can find a happy man, take his shirt, put it on the king—and the king will be cured."

The king sent his **emissaries** to search for a happy man. They traveled far and wide, but they could not find a happy man. There was no one who was completely satisfied. If a man was rich, he was ailing; if he was healthy, he was poor. If he was rich and healthy, he had an unhappy marriage; or if he had children, they were sick. Everyone had something to complain of.

Do you think it is true that people always find something to complain about? Do you know anyone you would call truly happy?

Finally, late one night, the king's son was passing by a poor little hut and he heard someone say:

"Now God be praised. I have finished my work. I have eaten my fill, and I can lie down and sleep. What more could I want?"

What would you say is the moral of this fable?

The king's son rejoiced and gave orders that the man's shirt be taken and carried to the king, and that the man be given as much money as he wanted.

The emissaries went in to take off the man's shirt, but the happy man was so poor that he had no shirt.

emissaries people who are sent on a mission

How the Fly Saved the River

Many, many years ago when the world was new, there was a beautiful river. Fish in great numbers lived in this river, and its water was so pure and sweet that all the animals came there to drink.

A giant moose heard about the river and he too came there to drink. But he was so big, and he drank so much, that soon the water began to sink lower and lower.

The beavers were worried. The water around their lodges was disappearing. Soon their homes would be destroyed. The muskrats were worried, too. What would they do if the water vanished? How could they live? The fish were very worried. The other animals could live on land if the water dried up, but they couldn't.

All the animals tried to think of a way to drive the moose from the river, but he was so big that they were too afraid to try. Even the bear was afraid of him. At last the fly said he would try to drive the moose away. All the animals laughed and **jeered**. How could a tiny fly frighten a giant moose?

The fly said nothing, but that day, as soon as the moose appeared, he went into action. He landed on the moose's foreleg and bit sharply. The moose stamped his foot harder, and each time he stamped, the ground sank and the water rushed in to fill it up. Then the fly jumped about all over the moose, biting and biting and biting until the moose was in a **frenzy**. He dashed madly about the banks of the river, shaking his head, stamping his feet, snorting and blowing, but he couldn't get rid of that pesky fly.

At last the moose fled from the river, and didn't come back. The fly was very proud of his achievement, and boasted to the other animals, "Even the small can fight the strong if they use their brains to think."

jeered made fun of	frenzy a state of near madness

As you read, decide which character is the hero in this fable. Why do you think the author chose this hero? What do you think is the author's purpose?

15

More Fables   by Leo Tolstoy and Ojibwa Fable

Directions   Choose the letter of the best answer or write the answer using complete sentences.

Comprehension: Identifying Facts

1. In "The King and the Shirt," what does the wise man say will cure the king?

   A half the kingdom

   B the shirt from a happy man

   C to lie down and sleep

   D more emissaries

2. In "How the Fly Saved the River," what is the moose doing to the water in the river?

3. What does the fly do to drive away the moose?

Comprehension: Putting Ideas Together

4. Who is the hero in "The King and the Shirt"?

   A the poor man   **C** the emissaries

   B the king   **D** the wise men

5. In "How the Fly Saved the River," why don't the other animals believe the fly can help them?

6. Why is the poor man in "The King and the Shirt" so happy?

Understanding Literature: Irony and Hero

In these fables you have seen how writers use irony and create heroes to build strong and interesting stories. Writers use irony when they lead readers to expect something to happen, but then a different thing happens. Heroes are the main characters of stories, even if they do not do anything brave.

7. Would you say it is ironic that the king's messengers in "The King and the Shirt" have so much trouble finding a happy man? Why or why not?

8. Explain why the fly in "How the Fly Saved the River" could be considered the hero of the fable.

Critical Thinking

9. What is the moral of "The King and the Shirt"? Use examples to support your answer.

Thinking Creatively

10. Many cultures have stories with plots that are like the plot of "How the Fly Saved the River." Small or weak characters defeat large or strong characters by doing what they do best. Why do you think many writers have used this plot?

Grammar Check

Writers have several ways in which they can end a sentence. They choose the one that helps them make sense for their readers. When they are making statements, authors end their sentences with periods. This tells the reader they have completed their thought about a certain subject. For example, try to read this paragraph:

At last the fly said he would try to drive the moose away all the animals laughed and jeered how could a tiny fly frighten a giant moose the fly said nothing but that day as soon as the moose appeared he went into action

Why doesn't this make sense to you? Now reread this paragraph in the story. What is the difference?

 Writing on Your Own

Rewrite "The King and the Shirt" using animal characters instead of people. Be sure that your fable has the same plot as Tolstoy's fable does, suggests the same moral, and follows the characteristics of fables.

 Speaking and Listening

Working in pairs, create a fable that gives listeners an important lesson that applies to life today. Make sure to include all the characteristics that fables have, such as flat characters and a moral. Tell your fable to another pair. How did they react?

 Viewing

What animals can you see in the border around the fable "How the Fly Saved the River"? Why do you think these animals were chosen? Are there any animals not pictured here that you expected to see, based on the story?

 Research

Tolstoy wrote his fable about a time in Russia when kings ruled the land. Use the Internet or books in the library to find out more details about this time in Russian history.

The Singing Turtle   by Philippe Thoby-Marcelin and Pierre Marcelin

Philippe Thoby-
Marcelin
1905–1972

Pierre Marcelin
1908–

Objectives

■ To determine the
moral of a fable

■ To explore how
dialect and
setting add to
the reading
experience

■ To explore fable
as a genre
of literature

About the Authors

Philippe Thoby-Marcelin and his younger brother Pierre
Marcelin were born in Port-au-Prince, the capital of Haiti, a
country in the West Indies. The brothers grew up in a home
where writers and important people often came to visit.

Together, the brothers wrote many stories and novels. They
wrote the first book by a writer from Haiti ever translated into
English. This book was called *Canape-Vert*, or *The Green Sofa*.
Like all the books the brothers wrote together, *Canape-Vert*
was first written in French.

In their novels and stories, the Marcelin brothers told about
the lives of the poorer people of their country. They described
ancient customs many people of Haiti shared, including the
vodun (voodoo) rituals they brought with them from Africa.
In doing this, the two writers helped preserve the native
culture of their Caribbean nation. They also introduced
Haitian literature to the world.

About the Selection

"The Singing Turtle" is part of a collection of Haitian folktales
called *Contes et Legendes d'Haiti (Tales and Legends of Haiti)*,
first published in 1967. These folktales have been part of the
culture of Haiti for many years. Since the Haitians speak
Creole French, this tale was first told in Creole French. The
Marcelins translated the story into English. However, they
still kept some Creole French words. For example, one of the
main characters is a person called Tonton Jean. *Tonton* is a
familiar form of the word for *uncle*. Haitians use this word to
talk to someone they know very well.

This fable tells an interesting story about a turtle that has
special powers. You know from the title that he can sing.
But what else can he do? And how does it change the life of
Tonton Jean?

Literary Terms People think of books, plays, and poems that share the same characteristics as being part of the same **genre** of literature. For example, fables are all fictional stories that have a moral. **Setting** is the term used to talk about the place and time stories take place. In fables, the setting is often outdoors and the time is usually in the past. Writers who create fables do not fully describe the story's setting. In order to add some flavor to a story, authors often use **dialect**. Dialect is the language spoken by people living in a particular part of a country.

genre a specific type, or kind, of literature

setting a story's time and place

dialect the speech of a particular part of a country, or of a certain group of people

Reading on Your Own As you read the story, look for examples of dialect and other details that help you learn more about the setting of this fable. What do they tell you about the kind of land the Marcelin brothers wrote about in this fable?

Writing on Your Own What would you do if you ever encountered an animal that sang to you? Write two paragraphs that describe how you would feel and what you would do.

Vocabulary Focus Verbs can tell readers when action occurs. For example, "the birds flew away" means they are already gone; "the bird will fly away" means it has not left yet; and "the bird flies high in the sky" means it is flying now. Each verb describes action at a different time. If you use the verb to talk about a past action, sometimes you have to change it slightly. Look for verbs in this fable that describe past actions. How do they end?

Think Before You Read What characteristics do you generally think of when you picture a turtle?

The Singing Turtle

As you read, look for clues about the setting for this fable.

Millet is a grass grown for its grain, which is used for food.

On the bank of the river where he lived, a turtle was quietly warming himself in the sun, when a flock of birds flew overhead.

"Where are you going?" asked the turtle.

"Over to Tonton Jean's garden to harvest the millet," the birds boldly replied.

And they invited the turtle to go along on the expedition.

"I would very much like to join you," he said, sighing, "but, alas, I have no wings! If Tonton Jean should catch us in his garden, you'll get away without any trouble, but I . . ."

"We'll give you wings," said the birds.

They all pulled a few of their feathers and gave them to the turtle, who fastened them to his shoulders with mud and took flight along with them. Finally they reached Tonton Jean's garden and began to fill their bags with millet. The turtle, who was a good musician, made up a very entertaining song to encourage his comrades in their work:

"Tonton Jean planted millet,
So the birds could eat it,
Waya, waya!
Tonton Jean planted millet,
So the birds could eat it,
Waya, waya . . ."

Waya, waya is an example of dialect. What other uses of dialect can you find in this fable?

After a while the turtle took off his wings because they hindered his movements and he lay them on a stone so that, in case of danger, he could easily get them again. Then, picking up two iron rods, he began striking them against each other:

"Ting ti-ting ting,
Ting ti-ting ting,
Ting ti-ting ting . . ."

And the birds joined in the song with him:

"Tonton Jean planted millet

So the birds could eat it,
Waya, waya . . ."

The harvesting was going along very well and their bags were three-quarters full when one of the robbers who was on the look-out sounded the alarm: "Here comes Tonton Jean: let's fly away, quick, my friends!"

All the birds flew away with their bags, while the turtle, who went to get his wings to fasten them on his shoulders again, was horrified to see that the sun had dried the mud. He tried to get away on foot. Alas! he had gone only a little way when Tonton Jean caught up with him. But, being clever, he began singing a very sad **ballad**:

"Colico, Tonton Jean, oh!
If I still had wings,
I would have flown away.
It is really a shame,
I no longer have them!
The pigeon gave me feathers,
The guinea hen gave me feathers,
The duck gave me feathers,
And the hen gave me some, too!

Why do you think the "clever" turtle sings this song when Tonton Jean catches him?

ballad a simple song

Colico, Tonton Jean, oh!
If I still had wings,
I would have flown away.
It is really a shame,
I no longer have them!"

Tonton Jean could not believe his ears. To make sure he had not been tricked, he asked the turtle to sing his song once more. You may be sure the turtle was glad to oblige. And when he finished singing, Tonton Jean took him home and carefully put him in a big earthenware jar. Then he went to the marketplace of the nearby town, where he publicly boasted about his great discovery. Everyone took Tonton Jean for a liar, but that was exactly what he expected.

"Who wants to bet that I don't have a singing turtle?" he asked in a **provocative** way.

At that very moment the king happened to pass by. He ordered his carriage stopped and asked the crowd what was going on. They explained that Tonton Jean claimed he had a turtle that could sing and was challenging all who did not believe him to bet he was not telling the truth.

"This man is an **impostor**," said the king to the **dignitaries** accompanying him.

Then, addressing Tonton Jean, "I bet two hundred dollars that you are lying."

"I am only a poor peasant," said Tonton Jean. "How can I bet such a big sum of money?"

"It doesn't matter," replied the king. "If you lose, I'll have you thrown in the river with a stone around your neck."

Meantime, Sor Mise—that was the name of Tonton Jean's wife—hearing that her husband had found a singing turtle, ran home as fast as she could. She uncovered the jar and asked the turtle to sing something for her.

"I can sing only on the riverbank," replied the turtle.

"Very well!" said Sor Mise.

And she took him to the riverbank.

Tonton Jean is eager to take bets on whether or not he has a singing turtle. He expects to make lots of money from the townspeople.

How did the turtle trick Sor Mise into letting him go?

provocative intended to stir up, anger, or excite	**impostor** one who pretends to be someone else	**dignitaries** important people

"You'll have to wet my feet," said the turtle.

"Very well!" said Sor Mise.

And she leaned over the water to wet the turtle's feet. But the animal slipped out of her hands and plunged into the river, where he disappeared like lightning.

At that very moment, paf! a silly toad fell to the ground a few feet away from Sor Mise, who, in her **disarray**, asked him: "Can you sing?"

"Yes," answered the toad, puffing out his chest.

"Then sing something for me," said Sor Mise sweetly. And our toad started in with his lips all puckered up:

"Ah! . . . Oh! . . . Oh! . . . Of! . . .
Ah! . . . Oh! . . . Oh! . . . Of! . . . "

"Sing something else for me," begged Sor Mise. "A real song, a very, very pretty one!"

But the toad, **imperturbable,** started up again:

"Ah! . . . Oh! . . . Oh! . . . Of! . . .
Ah! . . . Oh! . . . Oh! . . . Of! . . ."

"Brother," said Sor Mise, despairing, "your song is absolutely worthless!"

However, since she just had to have an animal that could sing, she caught hold of the toad, took it home, and simply put it in the jar, hoping that when her husband got back she would come out all right by pretending she did not know anything.

But when the king arrived, followed by Tonton Jean, the dignitaries, and the whole crowd of the curious, Sor Mise, imagining the fatal **consequences** of her foolish action, fell face down in a faint. No one paid attention to her, not even her husband, who walked over to the jar in smiles.

"Brother turtle, my little treasure," he said gently, "sing something for our king."

And the little treasure self-confidently started right up:

"Ah! . . . Oh! . . . Oh! . . . Of! . . .
Ah! . . . Oh! . . . Oh! . . . Of! . . ."

> What do you think will happen when Tonton Jean gets back?

disarray confusion, disorder	**imperturbable** calm, steady, impossible to upset	**consequences** results or effects

"Get hold of that impostor!" said the king coldly, pointing to Tonton Jean, "and throw him into the river with a stone around his neck!"

It so happened that the turtle had a kind heart. When he realized he would be to blame if they drowned Tonton Jean, he came up out of the water and spoke to the crowd of people gathered around.

"Don't kill my poor master!" he said. "He did not tell a lie."

And since the king was wide-eyed with astonishment, he added: "The proof is, ladies and gentlemen, that I am going to sing you a little song of my own."

Striking the little rods against each other,

"Ting ti-ting ting,
Ting ti-ting ting,
Ting ti-ting ting"
he sang:
"Colico, Tonton Jean, oh!
If I still had wings,
I would have flown away.
It is really a shame,
I no longer have them!
The pigeon gave me feathers,
The guinea hen gave me feathers,
The duck gave me feathers,
And the hen gave me some, too . . ."

The king, marveling, listened to the song till the end. Then, **apologizing** to Tonton Jean, he counted out the two hundred dollars of the bet. But it was the last time anyone heard of a turtle singing.

apologizing saying you are sorry

Directions Choose the letter of the best answer or write the answer using complete sentences.

Comprehension: Identifying Facts

1. Who asks the turtle to go to Tonton Jean's garden?
   - **A** Sor Mise
   - **B** Tonton Jean
   - **C** the birds
   - **D** the king

2. How does the turtle get to the garden?
   - **A** He flies.
   - **B** He runs.
   - **C** He walks slowly.
   - **D** He goes with Tonton Jean.

3. What does the turtle do to encourage his friends as they work?

4. What do the birds gather from the garden?

5. What happens to the turtle's wings after he lays them down?

6. How does the turtle save himself when Tonton Jean catches him in the garden?

7. What happens when Tonton Jean tells everyone that he has a singing turtle?

8. How does the turtle get back to the river?

9. What does Sor Mise put in the jar in place of the turtle?

10. How does the turtle save Tonton Jean?

Comprehension: Putting Ideas Together

11. When does the turtle show his cleverness?
    - **A** when he flies into the garden
    - **B** when he sings to Tonton Jean
    - **C** when he tells Sor Mise he can only sing on the riverbank
    - **D** in all three events

12. How do you think Sor Mise feels when she sees that the turtle has tricked her into letting him escape?
    - **A** embarrassed
    - **B** angry
    - **C** depressed
    - **D** confused

13. What kind of a character is the Singing Turtle?

14. Do you think the bet between Tonton Jean and the king is fair? Why or why not?

15. Why do you think the turtle decides to save Tonton Jean's life?

16. Why do you think the turtle never sings again?

17. How are all the settings in this story alike? How are they different?

After Reading continued on next page

The Singing Turtle by Philippe Thoby-Marcelin and Pierre Marcelin

18. Who is the hero of this fable? Why do you think so?

19. What do you think the moral of this fable is?

20. Why do you think the authors did not state a moral?

Understanding Literature: Setting and Dialect

Like all genres of literature, fables use settings, or the time and the place of the story, to help readers place themselves in the stories. If a fable is set in a particular area, the author may use the dialect of the people in that area. Dialect is the speaking customs of a particular area. The dialect of a region is usually made up of words, expressions, and pronunciations used only in that area or by one group of people. The use of dialect adds richness to stories.

21. What details about the setting do the authors give readers in this fable?

22. What other details about the setting do readers have to create in their imaginations?

23. What are some examples of dialect in "The Singing Turtle"?

24. How does the author's use of details of speech and customs of speaking help you as a reader to see the story better?

25. What are some words or expressions that you and your friends use that older people do not use?

Critical Thinking

26. How would you compare the way the birds treat the turtle with the way the turtle treats Tonton Jean? How are they the same? How are they different? How does this affect your opinion of the story?

27. This fable is taken from the Haitian culture. What are some clues in it that tell you this?

28. This fable is told with lots of humor. What are several examples of funny descriptions or events? Why do you think writers of fables often include humor along with a moral?

29. The authors are Haitian, growing up and living in the Caribbean. How might this fable be different if the Inuit people of Alaska and northern Canada told it?

Thinking Creatively

30. What are some other ways this fable might have ended? Would a different ending change the message, or moral of this fable?

Grammar Check

Fables were first passed down to other members of the community by telling them aloud. However, as people like Aesop began to pass the stories on to others, these people began to write them down.

Imagine that you are one of the first people to write down the fable of the Singing Turtle. Use your best handwriting to rewrite the first six paragraphs of the fable. Use your own words. Use the story as a sample for using quotation marks, capitalization, and punctuation.

Writing on Your Own

Use the Character Analysis Guide described in Appendix A to look closely at the character of Tonton Jean. Try to think about the difference between what the author tells you about this character and the details of his character that you have created in your mind. Write a paragraph to explain the differences.

Speaking

Practice saying the words of the song that the Singing Turtle sings in order to encourage the birds as they work.

Use a slow rhythm, a fast rhythm, and one in between as you explore the pace at which the turtle may have sung. Which pace sounds best for encouraging someone to work?

Listening

Form teams to read this fable aloud. Each person should take a turn reading. Close your eyes when someone else reads. What are you seeing?

Media

Music in movies can add a great deal to the storyline. If you were designing a cartoon version of this fable, what kind of music would you choose to accompany the events of the story? List the events of the story and the kind of music you would select for each.

Technology

The authors never say what kind of birds coax the Singing Turtle into Tonton Jean's garden. Use the Internet and a good search engine to find out which birds are native to Haiti and how they might look and behave.

Setting describes the place where a story, or an event in a story, happens. The place might be outdoors or indoors. It might be a particular city or region. Whatever the place, the writer usually gives details about it. For example, if a story or event happens outdoors, the writer might tell readers about the weather.

A story's setting also describes the time in which the story happens. Stories may happen in the past, the present, or the future. They may happen in the morning, afternoon, or night. Each choice affects the story.

The details of setting do two main things. First, they help readers see the story in their own minds. For example, if readers can remember the smells of a rainy night, or the sounds of an old, broken-down house, the details of this setting make the story more real.

Second, the details of setting can tell us something about the story or its characters. Rather than tell readers that a character is having money problems, an author might set the story in a rundown apartment. Rather than say that a girl loves to read, an author can mention the piles of books in her bedroom.

Many fables have an outdoor setting and take place sometime in the past. For example, "The Milkmaid and Her Pail" takes place on the road to the Milkmaid's home. "How the Fly Saved the River" takes place "when the world was new." Often, we do not learn more about a fable's setting than that. Just as they do with characters, the creators of fables depend on the reader's imagination to fill in the details.

Review

1. What is setting?

2. If a story has an outdoor setting, what details might the author describe?

3. How can settings help readers see the story?

4. How can the details of setting tell readers something about the characters?

5. What is the setting of many fables?

Writing on Your Own

Imagine that you are writing a fable whose moral is *You can catch more flies with honey than with vinegar.* This is the same moral as the one that ended the fable "The North Wind and the Sun." Describe the setting for your fable. Explain what readers might see in this setting. How could the setting help them understand your fable?

Unit 1　SUMMARY

Unit 1 presents examples of one of the oldest forms of stories: fables. The purpose of most fables is to teach something about life. This lesson is given in the form of a moral, which may either be stated or suggested.

Some of the world's most famous fables come from Aesop, a Greek slave who probably lived between 600 and 500 B.C. Aesop's fables, and many others that came later, share certain characteristics. They were first told orally, rather than written down. They are short and simply told. They usually feature animal characters that think, speak, and behave as human beings would. The characters are flat, meaning that not much is told about them. Each fable ends with a moral, or lesson about life.

Most of the cultures of the world enjoy fables. Fables are still being written today and will probably always be part of the world's literature.

Selections

- "The Dog in the Manger" by Aesop tells of a selfish dog who tries to keep the hungry cattle from getting to the fresh hay he is sleeping in.

- "The Dog and His Reflection" by Aesop tells of a greedy dog who jumps into the river to steal the bone he sees carried by his own reflection.

- "The North Wind and the Sun" by Aesop tells of an argument between the North Wind and the Sun over who is stronger. The North Wind foolishly agrees to let a traveler settle the question.

- "The Milkmaid and Her Pail" by Aesop tells of a milkmaid who is so busy dreaming about all she will gain when she sells the butter churned from her cows' rich milk that she spills the milk.

- "The King and the Shirt," by the Russian novelist Leo Tolstoy, tells of a search for a happy man whose shirt will cure the king. The happy man, it turns out, is too poor to own a shirt.

- "How the Fly Saved the River," an Ojibwa fable, tells of a tiny fly that drives away the giant moose who is drinking up the river water.

- "The Singing Turtle," a fable from Haiti, tells of a man who bets the king that he actually has caught a singing turtle.

Directions Choose the letter of the best answer or write the answer using complete sentences.

Comprehension: Identifying Facts

1. _____ is a moral of one of the fables in this unit.
   - **A** *A stitch in time saves nine*
   - **B** *Be kind to everyone*
   - **C** *A picture is worth 1,000 words*
   - **D** *Being greedy is very foolish*

2. Why do the Cattle think the Dog is selfish?

3. How does the Milkmaid carry the milk?

4. Why are the North Wind and the Sun quarreling?

5. Why are the animals afraid of the Moose?

Comprehension: Putting Ideas Together

6. Both the Fly in "How the Fly Saved the River" and the Turtle in "The Singing Turtle" are:
   - **A** greedy
   - **B** sad
   - **C** brave
   - **D** silly

7. Does the Dog in "The Dog in the Manger" show the moral of the story by what he does, or by what he doesn't do? How about the Dog in "The Dog and His Reflection"?

8. In your own words, what is the moral of "The Milkmaid and Her Pail"?

9. Why do you think Sor Mise puts a toad in the jar even though she knows it cannot sing?

10. In "The King and the Shirt," why do you think the wise men want to find a cure for the king?

Understanding Literature: Plot

A plot is the series of events that take place in a story. Each event leads to another, which builds the plot. A plot usually has a beginning, middle, and end. In the beginning of a story, the main ideas, problems, and characters are introduced. During the middle section, the story develops. At the end, the problem is usually resolved, or settled.

11. Define plot.

12. Outline the plot of "The King and the Shirt."

13. The plot of "The Dog and His Reflection" contains a series of events. Could Aesop have left out any of these events without changing the story in important ways? Explain your answer.

14. In your opinion, which fable in this unit has the most believable plot? Why?

15. Sometimes, when you start to read a fable or story, you know what is going to happen in the end. Stories like this have a predictable plot. Did any fables in this unit have a predictable plot? If so, did this make reading the fable more enjoyable or less enjoyable? Explain your opinion.

Critical Thinking

16. Suppose the Dog in "The Dog and His Reflection" crosses the bridge the same day, carrying another large bone. What do you think he will do?

17. Describe the irony in "The King and the Shirt."

18. Why is the North Wind a flat character?

19. Who is your favorite hero in these fables? Explain why.

Thinking Creatively

20. What do you think about the morals of fables? Do people living now need these kinds of messages?

Speak and Listen

What do you think Sor Mise would have told Tonton Jean if he had discovered her putting the toad in the jar in place of the singing turtle? Practice presenting a convincing explanation or a sincere apology with a partner.

Writing on Your Own

Write a fable using one of the following morals:

A stitch in time saves nine.
The squeaky wheel gets the oil.
Don't cry over spilt milk.
There's no place like home.

Your fable should have a setting, plot, and flat characters. Look at Appendix C for writing tips. Prewrite first; then write a draft; revise; edit and proof; then write your final draft.

Beyond Words

Many famous artists, including Alexander Calder, have created illustrations for fables. Calder also introduced the mobile to the art world. Create a mobile that features characters, objects, or events from a fable in this unit.

Test-Taking Tip

If you know you will have to define certain words or terms on a test, write each word on one side of a card. Write the definition on the other side. Use the cards as flash cards to test yourself or a partner.

Opening of Pandora's Box
Engraving, 19th Century

P eople from most of the world's cultures have created myths to explain what they did not understand. One important group of myths explains how the world began. Another group explains why events in nature, such as thunderstorms and earthquakes, happen. Myths were often part of people's religion, believed to be true. Unlike the animal characters in fables, the characters in myths are usually gods, goddesses, and heroes. These characters have unusual strengths and powers.

In this unit, you will read myths about the beginning of the world, about some reasons for natural events, and about the experiences of strong, powerful characters.

"Myths are early science, the result of men's first trying to explain what they saw around them."

—Edith Hamilton,
  Mythology, 1942

Unit 2

About Myths

People from every culture have created, told, and believed in myths. The peoples of ancient India, Greece, Rome, Mexico, North America, Scandinavia, Egypt, Indonesia, Babylon, and many other places had myths related directly to their own history and religious beliefs.

Like fables, myths are one of the oldest forms of stories. Many were first told orally, before being written down. Myths may include a message about life, just as fables do. Myths also have a plot, setting, and characters. However, the characters in myths are not the flat characters of fables. Usually, they are gods, goddesses, or heroes, with great powers and unusual strengths. We find out more about these characters than we do about the characters in fables.

Myths are also different from fables in the way people thought about them. Few people who heard Aesop's fables believed that animals could talk, think, and behave as human beings do. Myths, however, were part of people's religion. They were believed to be true. For example, the people living on the Trobriand Islands in the Pacific Ocean have a myth that explains how death came to be. When people were first created, the Trobriand myth says, they were immortal, meaning they never died. When they felt themselves growing old, they swam in a special pond and shed their old skin, just like a snake. They came out of the water with a brand-new skin. One day, a woman went to the pond and shed her old skin. When she returned to her home in her new skin, her frightened daughter didn't know who she was. Upset, the woman returned to the pond and took back her old skin. Ever since, the Trobriands believe, death has been part of life.

Most myths can be grouped according to the kind of story they tell.

People have always wondered how the world came to be. Before science could supply answers, myths did. One group of myths explains how the world and all its creatures came into being. These are called creation myths. Sometimes, these myths also tell how the world will end. In the myths of the ancient Greeks, the world began from nothingness. In the myths told by the Hopi Indians, all living things came from deep within the earth. The Polynesian creation myths, among others, tell of two parents who bring life to the earth. Still others, such as the myths of India, tell of an animal that dove deep into the sea to bring up a small piece of the earth. This small piece then grew into the world.

Zeus, Roman marble copy of a lost Greek original of the 4th century B.C.

A second group of myths explains why natural events such as earthquakes and eclipses happen. People are less afraid once they have reasons for things. For example, in ancient Norse myths, the god Thor created thunder and lightning when he threw a hammer at his enemies. The Greeks believed that thunderbolts were the weapons of the king of the gods, Zeus. For people in these cultures, thunderstorms happened when the gods were fighting. Some of the myths in this group tell us that parts of nature, such as fire and animals, were gifts from the gods.

This unit begins with three myths that were part of ancient Greek culture. "Prometheus" explains how people received one of their most precious gifts, fire. "Demeter and Persephone" offers an explanation of why we have seasons.

"Perseus and Medusa" tells of a hero's dangerous mission. "The Beginning and the End of the World," an American Indian myth from the Okanogan culture, explains how the world came to be and how it will end. "Loki and the Master Builder," an ancient Norse myth, tells what happens when the gods put their trust in Loki, a troublemaker. "The Moon Spirit and Coyote Woman," a modern folk myth, tells of the love of the magical Moon Spirit for Coyote Woman.

Greek Myths   *Anonymous*

Apollo
god of the arts,
especially poetry
and music

Athena
goddess of wisdom,
war, and crafts

Objectives

- To read and understand the purposes behind each myth
- To explore the concept of hero in literature and in myth
- To identify and understand simile, genre, and plot

About the Authors

The **myths** in this section come from ancient Greece. Historians believe the Greeks adapted their myths from other ancient cultures that lived near them. At first, ancient Greeks told these myths aloud, rather than writing them down. The Greek poets Homer and Hesiod first wrote these stories down in the 700s or 600s B.C.

About the Selections

In ancient Greece, gods, goddesses, and heroes were an important part of everyday life. The ancient Greeks felt that their gods and goddesses controlled the world. They included them in almost every part of their lives. In their homes, they would set up altars to certain gods. They would pray at these altars several times a day. Each Greek city chose a certain god or group of gods to honor and respect with temples and festivals. At the festivals, the people would hear the stories of their gods and goddesses retold by their culture's great poets. These are the stories that we know today as Greek myths.

The Greeks believed their gods and goddesses looked like human beings. These gods and goddesses ate, slept, quarreled, and fell in love, just as people do. However, these gods also had powers that people did not have. Some could fly. Some could change shape. Some could make people do things against their will. The gods and goddesses lived in a place called Olympus.

Heroes were a special class of people in Greek mythology. Like all people, they were mortal—meaning they died—unlike the gods and goddesses, who were immortal and never died. However, these heroes had unusual strength and power. They took on the most difficult and dangerous of tasks.

Literary Terms A **hero** is the leading character. In Greek myths, the hero can be a god, goddess, or a special human with great strength and power. In literature, the hero of the story is not always brave like the heroes in Greek mythology. In literature, heroes are simply the main characters of the story. The **plot**, or events in the story, tells what happens to these heroes. In a myth and other kinds of literature, the plot is the backbone of the story.

Reading on Your Own Before reading these three myths, preview the text. Look at the titles, the illustrations, and the words in bold. What clues do they give you about these stories? Based on this, which one would you like to read first?

Writing on Your Own Think about what you have learned about myths, either in this text, in other classes, or in everyday life. Based on that, list four characteristics that Greek myths might share as part of the same **genre**, or type of literature.

Vocabulary Focus   In creating the heroes of their stories, the Greek storytellers sometimes used **similes** to make the characters come alive for the reader or listener. "Horses that were as black as night" is an example of simile. Basically, the simile says: "Think of how black it is at night. That's how black the horses are." A simile always uses the words *like* or *as*. As you read these myths, look for examples of similes. How do they help you see the story and its characters in a more complete way?

Think Before You Read What kinds of things do you think you might learn by reading these myths?

---

myth an important story, often part of a culture's religion, that explains how the world came to be or why natural events happen, usually including gods, goddesses, or unusually powerful human beings

hero the leading character in a story, novel, play, or film

plot the series of events in a story

genre a specific type, or kind, of literature

simile a figure of speech in which two things are compared using a phrase that includes the word *like* or *as*

PROM

As you read, decide what the purpose of this myth is. Why do you think the Greeks told this myth?

Forethought means thinking or planning ahead. *Hindsight* means figuring something out after it happens.

Who is the hero of this myth?

Why was it dangerous for Prometheus to give people fire? Why does he do it anyway?

In the beginning of time, there was a group of giant gods known as the Titans. The twin brothers Prometheus and Epimetheus were part of this group. The gods gave the brothers the special task of bringing to life all mortal beings—animals and man. They had formed these beings from the soil and fire inside the earth. Still, they were nothing more than clay statues. They needed life.

Prometheus's name means *forethought*. Epimetheus's name means *hindsight*. That was the way the two behaved. Epimetheus acted first and thought later. Prometheus thought carefully first, made plans, and then acted.

As soon as the gods gave him this task, Epimetheus started working. Without a thought, he gave the animals all the best gifts of the gods. He made them strong and nimble, with special coverings to protect them from the wind and cold on earth.

When Prometheus saw what had happened, he was dismayed. There were no special gifts left to protect the humans on whom he had **lavished** so much thought and care. He thought for a long while before he found a solution to this problem. People might not have the protection of furs, feathers, or skins, as the animals to whom Epimetheus had given these gifts. Yet they would have something to keep them warm and safe. They would have fire, and Prometheus would give it to them.

Fire was a gift that only the gods enjoyed, and Zeus, the leader of the gods, had forbidden any mortal creature from having it. Nevertheless, Prometheus cared deeply about the unprotected people who might not **survive** if they did not have some protection. He sneaked into Olympus at night,

lavished given a great deal of   **survive** to go on living

and lit a torch from the flames of the **Chariot** of the Sun. He **extinguished** the flames, but carried the burning embers back to earth, hiding them in a stalk of fennel. Prometheus gave people his precious gift.

Fennel is an herb that has seeds.

When Zeus heard of this, he became enraged. How dare Prometheus defy him? How dare he give the **immortal** gods' special treasure to **mere** mortals? Prometheus would have to be punished. He ordered Hephaestus, the god of the blacksmiths and fire, to chain Prometheus to a rock in the Caucasus Mountains for **eternity**. Every day, a giant eagle swept down from the sky and ate the **lobes** of Prometheus's liver. Each night, the lobes would grow back. Prometheus endured this torture for 30,000 years.

The Caucasus Mountains form part of the border between Europe and Asia.

Zeus finally sent Hercules to set Prometheus free. Hercules shot the eagle with a special arrow and released Prometheus from his chains. However, Zeus could not go back on his word. He had ordered that Prometheus be bound for eternity and so he would be. Forevermore, Prometheus carried around a piece of the rock to which he was chained, **embedded** with a link in the chain that had kept him there.

Roman Mosaic of Prometheus Giving Fire to Man

chariot a two-wheeled cart

extinguished put out

immortal living forever; free from death

mere nothing more than

eternity forever

lobes rounded parts that stick out or down

embedded fixed or enclosed in something

DEMETER AND PERSEPHONE

As you read, decide what the purpose of this myth is. Why do you think the Greeks told this myth?

Zeus's sister, Demeter, was a kind and loving goddess who watched carefully over the harvest. She had taught people how to take seeds from fruits and vegetables and plant them. She cared for the young plants and protected them until they grew and bore fruit.

Demeter's daughter, Persephone, was even more beautiful than she. The two were rarely apart. Persephone brought great joy to her mother and all those around her. Everyone noticed her graciousness and beauty, including Hades, god of the underworld and death. He fell in love with the **captivating** girl.

The *underworld* was believed to be the place of souls of those who had died.

One bright morning, Persephone was playing with her friends in a great field of narcissuses. Gaea, the earth mother, had planted these bright yellow flowers to please Hades. As Persephone bent to pick one of these lovely flowers for her mother, the earth suddenly split open. Hades appeared, riding in a **chariot** pulled by horses that were as black as night. He grabbed the terrified girl, and urged his horses back into the **chasm**. As quickly as it had opened, the earth closed over. Persephone was gone.

"As black as night" is a simile. What two things are being compared?

Hades raced to his underground kingdom, a world full of darkness and shadows. As she walked slowly through this **melancholy** place, Persephone felt ever more alone. Nothing here was as it was in her home. In the garden, there were only whispering poplars and weeping willows. She could find no trace of the beautiful flowers she and her mother loved so much. The poor souls who lived here had none of the delicious fruits she loved to eat. The garden held only one tree—a **pomegranate**—that bore the food of the dead. The young girl fell to the ground, weeping.

Demeter soon realized that her precious child was missing. For nine long days, she **scoured** the earth, searching

captivating charming	**melancholy** sad	**scoured** searched thoroughly
chariot a two-wheeled cart	**pomegranate** a reddish-gold fruit with many seeds	
chasm a large opening		

for her beloved daughter. Finally, the sun god Helios, who sees everything, told her that Hades had taken Persephone to his kingdom. Demeter felt her grief turn to icy anger. Until her daughter returned, her carefully tended plants would not bear fruit. Cursed by the one who had cared so deeply for them, the crops withered and died in the fields. People everywhere starved.

When the gods saw the power of Demeter's curse, they were alarmed. They could not overlook this. The fate of many mortals depended on them. Zeus ordered his brother Hades to let Persephone come back to her mother. Hades knew he had to obey the wishes of his brother. **Reluctantly**, he let Persephone go.

As the young girl started to leave, she heard the wicked laugh of one of Hades's gardeners. She turned as he showed Hades a pomegranate with a few seeds missing. Persephone blushed. She had eaten a few of the seeds. Hades was **jubilant**. She had eaten the food of the dead. Persephone could leave, as Hades had promised his brother, but she would have to return to him.

Demeter was delighted when her lovely daughter came back to her. Yet her joy turned to fury when she found that Persephone had eaten the pomegranate seeds. She knew this meant that her daughter would have to go back to the underworld. The curse would remain. If she could not have her daughter, then people would not have their crops.

Rhea, the oldest and most respected goddess of all, offered a **compromise**. If Demeter agreed, Persephone could spend one part of the year with Hades. During the rest of the year, the girl would live with her mother. Demeter knew this was only fair. With **resignation**, she agreed to the bargain and lifted the curse.

In the spring, summer, and fall, Persephone would be by Demeter's side as she watched over the planting and harvest. In the winter, Persephone would go to the underworld, and the whole world would grieve with the lonely mother.

Proserpine, Dante Gabriel Rossetti

Why does Persephone have to return to Hades?

Why does Demeter lift the curse? Do you think the agreement is fair?

How might the plot of this myth have been different if Demeter had not agreed to a compromise?

reluctantly without wanting to	**compromise** an agreement that tries to satisfy both sides	**resignation** accepting with grace
jubilant joyful		

Medusa,
Caravaggio

PERSEUS AND MEDUSA

This myth is the story of a hero: a human being with unusual strength and power. As you read, notice the ways Perseus shows these characteristics. How is the focus on the actions of a hero typical of the genre of mythology?

When the people gathered at the feast heard his words, they gasped. He, Perseus, would kill the Gorgon Medusa. It was unthinkable. The Gorgons were crude and graceless creatures. Their hair was a mass of **writhing** snakes. One glance from a Gorgon would turn any living thing to stone. The people could not understand why such a handsome and strong man would choose to die in such a terrible way.

Perseus understood the danger, too. Yet, he had no other choice. The king, Polydectes, had tricked him. Polydectes had told his people that he was planning to be married. All the people in the kingdom had brought their king splendid gifts to honor the bride and groom. Perseus had nothing to give. In his shame, he decided to risk everything to bring the king the head of Medusa.

With great determination, Perseus set off on his journey. He asked many people, but no one could tell him how to find the Gorgons. Suddenly, Hermes and Athena appeared to him. They knew of his **quest.** They told him how to find the island where Medusa and her sisters lived. Each had a special gift

writhing wiggling   **quest** a search for something

for Perseus that he would need to **survive.** Hermes gave him a pair of winged sandals to fly over the sea. Athena presented him with a gleaming shield, warning him to use it as a mirror if he needed to look at the horrible Gorgon. As wonderful as these gifts were, they were not enough for him to succeed, the two warned. Perseus must gather other magical items from the Nymphs of the North.

However, finding the Nymphs of the North was not that easy. Only the Grey Women could tell Perseus where they lived. Living in a world as grey and murky as fog, these sisters were strange creatures who shared only one eye between them. When one of them wanted to look at something, she would snatch the eye and place it in her forehead. Hermes told Perseus that this would be his only chance. He was to grab the eye as they were exchanging it. Only then would the Grey Women tell him how to find the Nymphs.

Perseus followed the plan exactly, and the weird Grey Women told him what he needed to know. He sped to the island where the Nymphs of the North lived. The Nymphs were sympathetic to Perseus's story, and gave him two more gifts: a magic bag and the Cap of Darkness. The Cap would make anyone who wore it invisible. Thanking the Nymphs, Perseus flew once again. He was ready for his **ordeal.**

Even though Perseus was prepared, he still trembled when he saw the island of the Gorgons reflected in his polished shield. Scattered about the barren ground were many strangely shaped stones . . . stones that had once been living creatures. Medusa lay sleeping with her sisters, her hair a mass of snakes with darting tongues. Perseus put on the Cap of Darkness so that no one would see him coming, and swooped down. With one mighty blow, he cut off Medusa's horrific head, threw it quickly into his magic bag, and flew off.

Hermes is the god of merchants and the messenger of Zeus; Athena is the goddess of wisdom, war, and crafts.

Murky means dim, hard to see through. In the sentence using this word, what is the simile? What two things are being compared?

Why do you think the Greeks told this myth?

survive to go on living   **ordeal** a terrible experience

Directions Choose the letter of the best answer or write the answer using complete sentences.

Comprehension: Identifying Facts

1. To what group of gods do Prometheus and Epimetheus belong?

   A Zeus
   B Titans
   C Olympus
   D Caucasus

2. What gift does Prometheus bring to people?

   A strength
   B special coverings
   C fire
   D clay statues

3. How does Zeus punish Prometheus?

4. Who does Zeus send to free Prometheus?

5. As goddess of the harvest, what jobs does Demeter have?

6. What does Demeter do when she learns her daughter is gone?

7. Why does Persephone have to return to Hades's underground kingdom?

8. Why can't Perseus look at Medusa?

9. What special gifts does Perseus receive from the Nymphs of the North?

10. What does Perseus need from the Grey Women?

Comprehension: Putting Ideas Together

11. Who is the hero of the myth "Prometheus"?

   A Olympus
   B Zeus
   C Epimetheus
   D Prometheus

12. How did Prometheus feel about people?

   A He cared for them deeply.
   B He didn't know people existed.
   C He wanted them to obey his orders.
   D He didn't care about people.

13. Why is Prometheus's gift of fire so important to people?

14. Why do you think Zeus gives Prometheus such a severe punishment?

15. How is the character of Demeter similar to and different from the character of Hades in the myth "Demeter and Persephone"?

16. Why do you think the Greeks created the myth of Demeter and Persephone?

17. Why do Hermes, Athena, and the Nymphs of the North help Perseus try to kill Medusa?

18. How does Perseus use each of the gifts he receives?

19. How would you describe the Gorgon Medusa?

20. Based on what you read in "Perseus and Medusa," what kinds of character traits do you think the Greeks valued?

Understanding Literature: Heroes and Simile

In literature, the hero of the story is the main character around which all the action of the story revolves. In bringing these heroes to life, authors often use similes to help readers understand a character. A simile compares two things, using the word *like* or *as*.

21. Who is the hero, or main character, of the myth "Demeter and Persephone"?

22. What is a simile the author could have used to tell us more about this character?

23. Create two similes to describe Hades that other readers might find useful in helping them know more about this character.

24. How would you describe the character Perseus in the myth "Perseus and Medusa"?

25. Why could you consider Perseus to be the hero in the story and a hero in Greek mythology?

Critical Thinking

26. Which myth do you think was created to explain a natural event? Explain your choice.

27. Which character in these myths do you like the most? Why? How much do we learn about the character?

28. If you were Demeter, what would you have done when your daughter disappeared?

29. Fables often have a moral that is stated after the story, but most myths do not. However, myths often contain a message about life. What do you think is Prometheus's message about living? Explain.

Thinking Creatively

30. Are you more like Prometheus or Epimetheus? Explain.

After Reading continued on next page

Greek Myths   Anonymous

 Grammar Check

Many Greek words, or parts of Greek words, are used in other languages, including English. For example, the name *Prometheus* means "thinking beforehand." *Pro* is the part of the word that means before.

Use a dictionary to find the meaning of these words, all of which begin with *pro*. Write your own definition showing how this part of the word affects its meaning.

proactive   prototype   prologue

 Writing on Your Own

How would you feel if you were Prometheus, still wearing a part of a chain after so many years? Write an entry that might have appeared in his diary or journal. Tell about the way he feels.

 Speaking

If you were in a play based on the myth of Perseus, what items would you carry or have on stage? These items, called props, would help your audience know more about the character. Tell your class which props you would choose and why you would choose them.

 Listening

Active listeners often set a purpose for listening before the experience begins. What purpose would you set for yourself before listening to another Greek myth? For example, would you want to end your listening experience knowing the events of the plot—or the characteristics of the hero? Write a paragraph that explains your purpose for listening. Outline how you might accomplish that goal.

 Media and Technology

Even though Greek myths are very old, the basics of their characters and plots are still used today. For example, some people say that Neo, the hero in the movie *The Matrix*, is a modern-day Prometheus. Find out more about Neo and *The Matrix*. In your opinion, how does Neo's character compare with the character of Prometheus? Explore this question using words or art.

BEFORE READING THE SELECTION

The Beginning and the End of the World   Okanogan Traditional Myth

About the Authors

This myth comes from the Okanogan people, a group belonging to the Plateau Indians who first lived near the Columbia River in the Pacific Northwest. Their name may have come from a word meaning *meeting*. This word was first used as a name for a place on a nearby lake where native people from North America gathered to catch fish and exchange goods. The Okanogan were mainly fishers and gatherers. During the winter months, they lived in earth-covered pit houses that were partly underground. When the weather got warmer, the Okanogan moved to homes made of wood. Salmon from the river was an important part of their diet, but the group also hunted bear, deer, and elk, and gathered plants and berries from the nearby plains.

In 1872, the Colville Confederated Tribes (CCT) were set up on a reservation in north central Washington state. The Okanogan, along with other American Indian groups in the area, moved onto the 1.4 million-acre reservation, larger than the state of Rhode Island. Today, many thousands of Colville Indians live on this reservation, which has a tribal government and operates tourist, gaming, and forest product activities.

About the Selection

For centuries, cultures around the world tried to answer the question, "How did our people come to be?" "The Beginning and the End of the World" tells the story of how the Okanogan believed their land and their people were created. It also details the way the Okanogan believe their world will end. This myth is retold by Ella E. Clark, who drew on the tales Okanogans have passed down to their children through the years.

***Before Reading* continued on next page**

Objectives

- To read and explore a creation myth
- To understand myths as part of oral literature
- To understand character, setting, and anthology

The Beginning and the End of the World   Okanogan Traditional Myth

creation myth
a myth that tells
the story of the
beginning of the
world

oral literature
stories that were
first told, rather
than being written
down

character
a person or animal
in a story, poem,
or play

setting a story's
time and place

anthology
a collection of
stories, plays, or
poems by different
authors collected in
one book

Literary Terms Myths were created for many purposes.
One of these purposes was to help people understand how
their world and all the creatures in it began. Myths that tell
these kinds of stories are called **creation myths**. Like fables
and other myths from different cultures, these myths began
as **oral literature**. For years, communities gathered to share
these stories aloud. Finally, these myths were written down.
The **characters**—usually gods, goddesses, and heroes, their
setting—the place and time in which the story's events
happen, and their plots were recorded. Characters, setting,
and plot are always a part of myths, fables, and other stories
and plays.

Reading on Your Own "The Beginning and the End of the
World" is a creation myth. Based on what you have learned
about Greek myths, what do you expect to see in this myth?
How might it be similar? How might it be different?

Writing on Your Own An **anthology** is a collection of
literature. It is usually chosen from one genre, or type of
literature, by an editor. An anthology could be a collection
of poems or short stories. This textbook might also be
considered a kind of anthology. Write a short description
of other stories you might expect to find in an anthology of
American Indian myths.

Vocabulary Focus Setting describes when and where a
story takes place. As you read this myth, look for words that
help you determine the setting for this myth. The myth
begins "Long, long ago," on an "island far off" in the "middle
of the ocean." What other clues you can find?

Think Before You Read Why do you think the Okanogan
people wanted to know how their world began?

THE BEGINNING AND THE END OF THE WORLD

Long, long ago, when the sun was young and no bigger than a star, there was an island far off in the middle of the ocean. It was called Samah-tumi-whoo-lah, meaning White Man's Island. On it lived a race of giants—white giants. Their ruler was a tall white woman called Scomalt. Scomalt was great and strong, and she had Tahmahnawis powers. She could create whatever she wished.

For many years the white giants lived at peace, but at last they quarreled among themselves. Quarreling grew into war. The noise of the battle was heard, and many people were killed. Scomalt was made very, very angry.

"I will drive the wicked ones of these people far from me," she said. "Never again shall my heart be made sick by them. And they shall no longer trouble the peaceful ones of my people."

So she drove the wicked giants to one end of the White Man's Island. When they were gathered together in one place, she broke off that piece of land and pushed it out to sea. For many days the floating island drifted on the water, tossed by waves and wind. All the people on it died except one man and one woman.

They floated and drifted for many more days. The sun beat down upon them, and ocean storms swept over them. They became very hungry, until the man caught a whale. Seeing that their island was about to sink, they built a canoe, put the whale blubber into it, and paddled away.

As you read, think about whether this creation myth is just one story or several stories told together. What is explained by this myth?

Tahmahnawis powers were understood to be supernatural powers.

Who are the main characters in this myth?

Moonlight,
Isle of Shoals,
Frederick Childe Hassam

The mainland refers to a continent or the main part of a continent. Which continent do you think this is? What is the setting?

After paddling for many days and many nights, they came to some islands. They steered their way through them and at last reached the mainland. Here they stopped. The mainland was not so large as it is now, because it had not grown much yet. Wandering toward the sunrise, the man and woman came to the country now known as the Okanogan country. They liked that best, and there they stayed.

By this time they were so burned by the sun and whipped by the storm winds that their whiteness was entirely gone. Their skins were tanned a reddish brown. That is why the Indians have that color. All the Indians are the children of this first grandfather and grandmother.

Can you imagine this myth as oral literature, being told to people by a storyteller?

In time to come, the Okanogan Indians say, the lakes will melt the foundations of the world, and the rivers will cut the world loose. Then it will float as the island did many suns and snows ago. That will be the end of the world.

Directions Choose the letter of the best answer or write the answer using complete sentences.

Comprehension: Identifying Facts

1. What kind of powers does Scomalt have?
   A She had Tahmahnawis powers.
   B She had supernatural powers.
   C She could create whatever she wished.
   D all of the above

2. Why does Scomalt send the "wicked giants" away from her?

3. How do the last surviving man and woman giants get away when their island begins to sink?

Comprehension: Putting Ideas Together

4. In this myth, Scomalt drives away the people who made war. What does this say about the Okanogan people's view of war?
   A They are peace loving.
   B They often quarrel among themselves.
   C They like the noise of the battle.
   D Their heroes often lead them into battle.

5. In the Okanogan tradition, how did their people come to have the skin color they did?

6. How is the story about the beginning of the world similar to the Okanogan idea about the end of the world? How are the two different?

Understanding Literature: Oral Literature

Oral literature includes stories told from generation to generation. Sometimes the tellers would add, take away, or change details as they told the story. But, even though the details might change, the basic ideas of the story remain the same.

7. Describe the main events of this myth in the order in which they occurred.

8. What details may other storytellers add or subtract and still tell the same story?

Critical Thinking

9. Why do you think this creation myth includes an explanation of the people's skin color?

Thinking Creatively

10. How would you describe the character of Scomalt to someone who has not read this myth? How is she the same as and different from other female characters you have read about in stories or seen in movies?

After Reading continued on next page

The Beginning and the End of the World *Okanogan Traditional Myth*

 ### Grammar Check

Nouns are the names of people, animals, places, things, or ideas. In this myth, the names of the characters—*Scomalt*, the *giants*, the *man*, and the *woman*—are all nouns. Find 10 other nouns in this myth that are things, places, or ideas. List each noun and note whether it is a name of a thing, place, or idea.

 ### Writing on Your Own

Write the first draft of a description of the day Scomalt sent the white giants away. Be sure to include details about the way Scomalt may have felt. Review your work with a partner to see which parts need rewriting.

 ### Speaking and Listening

If you were going to tell someone else the myth of "The Beginning and the End of the World," what tone of voice would you use to retell the story? In other words, how would you make your voice sound? What tone would you use for a young audience? For an older audience? Explain how your tone might affect the people who are listening to you.

 ### Viewing

Look at the picture on page 50. What objects do you see in it? To which part of the myth do you think this painting is connected? Does this picture help you better understand the myth and the Okanogan people who created it? What other kinds of photographs and art might you add to help other readers better understand this myth?

 ### Research

If you wanted to learn more about the Okanogan people, what resources might you use? Brainstorm to think of ideas or topics you could research and sources of information about each. Make a list of the topics, ideas, and two or three places where you might look to find this information. You may want to use the Concept Map described in Appendix A to help you record your ideas.

BEFORE READING THE SELECTION

Loki and the Master Builder by Snorri Sturluson

About the Author

Like other civilizations, the Norse people of Scandinavia had a rich collection of myths about their gods, goddesses, and other important figures in their culture. As with most myths, Norse myths were first told orally. Snorri Sturluson was one of the first people to collect these myths into a written work.

Snorri Sturluson was born in 1179 in Hvammur, Iceland, where the Norse people had settled. Snorri was a leader of his people. He was elected to the highest office in the land, a position much like United States president. However, at that time, the king of Norway wanted to take control of Iceland. Afraid that Snorri might get in his way, he had Snorri killed in 1241.

Snorri also was a poet and historian. He is best known for two important works. The first, *Heimskringla*, tells the history of the kings of Norway from ancient times until 1177. The second, called *The Prose Edda*, is a handbook for poets. It also contains myths of the Scandinavian people, including "Loki and the Master Builder."

About the Selection

"Loki and the Master Builder" shows how powerful the Norse gods were. In Norse myths, Loki is a character who plays tricks and causes trouble. He can also change shape and sometimes appears as an old woman. Loki was a giant who lived among the gods, even though giants and gods were enemies. The Norse people would have known right away that they could expect trouble from Loki.

Objectives

■ To identify the problem in a myth

■ To understand how problems enrich plots

■ To explore how tricksters find solutions to the story's problem

Before Reading continued on next page

Loki and the Master Builder   *by Snorri Sturluson*

problem the focus, or main concern, of the plot of a story

trickster a character who uses his cleverness and quick thinking to outsmart enemies, sometimes by playing tricks on them

Literary Terms In literature, a **problem** is a situation that gives the plot a center of attention. The problem in "Loki and the Master Builder" is that a master builder has offered to build the gods a stronghold. They need this stronghold, which is a kind of fort or protected place, to be safe. But in return, the builder wants to marry Freyja, goddess of love, and also wants to own the sun and the moon. As the plot continues, things happen that make it difficult for Loki, the hero, to solve the problem. As you will see in this Norse myth, sometimes a problem is best solved by a **trickster**. A trickster is a sometimes-sly character who depends on his skills to find a clever and unexpected solution to the problem.

Reading on Your Own As you read this myth, look for the problem that is the center for all the other events that happen in the myth's plot. In literature, the story's problem sometimes seems to grow even larger as the story progresses, making its outcome even more uncertain. As you read, notice the events in the plot that complicate the situation. The events make you unsure if the problem presented in the myth will ever be solved. Reread the story if any of the events seem unclear.

Writing on Your Own Think about a character in a movie, play, or story you've read who could be called a trickster. Write a one-paragraph sketch of the character. Explain why you feel he or she has the characteristics of a trickster.

Vocabulary Focus Because this is a Norse myth, its author often uses terms that would be familiar to a Norse reader or listener. Skim the text to find several of these words, which are often defined for you. What do these terms add to the myth?

Think Before You Read Based on the title, what do you think this myth is about?

LOKI *and the Master Builder*

In the early days of the settlement of the gods, when they had established Midgard and made Valhalla, a builder came to them and offered to make a **stronghold** so excellent that it would be safe and secure against cliff giants and frost **ogres,** even if they got inside Midgard.

He **stipulated** that as his reward he was to have Freyja as his wife and possession of the sun and moon besides.

The Æsir had a conference, and they struck this bargain with the builder. He should receive what he asked for, if he succeeded in building the stronghold in one winter. But if, on the first day of summer, any part of it was unfinished, he was to forfeit his reward; nor was he to receive anyone's help in the work.

When they told him these terms, however, he asked them to let him have the help of his horse, which was called Svadilfari, and acting on the advice of Loki, the gods granted this to him.

Midgard is where the gods live. *Valhalla* is the home of heroes who have died in battle.

The Æsir are gods. They are sworn enemies of giants.

Loki is a trickster, shape-changer, and general troublemaker. Why do you think he gives this advice?

Loki trickster and shape-changer

Freyja goddess of fertility, death, love, and war

Thor god of thunder

stronghold a protected place, safe from enemies

ogres monsters

stipulated demanded as a condition of agreement

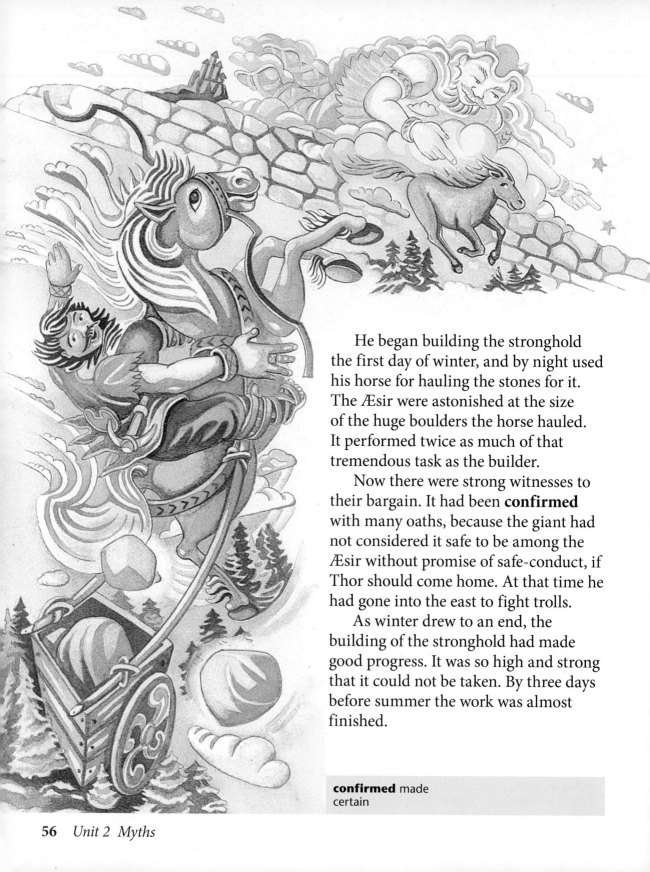

He began building the stronghold the first day of winter, and by night used his horse for hauling the stones for it. The Æsir were astonished at the size of the huge boulders the horse hauled. It performed twice as much of that tremendous task as the builder.

Now there were strong witnesses to their bargain. It had been **confirmed** with many oaths, because the giant had not considered it safe to be among the Æsir without promise of safe-conduct, if Thor should come home. At that time he had gone into the east to fight trolls.

As winter drew to an end, the building of the stronghold had made good progress. It was so high and strong that it could not be taken. By three days before summer the work was almost finished.

confirmed made certain

The gods then sat down in their judgment seats and sought for a way out. They **recalled** that it had been Loki who had given the advice to marry Freyja into Giantland and also to ruin the sky and heaven by giving the sun and moon to the giants. They threatened him with an evil death if he did not **devise** a plan whereby the builder would forfeit his wages. Loki swore that he would do this, no matter what it might cost him.

That same evening, when the builder was driving out after stones with his stallion Svadilfari, a mare ran out of a wood up to the horse and **whinnied** to him. The stallion became frantic and ran into the wood after the mare. The two horses galloped about all night, and the work was delayed.

The next day, when the builder saw that the work would not be finished, he flew into a rage. As soon as the Æsir saw for certain that it was a giant who had come there, they **disregarded** their oaths and called on Thor.

He came at once and raised the hammer Mjölnir **aloft.** Thor paid the builder his wages, and it was not the sun and the moon. He struck him such a blow that his skull shivered into **fragments,** and he sent him down to Niflhel.

Loki, however, had had such dealings with Svadilfari that some time later he bore a foal. It was gray and had eight legs, and amongst gods and men that horse is the best.

Why do you think the gods want a way out of their problem? Why did they make this bargain with the builder in the first place?

Loki has disguised himself as the mare.

recalled remembered

devise to think up; to invent

whinnied the sound a horse makes

disregarded paid no attention to

aloft up in the air

fragments small pieces

AFTER READING THE SELECTION

Loki and the Master Builder   *by Snorri Sturluson*

Directions Choose the letter of the best answer or write the answer using complete sentences.

Comprehension: Identifying Facts

1. What does the builder want as a reward for building a stronghold, or fort, for the Æsir?
   A a very strong horse
   B a fort of his own
   C to marry Freyja
   D one of Thor's thunderbolts

2. How did the builder move so many stones so easily?

3. What does Thor do to "pay" the builder?

Comprehension: Putting Ideas Together

4. Why do the gods blame Loki for accepting the terms of the bargain with the builder?
   A Loki wanted to marry Freyja.
   B Loki had used his magic hammer to kill other giants.
   C Loki had told them to accept the bargain.
   D Loki had a magic horse.

5. How important is it for the Norse gods to keep their word? Find evidence to support your answer.

6. The builder in this myth seems to be a giant. For what reasons might the Æsir have entered into a bargain with their sworn enemy?

Understanding Literature: Problem and Trickster

In literature, the problem is a situation that must be solved if the story is to end. Characters, especially trickster characters, can help solve the story's problem. Tricksters often have very creative solutions.

7. In your own words, what is the problem that focuses the myth about Loki and the master builder?

8. How does the trickster Loki help solve the problem? Were there other ways he could have helped?

Critical Thinking

9. It appears that the Æsir do not know for sure that the master builder is a giant until he goes into a rage about not finishing his job. How could they not know?

Thinking Creatively

10. In your opinion, is it fair of Thor to punish the builder? Explain your reasoning.

Grammar Check

An *appositive* is a noun or pronoun that appears beside another noun or pronoun to explain it. For example, look at this sentence: "Loki, a trickster, helped solve the problem in this myth." The noun in the sentence is *Loki*. The appositive is *trickster,* because it gives us more information about the noun. Look for appositives in the myth you have just read. How do appositives help you better understand what you are reading?

 Writing on Your Own

What do you think the master builder's stronghold looked like? What clues can you find about this in the myth? Use this information and your imagination to write a short description of the stronghold.

Speaking and Listening

Sometimes, listeners like to have a graphic organizer to look at as they listen to someone speak. This helps them listen carefully to the speaker's main points. Prepare a Sequence Chain described in Appendix A for listeners who might attend an event where you are planning to speak on what you have learned about Norse gods.

 Media

Which character would you feature on the cover of a program to give to the audience of a play based on this myth? Draw a picture of what the cover might look like. You can also use pictures cut from magazines.

 **Technology**

How would this myth be different if it were set in the present day? For example, would Thor have used a laser instead of a hammer? Rewrite the story showing the effect of modern technology.

The Moon Spirit and Coyote Woman   by Clive Grace

Clive Grace
1964–

Objectives

- To define a story-within-a-story
- To identify plot lines
- To name and determine the nature of a story's narrator

About the Author

Many people call themselves storytellers. Few of them are given that title officially. Clive Grace is one of them. In fact, he is qualified as a storyteller by the British library system. He has a Grade B rating, which means he is qualified to tell stories to young people from ages 11 to 13.

Clive Grace was born in North London in 1964 and now lives in the city of Bath, England, with his dog, Galen. A computer journalist by trade, Grace is deeply involved in creating and telling stories. Tanais the fox, a thoughtful storyteller himself, is one of Grace's most popular characters. Tanais is the featured character in a series of stories that Grace tells in person and on his Internet Web site. "The Moon Spirit and Coyote Woman" is part of this series. Grace calls this story "a sort of modern folk myth."

About the Selection

"The Moon Spirit and Coyote Woman" has many of the same characteristics as other myths in this unit do. It was created to be told orally; its characters have great powers; and it tells a story about the early days of the earth. However, this is a modern myth, full of descriptions about setting and characters, unlike the other myths in this unit. Unlike the characters in fables and other, older myths, the characters in this story are not flat characters. They are not chosen because they represent one trait, as the Dog in "The Dog in the Manger" was. They are more complex. They grow and change over the course of the story. The settings of this myth are also described in more detail than the settings in other myths included in this unit.

Literary Terms This myth is actually a **story-within-a-story**. This means that a second, inner story is told within the first, or framing, story. In this case, the **narrator,** or person who is telling the story, is Tanais the fox. Tanais then becomes the narrator of another story—the myth of "The Moon Spirit and Coyote Woman." Sometimes, authors use a story-within-a-story as a way to enrich the way readers experience their stories. They use the mood or details in one story to mirror the mood or details in the second story.

Reading on Your Own Readers often set a purpose for reading before they begin. They decide whether they want to read to learn new information, to perform a new task, or simply to have a literary experience. Sometimes they combine these goals. For example, someone reading a new myth might like to learn about the characters as well as enjoy the experience of reading literature. For what purposes might you read this myth?

Writing on Your Own What do you already know about coyotes? Use a Concept Map, described in Appendix A, to help you organize these thoughts.

Vocabulary Focus The author of this modern myth is British. He writes using the British spelling of some words, such as *favourite* instead of the common American spelling *favorite*. As you read this story, note other words that are spelled somewhat differently than Americans spell them. Why do you think these differences happen?

Think Before You Read The other myths in this unit have all had settings in the past. In what kind of a setting might you expect this myth to happen?

story-within-a-story a second story told within another story

narrator one who tells a story

The Moon Spirit and Coyote Woman

Why Coyotes Howl at the Moon

As you read, notice how the character of Tanais is developed and described. How is he different from the "flat" animal characters often found in fables?

To *catch your bearings* is an idiom that means to figure out where you are and where you're going.

Notice the details of setting. How would you describe the location of Tanais's midnight walk?

It was midnight and Tanais the fox was walking alone, deep in thought. It was a beautiful night, a full moon shone high in the sky and he could hear waves crashing against the distant shoreline. He felt a need to look out at the sea, so he decided to walk by himself in the moonlight for a while and maybe smoke his pipe a little. He didn't know *why* he felt this need to be alone, only that he needed it every now and then. Hoping he would feel a lot happier with the sound of waves and the smell of salt, he sniffed **expectantly** at the sea air to catch his bearings and started on his journey.

Leaving a long trail of paw prints behind him, Tanais walked the entire length of the beach occasionally puffing on his pipe. At one point he came across a walking stick tossed upon the sand. It was actually a short length of tree branch or a thick twig that had been **discarded** by the ocean; a few tiny **barnacles** had attached themselves to one end and it was still quite damp from floating in the sea, but it would dry out eventually, so he picked it up, brushed some seaweed off of it and continued on his journey, propping the stick on one shoulder.

Tanais especially liked to walk along the shoreline and watch the waves as they crashed against the rocks in the distance. It was a strangely magical night; at one point he thought he heard the sound of fluttering wings somewhere

expectantly as if looking forward to something

discarded thrown away or cast off

barnacles small sea animals that attach themselves to rocks or floating objects

deep in the darkness. Stopping to look around, he saw no one, so he shrugged—snuggling deeper into a scarf he had brought along for the night—continuing on his midnight walk.

Eventually he came upon a rocky cove; it was a favourite haunt of his and he found it ideal as a place of quiet **contemplation**—a place where he could get some thinking done at times like this.

A *haunt* is a place someone goes to a lot.

Finding his favourite spot in the cove, Tanais stared for a long while at the moon reflecting off the surface of the sea and felt a **pang** of loneliness. He felt this every now and then and indeed had come to live with it and accept it. He knew that the life of a wanderer is sometimes like that, but he wouldn't have it any other way.

Favourite is the British spelling of favorite. Later, you will see *colourful* for colorful and *centre* for center; *realise* for realize and *ploughing* for plowing. These are all British spellings.

The fox sat down on a smooth rock jutting out over a shallow pool of water; every now and then he puffed on his pipe, sending plumes of smoke into the cold air. Apart from the occasional crash of waves in the distance, all was quiet around him.

Watching the shadows of rocks made by the moon's reflection, Tanais quietly pondered how different everything looked at night; in the daytime the pool was home to tiny sea creatures caught in the low tide, but at night it became something quite different and enchanting. Tanais watched the water in the pool as it caught the moon's reflection, bathing nearby rocks and stones in a shimmering silver light. It was one of the most beautiful places Tanais knew of and he would often return there when he felt sad, lonely or just a little thoughtful.

As he puffed on his pipe Tanais remembered a story he had been told as a cub, a story about the moon and the sea and many other things besides. The moment was perfect for the telling of this particular tale, but there was no one around to hear it! So he sat with his head resting in both paws and looked out at the sea and the moon's reflection, pondering what to do with the story.

How would you describe Tanais's feelings as he sits on the rock looking at the moon's reflection on the water?

contemplation study; deep thought; **pang** a sharp pain

After a while, Tanais shrugged a little and looked thoughtfully at the moon. Try as hard as he might he couldn't get the tale out of his head. Suddenly an idea crossed his mind and he paused for a few moments, pondered quietly on his idea before turning his muzzle skywards where he addressed the moon with a smile. "Then I think I shall tell it to you, my friend. You know, I've never told a story to the moon before—I hope you like it." Shifting into a more comfortable position, Tanais paused only to push his scarf a little higher onto his shoulders and he began his tale:

"This story happened years ago," began Tanais a little uncertainly. "It happened many years before I, or anyone I know was born—at a time when this land was still quite young and when there were many places filled with wild magic."

Tanais reached for the stick he had found on the beach and started to draw shapes in the sand in front of him. "Of all the creatures, the most popular, and certainly the most **prolific** was the coyote," he said, his sketching rapidly turning into the outline of a coyote.

Here, Tanais becomes the narrator of a story-within-a-story. Who is the audience for his tale?

prolific producing
many young

"Some legends say that the coyotes were the first of the creatures to be made for the new land and that they were told by the creator to look after the land whilst he went off and made the rest of us." Tanais laughed a little. "Others say that the coyote was put here so that none of us would have an easy life." The fox's laugh trailed off into a **wistful** sigh. "I guess we shall never know exactly for sure," he said as he continued drawing. "Back in those days, people just lived by the fact that the sun always followed the moon and that Winter always followed Summer. They didn't have any need for clocks or calendars, choosing to sleep when they were tired and waking when the sun came up." With a flourish, Tanais finished his drawing and stopped for a moment to admire the **likeness.**

With a satisfied nod, Tanais looked back up at the moon. "This story is about one tribe of coyotes in particular," he said. "The other coyote tribes had **dispersed** throughout the land and had fallen into fights and **squabbles** with each other— mainly over land or food, but this tribe was different. Theirs was a peaceful tribe, working hard and quietly living off the land in their own way."

Becoming more elaborate with his drawing, Tanais started to sketch out some more coyotes in the sand; some were ploughing the land, others were harvesting fields or pulling fishing nets in small boats on the sea. Dotted around his picture were small teepee-like tents—out of which poked the faces and noses of coyote mothers with their cubs.

As Tanais drew each coyote he explained to the moon what each one was doing. "None of them were warriors. They lived a peaceful life in spite of their warring cousins," he concluded as he put the stick down. "Some were farmers, others herded cattle or rode horses, whereas a few would catch fish in the ocean."

Tanais brushed some sand off of his paws. "The other tribes lived far away and would fight and squabble amongst each other, fouling and spoiling wherever they went. The tribe by the sea was, by contrast, the smallest of all the coyote tribes

Whilst is an old spelling of *while.*

How do details from the first story help you understand the second story?

How does Tanais "illustrate" his story-within-a-story?

---

wistful sad	**likeness** a copy or picture	**dispersed** scattered
		squabbles arguments or quarrels

and their peacefulness didn't interest the others. As they never went attacking or plundering anyone, they never got attacked themselves. After a while they had been all but completely forgotten by the other tribes."

Tanais picked up the stick again and started to very carefully adapt the picture of the first coyote he drew. "Not very far away from the tribe lived a coyote woman," Tanais said. "She was very beautiful and wore a green and purple cape and the feather necklace of a medicine woman. Known only as *Why-ay-looh´*, or 'Coyote Woman,' she loved to take long walks by herself in the plains, searching for herbs and roots that she would later turn into powerful medicines.

As you read the story-within-a-story, look for details of the setting.

"One of her favourite places was a rocky cove; called Medicine Cove, it was shielded on all three sides by a sheer wall of rocks, **accessible** by a secret path that only she knew about. Coyote Woman would often spend many hours sitting in her cove, looking at the moon as it rose over the ocean. Sometimes she would sing to herself or **devise** new magic and medicine, sometimes she would braid colourful beads into her long golden fur or prepare her herbs. In the centre of the cove was a pool of water that she would often use to look into and think about things when she wanted to be by herself and not be disturbed.

How is Medicine Cove like the rocky cove that Tanais himself likes to visit?

"One night, Coyote Woman went to her cove and sat on an outcropping of rocks that looked over the pool. As she sat, braiding beads into her hair and humming a song to herself, she looked into the pool and saw to her surprise what looked like a face smiling up at her in the reflection of the moon. With a startled yelp, she jumped back and looked up at the moon shining high in the sky but saw nothing unusual there. Shaking her head, she looked back at the pool and stared into the water."

An *outcropping* is the part of a rock formation that appears at the surface of the ground.

Tanais looked down into the pool and saw his reflection looking up at him. The reflection of the moon had slid a little further into the pool and shone behind him, lighting the outline of his ears with an **eerie** glow. He thought about playing with his reflection using the stick he had just been

---

accessible reachable   **devise** to think up; to invent   **eerie** spooky

drawing with, but he thought better of it. He paused to remember where he was in the story, then continued.

"At first she thought it must have been some sort of **illusion**—that the reflection in the moon was her *own* face looking up at herself from the pool—so she peered a little closer. Although the face was indistinct and shimmered slightly as it rippled in the water, Coyote Woman found that if she squinted her eyes as she looked into the pool, she could quite clearly see the image of a pure white coyote staring up at her with his deep blue eyes.

"Nothing like this had ever happened before! She had **acknowledged** long ago that this was a very magical place but knowing about magic and coming face to face with it are two very different things."

Tanais looked into the pool again. As he told the story he noticed that the reflection of the moon had slid further into the centre of the pool, bathing even more of the surroundings in its eerie light. This made the rocks appear as if they were formed from glass and made the wet sand glisten with an icy blue **radiance** as the waves crashed and then drew back from the shoreline in a foaming silver-white carpet.

Although **entranced** by the beauty of the moment, Tanais remembered his audience; hard as it might be, once a story is started, it should always be finished. He took a **refreshing** gulp of sea air to bring him back to his story and continued.

"If Coyote Woman was surprised at what she saw from within the pool she was completely unprepared for what followed," said Tanais, looking around him. "The face in the pool became more real and more solid with each passing moment until after a minute or so *Hah-ah´*—a moon spirit— was shimmering in the pool, looking up at her with his blue eyes."

Tanais paused for a moment; the hairs on the back of his neck and all along his tail were **bristling** with excitement. The cool sea air had suddenly become as sharp as a razor's

illusion an unreal vision	**radiance** glowing light	**refreshing** giving back strength or life
acknowledged admitted; recognized	**entranced** filled with joy or delight	**bristling** standing up or out from the body

edge and seemed to fill the cove with an almost electrifying energy—like the moment just before a thunderstorm. Tanais waited with **bated** breath for something to happen; he half-expected the Coyote Woman or the spirit from the pool to appear at any moment, but the moment passed and nothing appeared—so he gathered his thoughts together and continued a little more cautiously, his whiskers twitching and one ear cocked to catch the slightest change around him.

"The story is a little unclear around this point . . ." said Tanais, scratching at an ear as he observed the pattern of rocks shimmering and glowing under the moon's light, ". . . but the **version** of the story I prefer tells of the Coyote Woman and the moon spirit falling in love with each other." Smiling, the fox continued. "You see, the moon spirit loved to look down on this pool from where he lived on one of the moon's highest mountains. When the moon was full and at her most powerful, the moon coyote would shine down on the pool, spreading his magic into the rocks and sand.

"Some say that magic attracts more magic and as the cove was one of the few places still left where wild magic was still very much alive, he naturally felt an **affinity** with the place. The fact that a beautiful Coyote Woman also loved this place merely added to his insistence that he should appear in front of her.

"Without a word, the moon spirit started to lift himself up out of the pool. First a pink nose pushed through the water, followed by a muzzle and then a pair of milky white ears. The moon coyote was pushing very hard against something as he slowly **heaved** more and more of his body out of the pool, pausing every now and then to catch his breath. Water didn't drip off of him, rather the water seemed to solidify and *become* part of him, drawing out into long strands of silver-white hair.

"Coyote Woman stood and watched breathless as Moon Coyote lifted more and more of himself out of the pool.

bated kept low and shallow	**version** a form or type	**affinity** a liking for something
		heaved lifted up and out

Fighting with all his might, he strained against the water that seemed to cling to him. It was as if it wanted to drag the moon coyote back down, but he continued, straining along with every muscle in his body until he finally leapt free of the pool and stood triumphant in the moonlight.

"The next morning, Coyote Woman and Moon Coyote went into the village. Seeing their medicine woman walking into the village with a stranger, the tribe immediately stopped what they were doing and came rushing to see who her strange new companion was. She padded to the Chief of the tribe's tent and knelt as the Chief of the tribe who was called *Le-ee´-oo* came out to see what was going on.

Moon Coyote is the moon spirit.

"'*Le-ee´-oo!*' said Coyote Woman, holding her head down, 'this is *Hah-ah´*,'" pointing at Moon Coyote. 'He came to me last night from out of the pool in Medicine Cove. I wish to marry him,' she said rather matter-of-factly. There was a gasp from the villagers as she said this because the medicine women normally didn't marry and when they did, they certainly didn't marry at such a young age.

"The Chief just nodded and looked at Moon Coyote as he slowly walked around him. Every now and then he sniffed and prodded at Moon Coyote and muttered to himself and exchanged words with his **advisers.** Everyone fell silent as he did this until finally the Chief looked deeply into his eyes, snorted to himself and nodded again.

"Turning to Coyote Woman, he looked at her and said rather gruffly, 'Medicine woman, *Hah-ah´* is a spirit, a moon coyote, he is not from this land. Why do you wish to marry him?'

"'Because I love him!' she said, still kneeling '. . . and because he loves me.'

"*Le-ee´-oo* snorted again, but this seemed to be what he wanted to hear, so he looked back at the moon coyote and asked, '. . . and do you love her *Hah-ah´*? Will you stay with her for as long as you live?'

"The moon coyote nodded and padded over to Coyote Woman and gently lifted her up off the ground. 'I do,' he said, 'I will love your medicine woman even after I die.'

"'Then let it be so,' said the Chief. Turning to the villagers the Chief proclaimed in a loud and very formal voice, 'Our medicine woman has a husband. He is *Hah-ah´* of the moon tribe. From now on he shall be known as "Moon Coyote."' With a nod and a gentle smile at the couple, *Le-ee´-oo* walked back into his tent, followed by his advisers. Coyote Woman and Moon Coyote were married."

Tanais frowned a little to himself. Had he ended the story there, it would have been a good place to stop, but even he would be the first to admit that nothing much happened and there was more. ". . . And I suspect you know there's more to the story, don't you?" said Tanais, eyeing the moon suspiciously as he sat down on his rock again. Looking at the shoreline and noticing the water was slowly crawling up the beach toward the pool, the fox reckoned that he would have just enough time to finish telling his tale without getting trapped by the rising tide, so settling down to finish the rest of the story, Tanais took one last puff from his pipe and continued:

"Of course Coyote Woman and Moon Coyote were very happy together; they went back to their home by the sea and

What do you think will happen next?

advisers people who give advice

watched the waves beating against the shore. Throughout the day they were visited by villagers and friends—bearing gifts and blessings for the newly-weds. Later in the afternoon, they decided to explore the beach and Coyote Woman showed her husband the places she liked to go and things she liked to see. Together they laughed and skipped in the sand, chasing each other up and down the beach as they played games with each other.

"In the evening, Coyote Woman went down to the beach and took her beads and herbs with her. Her husband had gone hunting with his new friends and tribe members, so she thought it would be a good time to sit by herself and **contemplate** how different her life had suddenly become. She thought lovingly about her husband and soon her thoughts drifted towards raising a family together."

Tanais sighed to himself as he pictured the image in his mind. "For the first time in her life Coyote Woman was truly contented."

Tanais stopped and shrugged as he remembered the story. "Coyote Woman was lost in her own dreams and braiding her hair when, all of a sudden, she heard the distant sound of a yelp followed by a cry of pain. Someone was hurt, and it wasn't far away by the sound of it. She rushed to the top of a sandy hillock to see better and, to her horror, saw her husband in the distance lying on the floor twitching.

A *hillock* is a small hill.

"As he was the newest member of the tribe and because he had just been married, it was agreed that the hunters were to go on an expedition and that Moon Coyote was to have the first try at pulling down a bison," explained Tanais, tapping the ashes from his pipe into the sand. "Moon Coyote had never hunted one of these before—being something of a **rarity** where he came from—and it came as no surprise that he had badly **miscalculated**. As he chased after his prey, it **swerved** madly in front of him, trampling him under its powerful hooves, lifting him into the air with its short, but nonetheless

An *expedition* is a trip. A *bison* is a buffalo, a large wild animal.

contemplate to study or think about

rarity something not usually seen

miscalculated judged or figured out wrongly

swerved turned sharply

Why do you think the hunters allowed Moon Coyote to go after the first bison, when he had no hunting experience?

lethal horns before dashing him on the floor with a sickening crack of bones.

"Seeing her husband lying there, Coyote Woman didn't hesitate, she grabbed her herbs and ran as fast as she could to his side. By the time she arrived, Moon Coyote was barely alive. He was unconscious and his breath was rasping—a thick pool of blood had soaked into the sand and the rear half of his body lay twisted on the floor. You didn't have to be a medicine woman to realise that his back had been broken.

"Nevertheless, Coyote Woman tried to help her husband; she applied her strongest and most powerful medicines—but everything she did to try and heal him was in vain. Moon Coyote's beautiful white coat was now a dull grey and was caked with blood where the bison had tossed him into the air. His deep blue eyes had started to mist over and his rasping breath got fainter with every passing breath. Coyote Woman's instincts told her that he was dying.

"She thought desperately of possible remedies and cures, but this was far beyond her healing capabilities. Eventually, and with tear-filled eyes, she admitted defeat and turned away from her husband to howl a cry so painful and so desperate that everyone for miles around stopped in their tracks and listened with dread at the pain in Coyote Woman's voice.

"There was nothing else to do but to look on helpless as her Moon Coyote's breath faded. She applied what little medicine she could to ease the pain away and just sat, watching Moon Coyote slowly die—lit by the moon as it rose slowly over the sea. Never before had she felt so helpless, if only there was something she could do!

"All of a sudden she had an idea! It was crazy and desperate, but then she *was* desperate. Lifting Moon Coyote's dying body in her paws, she ran down to Medicine Cove. The moon coyote was already so far gone that he only moaned **pitifully** and his breath started to rasp and become more ragged again.

"When she finally arrived, Coyote Woman spread her dying husband out in the shallow pool. Propping his head

Why do you think Coyote Woman brings Moon Coyote to Medicine Cove?

---

lethal deadly   **pitifully** causing sorrow

gently on her robes, she watched helpless as his life seemed to **ebb** from his body into the pool.

"Pointing her muzzle towards the moon, the Coyote Woman howled again, a lonely, broken howl. Moon Coyote sagged as the life finally left his body and he breathed his last. Coyote Woman looked on with bated breath, waiting for something to happen, but the moon just carried on its upward ascent into the night sky, shining down on the cove, the moon coyote and his **disconsolately** sobbing widow."

Tanais stared into the pool and sniffed. "The Moon felt that Moon Coyote's death was unfair and although she hadn't the power to bring Coyote Woman's husband back to life, she *was*, nevertheless, an important part of the wild magic—a magic that was in existence long before death came into the world. She looked down sadly on the sobbing Coyote Woman and decided to do something about it.

"After Coyote Woman had cried herself out, she looked miserably at where her husband lay in the pool and saw, to her astonishment, the ghostly **apparition** of her husband floating above his body. The moon's silver light was shining down on the pool—stronger and brighter than it had ever been before—and his body was still lying in the shallow pool, but the huge ugly blood stain in his side had been washed away by the pool. The spirit of her husband looked down on his body and sniffed at it before looking at his wife and, to her amazement, smiled at her."

Tanais stopped. Picking up his stick, he looked at the moon and frowned. "No one really knows what happened as the story ends there. The next day the other tribe members eventually found their way into Medicine Cove and discovered Coyote Woman's drowned body lying next to her husband in the pool.

"Some stories say that Coyote Woman died of a broken heart," Tanais looked carefully at the rising tide, "others say that she had drowned—too heartbroken to notice, or to care—I guess we shall never know," and he kicked a little at the sand. "But the stories all agree on one thing, however.

According to this myth, why do coyotes howl at the moon?

ebb to flow away	**disconsolately** impossible to comfort	**apparition** a vision or appearance

On the night they died, a star appeared next to the moon. It's one of the brightest stars in the sky and is the first to come out in the summer evenings. If you look at it very carefully, you'll see that it appears as if it is two stars joined closely together."

Tanais picked up his hat and looked at his drawings in the sand as the waves crawled closer up the shoreline. The cove was nearly filled with water now and he would have to hurry in order to get out and not get his paws wet. Soon his pictures would be gone—washed away as if they were never there. "Nothing's permanent," muttered the fox as he quickly gathered his belongings together and started on his journey home, his spirit strangely lifted by the telling of such a sad story.

As he turned to walk home, he took one last look at the water rolling **relentlessly** into the cove. The waves were much heavier now and the water was much higher than before. Nodding his head and sniffing the air one last time, Tanais raised his hat to the moon and walked off.

Had he been a little closer to the pool, Tanais would have seen the faces of two shimmering Coyotes—one white, the other golden—holding each other and looking at him as the water washed over them.

What other natural event does this myth explain?

relentlessly without softening or letting up

AFTER READING THE SELECTION

The Moon Spirit and Coyote Woman   *by Clive Grace*

Directions Choose the letter of the best answer or write the answer using complete sentences.

Comprehension: Identifying Facts

1. At what time of day does Tanais tell his story?
 A midnight
 B noon
 C morning
 D evening

2. To whom does he tell his story?
 A the sea
 B the rocks
 C the pool
 D the moon

3. What does Tanais do as he tells the story?

4. What details does Tanais give about the way Coyote Woman and Moon Coyote look?

5. What is Coyote Woman's favorite place to go?

6. How does Coyote Woman first meet the moon spirit?

7. How is Moon Coyote injured?

8. How does Coyote Woman try to help her wounded husband?

9. What happens in the heavens the night the two die?

10. What does Tanais fail to notice in the pool as he leaves?

Comprehension: Putting Ideas Together

11. How would you describe Tanais's mood as he begins to tell the story?
 A happy
 B upset
 C lonely
 D excited

12. What kind of mood or feeling does the setting of Tanais's story—a rocky cove at midnight—create?
 A lonely
 B magical
 C sad
 D thoughtful

13. Why do you think Tanais does not end his story with the wedding?

14. Give two examples of the importance of magic in the plot of this myth.

15. In what ways is this myth like a fable?

16. How are the animal characters in this myth like people?

17. What is one detail that is common to both the framing and the inner stories?

***After Reading* continued on next page**

18. Why does Coyote Woman bring her dying husband to Medicine Cove?

19. Why do you think Coyote Woman drowned?

20. In what ways does this myth explain its subtitle: *Why Coyotes Howl at the Moon*?

Understanding Literature: Story-Within-a-Story and Narrator

A story-within-a-story is a work with two separate plots. Each story is usually connected. Details in one story are sometimes repeated in the other. Each story has a narrator, or person who tells the story. Sometimes the narrator can be the same in both the framing story and the inner story.

21. Why would an author use a story-within-a-story?

22. Who is the narrator in the first or framing story that is part of "The Moon Spirit and Coyote Woman"? Who is the narrator in the second or inner story?

23. Outline the basic plot of Tanais's story.

24. Outline the basic plot of the myth of "The Moon Spirit and Coyote Woman."

25. Give two examples of ways in which Tanais's story helps you better understand the myth of "The Moon Spirit and Coyote Woman."

Critical Thinking

26. If Tanais the fox were a person, would you want him as a friend? Explain your opinion, using facts and details from the story that show how Tanais behaves.

27. How does the narrator describe the tribes of coyotes? How are these tribes different from and the same as the Okanogan peoples in the myth "The Beginning and the End of the World"?

28. Do you think that Clive Grace wants readers to believe this myth in the same way that ancient Greeks and Norse people believed in their myths? Explain your thinking.

29. Tanais says "knowing about magic and coming face to face with it are two very different things." What do you think this means?

Thinking Creatively

30. How do you think Tanais would have felt if he had seen the faces in the pool at the end of the story? Explain your answer.

Grammar Check

Verbs are action words. In sentences, they express physical or mental action, or describe a state of being. In our language, we use verbs in different forms to describe when the action happens—in the past, right now, and in the future. Since verbs are such powerful words, authors often work to make the verbs they use the most descriptive words possible. For example, Clive Grace could have said, "He *came* out of the water." Instead he said, "*Fighting* with all his might, he *strained* against the water that seemed to cling to him." The verbs he chose create a much stronger image for the reader.

Look in Appendixes B and C for other tips to strengthen your writing.

 ## Writing on Your Own

An *obituary* is a short article about someone who has died. It gives some details about the person's life as well as his or her death. Write an obituary for Moon Coyote and Coyote Woman.

 ## Speaking and Listening

In groups of four, take turns reading the inner story about Moon Coyote. Listen carefully as others read. How does listening affect the way you feel about the story?

 ## Media and Technology

As Tanais told his tale, he drew story details in the sand. What do you think they looked like? Use the Internet to locate images that show details of the story as Tanais may have drawn them in the sand, reflecting the events in the plot of this myth.

 ## Research

An interview is an effective way to gather more information about a story such as this. What details do you still want to know about the story? Who could you ask to find this information? List five good questions that you would ask. Avoid questions that can be answered with a "yes" or "no" answer.

One of the first decisions writers have to make is who will tell the story. Will the narrator—the storyteller—know everything about the plot? Or should the narrator be a character in the story? These choices all make a difference to the way the reader experiences the story.

If the person telling the story is also a character in it, we say the story is written in first person. First-person narrators use the pronouns *I* and *we*. If the narrator is not a character, the author is using a different point of view: third person. Third-person narrators use the pronouns *he*, *she*, *it*, and *they*. The myths in this unit were written using the third-person point of view.

Review

1. What role does the narrator play in a story?

2. In your own words, describe a third-person narrator.

3. A story begins, "As I looked around . . ." What does this tell you about the narrator?

4. How would the myth about Loki be different if Loki himself told the story?

5. Which kind of narrator do you prefer in the stories you read?

Writing on Your Own

One of Coyote Woman's favorite places was a rocky cove. Reread the description of the rocky cove. Write a paragraph that describes your favorite place. Write the paragraph from a first-person point of view.

First, gather your thoughts. Try to see the place in your mind. Write down notes to help you remember what you want to tell about your favorite place. Write a first draft. Review the draft carefully to make sure its words and grammar are correct. Make any changes needed and write a second draft.

Unit 2 has presented examples of another very old form of story: myth. All cultures have created myths to explain what they did not understand or what they thought of as holy. Unlike fables, myths were often part of religion. People believed them to be true.

Like fables, many myths were told orally before being written down. Myths have plots, settings, and characters, just as fables do, and they often have messages about life. However, the characters of myths are usually gods, goddesses, or heroes—human beings with unusual strengths and powers. We often find out more about the characters in myths than we do about the flat characters in fables.

Most myths can be grouped according to the kind of story they tell. Some myths explain how the world was created. Others explain events in nature, such as seasons and thunderstorms.

From myths, we can learn what people thought was important. We can also learn how people in different places explained the world, nature, and their own lives.

Selections

- "Prometheus," a Greek myth, explains what Prometheus suffered in order to give fire to human beings.

- "Demeter and Persephone," a Greek myth, tells how Demeter's curse explains why we have seasons.

- "Perseus and Medusa" is a Greek myth that describes how a brave hero killed a terrible monster.

- "The Beginning and the End of the World," from the Okanogan culture, explains how the world began and how it will end.

- "Loki and the Master Builder" is an ancient Norse myth first recorded by Snorri Sturluson. It tells what happened when the gods trusted Loki, the troublemaker.

- "The Moon Spirit and Coyote Woman," by Clive Grace, tells the tragic love story of two magical characters. It also explains why coyotes howl at the moon.

Directions Choose the letter of the best answer or write the answer using complete sentences.

Comprehension: Identifying Facts

1. The trickster character in the Norse myth about the Æsir is:
   A Thor
   B Freyja
   C the builder
   D Loki

2. What are some reasons that people have created myths?

3. How are myths different from fables? How are they the same?

4. To what compromise does Demeter agree to in order to see her daughter again?

5. How did the Okanogan people get the skin color they have, according to the myth?

Comprehension: Putting Ideas Together

6. What is the problem that focuses the myth of Perseus?
   A Perseus couldn't find his way home.
   B Perseus needed to kill Medusa.
   C Medusa was mad at him.
   D Perseus wanted to get married.

7. How is the myth of Prometheus like the myth of Loki and the Master Builder? How are the two myths different?

8. Compare the character of Prometheus with the character of Loki.

9. How would the myth of "The Moon Spirit and Coyote Woman" have been different if it was not told as a story-within-a-story?

10. Why are the characters in myths often gods, goddesses, and heroes with special powers? Does this add to or take away from the stories?

Understanding Literature: Simile

As you have read, similes are tools that writers use to compare objects and people. Similes include the word *like* or *as*. When Clive Grace writes that "The cool sea air had suddenly become *as sharp as a razor's edge*," he is using a simile. He is telling his readers to think of the air as the sharp edge of a razor, cutting into Tanais's fur. By using a simile, Grace tells us much more than if he had just said, "It was windy."

11. What do similes do?

12. How do similes help readers see a picture in their minds?

13. What character in this unit does this simile describe: *She was as angry as a hornet?*

14. Write a simile that describes the rocky cove in "The Moon Spirit and Coyote Woman."

15. What simile might people use to describe you?

Critical Thinking

16. If you were Perseus, would you have offered to kill Medusa? Why or why not?

17. If Perseus did not have the help of the gods, how might he complete his task?

18. How do you think Scomalt would feel if she were present as the Okanogan world ended?

19. If you were Freyja, how would you feel about being a prize in a contest over which you had no control?

Thinking Creatively

20. Which is your favorite myth in this unit? Explain why you like this work.

Speak and Listen

Prepare a brief oral report on one of the Greek or Norse gods or goddesses. You can use reference materials such as encyclopedias and books on mythology to gather information. Outline what you want to say. Use the outline to present your report to the class.

Writing on Your Own

Write a creation myth of your own, explaining how school may have been started. Your myth should have a setting, plot, and third-person narrator. Your characters should be gods, goddesses, or heroes. Review your work with a partner. Where can you make changes to help the reader understand your writing better?

Beyond Words

Create a collage that represents the characters or plot of the myth of Prometheus. You can use pictures and words from magazines, objects, and your own drawings to complete this project.

Test-Taking Tip

When studying for a test, use a marker to highlight important facts and terms in your notes. For a final review, read over the highlighted areas.

Paul Bunyan
Dave Fisher

Tall Tales and Legends

Tall tales and legends are important parts of American folklore. Like fables and myths, many tall tales and legends were first spread by word of mouth. Tall tales feature characters who are larger than life and have fantastic adventures. The stories often come from the American frontier and the colorful people who settled there. Legends are usually based on real people, places, or events. Some details may be true; others come straight from the storyteller's imagination.

In this unit, you will meet two colorful characters from tall tales, two legendary figures from American history, and in a modern legend, a man who has a strange adventure in the middle of the night.

"These are the stories that never, never die, that are carried like seed into a new country, are told to you and me and make in us new and lasting strengths."

—Meridel Le Sueur, *Nancy Hanks of Wilderness Road,* 1949

Unit 3

About Tall Tales and Legends

In every culture, people develop stories, customs, and traditions that they want to pass on to others. These all become part of the culture's folklore. Folklore includes stories and fairy tales, as well as sayings, games, songs, and dances. People living in an area or belonging to the same group preserve important parts of their history through their folklore. Many authors have used folklore as a basis for their work. However, folklore begins with ordinary people, not professional writers.

Tall tales and legends are important parts of American folklore. America's folklore has great variety. As people from different cultures settled in the United States, they brought their folklore with them. Some of their stories found their way into the American folklore. For example, stories in African folklore told about the adventures of Trickster Rabbit, who was clever enough to outsmart his enemies. These stories traveled with Africans when they came to the United States. Soon, Trickster Rabbit became B'rer Rabbit, a hero of many American folktales.

Folklore is part of oral literature. Most tall tales and legends, like fables and myths, were first told years ago and passed along by word of mouth. Telling stories, rather than writing them down, has many advantages. When you tell someone a story, you want to keep their attention. You spend time on the more interesting parts of the story and change details to suit your audience. The story is told a little differently each time, depending on whom you're telling it to. The basics of plot, character, and setting may stay the same, but the details change.

Tall tales are, first of all, stories. They all have a plot, characters, and setting. Very often, the setting and characters in American tall tales are drawn from the American frontier and the pioneers who settled there. The characters in these tales are larger than life. They tend to be taller, stronger, smarter, and braver than the usual person. For example, Joe Margarac could stir melted iron with his bare hands. Pecos Bill, another tall tale hero, rode a cyclone, creating Death Valley when he crashed as the storm "rained out." Tall tales show these characters using their great strengths to do things most of us could only imagine. In fact, tall tales are stories from the imagination. The ordinary rules of reason do not apply, much to the delight of the people who read or hear tall tales.

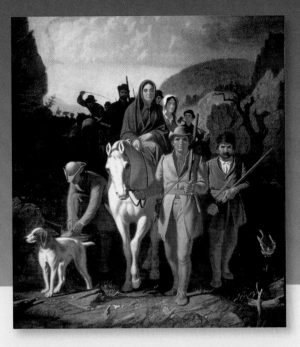

Daniel Boone escorting settlers through Cumberland Gap, 1851–1852, G. C. Bingham

Legends are another part of America's folklore. Legends are stories told about real people, places, or events. For example, in some legends, the characters are people who actually lived, such as Daniel Boone and Davy Crockett, or who may have actually lived, such as Joe Margarac or Annie Christmas, an eight-foot tall keelboat pilot. Other legends are built around a real event or a real place. When we listen to or read legends, we know that some details have been included just to make a good story. We also know that some parts of the story are true.

America's legends and tall tales give people a chance to look back at their past. We'll probably always enjoy these entertaining stories.

This unit includes two tall tales. "Babe the Blue Ox," as told by Esther Shephard, is about Paul Bunyan's huge ox and the wonderful things this animal could do. Walter Blair shows what can happen if you put your mind to it in "Feboldson, Western Scientist." Two legends, "John Henry" and "Life and Adventures of Calamity Jane, by Herself," tell the stories of two real characters from America's past. John Henry was an African American who helped build railways all along the Atlantic coast. Martha (Marthy) Cannary Burk had adventures that earned her the name Calamity Jane. The final story in the unit, "The Phantom Hitchhiker" by Daniel Cohen, is a modern urban legend about a driver who picks up a ghostly hitchhiker.

Babe the Blue Ox by Esther Shephard

Esther Shephard
1891–1975

Objectives

- To read and understand a tall tale
- To explore the characteristics of this genre of literature
- To identify and give examples of folklore, exaggeration, dialect, and humor

tall tale a story from the past that features larger-than-life characters who have unreal adventures

About the Author

Esther Shephard was born in Minneapolis, Minnesota, in 1891. The age of exploring the American frontier was drawing to a close. However, the spirit of this exciting time lives on in her works.

Her first book, *Paul Bunyan*, retold many of the **tall tales** about this famous imaginary hero of American stories. Shephard drew from many sources to create one of the best collections of Paul Bunyan stories. She also wrote books based on other stories that were part of the history of many cultures. These included *The Cowherd and the Sky Maiden*, her telling of a Chinese legend that was later made into an opera. Her other works include *Selected Poems*, a play called *Pierrette's Heart*, and *Walt Whitman's Prose*.

Shephard died in 1975 in San Francisco.

About the Selection

"Babe the Blue Ox" is a chapter in Esther Shephard's book, *Paul Bunyan*. The imaginary folk hero Paul Bunyan was a huge lumberjack (logger) who practiced his trade near the Great Lakes.

Stories about Paul Bunyan were probably first told around the campfires in logging camps in forests in the northern parts of the East and Midwest. These camps were places where people worked very hard. In the fall, groups of men would set up a camp and hire lumberjacks and other workers. All winter long, the lumberjacks would cut down trees and move them to a stockpile near a river or on a lake. When the spring came, they would float the logs down the river or drive them to market. They worked long hours in the cold. In the few moments they had to spare, they would entertain each other by telling stories such as the tall tale you are about to read. It features a man only a true lumberjack could create, strong and mighty, just as they imagined themselves to be.

Literary Terms America's **folklore** is a rich collection of stories, tall tales, and legends. The stories were created and shared by the many cultures who have called America home. Through **exaggeration**—using larger-than-life characters and events that stretch the truth—tall tales are an important part of that literary heritage. They tell amusing and amazing stories with **humor**. This makes people laugh at creatures as fascinating as a blue ox and the giant lumberjack who owned him.

Reading on Your Own Exaggeration is a key characteristic of most tall tales. As you read this tall tale about Paul Bunyan and his blue ox Babe, look for examples of exaggeration. You may want to read the first few paragraphs and list the examples you find there before you read the entire story. Review your list. What does the narrator say? How is it different from what the words mean?

Writing on Your Own Write three sentences that show how a tall tale writer might use exaggeration to say, "He was very tall." You may want to start your sentence with, "He was so tall that . . ."

Vocabulary Focus In this tall tale, Shephard chose to write in **dialect**, meaning in the language of a particular region. To do this, she probably drew heavily on the speech she heard in the logging camps during her childhood in Minnesota. Dialect is more a feature of the way people speak than of the way they write. By writing in dialect, Shephard created a story that sounds as if someone is telling it aloud. As you read this story, look for examples of dialect. What are the characters actually saying in plain English?

Think Before You Read What images come to mind when you think of the word "lumberjack"?

folklore stories and customs that are saved and passed along by people in an area or group

exaggeration in literature, making something seem more than it is; stretching the truth

humor writing intended to amuse

dialect the speech of a particular part of a country, or of a certain group of people

BABE
the Blue Ox

As you read, decide why this story is called a tall tale.

Paul Bunyan couldn't of done all the great loggin' he did if it hadn't been for Babe the Blue Ox. I believe I mentioned helpin' to take care of him for a couple of months when I first come to camp, and then I helped measure him once afterwards for a new **yoke** Ole had to make for him. He'd broke the one he had when Paul was doin' an extra quick job haulin' lumber for some **millmen** down in Muskegon one summer, and Ole had to make him a new one right away and so we had to take Babe's measurements.

I've forgot most of the other figgurs, but I remember he measured forty-two axhandles between the eyes—and a tobacco box—you could easy fit in a Star tobacco box after the last axhandle. That tobacco box was lost and we couldn't never take the measurements again, but I remember that's what it was. And he weighed accordin'. Though he never was weighed that I know of, for there never was any scales made that would of been big enough.

Dialect is the way people from a certain area speak. This narrator tends to drop the final 'g' from words like loggin' and helpin'. The sentences are long, strung together with and, the way someone might tell a story out loud.

Paul told Ole he might as well make him a new log chain too while he was at it, for the way Babe pulled on 'em, in just about a month or two what had been a chain would be pulled out into a solid bar and wouldn't be any good. And so we measured him up for the chain too.

Many of the exaggerations used in this tall tale concern Babe's great size.

Babe was so long in the body, Paul used to have to carry a pair of field glasses around with him so as he could see what he was doin' with his hind feet.

---

yoke a wooden bar or frame that joins two oxen

millmen people who work in a mill where wood is cut

One time Babe kicked one of the straw bosses in the head, so his brains all run out, but the cook happened to be handy and he filled the hole up with hotcake batter and plastered it together again and he was just as good as ever. And right now, if I'm not mistaken, that boss is runnin' camp for the Bigham Loggin' Company of Virginia, Minnesota.

Babe was so big that every time they shod him they had to open up a new iron mine on Lake Superior, and one time when Ole the Blacksmith carried one of his shoes a mile and a half he sunk a foot and a half in solid rock at every step.

His color was blue—a fine, pretty, deep blue—and that's why he was called the Blue Ox—when you looked up at him the air even looked blue all around him. His nose was pretty near all black, but red on the inside, of course, and he had big white horns, curly on the upper section—about the upper third—and kind of darkish brown at the tip, and then the rest of him was all that same deep blue.

He didn't use to be always that blue color though. He was white when he was a calf. But he turned blue standin' out in the field for six days the first winter of the Blue Snow, and he never got white again. Winter and summer he was always the

Straw bosses were in charge of the work gangs. If the cook replaced this straw boss's brains with hotcake (pancake) batter, what does that say about the man's intelligence?

When loggers *shod* their animals, they put iron horseshoes on them.

same, except probly in July—somewheres about the Fourth— he might maybe've been a shade lighter then.

I've heard some of the old loggers say that Paul brought him from Canada when he was a little calf a few days old— carried him across Lake Champlain in a sack so he wouldn't have to pay duty on him. But I'm thinkin' he must of been a mighty few days old at the time or Paul couldn't of done it, for he must of grown pretty fast when he got started, to grow the size he did. And then besides there's them that says Paul never had him at all when he was a little fellow like that, but that he was a pretty fair-sized calf when Paul got him. A fellow by the name of O'Regan down near Detroit is supposed to of had him first. O'Regan didn't have no more'n about forty acres or so under cultivation cleared on his farm and naturally that wasn't near enough to raise feed for Babe, and so he's supposed to of sold him the year of the Short Oats to Paul Bunyan. I don't know exactly. It's all before my time. When I went to work for Paul, and all the time I knowed him, the Ox was full grown.

Babe was as strong as the breath of a tote-teamster, Paul always said, and he could haul a whole section of timber with him at a time—Babe'd walk right off with it—the entire six hundred forty acres at one drag, and haul it down to the landin' and dump it in. That's why there ain't no section thirty-seven no more. Six trips a day six days a week just cleaned up a township, and the last load they never bothered to haul back Saturday night, but left it lay on the landin' to float away in the spring, and that's why there quit bein' section 37's, and you never see 'em on the maps no more.

The only time I ever saw Babe on a job that seemed to nearly stump him—but that sure did look like it was goin' to for a while, though—durin' all the time I was with Paul was one time in Wisconsin, down on the St. Croix. And that was when he used him to pull the crooks out of eighteen miles of loggin' road; that came pretty near bein' more'n the Ox could handle. For generally anything that had two ends to it Babe could walk off with like nothin'.

Duty is the tax paid on items taken from one country to another.

A *tote-teamster* drove a wagon load of logs to the mill.

But that road of all the crooked roads I ever see—and I've seen a good many in my day—was of all of 'em the crookedest, and it's no wonder it was pretty near too much for Babe. You won't believe me when I tell you, but it's the truth, that in that stretch of eighteen miles that road doubled back on itself no less than sixteen times, and made four figure 8's, nine 3's, and four S's, yes, and one each of pretty near every other letter in the alphabet.

Of course the trouble with that road was, there was too much of it, and it didn't know what to do with itself, and so it's no wonder it got into mischief.

You'd be walkin' along it, all unsuspectin', and here of a sudden you'd see a coil of it layin' behind a tree, that you never know'd was there, and layin' there lookin' like it was ready to spring at you. The teamsters met themselves comin' back so many times while drivin' over it, that it begun to get on their nerves and we come near havin' a crazy-house in camp there. And so Paul made up his mind that that there road was goin' to be straightened out right then and there, and he went after it accordin'.

Teamsters drive teams of horses.

What he done was, he went out and told Bill to bring up the Blue Ox right away, and hitch him to the near end of the road.

Then he went up and spoke somethin' kind of low to Babe, and then afterwards he went out kind of to one side himself, and Babe laid hold, and then is the time it come pretty near breakin' the Ox in two, like I said.

"Come on, Babe! Co-ome on, Ba-abe!" says Paul, and the Ox lays hold and pulls to the last ounce of him. If I live to be a hundred years old I never hope to see an ox pull like that again. His hind legs laid straight out behind him nearly, and his belly was almost down touchin' the ground.

It was one beeg job, as the Frenchmen would of said. And when the crooks finally was all out of that there piece of road, there was enough of it to lay around a round lake we skidded logs into that winter, and then there was enough left in the place where it'd been at first to reach from one end to the other.

I've always been glad I saw Babe on that pull, for it's the greatest thing I ever saw him do—in its way, anyway.

Bill, that took care of the Blue Ox, generally went by the name of Brimstone Bill at camp and the reason was because he got to be so awfully red-hot tempered. But I never blamed him, though. Havin' that Ox to take care of was enough to make a sinner out of the best fellow that ever lived. Of all the scrapin' and haulin' you'd have to do to keep him lookin' anywheres near **respectable** even, no one would ever think.

And the way he ate—it took two men just to pick the balin' wire out of his teeth at mealtimes. Four ton of grain wasn't nothin' for Babe to get away with at a single meal, and for the hay—I can't mention quantities, but I know they said at first, before he got Windy Knight onto cuttin' it up for nails to use in puttin' on the cook-house roof, Paul used to have to move the camp every two weeks to get away from the mess of haywire that got collected where Babe ate his dinner. And as for cleanin' the barn and haulin' the manure away—

I remember one night in our bunkhouse as plain as if it'd been yesterday. I can see it all again just like it was then. That was one time afterwards, when we was loggin' down in Wisconsin.

Brimstone is sulfur, which is used to make matches and gunpowder. Why is this a good nickname for Bill?

Baling wire holds the bales of hay together.

respectable decent; proper; fit to be seen

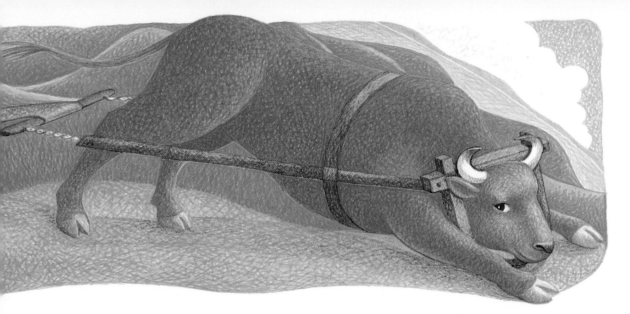

There was a new fellow just come to camp that day, a kind of college fellow that'd come to the woods for his health, and we was all sittin' around the stove that night spinnin' yarns like we almost always done of an evenin' while our socks was dryin'. I was over on one end, and to each side of me was Joe Stiles, and Pat O'Henry—it's funny how I remember it all— and a fellow by the name of Horn, and Big Gus, and a number of others that I don't **recollect** now, and over on the other end opposite me was Brimstone Bill, and up by me was this new fellow, but kind of a little to the side.

Spinnin' yarns means telling tall tales.

Well, quite a number of stories had been told, and some of 'em had been about the Blue Ox and different experiences men'd had with him different times and how the manure used to pile up, and pretty soon that there college chap begun to tell a story he said it reminded him of—one of them there old ancient Greek stories, he said it was, about Herukles cleanin' the Augaen stables, that was one of twelve other hard jobs he'd been set to do by the king he was workin' for at the time, to get his daughter or somethin' like that. He was goin' at it kind of fancy, describin' how the stables hadn't been cleaned for some time, and what a condition they was in as a **consequence,** and what a strong man Herukles was, and how he adopted the plan of turnin' the river right through the

The "college chap" is telling about one of the 12 labors of the Greek hero Herukles (Hercules). Later, Brimstone Bill will call him "Herik Lees."

recollect to remember **consequence** a result or effect

stables and so washin' the manure away that way, and goin' on describin' how it was all done. And how the water come through and floated the manure all up on top of the river, and how there was enough of it to spread over a whole valley, and then how the manure rolled up in waves again in the river when it got to where it was swifter—and it was a pretty good story and he was quite a talker too, that young fellow was, and he had all the men listenin' to him.

Well, all the time old Brimstone Bill he sat there takin' it all in, and I could see by the way his jaw was workin' on his tobacco that he was gettin' pretty riled. Everythin' had been quiet while the young fellow was tellin' the story, and some of us was smokin', some of us enjoyin' a little fresh Star or Peerless maybe and spittin' in the sandbox occasionally which was gettin' pretty wet by this time, and there wasn't no sound at all except the occasional sizzle when somebody hit the stove, or the movin' of a bench when somebody's foot or sock would get too near the fire, and the man's voice goin' along describin' about this Herukles and how great he was and how fine the stables looked when he got through with 'em, when all at once Brimstone Bill he busted right into him:

"You shut your blamed mouth about that Herik Lees of yourn," he says. "I guess if your Herik Lees had had the job I've got for a few days, he wouldn't of done it so easy or talked so smart, you young Smart Alec, you—" and then a long string of 'em the way Bill could roll 'em off when he got mad—I never heard any much better'n him—they said he could keep goin' for a good half hour and never repeat the same word twict—but I wouldn't give much for a lumberjack who couldn't roll off a few dozen straight—specially if he's worked with cattle—and all the time he was gettin' madder'n madder till he was fairly sizzlin' he was so mad. "I guess if that Mr. Lees had had Babe to take care of he wouldn't of done it so easy. Tell him he can trade jobs with me for a spell if he wants to, and see how he likes it. I guess if he'd of had to use his back on them one hundred and fifty jacks to jack up the barn the way I got to do he wouldn't of had enough strength left in him to brag so much about it. I just got through raisin' it another sixty foot this afternoon. When this job started we was workin' on the level, and now already Babe's barn is

Riled means angry.

Notice how the author uses humor in all the funny details in this long sentence beginning "Everythin' had been quiet. . ."

Bill is especially good at rolling off a string of curses and not repeating himself once.

Babe produces so much manure that his barn has to be jacked up higher and higher.

up sixteen hundred foot. I'd like to see the river that could wash that pile of manure away, and you can just tell that Herik Lees to come on and try it if he wants to. And if he can't, why, then you can just shut up about it. I've walked the old Ox and cleaned 'im and doctored 'im and rubbed 'im ever since he was first invented, and I know what it is, and I ain't goin' to sit here and let you tell me about any Mr. Lees or any other blankety blank liar that don't know what he's talkin' about tellin' about cleanin' barns—not if I know it." And at it he goes again blankety blank blank all the way out through the door, and slams it behind him so the whole bunkhouse shook, and the stranger he sits there and don't know hardly what to make of it. Till I kind of explained to him afterwards before we turned in, and we all, the rest of 'em too, told him not to mind about Bill, for he couldn't hardly help it. After he'd been in camp a few days he'd know. You couldn't hardly blame Bill for bein' **aggravated**—used to be a real good-natured man, and he wasn't so bad even that time I was helpin' him, but the Ox was too much for any man, no matter who.

And so I never held it against Bill much myself. He was fond of Babe too and made quite a pet of him, more so than the rest of us even, and we all did.

"I been with the beast a good long time," he used to say, "and I know the **cantankerous** old reptile most the

aggravated angry; upset	**cantankerous** hard to deal with

same's if I had been through him with a lantern. I know how to do for 'im, and all his little ways and all, and I don't want anybody else botherin' round and messin' things up for me. I can take care of 'im all right. All I want is to be let alone."

Afterwards when Paul got his hay farm down in Wisconsin it made it easier for Bill. Then we'd just rake the hay up in windrows and let it freeze that way layin' out across the fields, and in the winter they'd haul it in one end first in the stable and cut it up in chunks for Babe, just pullin' it up a little each time. That way you could get away from the nuisance of the haywire, and didn't have that to bother with.

In any of his small camps Paul couldn't never keep Babe but a day or so at a time, because it took the tote-teamsters a year to haul a day's feed for him.

Babe was a kind of playful fellow too. Sometimes he'd step in a river and lay down there and so make the water rise and leave a boom of logs that was below there up high and dry, and again sometimes he'd step on a ridge makin' a lakeshore maybe, and smash it down and let out the water to flood a river and drown out some low water drive.

Around the camp he'd play with almost any of us who was willin' to play with him after the day's work. We used to feed him hotcakes sometimes and he got awful fond of 'em. Them big ones we made on the big griddle we used to fold up in quarters and put clover hay in between and give it to him for a sandwich and he liked that powerful well. But we shouldn't of done it, I know that now. I've thought many times since, it's too bad, for that's what got him started, and once started he seemed he couldn't never stop. Poor old Babe. It proved to be the death of him at last. It was all wrong of us, but of course we didn't think about it then, and had no notion what it would lead to in the end.

Paul Bunyan was sure fond of his Ox, and mighty proud of him too, as he'd a right to be.

"Be faithful" he used to say to him low under his breath as he walked along beside him. "Be faithful, my Babe. Faithful."

Windrows are rows of hay raked up to dry before being baled or stored.

A *boom* is a chain, cable, or line of connected floating logs. In a *drive*, floating logs are guided downstream to a mill.

Why might this story be considered a good example of America's folklore?

AFTER READING THE SELECTION

Babe the Blue Ox   by Esther Shephard

Directions Choose the letter of the best answer or write the answer using complete sentences.

Comprehension: Identifying Facts

1. What kind of work does Paul Bunyan do?
   A He is a logger.
   B He makes new yokes.
   C He is a millman.
   D He measures axhandles.

2. Why can't Babe be measured again?
   A They lost the ax.
   B The chain was too short.
   C They lost the tobacco box.
   D He needed a new yoke.

3. How does Paul see around Babe?

4. What has to happen every time they make new shoes for Babe?

5. How does Babe get his blue color?

6. How does Paul Bunyan get Babe across Lake Champlain?

7. What job nearly defeats Babe?

8. Why does Paul Bunyan have to move his camp so often?

9. What story does the "college fellow" tell the other loggers?

10. What is Bill's job at camp?

Comprehension: Putting Ideas Together

11. What happens when Ole the Blacksmith carries one of Babe's shoes a mile and a half?
    A They need to open a new iron mine.
    B He sunk in the mud with every step.
    C They need to measure Babe with an axhandle.
    D Paul needs to carry field glasses.

12. Why aren't there any more timber section 37's?
    A Paul straightened them out.
    B Bill fed them to Babe.
    C Babe hauled all the timber away.
    D They sank.

13. Why was Paul such a good logger?

14. What was the trouble with the crooked logging road?

15. Why do the loggers "come near havin' a crazy-house in camp" before Babe straightens the logging road?

16. How does Babe get the crooks out of the road?

17. Why does the college student's story make Brimstone Bill so angry?

After Reading **continued on next page**

Babe the Blue Ox by Esther Shephard

18. Why does Bill need to jack up Babe's barn?

19. How do the narrator and the other loggers feel about Babe?

20. Why is it easier for Bill once Paul Bunyan gets his hay farm in Wisconsin?

Understanding Literature: Exaggeration and Humor

Exaggeration is an important part of the humor in all tall tales. Their characters, plots, and sometimes even settings are often stretched way beyond what could be true. By exaggerating, writers push the limits of truth to create humor. For example, when the narrator talks about a curving road, he reports that "in that stretch of eighteen miles that road doubled back on itself no less than sixteen times, and made four figure 8's, nine 3's, and four S's, yes, and one each of pretty near every other letter in the alphabet." The piling on of one exaggeration after another all through the tall tale keeps us reading and laughing.

21. How does exaggeration help create humor?

22. How did Babe change the geography near the logging camp? Why is this exaggeration?

23. Is Brimstone Bill an exaggerated character? Explain your thinking.

24. Give an example of a funny, exaggerated event in the plot of this story.

25. Describe a funny event in your own life, using exaggeration.

Critical Thinking

26. Why do you think the storyteller's sentences get longer when he reaches especially exciting parts of his tale?

27. In what ways is the myth of "Herukles" told by the college student similar to the tall tales about Babe the Blue Ox? What are some differences between myths and tall tales?

28. Do you think people like Paul Bunyan, Ole the Blacksmith, and Brimstone Bill ever existed? Explain your thinking.

29. What do you learn in this story about logging and the people who worked in the industry?

Thinking Creatively

30. Why do you think that feeding Babe hotcakes "proved to be the death of him at last"?

Grammar Check

When people speak, they sometimes use different word choices than they would if they were writing. One of those word choices involves the words *of* and *have*. For example, people sometimes say, "I should *of* gone home." Using *have* instead of *of* is expected in writing that is more formal. Generally, authors would write: "I should *have* gone home."

Look at the beginning of this sentence: "Paul Bunyan couldn't *of* done all the great logging he did . . ." Why do you think Esther Shephard made this word choice? Find other examples where the author chose to use the informal *of* instead of the more formal *have*.

 Writing on Your Own

How would you summarize this story to give people living in other parts of the world a good word picture about Babe the Blue Ox? Write a brief description.

 Speaking

In small groups, practice reading the sentences in this tall tale that you particularly like. Try to read them using expression, paying close attention to dialect (the way it is said) and sentence meaning.

 Listening

If you were listening to someone tell you the story of Babe the Blue Ox, how would you show them that you were interested in what they were saying? Make a list of five things you can do to show the storyteller that you are listening carefully.

 Research

Taking notes on information you gather is an important technique for any writer. When you take notes, you do not copy every bit of information you find, word for word. You summarize the main points. For example, if you took notes on the first page of this tall tale, they might look like this:

> Babe helped Paul be a great logger
>
> Babe needed new yoke; people measured him using an axe handle and a tobacco box

Practice this skill by taking notes on the second page of the story.

Feboldson, Western Scientist by Walter Blair

Walter Blair
1900–1992

About the Author

Walter Blair was born in Spokane, Washington. He got to know a number of great storytellers. He listened eagerly to their jokes, yarns, and tall tales.

Wherever he went, Blair collected stories. When he went off to graduate school, all these tales went with him. He began to look at these stories as a scholar would, trying to see how they related to each other and what they showed about America. In fact, he became one of the first Americans to study American humor in a scholarly way.

As he worked, he became a skilled storyteller himself. Walter Blair was especially proud of two of his books: *Davy Crockett: Truth and Legend* and *Tall Tale America*. A special version of *Tall Tale America* was sent by the U.S. Armed Services to military people serving around the world. At one time, this book was the only example of folklore in the White House Presidential Library.

About the Selection

This story is about Febold Feboldson, an imaginary, no-nonsense Nebraska farmer. Feboldson made his appearance at a time when Americans were settling states like Nebraska. Before this point, pioneers rushed west looking for gold. They thought it was too hot and too dry to settle in places like Nebraska. And it was. But there was also plenty of land there.

One thing set Feboldson apart from the other settlers. He was an inventor whose uncommon sense eventually made perfect sense.

People think that Febold Feboldson was created by Wayne Carroll, a lumber dealer. Tall tales about this brainy folk hero were first published in 1923 in the *Independent*, a newspaper published in Gothenburg, Nebraska.

Literary Terms "Feboldson, Western Scientist" is an **excerpt,** or small part, from Walter Blair's book *Tall Tale America.* In it, Blair explores the **character traits** of many of America's tall tale heroes. He shows how the heroes thought and behaved as they faced impossible problems and handily solved them. Feboldson makes up in brain power what he lacks in physical strength. Walter Blair's **characterization** makes this inventor come to life. In the story, Feboldson deals with other characters and the great Nebraska plains around him.

Reading on Your Own When you get to know people, you often listen to what they say, the way they say it, and the way people react to them. As you read, ask yourself the same kinds of questions about each character that you would ask when you first meet a person: What do the characters say? What do the narrator and other characters say about them? How do other characters treat them?

Writing on Your Own What do you know about Nebraska? Write the first ideas that come into your mind.

Vocabulary Focus As you read, you might find words whose meanings you don't know. Sometimes, you can use the words around the unknown word to figure out what the word means. This is called using *context clues.* For example, in this sentence: "Send along a *gross* of your fanciest fog-cutters . . .", you probably know that *gross* doesn't mean *disgusting.* By using the other words around *gross,* you might see that *gross* refers to a certain number of fog-cutters. While you don't have to know exactly how much a *gross* is, you could probably figure out that a *gross* is quite a few, just by using context clues. As you read, look for other words whose meanings you don't know. Use context clues to determine their meanings.

Think Before You Read How do you think this tall tale might be different from "Babe the Blue Ox"?

excerpt a short passage from a longer piece of writing

character trait a character's way of thinking, behaving, or speaking

characterization the way a writer develops characters' qualities and personality traits

Feboldson,

Western Scientist

Like all tall tales, this excerpt creates humor by using exaggeration. Look for examples as you read.

Tableland is a broad, level, raised area.

A *let* is a block, or something that gets in the way.

Febold, as a *natural scientist,* studies nature. As you read, notice his character traits.

Mercury is the liquid in some thermometers.

Nebraska, at the start, was big enough so great hunks could be chopped off and handed over to Colorado, Dakota and Idaho without anybody in Nebraska getting worried. After these gifts had been passed out, it was seen that every dratted mountain in the whole vicinity had been handed over to some other state. Result was that the whole of Nebraska was nothing but valleys, tableland and rolling prairies, all with a southwestern **exposure**. This meant that all the weather and all the wild life that came along had plenty of room to work and play in without natural let or **hindrance**.

Febold Feboldson settled down out there about the time the weather began to feel its strength. He got his farm and his family started, took on the job of Indian Agent . . . and then started his great work as a natural scientist.

One of the first things he had to cope with was the Great Fog that came along the year of the Great Heat. The Great Heat was bad enough, Heaven knows. Looking back, many people said that one of the most **fiendish** things about it was the way the mercury in thermometers everywhere shot up the tubes and spewed out the top like a fountain, so people couldn't *tell* how hot it was. Over in Saline County, though, one fellow with a big thermometer that'd take two hundred

---

exposure how something is placed so it is not sheltered from weather

hindrance something that gets in the way

fiendish unpleasant; bad

and thirty-two degrees, stood by it day and night with a cake of ice, bound and determined to save his thermometer. And he said the heat never went below a hundred and fifty degrees all those weeks, leastwise when he could see the thermometer with the help either of the sun, the moon or a lantern.

That was bad enough, as you can imagine. But one day Febold looked at the sky, fiddled around with some of his instruments, and made a horrible discovery. "That's bad," he said. "Got to do something **drastic**."

What he did was send a cable to London that read this way: "Send along a gross of your fanciest fog-cutters soon as possible, C.O.D. Febold Feboldson."

Being a scientist, you see, Febold had figured out right away what a horrible time Nebraska was in for. He told Mrs. Feboldson about the steps he'd taken that very evening while they were sitting in the sitting room trying to cool off a bit.

"Cabled over to London today for a gross of fog-cutters," he said.

Mrs. Feboldson's eyes stuck out so far they appeared to be on stems. "Fog-cutters?" she said, dazed-like.

"Yes, fog-cutters, Mother," he said. "You see, they have the thickest fogs in London that they have anywhere except on the ocean. And they're inventive there, you know—a right smart race. So they've doubtless got the best fog-cutters you can find anywhere."

"Of course, Febold, but I can't see as we need any fog-cutters. What would we do with them?"

"Cut the fog."

"It's been hot enough to make me wish we could cut the heat," says Mrs. Feboldson. "But if you look out the window there, you'll notice there's no fog—nothing but level land and sky, as far as you can look, with a hundred thousand heat-waves, just what you usually see out that living room window."

"Some unusual things out there, too," says Febold. "What's that dark gray thing up in the sky yonder—a dark gray thing no bigger than a man's hand?"

> A *gross* is 12 dozen or 144. *C.O.D.* means *cash on delivery.* You pay for the shipment when it arrives.

drastic very forceful

"Why!" Mrs. Feboldson said. "It's a cloud—first one I've seen since the Great Heat started pestering us. Looks as if it might be a rain cloud."

Febold nodded. "How about that little toe of yours that warns you when we're to have rain? How's it feel?"

Mrs. Feboldson noticed her toe for a minute, then, "I'll swan, it's a-twitching," she told him.

"I've fiddled around with my **barometers**, looked at the moon, and listened to the bullfrogs, and they all say the same thing," Febold said. "What's more, they say it's going to be a regular Bible storm—forty days and forty nights. Oh, we'll need those fog-cutters all right, Mother."

"Do they cut rain as well as fogs?"

"No, they just cut fogs, I reckon. But we'll need them. You'll see. Let's turn in."

Along toward morning, there was the beginning of that horrible sound that people in Nebraska (and parts of the neighboring territories) kept nearly being driven crazy by

barometers
instruments for measuring air pressure

for the next forty days and forty nights. People that tried to describe it later said it was like the sound of steam shooting out of three million tea-kettles at once—big kettles, too, boiling like fury—just one long burbling hiss.

As soon as Febold came in from milking, Mrs. Feboldson asked him what that horrible noise was.

"It's working the way I figured it would," he said. "The rain's coming down like a dribbled ocean. But up there ten miles or so, it's spattering down on the hot air that was piled up around here by the Great Heat. As soon as the rain hits the hot air, it turns to steam and makes that hissing noise. The steam will be the fog."

"But the steam's staying up there," Mrs. Feboldson said. "Out the window, all you can see is level land and sky as far as you can look, same as usual, only gray because there's no sun today."

"Pretty soon, Mother, the rain will hammer the fog down to the ground, and what'll pile up will be the fog. Hope those Englishmen hurry up with those fog-cutters. Things are going to be bad."

Febold was right, as usual. There was a little fog at first, then more and more of it, until taking a walk alone was impossible. At least two people would be needed so one could part the fog and hold it apart while the other one walked through. Cattle didn't have to be watered, because they could drink the fog. But the dirt farmers were scared speechless, because their crops were in a bad way. You see, some of the seeds had figured that the closest sunshine was in China, and had started growing downward.

Around Thanksgiving, when the fog was so thick that portions had turned to three hundred thousand gallons of slush, both farmers and stockmen by the hundreds had about decided to pull out of Nebraska. "Too crowded by this danged fog," they said. "We need elbow room."

It was when things had come to this kind of a pass that the fog-cutters arrived, C.O.D. Febold used one of them to cut red tape so he could pay for them. . . . Then he started to use them on the fog—to slice it into big neat strips. Soon, when he had great piles of these strips, it was needful that he figure out where to put them.

To cut red tape means to get around rules that slow things up.

"Can't leave them lying out there on the fields," he told Mrs. Feboldson, "or all the seeds will keep growing downward. I know! I'll lay them out along the roads."

Upshot was that he put those fog strips end to end all along the dirt roads of Nebraska. And before long some of the slush-fog seeped down, and some got so covered with dust that nobody could see where Febold had buried the Great Fog.

Upshot means the final result.

Only one serious bad result came of the whole thing. Every spring, when the sun begins to shine and the thaw comes, some of this old fog seeps up on the dirt roads, turning them into the gooiest mess you ever got stuck in.

And if you don't believe this, just go out to Nebraska some spring and try driving on one of those roads.

What do you learn about the setting—Nebraska—in this tall tale?

AFTER READING THE SELECTION

Feboldson, Western Scientist by Walter Blair

Directions Choose the letter of the best answer or write the answer using complete sentences.

Comprehension: Identifying Facts

1. What is Febold Feboldson's "great work"?
   A a natural scientist
   B a husband
   C a fog-cutter
   D an Indian agent

2. What does Febold order from London?

3. What does Febold do with the strips of fog he cuts?

Comprehension: Putting Ideas Together

4. How does Febold know it is going to rain?
   A The mercury in thermometers shot up.
   B He received a cable from London.
   C He fiddled with his barometer.
   D He saw a hundred thousand heat waves.

5. For which natural events and facts of geography does this tall tale give imaginative explanations?

6. What is the "one serious bad result" of Febold's actions?

Understanding Literature: Character Traits

Character traits—ways of behaving, talking, or thinking—show a person's nature. These traits show readers how to see a character's importance in the setting and plot of a story.

Writers do not usually list character traits. Instead, they let characters speak and act for themselves. By reading carefully, we get to know these characters through what they say and do.

When writers use flat characters in a story, as in fables, we learn only one or two of the characters' traits. When writers create round characters, they give readers many clues about the traits of each character. By understanding a character's traits, readers gain a better understanding of the story as a whole.

7. What adjectives would you use to describe Febold's character traits?

8. Do you think Febold is a round or flat character? Why?

Critical Thinking

9. How might the plot, characters, and setting of this tall tale be different if there was no exaggeration?

After Reading continued on next page

Feboldson, Western Scientist by Walter Blair

Thinking Creatively

10. Do you think Febold Feboldson is a true scientist? Support your opinion with evidence from the story.

 Grammar Check

Sentences that ask questions always end with a punctuation mark called a *question mark*. These sentences sometimes begin with questioning words such as *who*, *which*, *how*, and *why*. They are called *interrogative* (Latin for *asking*) sentences.

Look for sentences in the tall tale that ask questions. Pick three of them and rewrite them as sentences that state a fact. For example, "What's that dark gray thing up in the sky?" could be changed into this statement: "There is a dark, gray cloud up in the sky."

 Writing on Your Own

What if Febold Feboldson saw Babe the Blue Ox? Use the Story Map described in Appendix A to outline the setting, characters, problems, events, and solution for your story. Write a short play based on these notes.

 Speaking and Listening

There are many points in this tall tale where Mr. and Mrs. Feboldson share a conversation. Pick a partner and read these conversations aloud to each other. Afterward, talk about what you did. Do you think an audience would be interested in the way you read? What might you do to make the conversation more interesting to the audience?

 Media and Technology

Use a computer and presentation software to create a show about the things that American tall tales tell us we value as a culture. Outline your work first to plan enough space for your ideas. Find information, pictures, and music from online sources or elsewhere to help you design an interesting presentation.

 Research

Find more details about the people who settled in Nebraska during the early 1900s. Which of the sources below do you think would help you? List the sources and explain what information you might get from each.

- Atlas
- Almanac
- Speech
- Historical magazine
- Newspaper

BEFORE READING THE SELECTION

John Henry   *Anonymous*

About the Author and Selection

No one knows who actually created the character of John Henry and his work. The story of John Henry may have begun with one author. However, it was probably passed on by many generations of storytellers. The storytellers probably added their own details and ideas to the story. Because of this, no one can actually name the person who first told the world about John Henry.

Railway Tunnel Under Construction

John Henry was a powerful African American steel driver. Some think he was born a slave, but started working for the railroads after he was freed. His **legend,** or story, began just after the Civil War near the small town of Talcott, West Virginia. There, around 1870, the Chesapeake and Ohio Railroad (C and O) was building a tunnel straight through a mountain. The tunnel was over a mile long. The work was done by pairs of men—each pair had a steel driver and a shaker. The shaker would hold a metal drill against the rock. The steel driver would strike the drill with a hammer. Then the shaker would turn the drill slightly, and the driver would hit it again. When they had drilled a large enough hole, they placed gunpowder in it and blew apart the rock. It took a long time to make progress. When the steam driver machine was invented, some thought it could do a faster and better job of drilling through rock. But John Henry did not agree.

Some versions of this legend say John Henry was born with a hammer in his hand. Some say he was born all grown up—standing over eight feet tall. Others say he had the strength of 30 men. But all agree that John Henry was a hard-working man.

Objectives

■ To read and enjoy a ballad

■ To explore how legends become part of a culture

■ To define and give examples of ballads, stanzas, refrains, and mood

legend a story from folklore that features characters who actually lived, or real events or places

Before Reading continued on next page

John Henry *Anonymous*

ballad a form of poetry that tells a story, passed from person to person, often as a simple song with rhyming words and a refrain

stanza a group of lines that forms a unit in a poem

refrain repeated line in a poem or song that creates mood or gives importance to something

Literary Terms This **ballad** presents one version of the legend of John Henry. A ballad is a form of poetry. "John Henry" tells about a contest between man and machine. A ballad is a simple song that usually uses rhyming words, or words with similar sounds. Ballads often include words that are repeated at the end of each section or **stanza**. These repeated words are called a **refrain**. Ballads about John Henry have been sung, read, spoken, and enjoyed for well over a century.

Reading on Your Own Before you read this ballad, think about what you already know about John Henry, the railroads, and the people that built them. Use the first column of the K-W-L chart, described in Appendix A, to record your thoughts. Based on this, what new information do you predict this ballad might tell you?

Writing on Your Own Think about how you might feel if your boss tells you that a machine is now going to do your work. You are out of a job. Write four sentences that describe your reaction.

Vocabulary Focus Two related words that are sometimes confused are the verbs lay and lie. *Lie* means to rest or recline, as in this sentence: "There *lies* my steel-driving man." *Lay* means to put something down. Because of this, a sentence using *lay* always has to explain what is being laid down. What is being put down is called the object of the verb. In this sentence, "They *laid* him in the sand," the object of the verb is *him*. Look for another example of using lie or lay in this ballad. Why is this use of the word correct?

Think Before You Read What people or objects are so important to you that you would risk your life to save them?

John Henry

When John Henry was a little tiny baby
Sitting on his mama's knee,
He picked up a hammer and a little piece of steel
Saying, "Hammer's going to be the death of me, Lord, Lord,
5   Hammer's going to be the death of me."

John Henry was a man just six feet high,
Nearly two feet and a half across his breast.
He'd hammer with a nine-pound hammer all day
And never get tired and want to rest, Lord, Lord,
10   And never get tired and want to rest.

John Henry went up on the mountain
And he looked one eye straight up its side.
The mountain was so tall and John Henry was so small,
He laid down his hammer and he cried, "Lord, Lord,"
15   He laid down his hammer and he cried.

John Henry said to his captain,
"Captain, you go to town,
Bring me back a TWELVE-pound hammer, please,
And I'll beat that steam drill down, Lord, Lord,
20   I'll beat that steam drill down."

The captain said to John Henry,
"I believe this mountain's sinking in."
But John Henry said, "Captain, just you stand aside—
It's nothing but my hammer catching wind, Lord, Lord,
25   It's nothing but my hammer catching wind."

John Henry said to his shaker,
"Shaker, boy, you better start to pray,
'Cause if my TWELVE-pound hammer miss that little piece of steel,
Tomorrow'll be your burying day, Lord, Lord,
30   Tomorrow'll be your burying day."

As you read, see what character traits make John Henry the hero of a legend.

Notice the refrain at the end of each stanza of the ballad. How does each one affect the mood of the ballad?

John Henry's *captain* was his boss.

John Henry's *shaker* held the drill and gave it a twist by hand after each blow of the steel driver's hammer.

John Henry said to his captain,
"A man is nothing but a man,
But before I let your steam drill beat me down,
I'd die with this hammer in my hand, Lord, Lord,
35   I'd die with this hammer in my hand."

The man that invented the steam drill,
He figured he was mighty high and fine,
But John Henry sunk the steel down fourteen feet
While the steam drill only made nine, Lord, Lord,
40   The steam drill only made nine.

John Henry hammered on the right-hand side,
Steam drill kept driving on the left.
John Henry beat that steam drill down,
But he hammered his poor heart to death, Lord, Lord,
45   He hammered his poor heart to death.

Well, they carried John Henry down the tunnel
And they laid his body in the sand.
Now every woman riding on a C and O train
Says, "There lies my steel-driving man, Lord, Lord,
50   There lies my steel-driving man."

AFTER READING THE SELECTION

Directions Choose the letter of the best answer or write the answer using complete sentences.

Comprehension: Identifying Facts

1. As a child, what does John Henry say is going to cause his death?
   A a shaker
   B a hammer
   C a machine
   D the captain

2. What does John Henry think he can do with a 12-pound hammer?

3. Where did the people take John Henry's body after he died?

Comprehension: Putting Ideas Together

4. What hints does the ballad give you that John Henry was a larger-than-life character?
   A He spoke in sentences as a baby.
   B He played with a hammer and steel.
   C He never got tired.
   D all of the above

5. Some people say that the machine won in the end, because John Henry dies trying to beat it. What do you think?

6. Why do you think John Henry has become an American folk hero?

Understanding Literature: Refrain

Ballads are part of the oral literature of a culture. People would learn a ballad by hearing it sung. Like some stories and poems, ballads often include refrains, or words and sentences that are repeated. By repeating, the people who passed these works on to others did two things. First, they helped their audience pay attention to certain details of the story. Second, repeating made it easier for people to remember the stories.

7. What word is part of each refrain in the ballad of John Henry? What is the effect of repeating that word?

8. To what details of the story do the refrains in this ballad call attention?

Critical Thinking

9. Imagine that you are nearby when John Henry takes up the captain's challenge to try his strength against the steam drill. Which one would you pick to be the winner? Why?

Thinking Creatively

10. In 1996, the U.S. Postal Service issued a stamp honoring John Henry. Suggest some other ways Americans today could honor his courage and hard work.

After Reading continued on next page

John Henry   *Anonymous*

 Grammar Check

In the ballad about John Henry, look at the use of the noun, *captain*. When is it spelled with a lowercase *c*? When is it spelled with an uppercase *C*? When nouns begin with an uppercase letter, they are *capitalized*. Nouns are usually capitalized when they are the names of a specific person, place, or thing. This is called a *proper noun*. Do you think this is the reason *captain* is sometimes capitalized?

 Writing on Your Own

Some people claim that the tunnel John Henry helped dig was in West Virginia. Others say it was in Alabama. How might you be able to find out a possible answer to this question? Outline a research plan that details the steps you would take.

 Speaking

Some speakers use note cards to remind themselves of the main points they want to make. Prepare a series of 5–7 note cards that would be good reminders if you wanted to tell young people the legend of John Henry.

 Listening

There are many versions of this ballad online. Use a search engine to look for John Henry + recordings. Listen to at least two versions. How are the versions different from each other? How are they the same?

 Media

What location would you choose to film a documentary on the life of John Henry? Think about places you know that fit the mood of this ballad. Write a brief description of the place and why you chose it.

 Research

In using the Internet to research, you have to be very careful of the sources you use. Some are not written by experts in the field and may contain false information. Look for Web sites that have a ".gov" or ".edu" as part of their address. These are sites sponsored by the government and schools or colleges. Find four reliable sources for more information on John Henry and list their addresses (URLs).

BEFORE READING THE SELECTION

Life and Adventures of Calamity Jane, by Herself by Martha (Marthy) Cannary Burk

About the Author

Calamity Jane is a legendary figure of the American West. Martha Jane Cannary (she calls herself "Marthy") was born in Princeton, Missouri. According to her own accounts, Calamity Jane moved west on a wagon train with her family. Her mother died during the trip, and her father soon afterward. She was on her own for most of her life, traveling from Montana to Wyoming and South Dakota. In 1876, Calamity Jane appeared in Deadwood, South Dakota, dressed in men's clothes, and bragged about her adventures as a pony-express rider and army scout. She later married Clinton Burk and, she says, had a daughter.

Martha Cannary Burk "Calamity Jane" 1852–1903

Calamity Jane toured with the Wild West shows from 1895 to 1901. These shows featured characters of the old West. During the shows, performers showed off their sharpshooting and expert horseback riding skills. Calamity Jane later returned to Deadwood, in the territory she loved. At her request, she is buried there next to Wild Bill Hickok.

Objectives

- To read and appreciate a legend
- To define and give examples of anecdote, pamphlet, and autobiography

About the Selection

In "Life and Adventures of Calamity Jane, by Herself," the author tells the story of her life, including details of the way she earned her nickname—Calamity Jane. This text first appeared in 1896, when Calamity Jane started performing in Wild West shows. She would sell her story to people coming to the shows.

Her story starts just as the Civil War was ending and the gateways to the West were opening. She and her family became one of the many Americans who moved west to find a new and secure life. Many of them were very brave and ready for an adventure, including the young woman who grew to be a real American legend.

Before Reading continued on next page

Life and Adventures of Calamity Jane, by Herself *by Martha (Marthy) Cannary Burk*

anecdote a short account of an interesting event in someone's life

pamphlet a short printed story or paper with no cover, or with a paper cover

autobiography the story of a person's life, written by that person

Literary Terms Calamity Jane's story is a short collection of **anecdotes** about the remarkable adventures of this frontier woman. An anecdote is an interesting story. It was published as a **pamphlet** or booklet that people who came to her shows could buy, perhaps as a souvenir. While Calamity claimed this pamphlet was an **autobiography**, or a true account of her life that she herself wrote, others have doubts. People who knew Calamity Jane and Wild West experts have said many story details could never have happened. Others claim this pamphlet was actually written by Josephine Brake, a newspaper writer from Buffalo, New York.

Reading on Your Own Calamity Jane tells about many events in her life in this pamphlet—both real and imagined. As you read, use sticky notes to label each event. On each note, write what the event is and whether or not you believe it actually happened.

Writing on Your Own Think about an event in your own life. Write about it in two ways. First, write about it as if it was the worst thing that ever happened. Then, write about the event as if it was the most wonderful thing that ever happened.

Vocabulary Focus A calamity is great misfortune or serious trouble. Some *synonyms,* or words that have the same meaning, of calamity are *disaster* and *tragedy.* In fact, if you call someone a "Calamity Jane," you are saying that person causes disasters. As you read this story, look for the part of the story in which Martha Cannary explains how she got her nickname. Do you think she was proud to be called "Calamity Jane"?

Think Before You Read What have you heard, read, or seen about life in the Wild West? What are some images that come to mind?

LIFE AND ADVENTURES OF CALAMITY JANE,
by Herself

My maiden name was Marthy Cannary. I was born in
Princeton, Missourri, May 1st, 1852. Father and mother were
natives of Ohio. I had two brothers and three sisters, I being
the oldest of the children. As a child I always had a fondness
for adventure and out-door exercise and especial fondness for
horses which I began to ride at an early age and continued
to do so until I became an expert rider being able to ride
the most vicious and stubborn of horses, in fact the greater
portion of my life in early times was spent in this manner.

In 1865 we **emigrated** from our homes in Missourri by the
overland route to Virginia City, Montana, taking five months
to make the journey. While on the way the greater portion of
my time was spent in hunting along with the men and hunters
of the party, in fact I was at all times with the men when
there was excitement and adventures to be had. By the time
we reached Virginia City I was considered a remarkable good
shot and a fearless rider for a girl of my age. I remember many
occurrences on the journey from Missourri to Montana.
Many times in crossing the mountains the conditions of the
trail were so bad that we frequently had to lower the wagons
over ledges by hand with ropes for they were so rough and
rugged that horses were of no use. We also had many exciting
times **fording** streams for many of the streams in our way

Missourri is a
misspelling of
Missouri. *Marthy*
may also be a
misspelling of
Martha, or it may
be a nickname.

In an
autobiography, we
usually get a
detailed picture of
the author, who is
also the main
character. As
you read, decide
what kind of a
person Calamity
Jane was—or, at
least, what kind of
person she wants
us to think she was.
How did she think
of herself?

emigrated left one's homeland	**occurrences** happenings or events	**fording** crossing a body of water

Calamity Jane on Horseback, 1901

As you read the anecdotes in this autobiography, decide which you think might have been true. Which do you think the author either made up or greatly exaggerated?

were noted for quicksands and boggy places, where, unless we were very careful, we would have lost horses and all. Then we had many dangers to **encounter** in the way of streams swelling on account of heavy rains. On occasions of that kind the men would usually select the best places to cross the streams, myself on more than one occasion have mounted my pony and swam across the stream several times merely to amuse myself and have had many narrow escapes from having both myself and pony washed away to certain death, but as the pioneers of those days had plenty of courage we **overcame** all **obstacles** and reached Virginia City in safety.

| **encounter** meet or come upon | **overcame** won against or got the better of | **obstacles** things that get in the way |

Mother died at Black Foot, Montana, 1866, where we buried her. I left Montana in Spring of 1866, for Utah, arriving at Salt Lake city during the summer. Remained in Utah until 1867, where my father died, then went to Fort Bridger, Wyoming Territory, where we arrived May 1, 1868, then went to Piedmont, Wyoming, with U.P. Railway. Joined General Custer as a scout at Fort Russell, Wyoming, in 1870, and started for Arizona for the Indian Campaign. Up to this time I had always worn the costume of my sex. When I joined Custer I donned the uniform of a soldier. It was a bit awkward at first but I soon got to be perfectly at home in men's clothes.

Was in Arizona up to the winter of 1871 and during that time I had a great many adventures with the Indians, for as a scout I had a great many dangerous missions to perform and while I was in many close places always succeeded in getting away safely for by this time I was considered the most reckless and daring rider and one of the best shots in the western country.

After that campaign I returned to Fort Sanders, Wyoming, remained there until spring of 1872, when we were ordered out to the Muscle Shell or Nursey Pursey Indian outbreak. In that war Generals Custer, Miles, Terry and Crook were all engaged. This campaign lasted until fall of 1873.

It was during this campaign that I was christened Calamity Jane. It was on Goose Creek, Wyoming, where the town of Sheridan is now located. Capt. Egan was in command of the Post. We were ordered out to **quell** an uprising of the Indians, and were out for several days, had numerous **skirmishes** during which six of the soldiers were killed and several severely wounded. When on returning to the Post we were **ambushed** about a mile and a half from our destination. When fired upon Capt. Egan was shot. I was riding in advance and on hearing the firing turned in my saddle and saw the Captain reeling in his saddle as though about to fall.

After becoming a Civil War hero, General George Armstrong Custer fought against American Indians in the West and Southwest. He and his army were killed in 1876 during the Battle of Little Big Horn, against the Sioux led by Sitting Bull and Crazy Horse.

To *don* means to wear. Do you think Custer and his soldiers knew Calamity Jane was a woman?

A *calamity* is a disaster, a terrible event. Why do you think Captain Egan chose that name?

quell to quiet down or stop

skirmishes small battles

ambushed attacked by surprise

Pony Express Rider, **undated watercolor illustration**

I turned my horse and galloped back with all haste to his side and got there in time to catch him as he was falling. I lifted him onto my horse in front of me and succeeded in getting him safely to the Fort. Capt. Egan on recovering, laughingly said: "I name you Calamity Jane, the heroine of the plains." I have **borne** that name up to the present time. We were afterwards ordered to Fort Custer, where Custer city now stands, where we arrived in the spring of 1874; remained around Fort Custer all summer and were ordered to Fort Russell in fall of 1874, where we remained until spring of 1875; was then ordered to the Black Hills to protect miners, as that country was controlled by the Sioux Indians and the government had to send the soldiers to protect the lives of the miners and settlers in that section. Remained there until fall of 1875 and wintered at Fort Laramie. In spring of 1876, we

borne carried

were ordered north with General Crook to join Gen'ls Miles, Terry and Custer at Big Horn river. During this march I swam the Platte river at Fort Fetterman as I was the bearer of important **dispatches**. I had a ninety mile ride to make, being wet and cold, I contracted a severe illness and was sent back in Gen. Crook's ambulance to Fort Fetterman where I laid in the hospital for fourteen days. When able to ride I started for Fort Laramie where I met Wm. Hickock, better known as Wild Bill, and we started for Deadwood, where we arrived about June.

During the month of June I acted as a pony express rider carrying the U.S. mail between Deadwood and Custer, a distance of fifty miles, over one of the roughest trails in the Black Hills country. As many of the riders before me had been held up and robbed of their packages, mail and money that they carried, for that was the only means of getting mail and money between these points. It was considered the most dangerous route in the Hills, but as my reputation as a rider and quick shot was well known, I was **molested** very little, for the toll gatherers looked on me as being a good fellow, and they knew that I never missed my mark. I made the round trip every two days which was considered pretty good riding in that country. Remained around Deadwood all that summer visiting all the camps within an area of one hundred miles. My friend, Wild Bill, remained in Deadwood during the summer with the **exception** of occasional visits to the camps. On the 2nd of August, while setting at a gambling table in the Bell Union saloon, in Deadwood, he was shot in the back of the head by the **notorious** Jack McCall, a desperado. I was in Deadwood at the time and on hearing of the killing made my way at once to the scene of the shooting and found that my friend had been killed by McCall. I at once started to look for the **assassin** and found him at Shurdy's butcher shop and grabbed a meat cleaver and made him throw up his

James Butler (Wild Bill) Hickok, born in Illinois in 1837, was a scout, stagecoach driver, and frontier marshal in Kansas. His shoot-outs with various outlaws made him a legend.

A *desperado* is a bandit, or an outlaw.

dispatches messages

molested bothered

exception something that is left out

notorious well-known, especially for something bad

assassin a killer

Wild Bill Hickok

The Black Hills are in southwest South Dakota and northeast Wyoming. Gold mining began there in 1874; Calamity Jane refers to the *camps* and *claims* of the gold prospectors. Deadwood is in present-day South Dakota.

Prospecting means looking for gold.

hands; through the excitement on hearing of Bill's death, having left my weapons on the post of my bed. He was then taken to a log cabin and locked up, well secured as every one thought, but he got away and was afterwards caught at Fagan's ranch on Horse Creek, on the old Cheyenne road and was then taken to Yankton, Dak., where he was tried, sentenced and hung.

I remained around Deadwood locating claims, going from camp to camp until the spring of 1877, where one morning, I saddled my horse and rode towards Crook city. I had gone about twelve miles from Deadwood, at the mouth of Whitewood creek, when I met the overland mail running from Cheyenne to Deadwood. The horses on a run, about two hundred yards from the station; upon looking closely I saw they were **pursued** by Indians. The horses ran to the barn as was their custom. As the horses stopped I rode along side of the coach and found the driver John Slaughter, lying face downwards in the boot of the stage, he having been shot by the Indians. When the stage got to the station the Indians hid in the bushes. I immediately removed all baggage from the coach except the mail. I then took the driver's seat and with all **haste** drove to Deadwood, carrying the six passengers and the dead driver.

I left Deadwood in the fall of 1877, and went to Bear Butte Creek with the 7th **Cavalry**. During the fall and winter we built Fort Meade and the town of Sturgis. In 1878 I left the command and went to Rapid city and put in the year prospecting.

In 1879 I went to Fort Pierre and drove trains from Rapid City to Fort Pierre for Frank Witc then drove teams from Fort Pierce to Sturgis for Fred. Evans. This teaming was done with oxen as they were better fitted for the work than horses, owing to the rough nature of the country.

pursued chased	**haste** speed	**cavalry** soldiers on horseback

Deadwood,
South Dakota,
1877

In 1881 I went to Wyoming and returned in 1882 to Miles city and took up a ranch on the Yellow Stone, raising stock and cattle, also kept a way side inn, where the weary traveler could be **accommodated** with food, drink, or trouble if he looked for it. Left the ranch in 1883, went to California, going through the States and territories, reached Ogden the **latter** part of 1883, and San Francisco in 1884. Left San Francisco in the summer of 1884 for Texas, stopping at Fort Yuma, Arizona, the hottest spot in the United States. Stopping at all points of interest until I reached El Paso in the fall. While in El Paso, I met Mr. Clinton Burk, a native of Texas, who I married in August 1885. As I thought I had travelled through

Setting describes both place and time. What does Calamity Jane tell us about her times and about the places she lived in?

accommodated
supplied someone's
needs; helped

latter toward the end

What would you say is the *temper*— or usual state of mind and feeling— of this baby's mother, Calamity Jane?

life long enough alone and thought it was about time to take a partner for the rest of my days. We remained in Texas leading a quiet home life until 1889. On October 28th, 1887, I became the mother of a girl baby, the very image of its father, at least that is what he said, but who has the temper of its mother.

When we left Texas we went to Boulder, Colo., where we kept a hotel until 1893, after which we travelled through Wyoming, Montana, Idaho, Washington, Oregon, then back to Montana, then to Dakota, arriving in Deadwood October 9th, 1895, after an absence of seventeen years.

My arrival in Deadwood after an absence of so many years created quite an excitement among my many friends of the past, to such an extent that a vast number of the citizens who had come to Deadwood during my absence who had heard so much of Calamity Jane and her many adventures in former years were anxious to see me. Among the many whom I met were several gentlemen from eastern cities who advised me to allow myself to be placed before the public in such a manner as to give the people of the eastern cities an opportunity of seeing the Woman Scout who was made so famous through her daring career in the West and Black Hill countries.

The Wild West shows of the time were very popular. The most famous was started by "Buffalo Bill," William Frederick Cody, in 1883.

An agent of Kohl & Middleton, the celebrated Museum men came to Deadwood, through the **solicitation** of the gentleman who I had met there and arrangements were made to place me before the public in this manner. My first engagement began at the Palace Museum, Minneapolis, January 20th, 1896, under Kohl and Middleton's management.

Hoping that this little history of my life may interest all readers, I remain as in the older days,

Why is Calamity Jane's story called a legend?

Yours,

Mrs. M. Burk
Better known as Calamity Jane

---

solicitation an invitation

Directions Choose the letter of the best answer or write the answer using complete sentences.

Comprehension: Identifying Facts

1. What does Calamity Jane say her real name is?
   A Nursey Pursey
   B Marthy Cannary Burk
   C Jane Slaughter
   D General Custer

2. How does Calamity Jane spend much of her time as a child?
   A as a pony express rider
   B locating claims, going from camp to camp
   C protecting miners in the Black Hills
   D riding horses and traveling with her family

3. When does her family leave Missouri for Montana?

4. When does Calamity Jane start dressing in men's clothing?

5. How does Calamity Jane get her name?

6. Where does Calamity Jane meet Wild Bill Hickok?

7. Between what cities does Calamity Jane say she carried the mail for the pony express?

8. Who shot Wild Bill Hickok?

9. What do Calamity Jane and her husband do to earn money?

10. What do the "gentlemen from eastern cities" persuade Calamity Jane to do?

Comprehension: Putting Ideas Together

11. Why are Calamity Jane's skills as a horseback rider important to her life?
    A She was a pony express rider.
    B She protected miners in the Black Hills.
    C She kept a wayside inn.
    D She made friends with Wild Bill.

12. What does Calamity Jane say about her skill as a rider and shooter?
    A She was a fair shot.
    B She was a poor rider.
    C She was a good rider and could shoot well.
    D She hated to shoot her gun.

13. How might her parents' deaths have affected Calamity Jane?

14. Why did Calamity Jane begin to dress as a man?

15. How would you describe Calamity Jane's duties as a scout?

16. Why isn't Calamity Jane robbed when she works as a pony express rider?

After Reading continued on next page

Life and Adventures of Calamity Jane, by Herself *by Martha (Marthy) Cannary Burk*

17. How does Calamity Jane react to the news of Wild Bill's murder?

18. How does Calamity Jane describe her daughter?

19. How does Calamity Jane describe her welcome when she returns to Deadwood after 17 years?

20. Why does Calamity Jane decide to tour the country?

Understanding Literature: Anecdote

An anecdote is a brief account of an interesting event in someone's life. "Life and Adventures of Calamity Jane, by Herself" is filled with anecdotes about her adventurous life. These accounts are brief. For example, we learn only certain details about Calamity Jane's time as a pony express rider. She says that she was rarely bothered on her dangerous route and that she made her round trip of 50 miles every two days. We do not know how she felt as she rode along or what the territory looked like. She knew that simply telling people she rode with the pony express would amaze them. Her audience would supply the details as they imagined what it must have been like.

21. How is an anecdote different from a story?

22. Why might an author tell about events through anecdotes?

23. Do you as a reader expect anecdotes to be true? Why?

24. Which of Calamity Jane's anecdotes are funny? Why do you think so?

25. Which anecdote in Calamity Jane's story is most exciting, or well described? How does it hold your interest?

Critical Thinking

26. Is it important to you as a reader that Calamity Jane may have invented, rather than lived, some of these anecdotes? Explain your answer.

27. How might dressing in men's clothing have helped Calamity Jane? How might her style of dress have hurt her? Explain.

28. Why do you think Calamity Jane wanted to be buried in the same place as Wild Bill Hickok?

Thinking Creatively

29. How does the legend of Calamity Jane compare with the legend of John Henry?

30. Do you think people living today could create stories about themselves the way it appears Calamity Jane did? Explain your thinking.

Grammar Check

A complete sentence must have a subject and a verb. A sentence fragment lacks one of these parts. For example, look at this sentence: "Was in Arizona up to the winter of 1871." Even though it looks like a sentence, it is not. It doesn't have a subject. You don't know who was in Arizona. Look for five other examples of sentence fragments in the story. Rewrite them as complete sentences.

 Writing on Your Own

How would you persuade an audience that Calamity Jane is a real legend of the Wild West? Outline what you would say, making sure to present details from her pamphlet.

 Speaking and Listening

Prepare to tell your class an interesting anecdote from your own life. Use an organizer such as the Concept Map, described in Appendix A, to help you plan your presentation. Listen as each person talks. Did they organize their presentation in a logical and interesting way?

 Media

Write an article about Calamity Jane for a travel magazine featuring the western United States. Create a map to illustrate the article, showing places Calamity Jane mentions in her pamphlet.

 Viewing

The story of Calamity Jane has been part of several movies, plays, and television series. Locate a video of one of these and view it. How is it different from and the same as the story Calamity Jane told herself?

 Research and Technology

You should use many sources when you write about a historical event. Primary source documents are records from the actual time period. They were written by the people as they lived the events. They are private and factual records. Secondary source documents are records written after an event occurs. They are what someone thinks happened based on primary source documents. Use the Internet or print resources from the library to find four sources of information about Calamity Jane. Decide which are primary sources and which are secondary sources.

The Phantom Hitchhiker   by Daniel Cohen

Daniel Cohen
1936–

Objectives

- To read and understand a modern legend
- To identify and give examples of foreshadowing and explain how it contributes to the mood of a story

About the Author

Daniel Cohen has had a long writing career. He has written about ghosts and other strange things. However, he says, "I don't make up ghost stories. I deal with legends and factual accounts." Some of his books on this subject are *The Encyclopedia of Ghosts, Real Ghosts,* and *Ghost in the House.*

Cohen was born in Chicago. He was a managing editor of *Science Digest* magazine. In 1969, he retired so that he could write all the time. He has created a great number of books on many different subjects, including biographies of sports, television, music, and film stars; world history; animals and nature; and science and technology. His stories became so popular that he needed help in writing them. He turned to his wife, Susan Handler Cohen, for help. She was already a published author. They have worked together on a number of texts, including several books about Olympic athletes and heroes of America's space program. They live, with an assortment of cats and dogs, in New Jersey.

About the Selection

"The Phantom Hitchhiker" is probably the best-known American legend. For over a hundred years, people have told each other this tale. Some say this story actually began in early Europe with stories of people traveling on horseback. Like the other stories in this unit, the details may change slightly as the tale travels from place to place and person to person. But the basic plot remains the same.

You might even have heard the story yourself from a friend, who claims to have heard it from another friend. Like others who have told this legend, your friend may insist it is true. That's the way legends travel from person to person today. That's the way they have always traveled.

Literary Terms One of the reasons this legend has remained so popular is that, from the very beginning of the story, readers know that something strange is going to happen. They realize this because the storyteller gives them clues along the way. These clues are called **foreshadowing**. Through foreshadowing, authors build suspense and other elements of a story's **mood**. Mood is the feeling that a piece of writing creates.

foreshadowing clues or hints that a writer gives about something that has not yet happened

mood the feeling created by a piece of writing

Reading on Your Own As you read this story, place yourself in the story's setting. It's raining and Joel has been driving a long time. He feels a sense of danger. Would you feel the same way? Would you react the way he did? As you continue to read, look at things through Joel's eyes. Compare what he says and does with what *you* might say and do in the same situation.

Writing on Your Own What is the most frightening movie you've ever seen? Write a short review of the film that might appear in your school newspaper. Provide enough details so that others will want to see the movie.

Vocabulary Focus The word *phantom* can have several meanings, depending on how the writer or speaker uses it. Phantom can be used as a noun. It means a ghost or spirit, something that seems to be there but really isn't. Phantom can also be used as an adjective, giving us more information about a noun. The adjective means being like a ghost or a spirit. In the title of this story, how do you think the word *phantom* is used? What does it tell you about what to expect from the story?

Think Before You Read Hitchhiking is now illegal in many places. Why do you think people made this law? How might hitchhiking be dangerous?

The Phantom Hitchhiker

As you read, notice details about time and place that help create the mood. What is the mood of this story?

Joel Harris was tired, so tired that he shouldn't have been driving at all. It was nearly three A.M., and he had been up since six o'clock the previous morning.

"Too hard," he muttered to himself. "I'm pushing myself too hard."

To make matters worse it had begun to rain. Joel had to strain his eyes to keep the deserted road in front of him in view.

"Thank God, it's only thirty more miles."

It was the sort of situation in which an ordinary driver might have been tempted to speed a bit, thinking that by getting home faster he could beat the rain and the fatigue. But Joel Harris was one of those instinctively cautious drivers. He automatically slowed his speed to adjust to the **deteriorating** driving conditions. A sense of real danger cut through the weariness and made him more alert.

Instinctively cautious means naturally careful.

That's why Joel became aware of the figure at the side of the road before most people would have. First it was just a flash of white in his headlights, but as the car drew closer he could see it was a girl. She was young, about eighteen he guessed, and she was wearing a white party dress. She wasn't actually thumbing a ride, she was just standing there. As the car came closer Joel made eye contact with her. She looked at him pleadingly.

Why do you think this story is called a modern legend?

A young girl, alone at night on a deserted road, wearing only a **flimsy** dress, with the rain beginning to really come down. There was no way he was just going to pass her by.

Joel stopped and leaned out the window. "Hey, you need a lift?"

She was already walking toward the car. "Sure do, mister. Thanks."

deteriorating getting worse   **flimsy** thin, not strongly made

"You're lucky it's me. You can stand on this road for hours at this time of night without seeing a car. And then you never can tell who is going to stop. You hear about all sorts of terrible things that can happen."

The girl didn't say anything. She just climbed into the back seat of the car.

"Where you going?" Joel asked.

"Middletown."

"This is your lucky day, that's where I'm going too. Where in Middletown do you live? I'll take you right home. No sense in your wandering around town in the dark."

She gave him an address, which Joel recognized as being in one of the older and poorer sections of town. He didn't know that part of town well, but he figured he could find it easily enough.

Joel switched on the interior light and turned to get a look at his passenger. Perhaps he had overestimated her age. She might have been only sixteen, it was hard to tell. She was quite pretty, but looked worn and tired. Her hair, wet from the rain, hung down to her shoulders. Her dress was also wet and rumpled, and had a curiously old-fashioned look. Probably second hand, he thought.

Joel had wanted to ask the girl what she was doing on the road at three in the morning, but there was something about the way she looked at him that made him feel he shouldn't ask that question. It was really none of his business anyway. If she wants to tell me, she'll tell me, he thought.

The girl shivered slightly.

"You must be cold. I'll turn the heater up, and here, take my jacket."

The girl's old-fashioned dress and Joel's jacket are examples of foreshadowing. What other examples of foreshadowing do you find in this story?

The girl thanked him, wrapped the jacket around her shoulders, and lay back in the seat, her eyes closed. She seemed to fall asleep almost instantly.

Poor kid, thought Joel. She must be exhausted. I wonder what happened.

Joel drove on in silence. He didn't even turn the radio on for fear of waking his sleeping passenger.

It didn't take long to reach town, and he found the address the girl had given him without much trouble. It was the worst house on a bad street. In fact, the house was so **dilapidated** that it looked deserted, and Joel wondered if he had somehow gotten the address wrong.

"Is this the place?"

There was no answer, so he repeated the question more loudly. Still no answer. Sound sleeper, he thought. He turned around. The back seat was empty.

Joel's first **reaction** was surprise, but that was quickly replaced by fear. He hadn't stopped the car since he had first picked up the girl. He checked both back doors, and they were locked from the inside. There was no possible way for anyone to have gotten out of the car. Yet the girl in the white dress was gone.

Joel just wanted to drive away and forget the whole thing. But he couldn't. He had to try and find out what had happened. He went up to the house, half hoping that no one would be there. But as soon as he knocked he saw a light go on inside.

The door was answered by a thin, sad-looking old woman wearing a shabby robe.

"Yes?"

For a moment Joel was startled, for as he stared at the old woman's eyes they reminded him strongly of the eyes of the girl in the white dress.

"I'm sorry to disturb you at this hour," he began haltingly. "I know what I'm going to say will sound crazy. But I've just had the strangest experience of my life."

To speak *haltingly* means to speak unsurely, without confidence. Why would Joel speak haltingly to the old woman?

dilapidated rundown, falling apart   **reaction** a response

Joel began to relate the story of the girl he had picked up on the deserted road. As he talked it sounded more and more unbelievable, and he began to feel more and more foolish.

But he told the story all the way through, with all the details he could remember.

The woman listened patiently, her lined face registering no **emotion**. Indeed, she looked as if she were listening to a familiar tale. When Joel finished she said, "Where did you say you picked the girl up?"

Joel told her.

"That's my daughter Laura," the old woman said. "She's dead. She was killed in an automobile accident on that road ten years ago. She was coming home from a party.

"You're not the first young man to have had this experience. It usually happens on rainy nights. She was killed on a rainy night like this one. She seems to be trying to get home.

"Laura's buried in Oaklawn Cemetery just outside of town."

Joel had expected to be called crazy, but he never expected to hear a story even crazier than the one he told. He didn't know what to say. He just mumbled something about being terribly sorry, and walked away. Before he did, he caught a glimpse of the name on the door of the house. It was Kearns.

By the time Joel got back into his car and drove away, he had begun to convince himself that the whole experience had never taken place, that it was all a **hallucination** brought on by extreme fatigue. Things like that happen, he thought. That must be it.

He shivered in the cold. Only then did Joel realize that he didn't have his jacket on. He stopped the car and searched for his jacket. It wasn't there. He had given it to the girl in the white dress, and she had taken it away with her.

Now Joel could not let the matter rest. The following day he went to Oaklawn Cemetery. With the help of the caretaker he was able to locate the Kearns family plot. Sure enough, there was the grave of Laura Kearns. She had been just sixteen when she died, ten years earlier.

Draped over the tombstone, neatly folded, was Joel's jacket.

emotion a feeling	**hallucination** a vision that is not real

AFTER READING THE SELECTION

The Phantom Hitchhiker   by Daniel Cohen

Directions Choose the letter of the best answer or write the answer using complete sentences.

Comprehension: Identifying Facts

1. As the story begins, what is the time and place?
   A The sun is setting and Joel is driving.
   B Joel is driving and the sun is in his eyes.
   C It is 3 A.M. and Joel is driving while tired.
   D all of the above

2. What does Joel do when he sees the girl shiver?

3. Who is Joel's hitchhiker, according to the old woman?

Comprehension: Putting Ideas Together

4. What does Joel notice about the girl's dress that is important to the story?
   A It is white.
   B It is flimsy.
   C It looks old-fashioned.
   D all of the above

5. Why does Joel go up to the house after the girl disappears?

6. What does Joel find when he visits the cemetery?

Understanding Literature: Foreshadowing

When writers use foreshadowing, they give clues or hints about something that is going to happen. In "The Phantom Hitchhiker," foreshadowing is used to create suspense.

Writers sometimes foreshadow events through their descriptions of setting. For example, Daniel Cohen opens this story by saying it is 3 A.M. Readers expect something strange to happen at this time of night. Writers can also foreshadow through the actions of their characters. When the girl wraps Joel's jacket around her shoulders, this foreshadows Joel's discovery of his jacket draped over her tombstone.

7. In your opinion, why is foreshadowing effective in a story such as this?

8. How does the description of the girl's dress foreshadow the plot of the story?

Critical Thinking

9. What do we learn about Joel Harris's character? Use evidence from the story to support your answer.

Thinking Creatively

10. Why do you think this story, in hundreds of local versions, is one of the most popular and widespread of all modern American legends?

 Grammar Check

Authors usually vary the kinds of sentences they create in a single text. They vary the length. Some have many words; others have few. They also vary them in structure. They can make them active or passive sentences. In active sentences, the subject performs the action. This is an active sentence: "He shivered in the cold." The subject *he* is doing the action *shiver*. But, look at the last sentence in this story. It is a passive sentence. "Draped over a tombstone, neatly folded, was Joel's jacket." The sentence does not say who completed the action. Why do you think the author chose to end the story with a passive sentence?

 Writing on Your Own

Epitaphs are short sayings written on tombstones. They usually tell something about the person who is buried there, or about death itself. Write an epitaph for Laura Kearns's tombstone.

 Speaking

Think of the moment in the story when Joel found out Laura was killed 10 years before. How was his posture? What other clues about the way he felt might have he given? Practice this scene with a partner. Take turns being Mrs. Kearns and Joel. How does your posture change from one role to the other?

 Listening

What sound effects might you add to a reading of this story to add to its mood? Make a list of 10 effects and note the place where you would add them to the story. Describe how you might create the sound or music or list a source where you might find it.

 Media

A collage is a work of art made by using pictures, photos, materials, and found objects. Create a collage that tells the story of "The Phantom Hitchhiker," using pictures you find in magazines, objects, or images you draw yourself.

The characters of a story bring readers into the story. Because of this, authors take great care in creating and developing characters. As we learn more about characters, they become real to us.

Writers develop characters in several ways. Through their narrators, they can tell readers about a character. They can let other characters tell about a character. They can also let characters reveal themselves by what they do, say, and think.

In "The Phantom Hitchhiker," the author tells us that Joel is tired and knows he has been pushing himself too hard. He also tells us that Joel is not "an ordinary driver," tempted to speed through the rain and his own fatigue. Instead, Joel becomes more alert.

Cohen also tells us about Joel through the other characters in the story. We see that the young girl trusts him enough to accept a ride from him and, later, to fall asleep in his car. Laura's mother opens the door to him and listens patiently to his story.

Cohen also reveals Joel's character by the things he does, says, and thinks. Despite his fear and fatigue, he goes after answers to the mystery of his hitchhiker.

Review

1. In what ways can an author develop a character?

2. What does Daniel Cohen tell us about Joel?

3. What do the other characters tell us about Joel?

4. What do we learn about Joel through what he does, says, and thinks?

5. Which of these methods is most important in this story? Why do you think so?

Writing on Your Own

Assume that you are Joel. Write a short letter or e-mail message to your parents, letting them know what you thought about Laura. What kind of a person do you think she was?

People everywhere have created folklore: stories, customs, and traditions that they preserve and pass along to their children. American folklore is especially rich in tall tales and legends.

The settings and characters in American tall tales are often drawn from the frontier and the colorful people who lived and worked there. The characters in tall tales are imaginary, larger than life. They are bigger, braver, and smarter than anyone else, and they have fantastic adventures.

Legends are based on real people, real places, or real events. These stories include details that are true and details that are purely imaginary. Part of the fun of reading legends is not knowing which are which!

Most tall tales and legends are part of oral literature, told first not by professional writers but by ordinary people. This folklore tells us a lot about what people over the years have considered important, unique, and funny in their lives.

Selections

- "Babe the Blue Ox," by Esther Shephard, is a tall tale about the great deeds of Paul Bunyan's huge ox.

- "Feboldson, Western Scientist," by Walter Blair, is a tall tale about a no-nonsense Nebraska problem solver during the Great Heat and the Great Fog.

- "John Henry" is a ballad that tells about the legendary contest between a steel-driving man and a machine.

- "Life and Adventures of Calamity Jane, by Herself," by Martha (Marthy) Cannary Burk, is legendary Calamity Jane's own telling of anecdotes from her adventurous life.

- "The Phantom Hitchhiker," by Daniel Cohen, is a modern legend about the adventure of a late-night driver who picks up a mysterious hitchhiker.

Directions Choose the letter of the best answer or write the answer using complete sentences.

Comprehension: Identifying Facts

1. What job seems to stump Babe at first?

  A pulling the crooks out of a logging road

  B logging six hundred forty acres

  C eating hotcakes off of a big griddle

  D all of the above

2. After Nebraska gave out chunks of itself, what was left over?

3. How much does the hammer John Henry uses in the contest weigh?

4. Who gives Martha Cannary the nickname of Calamity Jane?

5. Where does the hitchhiker tell Joel she is headed?

Comprehension: Putting Ideas Together

6. How does Babe help Paul and the other loggers?

  A He pulls timber from the forest.

  B He straightens out a logging road.

  C He plays after a day's work.

  D all of the above

7. What roles do Brimstone Bill and Ole play in the logging camp?

8. How does Feboldson know he would need fog-cutters?

9. How do we know the people who knew Calamity Jane respected her?

10. Why is Joel sure that his passenger couldn't have left his car by normal means?

Understanding Literature: Autobiography and Biography

Autobiographies and biographies are two related kinds of literature. A *biography* is the story of a person's life, written by another person. An *autobiography* is the story of a person's life, written by that person.

From its title, we expect "Life and Adventures of Calamity Jane, by Herself" to be an autobiography. We expect that most of its details are based on fact. However, there is a lot of evidence showing that many of the details in this pamphlet are not true.

11. How is an autobiography different from a biography?

12. Could a tall tale be a biography or autobiography? Explain.

13. Why might people want to write their autobiographies?

14. Why do you think Calamity Jane changed some of the details of her life in this pamphlet?

15. What details of the legend might a biography of John Henry include?

Critical Thinking

16. What tasks would be easier for you to do if you had an ox like Babe?

17. From what you know of Febold Feboldson's character traits, how might he have handled a Great Snowstorm?

18. How would "John Henry" be different if it was written from his boss's point of view?

19. If you were Joel Harris, what would you have done after you found your jacket on Laura's grave?

Thinking Creatively

20. If you were creating a tall tale for American readers today, who would be the main character? What story would you tell about this character?

Speak and Listen

Record a scary story that you have heard before. Give the recording to a partner to listen to. After a week, have your partner record his or her version of the story. Listen to both recordings and compare them. Did any details change? How did the changes affect the story?

Writing on Your Own

Explore the characterization of one of the characters in this unit. Use the Character Analysis Guide graphic organizer described in Appendix A. Based on this graphic, write a first draft of a one-page essay. Show how the author presented this character to readers. With a partner, review your first draft for factual or writing errors. Make corrections and complete a final draft.

Beyond Words

How has the map of the United States changed since the days of Paul Bunyan and Febold Feboldson? Draw or build two versions of a map of this country. One should show the way the country looked in 1900. The other should show how it looks today. Summarize the differences in a chart.

Test-Taking Tip

Studying together in small groups, summarizing each selection, and asking questions of one another is one way to review material for literature tests.

Embracing Vacation
Tsing-Fang Chen, 1997

Unit 4

The Short Story

hort stories are brief works of fiction. Fiction stories are made up by the person who writes them. They first appeared in the 1800s. Because short stories are brief, they usually take place over a short time period, in one main place. Their plots include only the most important descriptive details. They usually have only a few characters. As this form of fiction has developed, authors have changed what the short story is and what it can do. Readers continue to enjoy the very different kinds of characters, plots, and themes found in the world of the short story.

In this unit, you will read short stories that show how different this form of fiction can be.

"The unread story is not a story; it is little black marks on wood pulp. The reader, reading it, makes it live: a live thing, a story."

—Ursula K. Le Guin, *Dancing at the Edge of the World,* 1989

Unit 4

About the Short Story

The storytelling of fables, myths, tall tales, and legends continues in the short story. People have been telling and writing short stories for many years. Modern short stories first developed in the 1800s. At that time, American writers such as Washington Irving, Nathaniel Hawthorne, and Edgar Allan Poe were popular. People became interested in this form of literature. Short stories are still very popular today.

All short stories have plot, setting, characters, point of view, and theme. The series of events in a short story makes up its plot. The setting is the time and place of the story. There are usually very few characters in a short story. The main character is also called the protagonist or hero. The antagonist is the person or force trying to keep the protagonist from reaching his or her goal. Short stories are told by a narrator. The narrator's point of view may be from inside the story (first person) or as someone who is watching the story happen (third person). The theme is the story's main idea.

> **Plot:** the series of events in a story
> **Setting:** a story's time and place
> **Character:** a person or animal in a story
> **Point of view:** the relationship of the narrator to the story
> **Theme:** the main idea of a story

Fables, myths, legends, and tall tales all have these same characteristics. What makes short stories different?

■ Short stories are brief, much shorter than novels, for example. Edgar Allan Poe said these stories should be short enough to read in one sitting. Whether this is true or not, readers can usually finish short stories quickly.

■ Because they are brief, short stories usually take place in a short period of time. They may be set in only one place. The time frame of a novel, on the other hand, is often much longer. Novels may also have many settings.

■ Writers of short stories focus on the basics of the story. They have less room for description than novelists do. Short-story writers tend to include only the most important details.

■ Short stories are a form of fiction. This means that they did not actually happen. The author creates the characters and the story they live. Writers of fiction may get ideas from the people they meet and the events they observe. However, they change this information to serve the story.

■ Short stories are included in the kind of literature called prose. Literature can be divided into two forms: prose and poetry. Poetry includes all forms

Winter Moonlight,
Currier & Ives, 1866

of writing that use special patterns of words and rhythm. Prose includes all other writing, such as short stories, novels, fables, myths, tall tales, and legends. Some people think of prose as writing that sounds like ordinary language, or writing that is organized into paragraphs. Recall, however, that "John Henry," in Unit 3, tells its legend in a ballad. A ballad is a form of poetry. So, even though the subject of this ballad was originally a legend, its rhyming words and rhythm make it a poem.

Building on the basic characteristics of short stories, today's authors continue to change what a short story is and does. In the 1800s, short stories were often about ghostly or amazing events. Today's short stories often focus on the familiar details of life. The plots of older short stories usually had clear beginnings, middles, and ends. Modern short stories sometimes just stop.

Each of the short stories in this unit has a very different style and effect. Mark Twain's "The Celebrated Jumping Frog of Calaveras County" gives readers a funny snapshot of life in one of the California mining towns that sprang up during the Gold Rush. "Everyday Use," by Alice Walker, takes a look at the changing and unchanging world of an African American family. In "American History," Judith Ortiz-Cofer brings readers into the sometimes-painful life of a young Latina girl growing up in Paterson, New Jersey. Langston Hughes's "Thank You, M'am" tells the story of a boy looking for trouble and the woman who makes him stop and think. The last story, "Unfinished Message" by Toshio Mori, deals with a startling event in the life of a Japanese American family dealing with World War II.

The Celebrated Jumping Frog of Calaveras County *by Mark Twain*

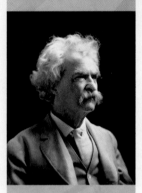

Mark Twain
1835–1910

Objectives

- To read and understand a short story
- To explain how the use of caricatures and humor adds to a story
- To define and give examples of story-within-a-story, short stories, and dialogue

pen name a false name used for writing

novel fiction that is book-length and has more plot and details than a short story

About the Author

Samuel Langhorne Clemens, better known as Mark Twain, was born in Missouri. His childhood was not ideal. He later said that for the first seven years of his life he was an "uncertain" child, always taking some medicine or the other. He made up for those years as soon as he could.

Clemens worked as a printer's helper, a Mississippi riverboat pilot, and a newspaper reporter and editor. He moved west to follow the Gold Rush. It was there that he first used the name Mark Twain. He had been looking for a **pen name** for a long time. Writers then often wrote using other names. After a few tries, he decided on Mark Twain. "Mark twain" was the call that steamboat pilots used to say that the river was deep enough for boats to pass.

Twain's earliest published writings were funny sketches that appeared in newspapers. These were soon followed by several books about travel, including *Innocents Abroad.* He also wrote several full-length **novels**, or fiction books. His best-known novels—*Tom Sawyer, The Prince and the Pauper,* and *Huckleberry Finn*—are classics of American literature.

About the Selection

"The Celebrated Jumping Frog of Calaveras County" was the story that first made people pay attention to Mark Twain. An early biography of Twain says that the writer first heard the tale from a gold miner he met in California. The story was first published in 1865 as "Jim Smiley and His Jumping Frog." In that version, Twain wrote the story as if it was a letter to an old friend. Twain rewrote the story several times during his life.

Literary Terms A **short story** is a brief work of **fiction**, or a story the author creates. The short story you are about to read is actually a **story-within-a-story**. The narrator meets a character named Simon Wheeler who then tells the story of Jim Smiley. Twain, an excellent **humorist,** wrote this story to amuse readers. In it, he uses **caricature**, or exaggerated descriptions of characters, and great storytelling. These same characteristics were part of everything Twain wrote, from essays and novels to many other forms of **prose**. Prose is any writing that is not poetry.

Reading on Your Own The dialect that Simon Wheeler uses to tell his tale shows certain speech patterns. The **dialogue**, or conversation, is often hard to read because it doesn't follow the speech patterns that we are used to hearing. As you read, say Wheeler's words aloud. Listen to their rhythms and think about what he is actually saying. Think about how you might say the same thing if you were talking with your friends.

Writing on Your Own If you were a miner in Angel's Camp, what might you think if you met Mark Twain? Create five lines of dialogue that the miner and Twain may have shared.

Vocabulary Focus In formal English, it is not correct to use two negative words in one sentence. Negative words are words like *no*, *not*, and *none*. Mark Twain uses dialect in this story. "He *never* done *nothing* for these three months" contains two negative words. "He did nothing for these three months" would be the correct way to write it. As you read this story, look for other sentences that have *double negatives* in them. Why do you think Twain used dialect to write this way?

Think Before You Read What do you already know about the California Gold Rush?

---

short story
a brief work of prose fiction that includes plot, setting, characters, point of view, and theme

fiction writing in which the author creates the events and characters

story-within-a-story a second story told within another story

humorist someone who writes funny works

caricature a character description that is exaggerated—overstated—to make people laugh

prose all writing that is not poetry

dialogue the conversation among characters in a story or play

The Celebrated Jumping Frog of Calaveras County

As you read, note the various parts of a short story: plot, characters, setting, point of view, and theme. Notice that this story uses a first-person narrator.

Hereunto append means that the narrator is about to state the result of his questioning of Simon Wheeler.

In **compliance** with the request of a friend of mine, who wrote me from the East, I called on good-natured, **garrulous** old Simon Wheeler, and inquired after my friend's friend, *Leonidas W.* Smiley, as requested to do, and I hereunto append the result. I have a lurking suspicion that *Leonidas W.* Smiley is a myth; that my friend never knew such a personage; and that he only **conjectured** that, if I asked old Wheeler about him, it would remind him of his **infamous** *Jim* Smiley, and he would go to work and bore me nearly to death with some **infernal reminiscence** of him as long and tedious as it should be useless to me. If that was the design, it certainly succeeded.

I found Simon Wheeler dozing comfortably by the barroom stove of the old, **dilapidated** tavern in the ancient mining camp of Angel's, and I noticed that he was fat and bald-headed, and had an expression of winning gentleness

compliance the act of doing what is asked

garrulous talkative

conjectured guessed or supposed

infamous well known because of bad or disagreeable things

infernal tiresome; unpleasant

reminiscence something remembered; memory

dilapidated run-down, falling apart

and simplicity upon his **tranquil countenance.** He roused
up and gave me good-day. I told him a friend of mine had
commissioned me to make some **inquiries** about a cherished
companion of his boyhood named *Leonidas W.* Smiley—*Rev.
Leonidas W.* Smiley—a young minister of the Gospel, who
he had heard was at one time a resident of Angel's Camp. I
added, that, if Mr. Wheeler could tell me anything about this
Rev. Leonidas W. Smiley, I would feel under many **obligations**
to him.

Simon Wheeler backed me into a corner and **blockaded**
me there with his chair, and then sat me down and reeled
off the **monotonous narrative** which follows this paragraph.

tranquil calm; peaceful	**inquiries** requests for information	**blockaded** prevented escape
countenance face; appearance	**obligations** feelings of gratitude	**monotonous** boring; unchanging
		narrative a story

He never smiled, he never frowned, he never changed his voice from the gentle-flowing key to which he tuned the initial sentence, he never betrayed the slightest **suspicion** of enthusiasm; but all through the **interminable** narrative there ran a vein of **impressive** earnestness and sincerity, which showed me plainly that, so far from his imagining that there was anything ridiculous or funny about his story, he regarded it as a really important matter, and admitted its two heroes as men of **transcendent** genius in *finesse*. To me, the spectacle of a man drifting **serenely** along through such a queer yarn without ever smiling, was **exquisitely** absurd. As I said before, I asked him to tell me what he knew of Rev. Leonidas W. Smiley, and he replied as follows. I let him go on in his own way, and never interrupted him once:

There was a feller here once by the name of *Jim* Smiley, in the winter of '49—or maybe it was the spring of '50—I don't **recollect** exactly, somehow, though what makes me think it was one or the other is because I remember the big flume wasn't finished when he first came to the camp; but anyway, he was the curiousest man about always betting on anything that turned up you ever see, if he could get anybody to bet on the other side; and if he couldn't, he'd change sides. Any way what suited the other man would suit him—any way just so's he got a bet, *he* was satisfied. But still he was lucky, uncommon lucky—he most always come out winner. He was always ready and laying for a chance; there couldn't be no solit'ry thing mentioned but that feller'd offer to bet on it, and take any side you please, as I was just telling you. If there was a horse-race, you'd find him flush, or you'd find him busted at the end of it; if there was a dog-fight, he'd bet on it; if there was a cat-fight, he'd bet on it; if there was a chicken-fight, he'd bet on it; why, if there was two birds setting on a fence, he would bet you which one would fly first; or if there was a camp meeting, he would be there reg'lar, to bet

Finesse comes from a French word meaning *the end*. It usually means skill in handling a situation.

Here begins the story-within-a-story. Notice that the second narrator, Simon Wheeler, talks in dialect.

Gold miners would cut a *flume*, or channel, to run water through in order to find gold.

suspicion hint; trace

interminable endless

impressive able to fix firmly in the mind

transcendent far beyond the usual

serenely calmly; not at all upset

exquisitely perfectly

recollect to remember

on Parson Walker, which he judged to be the best **exhorter** about here, and so he was, too, and a good man. If he even seen a straddle-bug start to go anywheres, he would bet you how long it would take him to get wherever he was going to, and if you took him up, he would foller that straddle-bug to Mexico but what he would find out where he was bound for and how long he was on the road. Lots of the boys here has seen that Smiley, and can tell you about him. Why, it never made no difference to *him*—he would bet on *any*thing—the dangdest feller. Parson Walker's wife laid very sick once, for a good while, and it seemed as if they warn't going to save her; but one morning he came in, and Smiley asked how she was, and he said she was considerable better—thank the Lord for his inf'nit mercy—and coming on so smart that, with the blessing of Prov'dence, she'd get well yet; and Smiley, before he thought, says, "Well, I'll risk two-and-a-half that she don't, anyway."

Thish-yer Smiley had a mare—the boys called her the fifteen-minute nag, but that was only in fun, you know, because, of course, she was faster than that—and he used to win money on that horse, for all she was so slow and always had the asthma, or the distemper, or the consumption, or something of that kind. They used to give her two or three hundred yards start, and then pass her under way; but always at the fag-end of the race she'd get excited and desperate-like, and come cavorting and straddling up, and scattering her legs around **limber**, sometimes in the air, and sometimes out to one side amongst the fences, and kicking up m-o-r-e dust, and raising m-o-r-e racket with her coughing and sneezing and blowing her nose—and always fetch up at the stand just about a neck ahead, as near as you could **cipher** it down.

And he had a little small bull pup, that to look at him you'd think he wan't worth a cent but to set around and look ornery and lay for a chance to steal something. But as soon

A camp meeting was an open-air religious gathering. Parson Walker, a minister, appears to have given the most enthusiastic sermons.

Smiley is a famous Twain caricature. As you read, see which parts of his personality are exaggerated or overstated.

Picture Smiley's horse in a race, lagging behind until the very end. Then, "desperate-like," she'd come up skidding, kicking, coughing, sneezing, her legs going every which way—and win the race!

exhorter one who strongly urges another to do or believe something

limber moving easily

cipher to use arithmetic

as money was up on him, he was a different dog; his under-jaw'd begin to stick out like the fo'castle of a steamboat, and his teeth would uncover, and shine savage like the furnaces. And a dog might tackle him, and bullyrag him, and bite him, and throw him over his shoulder two or three times, and Andrew Jackson—which was the name of the pup—Andrew Jackson would never let on but what *he* was satisfied, and hadn't expected nothing else—and the bets being doubled and doubled on the other side all the time, till the money was all up; and then all of a sudden he would grab that other dog jest by the j'int of his hind leg and freeze to it—not claw, you understand, but only jest grip and hang on till they throwed up the sponge, if it was a year. Smiley always come out winner on that pup, till he harnessed a dog once that didn't have no hind legs, because they'd been sawed off by a circular saw, and when the thing had gone along far enough, and the money was all up, and he come to make a snatch for his pet holt, he saw in a minute how he'd been imposed on, and how the other dog had him in the door, so to speak, and he 'peared surprised, and then he looked sorter discouraged-like, and didn't try no more to win the fight, and so he got shucked out bad. He give Smiley a look, as much to say that his heart was broke and it was *his* fault for putting up a dog that hadn't no hind legs for him to take holt of, which was his main **dependence** in a fight, and then he limped off a piece and laid down and died. It was a good pup, was that Andrew Jackson, and would have made a name for hisself if he'd lived, for the stuff was in him, and he had genius—I know it, because he hadn't no opportunities to speak of, and it don't stand to reason that a dog could make such a fight as he could under them **circumstances**, if he hadn't no talent. It always makes me feel sorry when I think of that last fight of his'n, and the way it turned out.

Well, thish-yer Smiley had rat-terriers, and chicken-cocks, and tomcats, and all them kind of things, till you couldn't

dependence	**circumstances**
something that is necessary	conditions

rest, and you couldn't fetch nothing for him to bet on but he'd match you. He ketched a frog one day, and took him home, and said he cal'klated to edercate him; and so he never done nothing for these three months but set in his back yard and learn that frog to jump. And you bet you he *did* learn him, too. He'd give him a little punch behind, and the next minute you'd see that frog whirling in the air like a doughnut—see him turn one summerset, or maybe a couple, if he got a good start, and come down flat-footed and all right, like a cat. He got him up so in the matter of catching flies, and kept him in practice so constant, that he'd nail a fly every time as far as he could see him. Smiley said all a frog wanted was education, and he could do most anything—and I believe him. Why, I've seen him set Dan'l Webster down here on this floor—Dan'l Webster was the name of the frog—and sing out, "Flies, Dan'l, flies!" and quicker'n you could wink, he'd spring straight up, and snake a fly off'n the counter there, and flop down on the floor again as solid as a gob of mud, and fall to scratching the side of his head with his hind foot as **indifferent** as if he hadn't no idea he's been doin' any more'n any frog might do. You never see a frog so modest and straight-for'ard as he was, for all he was so gifted. And when it come to fair and square jumping on the dead level, he could get over more ground at one straddle than any animal of his breed you ever see. Jumping on a dead level was his strong suit, you understand; and when it come to that, Smiley would ante up money on him as long as he had a red. Smiley was monstrous proud of his frog, and well he might be, for fellers that had traveled and been everywhere all said he laid over any frog that ever *they* see.

Well, Smiley kept the beast in a little lattice box, and he used to fetch him downtown sometimes and lay for a bet. One day a feller—a stranger in the camp, he was—come across him with his box, and says:

"What might it be that you've got in the box?"

Summerset is another word for somersault.

To *ante up*, as in poker, means to put your money into the pot.

As you read, see how Twain creates humor with his dialogue.

indifferent uncaring; uninterested

And Smiley says, sorter indifferent like, "It might be a parrot or it might be a canary, maybe, but it ain't—it's only just a frog."

An' the feller took it, and looked at it careful, and turned it round this way and that, and says, "H'm—so 'tis. Well, what's *he* good for?"

"Well," Smiley says, easy and careless, "he's good enough for *one* thing, I should judge—he can outjump any frog in Calaveras county."

The feller took the box again, and took another long, particular look, and give it back to Smiley, and says, very **deliberate**, "Well, I don't see no p'ints about that frog that's any better'n any other frog."

"Maybe you don't," Smiley says. "Maybe you understand frogs, and maybe you don't understand 'em; maybe you've had experience, and maybe you ain't only a amature, as it were. Anyways, I've got *my* opinion, and I'll risk forty dollars that he can outjump any frog in Calaveras county."

And the feller studied a minute, and then says, kinder sad-like, "Well, I'm only a stranger here, and I ain't got no frog; but if I had a frog, I'd bet you."

And then Smiley says, "That's all right—that's all right—if you'll hold my box a minute, I'll go and get you a frog." And so the feller took the box, and put up his forty dollars along with Smiley's, and set down to wait.

So he set there a good while thinking and thinking to hisself, and then he got the frog out and pried his mouth open and took a teaspoon and filled him full of quail shot—filled him pretty near up to his chin—and set him on the floor. Smiley he went to the swamp and slopped around in the mud for a long time, and finally he ketched a frog, and fetched him in, and give him to this feller, and says:

"Now, if you're ready, set him alongside of Dan'l with his forepaws just even with Dan'l, and I'll give the word." Then he says, "One—two—three—jump!" and him and the feller

By *amature,* Smiley means amateur, in this case someone who doesn't know what he's talking about.

deliberate carefully saying and meaning every word

touched up the frogs from behind, and the new frog hopped off, but Dan'l give a heave, and hysted up his shoulders—so—like a Frenchman, but it wasn't no use—he couldn't budge; he was planted as solid as an anvil, and he couldn't no more stir than if he was anchored out. Smiley was a good deal surprised, and he was disgusted too, but he didn't have no idea what the matter was, of course.

The feller took the money and started away; and when he was going out the door, he sorter jerked his thumb over his shoulder—this way—at Dan'l, and says again, very deliberate, "Well, *I* don't see no p'ints about that frog that's any better'n any other frog."

Smiley he stood scratching his head and looking down at Dan'l a long time, and at last he says, "I do wonder what in the nation that frog throw'd off for—I wonder if there ain't something the matter with him—he 'pears to look mighty baggy, somehow." And he ketched Dan'l by the nap of the neck, and lifted him up and says, "Why, blame my cats, if he don't weigh five pounds!" and turned him upside down, and he belched out a double handful of shot. And then he see how it was, and he was the maddest man—he set the frog down and took out after the feller, but he never ketched him. And—

At this point, the first narrator of the story returns to narrate the end.

(Here Simon Wheeler heard his name called from the front yard, and got up to see what was wanted.) And turning to me as he moved away, he said: "Just set where you are, stranger, and rest easy—I ain't going to be gone a second."

But, by your leave, I did not think that a continuation of the history of the **enterprising vagabond** *Jim* Smiley would be likely to afford me much information concerning the *Rev. Leonidas W.* Smiley, and so I started away.

At the door I met the sociable Wheeler returning, and he buttonholed me and recommenced:

"Well, thish-yer Smiley had a yeller one-eyed cow that didn't have no tail, only jest a short stump like a bannanner, and—"

"Oh, hang Smiley and his **afflicted** cow!" I muttered, good-naturedly, and bidding the old gentleman good-day, I **departed**.

Buttonholed me means he tried to keep him there to continue the conversation.

enterprising marked by a readiness to act	**afflicted** troublesome
vagabond wandering	**departed** went away; left

Directions Choose the letter of the best answer or write the answer using complete sentences.

Comprehension: Identifying Facts

1. Why does the first narrator go to call on Simon Wheeler?
   A He had heard about his frog.
   B He knew he told good stories.
   C A friend has asked him to.
   D He was in the neighborhood.

2. Where does Wheeler live?
   A in the East
   B in a mining camp
   C on a farm
   D on a riverboat

3. What is Jim Smiley's favorite thing to do?

4. What bet does Smiley offer to Parson Walker?

5. How does Smiley's mare win races?

6. What is Smiley's dog's name?

7. How does the dog win dog fights?

8. What is Smiley's frog's name?

9. What does the stranger do to Smiley's frog while Smiley is away?

10. Who wins the bet—Smiley or the stranger?

Comprehension: Putting Ideas Together

11. Why do the other men call Smiley's mare "the fifteen-minute nag"?
    A It took her 15 minutes to eat.
    B She was angry.
    C She was born in 15 minutes.
    D She was slow.

12. Why does Smiley's dog lose his last fight?
    A The other dog has no hind legs.
    B Parson Walker's wife was ill.
    C Smiley's dog had no talent.
    D The bets had been doubled.

13. What does Smiley teach his frog to do?

14. Why does Wheeler say Smiley's frog was "modest"?

15. Why does Smiley leave the stranger alone with his frog?

16. How does Smiley feel when he finds out what the stranger has done to his frog?

17. How would you describe the way Wheeler tells his tales of Jim Smiley?

18. Why does the narrator try to leave when Simon Wheeler is called away?

After Reading **continued on next page**

The Celebrated Jumping Frog of Calaveras County   by Mark Twain

19. What happens when Wheeler returns before the narrator can leave?

20. From what he says, how do you think Wheeler feels about Jim Smiley?

Understanding Literature: Caricature

Humorists use many different techniques to make their readers laugh. One is caricature, a way of describing characters. Artists have always used caricatures to create pictures of people, both in painting and cartooning. In literature, authors use caricature by exaggerating, or stretching the truth about, one or two of a character's traits in order to amuse readers. They also create caricatures by oversimplifying other character traits. In the end, their characters become a collection of all the unusual things the author has said about them. Instead of full and round characters, they become more like cartoons.

21. In your opinion, why do authors use caricature?

22. Is this story's narrator a caricature? Explain why you feel that way.

23. What do you learn about Simon Wheeler in the second and third paragraphs of the story?

24. Which of Wheeler's character traits are exaggerated here?

25. How is the description of Smiley's pup, Andrew Jackson, a caricature?

Critical Thinking

26. How would you describe the first narrator of Twain's story? How good an observer is he? How is his storytelling voice different from Simon Wheeler's storytelling voice?

27. Why do you think Mark Twain presents his tales of Smiley as a story-within-a-story? In what ways does Wheeler's style of storytelling make the events he describes even funnier?

28. "Before he thought," Smiley offers Parson Walker a bet that his wife will die. What does that tell you about Smiley's character?

29. Why is it important to the story that Smiley leaves his frog with the stranger?

Thinking Creatively

30. In what ways is "The Celebrated Jumping Frog of Calaveras County" a tall tale?

Grammar Check

Many authors like to create vivid pictures of the characters, settings, and plots in their stories. Using adjectives to describe nouns in the sentences helps them do this. An adjective is what modifies a noun, or changes the picture readers might have about the noun. For example, Twain talks about Wheeler dozing in front of an "old, dilapidated tavern." *Old* and *dilapidated* are adjectives that give the reader more information about the tavern. It is old and run-down. Review the story to find the adjectives below and the nouns they describe. How do they change the way you picture these nouns?

> "the curiousest man"
> "a little small bull pup"
> "a yeller one-eyed cow"

 ## Writing on Your Own

Rewrite the tale of Smiley's frog's defeat from the point of view of the frog Dan'l Webster.

 ## Speaking

With a partner, practice a section of dialogue from this story. What tone of voice and pace of speaking can you find that make the dialogue sound the funniest?

 ## Listening

Pretend you were listening to Wheeler tell his stories. What were some clues you would have picked up on as a listener that would have told you that he might be exaggerating the truth?

 ## Media

Each May since 1928, Calaveras County, California, holds the Jumping Frog Jubilee in honor of Mark Twain and Dan'l Webster, the jumping frog in this story. The highlight of the jubilee is a frog-jumping contest. Use a word processor to create an entry form for contestants who want to enter their frogs in the jumping contest.

 ## Research and Technology

Most people think that Dan'l Webster was a red-legged frog, the largest native frog in the West. Today, red-legged frogs are protected as a threatened species in danger of disappearing. Use the Internet to find out more about red-legged frogs. As you find information, record it on a Main Idea Graphic described in Appendix A.

BEFORE READING THE SELECTION

Everyday Use   by Alice Walker

Alice Walker
1944–

About the Author

Alice Walker was the eighth child in a family of Georgia sharecroppers—farmers who work another person's land. She spent her junior year of college in Africa as an exchange student. After graduating, she settled in Mississippi.

Alice Walker has written fiction and poetry about her childhood, about the experiences of African Americans, particularly women, and about her travels in Africa. She is still active in politics, working toward a better life for African Americans and women.

Walker is probably best known for her novel *The Color Purple*, for which she received the Pulitzer Prize and an American Book Award. Her other novels include *The Temple of My Familiar, Possessing the Secret of Joy,* and *Meridian*. She has also published several books of poetry and many essays.

About the Selection

This story first appeared in a collection of short stories called *In Love and Trouble*. It was published in 1973. At the time, the Black Pride movement was just getting under way. African Americans wanted to find both old and new ways to celebrate their roots and find joy in their culture.

"Everyday Use" is about three African American women, a mother and her two daughters. As in most short stories, the time frame is short. It takes place during a single day, during which a young woman goes to visit her family. The young woman, Dee, has begun a new way of life that she thinks is more suitable for an African American woman. She has a new boyfriend, a new hairdo, and new clothes. Are these new things going to help her discover more about her cultural roots? Or is the answer in the hard but satisfying life her sister and mother share?

Literary Terms   "Everyday Use" is told from the **point of view** of Mama, who is Dee and Maggie's mother. She is the story's narrator. Because Mama is also a character in the story, she is telling the story from an inside view. In literary terms, she is a **first-person** narrator. There's more to this story than just what happens during Dee's visit. Look carefully at the details Walker includes in her story. For example, the mother's quilts play an important role, both in the plot and as **symbols**. A symbol in literature is a person, place, or object that stands for something beyond itself. By looking at symbols such as the quilts, we can better understand the **theme**, or main idea, of the story.

Reading on Your Own   Brainstorm ways in which point of view might change the shape of a story. Think about details a narrator who is also a character in the story might leave out or exaggerate. As you read, imagine that you are looking in on the story from the outside. What details might you focus on, leave as is, or omit as you tell the story?

Writing on Your Own   What important items do you have that once belonged to a relative? Write a paragraph describing one of them.

Vocabulary Focus   *Synonyms* are words that mean almost the same thing. For example, *normal* is a synonym for *everyday*. Brainstorm other synonyms for *everyday*. As you read this story, look for items or events that you could call ordinary or everyday. Use a Main Idea Graphic, described in Appendix A, to record what you find.

Think Before You Read   Have you ever seen a handmade quilt? What was it like? What do you think it meant to the person who made it?

point of view the relationship of the narrator to the story

first person a point of view where the narrator is also a character, using the pronouns *I* and *we*

symbol something that represents something else

theme the main idea of a story or play

Everyday Use

for your grandmama

As you read, pay attention to the mother's voice and first-person point of view as she narrates the story. Notice how she describes herself and both her daughters.

I will wait for her in the yard that Maggie and I made so clean and wavy yesterday afternoon. A yard like this is more comfortable than most people know. It is not just a yard. It is like an extended living room. When the hard clay is swept clean as a floor and the fine sand around the edges lined with tiny, **irregular** grooves, anyone can come and sit and look up into the elm tree and wait for the breezes that never come inside the house.

Maggie will be nervous until after her sister goes: she will stand hopelessly in corners, homely and ashamed of the burn scars down her arms and legs, eying her sister with a mixture of envy and awe. She thinks her sister has held life always in

irregular uneven

the palm of one hand, that "no" is a word the world never learned to say to her.

You've no doubt seen those TV shows where the child who has "made it" is **confronted**, as a surprise, by her own mother and father, tottering in weakly from backstage. (A pleasant surprise, of course: What would they do if parent and child came on the show only to curse out and insult each other?) On TV mother and child embrace and smile into each other's faces. Sometimes the mother and father weep, the child wraps them in her arms and leans across the table to tell how she would not have made it without their help. I have seen these programs.

In the early days of television, there was a popular show called "This Is Your Life," which the narrator describes here.

Sometimes I dream a dream in which Dee and I are suddenly brought together on a TV program of this sort. Out of the dark and soft-seated **limousine** I am ushered into a bright room filled with many people. There I meet a smiling, gray, sporty man like Johnny Carson who shakes my hand and tells me what a fine girl I have. Then we are on the stage and Dee is **embracing** me with tears in her eyes. She pins on my dress a large orchid, even though she has told me once she thinks orchids are tacky flowers.

Johnny Carson hosted late-night television's "The Tonight Show" from 1962 to 1992.

In real life I am a large, big-boned woman with rough, man-working hands. In the winter I wear flannel nightgowns to bed and overalls during the day. I can kill and clean a hog as mercilessly as a man. My fat keeps me hot in zero weather. I can work outside all day, breaking ice to get water for washing; I can eat pork liver cooked over the open fire minutes after it comes steaming from the hog. One winter I knocked a bull calf straight in the brain between the eyes with a sledge hammer and had the meat hung up to chill before nightfall. But of course all this does not show on television. I am the way my daughter would want me to be: a hundred pounds lighter, my skin like an uncooked barley pancake. My hair glistens in the hot bright lights. Johnny Carson has much to do to keep up with my quick and witty tongue.

The mother believes that Dee would like her to be a "TV mom"— thinner, lighter-skinned, witty. What does this tell you about Dee and her relationship with her mother?

| **confronted** met face to face | **limousine** a large, fancy car | **embracing** hugging |

But that is a mistake, I know even before I wake up. Who ever knew a Johnson with a quick tongue? Who can even imagine me looking a strange white man in the eye? It seems to me I have talked to them always with one foot raised in flight, with my head turned in whichever way is farthest from them. Dee, though. She would always look anyone in the eye. Hesitation was no part of her nature.

"How do I look, Mama?" Maggie says, showing just enough of her thin body **enveloped** in pink skirt and red blouse for me to know she's there, almost hidden by the door.

"Come out into the yard," I say.

Have you ever seen a lame animal, perhaps a dog run over by some careless person rich enough to own a car, sidle up to someone who is ignorant enough to be kind to him? That is the way my Maggie walks. She has been like this, chin on chest, eyes on ground, feet in shuffle, ever since the fire that burned the other house to the ground.

Dee is lighter than Maggie, with nicer hair and a fuller figure. She's a woman now, though sometimes I forget. How long ago was it that the other house burned? Ten, twelve years? Sometimes I can still hear the flames and feel Maggie's arms sticking to me, her hair smoking and her dress falling off her in little black papery flakes. Her eyes seemed stretched open, blazed open by the flames reflected in them. And Dee, I see her standing off under the sweet gum tree she used to dig gum out of; a look of concentration on her face as she watched the last **dingy** gray board of the house fall in toward the red-hot brick chimney. Why don't you do a dance around the ashes? I'd wanted to ask her. She had hated the house that much.

I used to think she hated Maggie, too. But that was before we raised the money, the church and me, to send her to Augusta to school. She used to read to us without pity; forcing words, lies, other folks' habits, whole lives upon us two, sitting trapped and ignorant underneath her voice. She washed us in a river of make-believe, burned us with a lot of knowledge

To *sidle* is to move sideways, as if frightened or ashamed. Notice the differences the narrator sees between her two daughters, Dee and Maggie.

Augusta, in eastern Georgia, is the location of Paine College.

enveloped completely covered   **dingy** dirty; discolored

we didn't necessarily need to know. Pressed us to her with the serious way she read, to shove us away at just the moment, like dimwits, we seemed about to understand.

Dee wanted nice things. A yellow organdy dress to wear to her graduation from high school; black pumps to match a green suit she'd made from an old suit somebody gave me. She was determined to stare down any disaster in her efforts. Her eyelids would not flicker for minutes at a time. Often I fought off the **temptation** to shake her. At sixteen she had a style of her own: and knew what style was.

I never had an education myself. After second grade the school was closed down. Don't ask me why: in 1927 colored asked fewer questions than they do now. Sometimes Maggie reads to me. She stumbles along good-naturedly, but can't see well. She knows she is not bright. Like good looks and money, quickness passed her by. She will marry John Thomas (who has mossy teeth in an earnest face) and then I'll be free to sit here and I guess just sing church songs to myself. Although I never was a good singer. Never could carry a tune. I was always better at a man's job. I used to love to milk till I was hooked in the side in '49. Cows are soothing and slow and don't bother you, unless you try to milk them the wrong way.

"Hooked in the side" means kicked by a cow.

I have **deliberately** turned my back on the house. It is three rooms, just like the one that burned, except the roof is tin; they don't make shingle roofs any more. There are no real windows, just some holes cut in the sides, like the portholes on a ship, but not round and not square, with rawhide holding the shutters up on the outside. This house is in a pasture, too, like the other one. No doubt when Dee sees it she will want to tear it down. She wrote me once that no matter where we "choose" to live, she will manage to come see us. But she will never bring her friends. Maggie and I thought about this and Maggie asked me, "Mama, when did Dee ever *have* any friends?"

temptation an urge to do something

deliberately knowing exactly what one is doing

She has a few. **Furtive** boys in pink shirts hanging about on washday after school. Nervous girls who never laughed. Impressed with her they worshiped the well-turned phrase, the cute shape, the **scalding** humor that **erupted** like bubbles in **lye**. She read to them.

When she was courting Jimmy T she didn't have much time to pay to us, but turned all her faultfinding power on him. He *flew* to marry a cheap city girl from a family of ignorant flashy people. She hardly had time to **recompose** herself.

When she comes I will meet—but there they are!

Maggie attempts to make a dash for the house, in her shuffling way, but I stay her with my hand. "Come back here," I say. And she stops and tries to dig a well in the sand with her toe.

It is hard to see them clearly through the strong sun. But even the first glimpse of leg out of the car tells me it is Dee. Her feet were always neat-looking, as if God himself had shaped them with a certain style. From the other side of the car comes a short, stocky man. Hair is all over his head a foot long and hanging from his chin like a **kinky** mule tail. I hear Maggie suck in her breath. "Uhnnnh," is what it sounds like. Like when you see the wriggling end of a snake just in front of your foot on the road. "Uhnnnh."

Dee next. A dress down to the ground, in this hot weather. A dress so loud it hurts my eyes. There are yellows and oranges enough to throw back the light of the sun. I feel my whole face warming from the heat waves it throws out. Earrings gold, too, and hanging down to her shoulders. Bracelets dangling and making noises when she moves her arm up to shake the folds of the dress out of her armpits. The dress is loose and flows, and as she walks closer, I like it. I hear Maggie go "Uhnnnh" again. It is her sister's hair. It

At this point, think about what you have learned about Dee's character. Compare her mother's memories and thoughts with the way Dee behaves when she appears. How is Dee the same kind of person she always was? How has she changed?

Dee seems to be wearing an African-inspired dress, jewelry, and hairdo.

furtive secret; sly

scalding burning

erupted rose up

lye a strong solution used in making soap

recompose restore calmness

kinky tightly curled

stands straight up like the wool on a sheep. It is black as night and around the edges are two long pigtails that rope about like small lizards disappearing behind her ears.

"Wa-su-zo-Tean-o!" she says, coming on in that gliding way the dress makes her move. The short stocky fellow with the hair to his navel is all grinning and he follows up with "Asalamalakim, my mother and my sister!" He moves to hug Maggie but she falls back, tight up against the back of my chair. I feel her trembling there and when I look up I see the perspiration falling off her chin.

"Don't get up," says Dee. Since I am stout it takes something of a push. You can see me trying to move a second or two before I make it. She turns, showing white heels through her sandals, and goes back to the car. Out she peeks next with a Polaroid. She stoops down quickly and lines up picture after picture of me sitting there in front of the house with Maggie **cowering** behind me. She never takes a shot without making sure the house is included. When a cow comes nibbling around the edge of the yard she snaps it and me and Maggie *and* the house. Then she puts the Polaroid in the back seat of the car, and comes up and kisses me on the forehead.

Meanwhile Asalamalakim is going through motions with Maggie's hand. Maggie's hand is as limp as a fish, and probably as cold, despite the sweat, and she keeps trying to pull it back. It looks like Asalamalakim wants to shake hands but wants to do it fancy. Or maybe he don't know how people shake hands. Anyhow, he soon gives up on Maggie.

"Well," I say, "Dee."

"No, Mama," she says. "Not 'Dee,' Wangero Leewanika Kemanjo!"

"What happened to 'Dee'?" I wanted to know.

"She's dead," Wangero said. "I couldn't bear it any longer, being named after the people who **oppress** me."

"You know as well as me you was named after your aunt Dicie," I said. Dicie is my sister. She named Dee. We called her "Big Dee" after Dee was born.

Wa-su-zo-Tean-o is the greeting used by Black Muslims, the popular name for members of an African American nationalist religious movement in the United States. *Asalamalakim* is a Muslim greeting that means "Peace be with you."

Dee has taken an African name, as did most followers of the Black Muslims.

cowering hiding, as if in fear	**oppress** to wrong someone; to abuse one's power over someone

"But who was *she* named after?" asked Wangero.

"I guess after Grandma Dee," I said.

"And who was she named after?" asked Wangero.

"Her mother," I said, and saw Wangero was getting tired. "That's about as far back as I can trace it," I said. Though, in fact, I probably could have carried it back beyond the Civil War through the branches.

"Well," said Asalamalakim, "there you are."

"Uhnnnh," I heard Maggie say.

"There I was not," I said, "before 'Dicie' cropped up in our family, so why should I try to trace it that far back?"

He just stood there grinning, looking down on me like somebody inspecting a Model A car. Every once in a while he and Wangero sent eye signals over my head.

"How do you pronounce this name?" I asked.

"You don't have to call me by it if you don't want to," said Wangero.

"Why shouldn't I?" I asked. "If that's what you want us to call you, we'll call you."

"I know it might sound awkward at first," said Wangero.

"I'll get used to it," I said. "Ream it out again."

Well, soon we got the name out of the way. Asalamalakim had a name twice as long and three times as hard. After I tripped over it two or three times he told me to just call him Hakim-a-barber. I wanted to ask him was he a barber, but I didn't really think he was, so I didn't ask.

"You must belong to those beef-cattle peoples down the road," I said. They said "Asalamalakim" when they met you, too, but they didn't shake hands. Always too busy: feeding the cattle, fixing the fences, putting up salt-lick shelters, throwing down hay. When the white folks poisoned some of the herd the men stayed up all night with rifles in their hands. I walked a mile and a half just to see the sight.

Hakim-a-barber said, "I accept some of their **doctrines**, but farming and raising cattle is not my style." (They didn't

The Ford Model A replaced the Model T in the late 1920s. "Asalamalakim" is looking at the mother as a kind of human antique, pleasant but very old-fashioned. The Model A, however, was known for being a finely made and long-lasting car.

Salt-lick shelters were built to keep rain from dissolving the large blocks of salt on poles for cattle.

doctrines beliefs or teachings

tell me, and I didn't ask, whether Wangero (Dee) had really gone and married him.)

We sat down to eat and right away he said he didn't eat collards and pork was unclean. Wangero, though, went on through the chitlins and corn bread, the greens and everything else. She talked a blue streak over the sweet potatoes. Everything delighted her. Even the fact that we still used the benches her daddy made for the table when we couldn't afford to buy chairs.

"Oh, Mama!" she cried. Then turned to Hakim-a-barber. "I never knew how lovely these benches are. You can feel the rump prints," she said, running her hands underneath her and along the bench. Then she gave a sigh and her hand closed over Grandma Dee's butter dish. "That's it!" she said. "I knew there was something I wanted to ask you if I could have." She jumped up from the table and went over in the corner where the churn stood, the milk in it clabber by now. She looked at the churn and looked at it.

"This churn top is what I need," she said. "Didn't Uncle Buddy whittle it out of a tree you all used to have?"

"Yes," I said.

"Uh huh," she said happily. "And I want the dasher, too."

"Uncle Buddy whittle that, too?" asked the barber.

Dee (Wangero) looked up at me.

"Aunt Dee's first husband whittled the dash," said Maggie so low you almost couldn't hear her. "His name was Henry, but they called him Stash."

"Maggie's brain is like an elephant's," Wangero said, laughing. "I can use the churn top as a centerpiece for the **alcove** table," she said, sliding a plate over the churn, "and I'll think of something artistic to do with the dasher."

When she finished wrapping the dasher the handle stuck out. I took it for a moment in my hands. You didn't even have to look close to see where hands pushing the dasher up and down to make butter had left a kind of sink in the wood.

Collards and *chitlins* are foods enjoyed by many people in the American South. Collards are greens; chitlins, or chitterlings, are the intestines of hogs. Muslims don't eat pork.

Clabber is curdled, or sour, milk.

The *dasher* on a churn has blades that swirl the milk around.

Notice that these are the first words Maggie has spoken to the visitors.

alcove a small, set-in section of a room

Compare the attitudes of the mother, Maggie, and Dee toward the dasher. In what sense can the dasher be considered a symbol in this story—an object standing for something beyond itself?

In fact, there were a lot of small sinks; you could see where thumbs and fingers had sunk into the wood. It was beautiful light yellow wood, from a tree that grew in the yard where Big Dee and Stash had lived.

After dinner Dee (Wangero) went to the trunk at the foot of my bed and started rifling through it. Maggie hung back in the kitchen over the dishpan. Out came Wangero with two quilts. They had been pieced by Grandma Dee and then Big Dee and me had hung them on the quilt frames on the front porch and quilted them. One was in the Lone Star pattern. The other was Walk Around the Mountain. In both of them were scraps of dresses Grandma Dee had worn fifty and more years ago. Bits and pieces of Grandpa Jarrell's Paisley shirts. And one teeny faded blue piece, about the size of a penny matchbox, that was from Great Grandpa Ezra's uniform that he wore in the Civil War.

"Mama," Wangero said sweet as a bird. "Can I have these old quilts?"

I heard something fall in the kitchen, and a minute later the kitchen door slammed.

"Why don't you take one or two of the others?" I asked. "These old things was just done by me and Big Dee from some tops your grandma pieced before she died."

"No," said Wangero. "I don't want those. They are stitched around the borders by machine."

"That'll make them last better," I said.

"That's not the point," said Wangero. "These are all pieces of dresses Grandma used to wear. She did all this stitching by hand. Imagine!" She held the quilts securely in her arms, stroking them.

"Some of the pieces, like those lavender ones, come from old clothes her mother handed down to her," I said, moving up to touch the quilts. Dee (Wangero) moved back just enough so that I couldn't reach quilts. They already belonged to her.

"Imagine!" she breathed again, clutching them closely to her bosom.

"The truth is," I said, "I promised to give them quilts to Maggie, for when she marries John Thomas."

She gasped like a bee had stung her.

"Maggie can't appreciate these quilts!" she said. "She'd probably be backward enough to put them to everyday use."

"I reckon she would," I said. "God knows I been saving 'em for long enough with nobody using 'em. I hope she will!" I didn't want to bring up how I had offered Dee (Wangero) a quilt when she went away to college. Then she had told me they were old-fashioned, out of style.

"But they're *priceless!*" she was saying now, furiously; for she has a temper. "Maggie would put them on the bed and in five years they'd be in rags. Less than that!"

"She can always make some more," I said. "Maggie knows how to quilt."

Dee (Wangero) looked at me with hatred. "You just will not understand. The point is these quilts, *these* quilts!"

The mother hears Maggie's reaction to Dee's request for the quilts. Why do you think Maggie is upset?

The name of this short story is "Everyday Use." How are these words important to the story? What use are these quilts to Maggie and her mother? What use are they to Dee? Why do you think Dee now wants the quilts she rejected once as old-fashioned?

Notice that the
quilts, also, are
symbols in this
story. How are
they similar to the
dasher in their
meaning?

"Well," I said, stumped. "What would *you* do with them?"

"Hang them," she said. As if that was the only thing you
could do with quilts.

Maggie by now was standing in the door. I could almost
hear the sound her feet made as they scraped over each other.

"She can have them, Mama," she said, like somebody used
to never winning anything, or having anything reserved for
her. "I can 'member Grandma Dee without the quilts."

I looked at her hard. She had filled her bottom lip with
checkerberry snuff and it gave her face a kind of dopey,
hangdog look. It was Grandma Dee and Big Dee who taught
her how to quilt herself. She stood there with her scarred

hands hidden in the folds of her skirt. She looked at her sister with something like fear but she wasn't mad at her. This was Maggie's portion. This was the way she knew God to work.

When I looked at her like that something hit me in the top of my head and ran down to the soles of my feet. Just like when I'm in church and the spirit of God touches me and I get happy and shout. I did something I never had done before: hugged Maggie to me, then dragged her on into the room, snatched the quilts out of Miss Wangero's hands and dumped them into Maggie's lap. Maggie just sat there on my bed with her mouth open.

"Take one or two of the others," I said to Dee.

But she turned without a word and went out to Hakim-a-barber.

"You just don't understand," she said, as Maggie and I came out to the car.

"What don't I understand?" I wanted to know.

"Your **heritage**," she said. And then she turned to Maggie, kissed her, and said, "You ought to try to make something of yourself, too, Maggie. It's really a new day for us. But from the way you and Mama still live you'd never know it."

She put on some sunglasses that hid everything above the tip of her nose and her chin.

Maggie smiled; maybe at the sunglasses. But a real smile, not scared. After we watched the car dust settle I asked Maggie to bring me a dip of snuff. And then the two of us sat there just enjoying, until it was time to go in the house and go to bed.

What has happened here? What has "hit" the mother to make her do what she does at this point?

There are differences in the ways Maggie, her mother, and Dee view their heritage as African American women. What are those differences? How is the importance of heritage a theme in this story?

What changes do you notice here in Maggie and in the relationship between Maggie and her mother?

heritage what is handed down from one generation to the next

Directions Choose the letter of the best answer or write the answer using complete sentences.

Comprehension: Identifying Facts

1. What have Maggie and her mother done to prepare for Dee's visit?
  A found a new job
  B cleaned the yard
  C made a new quilt
  D gone on a television show

2. What does Mama dream about?
  A She and Dee are on TV.
  B She has pretty clothes.
  C Maggie doesn't have any scars.
  D Dee has a new boyfriend.

3. How does Mama say Maggie walks?

4. What does Mama say about Maggie's future plans?

5. What does Mama notice first when Dee gets out of the car?

6. Whom does Dee bring with her?

7. Why does Dee say she has changed her name?

8. Why does Dee want the churn top and the dasher?

9. Why does Dee think that Maggie should not have the quilts?

10. What does Dee say her mother doesn't understand?

Comprehension: Putting Ideas Together

11. Why does Maggie have "burn scars down her arms and legs"?
  A She has a bad sunburn.
  B She was a clumsy cook.
  C Her home burned down.
  D Mama used to mistreat her.

12. How would you describe Maggie and Dee's experience of the fire?
  A Maggie was injured.
  B Maggie was frightened.
  C Dee was glad to see the house burn.
  D all of the above

13. What do you think Dee was like when she was 16?

14. How does the new house compare with the old house?

15. How does the way Mama and Dee think about their family home differ?

16. Why does Dee want to be called by her African name?

17. Why are the quilts important to Dee?

18. Why are the quilts important to Mama and Maggie?

19. Why didn't Mama give Dee the quilts she wanted?

20. Why does Dee say her mother doesn't understand her heritage?

Understanding Literature: Symbol

A symbol is something that has meaning in itself, and also stands for something else. For example, the American flag is both a special piece of cloth and a symbol of what the United States stands for.

In literature, symbols are real parts of the story. They also stand for or suggest something more. In "Everyday Use," certain objects are parts of Maggie and her mother's everyday life. They see them in one way. Dee sees them in another. These objects are symbols. They help the reader understand the different ways the three women think about their lives.

21. In your own words, what is a symbol?

22. What are the churn top, dasher, and quilts symbols of to Dee? What are they symbols of to Maggie and her mother?

23. In what way is Dee's new name also a symbol in the story?

24. In what ways are Maggie's burn scars used as symbols in the story?

25. Why are the quilts especially good symbols for the theme of this story?

Critical Thinking

26. Why do you think Alice Walker dedicates the story "for your grandmama"?

27. In what ways does the last paragraph of the story suggest a change in Maggie? What do you think has caused this change?

28. Dee says that her mother doesn't understand her heritage. Do you agree with Dee? Why or why not?

29. How would you describe the character of the mother in this story? How does her point of view add to the reader's understanding of the story's theme?

Thinking Creatively

30. In an interview, Alice Walker said that her African background was important to her but that her family—her parents and grandparents—was more important. How is this idea part of the story?

After Reading **continued on next page**

Everyday Use   *by Alice Walker*

 Grammar Check

In addition to describing nouns, adjectives can also tell us how two nouns relate to each other. For example, in this sentence, Alice Walker is comparing the two sisters. "Dee is *lighter* than Maggie, with *nicer* hair and a *fuller* figure." Lighter, nicer, and fuller are comparative adjectives. They tell us how two nouns (sisters) compare with each other. Use a Venn Diagram, described in Appendix A, to tell about the two sisters. Use comparative adjectives you find in the story or that you think of on your own.

 Writing on Your Own

What object in your life could be a symbol of what you are and the way you think about things? Write a paragraph describing the object and what it says about you. Try to use vivid adjectives to create a piece that encourages readers to use all their senses as they read.

 Speaking

Who do you think was the strongest character in this short story? Plan a speech to present to your class. Use the Character Analysis Guide, described in Appendix A, to name the strongest character. List four traits of this character and the supporting events from the story. Use this information in your speech.

 Listening

Sometimes speakers try to persuade people by saying that everyone thinks a certain way, or everyone is doing a certain thing. Which character in "Everyday Use" tries to do this? What does this character say that shows you, as a listener, that he or she is using this technique? How do the other characters react to what he or she says? Would you as a listener react the same way?

 Media and Technology

What did Mama's quilts look like? Use a drawing program on your computer to create one of the family's quilts. You can look for patterns to inspire you by using the Internet or resources in your school's library.

BEFORE READING THE SELECTION

American History   by Judith Ortiz-Cofer

About the Author

Judith Ortiz-Cofer was born in Puerto Rico but moved to Paterson, New Jersey, when she was a child. She spoke Spanish and ate Puerto Rican food bought at local shops. The customs and cultures of both Puerto Rico and the United States became a part of her life. In her writing, she bridges both worlds.

Ortiz-Cofer has written many essays, poems, and short stories. In 1989, the New York City Library System listed her first novel, *The Line of the Sun,* as one of "25 Books to Remember." Her recent books include *Call Me Maria*, a young adult novel; *The Meaning of Consuelo*, a novel; and *Woman in Front of the Sun: On Becoming a Writer*, a collection of essays.

This writer now lives in Georgia and is the Franklin Professor of English and Creative Writing at the University of Georgia. She also travels around the country to share her experiences as a Latina poet, essayist, and novelist.

About the Selection

"American History" is fiction—the author created the story. But it is a story about an important day in the life of all Americans. Elena is a Puerto Rican girl living in a run-down part of Paterson, New Jersey. Paterson is a city in northern New Jersey that has many factories. At the time the story takes place, there were many families from other lands living in Paterson. They came to work in the factories in the area.

People often wonder if Judith Ortiz-Cofer is Elena in this story. Even though this author once lived in Paterson, she says she isn't the person in this story. She drew on her memories of life at that time and place to create this short story. Her realistic details help make the events of this fictional story come alive.

Judith Ortiz-Cofer
1952–

Objectives

- To appreciate an image in a short story
- To describe the characteristics of fiction
- To define and give examples of the ways authors use epiphanies and flashbacks
- To understand the author's purpose in a story

Before Reading **continued on next page**

American History by Judith Ortiz-Cofer

flashback a look into the past at some point in a story

epiphany the moment in a story when a character recognizes an important truth

image a picture in the reader's mind created by words

author's purpose the reason(s) for which the author writes

Literary Terms "American History" is told from Elena's point of view. In it, this narrator provides a **flashback** to some events that happened earlier. The beauty of this flashback contrasts sharply with the other events in the story. In the end, Elena comes to realize a hard truth about her life. In literature, this sudden, important realization is called an **epiphany.** The story ends with a striking **image** of snow falling that helps readers see Elena's epiphany more fully.

Reading on Your Own What do you think the **author's purpose** might be for choosing the title "American History" for this story? For example, do you think Ortiz-Cofer chose this title because she wanted to give people more information about American history? What else might she have wanted to accomplish? Remember your prediction as you read. You can always change it as you get further into the story.

Writing on Your Own   Have you ever come to an important realization in your life (an epiphany)—either about yourself or someone you know very well? Write a short poem or song describing this moment. The poem does not have to rhyme unless you want it to do so.

Vocabulary Focus This selection has many Spanish words and phrases. As you read, write the Spanish term and its meaning on a sheet of paper. Your list would include *salsas*—popular music, and *señorita*—young woman. What other Spanish terms can you find in this selection? What do they mean?

Think Before You Read What unforgettable historical events have you personally experienced? Were they important to the people around you or only to you?

AMERICAN HISTORY

I once read in a "Ripley's Believe It or Not" column that Paterson, New Jersey, is the place where the Straight and Narrow (streets) **intersect**. The Puerto Rican **tenement** known as *El Building* was one block up from Straight. It was, in fact, the corner of Straight and Market; not "at" the corner, but *the* corner. At almost any hour of the day, El Building was like a monstrous jukebox, blasting out *salsas* from open windows as the residents, mostly new immigrants just up from the island, tried to drown out whatever they were currently enduring with loud music. But the day President Kennedy was shot there was a **profound** silence in El Building; even the abusive tongues of **viragoes**, the cursing of the unemployed, and the screeching of small children had been somehow **muted**. President Kennedy was a saint to these people. In fact, soon his photograph would be hung alongside the Sacred Heart and over the spiritist altars that many women kept in their apartments. He would become part of the **hierarchy** of **martyrs** they prayed to for favors that only one who had died for a cause would understand.

As you read, notice what the narrator reveals about herself and her life as a young girl.

Salsa is a popular form of Latin American music.

John F. Kennedy, who became president of the United States in 1961, was shot and killed in Dallas on November 22, 1963.

intersect meet

tenement a city apartment for poorer families that is usually unclean, unsafe, uncomfortable

profound deep

viragoes loud, harsh-sounding women

muted quieted; softened

hierarchy a list in order of importance

martyrs people who die for a cause or religious belief

On the day that President Kennedy was shot, my ninth grade class had been out in the fenced playground of Public School Number 13. We had been given "free" exercise time and had been ordered by our P.E. teacher, Mr. DePalma, to "keep moving." That meant that the girls should jump rope and the boys toss basketballs through a hoop at the far end of the yard. He in the meantime would "keep an eye" on us from just inside the building.

It was a cold gray day in Paterson. The kind that warns of early snow. I was miserable, since I had forgotten my gloves, and my knuckles were turning red and raw from the jump rope. I was also taking a lot of abuse from the black girls for not turning the rope hard and fast enough for them.

"Hey, Skinny Bones, pump it, girl. Ain't you got no energy today?" Gail, the biggest of the black girls had the other end of the rope, yelled, "Didn't you eat your rice and beans and pork chops for breakfast today?"

The other girls are making fun of Elena for what they think Puerto Ricans eat for breakfast.

The other girls picked up the "pork chop" and made it into a **refrain**: "pork chop, pork chop, did you eat your pork chop?" They entered the double ropes in pairs and exited without tripping or missing a beat. I felt a burning on my cheeks and then my glasses fogged up so that I could not manage to **coordinate** the jump rope with Gail. The chill was doing to me what it always did; entering my bones, making me cry, **humiliating** me. I hated the city, especially in winter. I hated Public School Number 13. I hated my skinny flatchested body, and I envied the black girls who could jump rope so fast that their legs became a blur. They always seemed to be warm while I froze.

Here, the first-person narrator provides a flashback to an earlier time.

There was only one source of beauty and light for me that school year. The only thing I had **anticipated** at the start of the semester. That was seeing Eugene. In August, Eugene and his family had moved into the only house on the block that had a yard and trees. I could see his place from my window

---

refrain repeated words

coordinate to move or act smoothly with someone else

humiliating embarrassing deeply

anticipated looked forward to

in El Building. In fact, if I sat on the fire escape I was **literally** suspended above Eugene's backyard. It was my favorite spot to read my library books in the summer. Until that August the house had been occupied by an old Jewish couple. Over the years I had become part of their family, without their knowing it, of course. I had a view of their kitchen and their backyard, and though I could not hear what they said, I knew when they were arguing, when one of them was sick, and many other things. I knew all this by watching them at mealtimes. I could see their kitchen table, the sink, and the stove. During good times, he sat at the table and read his newspapers while she fixed the meals. If they argued, he would leave and the old woman would sit and stare at nothing for a long time. When one of them was sick, the other would come and get things from the kitchen and carry them out on a tray. The old man had died in June. The last week of school I had not seen him at the table at all. Then one day I saw that there was a crowd in the kitchen. The old woman had finally emerged from the house on the arm of a stocky, middle-aged woman, whom I had seen there a few times before, maybe her daughter. Then a man had carried out suitcases. The house had stood empty for weeks. I had had to resist the **temptation** to climb down into the yard and water the flowers the old lady had taken such good care of.

By the time Eugene's family moved in, the yard was a tangled mass of weeds. The father spent several days mowing, and when he finished, from where I sat, I didn't see the red, yellow, and purple clusters that meant flowers to me. I didn't see his family sit down at the kitchen table together. It was just the mother, a red-headed tall woman who wore a white uniform—a nurse's, I guessed it was; the father was gone before I got up in the morning and was never there at dinner time. I only saw him on weekends when they sometimes sat on lawn-chairs under the oak tree, each hidden behind a section of the newspaper; and there was Eugene. He was tall and blond, and he wore glasses. I liked him right away

literally actually; really	**temptation** an urge to do something

White Tenements,
Robert Spencer

Here Elena refers to her school as P.S. 13—Public School 13. Some large school districts in the East number their schools instead of giving them names.

because he sat at the kitchen table and read books for hours. That summer, before we had even spoken one word to each other, I kept him company on my fire escape.

Once school started I looked for him in all my classes, but P.S. 13 was a huge, **over-populated** place and it took me days and many **discreet** questions to discover that Eugene was in honors classes for all his subjects; classes that were not open to me because English was not my first language, though I was a straight A student. After much **maneuvering** I managed "to run into him" in the hallway where his locker was—on the other side of the building from mine—and in study hall at the library where he first seemed to notice me, but did not speak; and finally, on the way home after school one day when I decided to approach him directly, though my stomach was doing somersaults.

over-populated very crowded	**discreet** careful, showing good judgment	**maneuvering** planning a movement to gain you something

I was ready for **rejection**, snobbery, the worst. But when I came up to him, practically panting in my nervousness, and blurted out: "You're Eugene. Right?" he smiled, pushed his glasses up on his nose, and nodded. I saw then that he was blushing deeply. Eugene liked me, but he was shy. I did most of the talking that day. He nodded and smiled a lot. In the weeks that followed, we walked home together. He would **linger** at the corner of El Building for a few minutes then walk down to his two-story house. It was not until Eugene moved into that house that I noticed that El Building blocked most of the sun, and that the only spot that got a little sunlight during the day was the tiny square of earth the old woman had planted with flowers.

I did not tell Eugene that I could see inside his kitchen from my bedroom. I felt dishonest, but I liked my secret sharing of his evenings, especially now that I knew what he was reading since we chose our books together at the school library.

One day my mother came into my room as I was sitting on the window staring out. In her **abrupt** way she said: "Elena, you are acting 'moony'." *Enamorada* was what she really said, that is—like a girl stupidly **infatuated**. Since I had turned fourteen and started menstruating my mother had been more **vigilant** than ever. She acted as if I was going to go crazy or explode or something if she didn't watch me and nag me all the time about being a *señorita* now. She kept talking about **virtue**, **morality**, and other subjects that did not interest me in the least. My mother was unhappy in Paterson, but my father had a good job at the bluejeans factory in Passaic and soon, he kept assuring us, we would be moving to our own house there. Every Sunday we drove out to the suburbs of Paterson, Clifton, and Passaic, out to where people mowed grass on Sundays in the summer, and where children made snowmen in the winter from pure white snow, not like the

Snobbery means to ignore people you consider to be of low quality.

Being a *señorita* means being a young woman, rather than a child.

rejection refusal to accept or hear	**abrupt** said or done suddenly, without much explanation	**vigilant** watchful
linger stay		**virtue** goodness
	infatuated foolishly in love	**morality** a system of good behavior

gray slush of Paterson which seemed to fall from the sky in that hue. I had learned to listen to my parents' dreams, which were spoken in Spanish, as fairy tales, like the stories about life in the island paradise of Puerto Rico before I was born. I had been to the island once as a little girl, to grandmother's funeral, and all I remembered was wailing women in black, my mother becoming **hysterical** and being given a pill that made her sleep two days, and me feeling lost in a crowd of strangers all claiming to be my aunts, uncles, and cousins. I had actually been glad to return to the city. We had not been back there since then, though my parents talked constantly about buying a house on the beach someday, retiring on the island—that was a common topic among the residents of El Building. As for me, I was going to go to college and become a teacher.

But after meeting Eugene I began to think of the present more than of the future. What I wanted now was to enter that house I had watched for so many years. I wanted to see the other rooms where the old people had lived, and where the boy spent his time. Most of all, I wanted to sit at the kitchen table with Eugene like two adults, like the old man and his wife had done, maybe drink some coffee and talk about books. I had started reading *Gone With the Wind*. I was **enthralled** by it, with the daring and the **passion** of the beautiful girl living in a mansion, and with her devoted parents and the slaves who did everything for them. I didn't believe such a world had ever really existed, and I wanted to ask Eugene some questions since he and his parents, he had told me, had come up from Georgia, the same place where the novel was set. His father worked for a company that had transferred him to Paterson. His mother was very unhappy, Eugene said, in his beautiful voice that rose and fell over words in a strange, **lilting** way. The kids at school called him "the hick" and made fun of the way he talked. I knew I was his only friend so far, and I liked that, though I felt sad for

Gone With the Wind, by Margaret Mitchell, is a novel about life in the American South before, during, and after the Civil War.

hysterical not able to stop crying

enthralled charmed

passion strong feeling

lilting musical

him sometimes. "Skinny Bones" and the "Hick" was what they called us at school when we were seen together.

The day Mr. DePalma came out into the cold and asked us to line up in front of him was the day that President Kennedy was shot. Mr. DePalma, a short, **muscular** man with slicked-down black hair, was the science teacher, P.E. coach, and **disciplinarian** at P.S. 13. He was the teacher to whose homeroom you got assigned if you were a troublemaker, and the man called out to break up playground fights, and to escort **violently** angry teen-agers to the office. And Mr. DePalma was the man who called your parents in for "a conference."

That day, he stood in front of two rows of mostly black and Puerto Rican kids, **brittle** from their efforts to "keep moving" on a November day that was turning bitter cold. Mr. DePalma, to our complete shock, was crying. Not just silent adult tears, but really sobbing. There were a few titters from the back of the line where I stood shivering.

"Listen," Mr. DePalma raised his arms over his head as if he were about to conduct an orchestra. His voice broke, and he covered his face with his hands. His barrel chest was **heaving**. Someone giggled behind me. "Listen," he repeated, "something awful has happened." A strange gurgling came from his throat, and he turned and spat on the cement behind him.

muscular strongly built	**violently** done with strong, rough force	**heaving** moving up and down
disciplinarian one who punishes	**brittle** stiff	

"Gross," someone said, and there was a lot of laughter.

"The President is dead, you idiots. I should have known that wouldn't mean anything to a bunch of losers like you kids. Go home." He was shrieking now. No one moved for a minute or two, but then a big girl let out a "Yeah!" and ran to get her books piled up with the others against the brick wall of the school building. The others followed in a mad scramble to get to their things before somebody caught on. It was still an hour to the dismissal bell.

A little scared, I headed for El Building. There was an eerie feeling on the streets. I looked into Mario's drugstore, a favorite hangout for the high school crowd, but there were only a couple of old Jewish men at the soda-bar talking with the short order cook in tones that sounded almost angry, but they were keeping their voices low. Even the traffic on one of the busiest intersections in Paterson—Straight Street and Park Avenue—seemed to be moving slower. There were no horns blasting that day. At El Building, the usual little group of unemployed men were not hanging out on the front stoop making it difficult for women to enter the front door. No music spilled out from open doors in the hallway. When I walked into our apartment, I found my mother sitting in front of the grainy picture of the television set.

She looked up at me with a tear-streaked face and just said: "Dios mio," turning back to the set as if it were pulling at her eyes. I went into my room.

Dios mio means "My God."

Though I wanted to feel the right thing about President Kennedy's death, I could not fight the feeling of **elation** that stirred in my chest. Today was the day I was to visit Eugene in his house. He had asked me to come over after school to study for an American History test with him. We had also planned to walk to the public library together. I looked down into his yard. The oak tree was bare of leaves and the ground looked gray with ice. The light through the large kitchen window of his house told me that El Building blocked the sun to such an extent that they had to turn lights on in the middle of the day.

---

elation great happiness

I felt ashamed about it. But the white kitchen table with the lamp hanging just above it looked cozy and inviting. I would soon sit there, across from Eugene, and I would tell him about my perch just above his house. Maybe I should.

In the next thirty minutes I changed clothes, put on a little pink lipstick, and got my books together. Then I went in to tell my mother that I was going to a friend's house to study. I did not expect her **reaction**.

"You are going out *today*?" The way she said "today" sounded as if a storm warning had been issued. It was said in **utter** disbelief. Before I could answer, she came toward me and held my elbows as I clutched my books.

"*Hija*, the President has been killed. We must show respect. He was a great man. Come to church with me tonight."

Hija means daughter.

She tried to embrace me, but my books were in the way. My first impulse was to comfort her, she seemed so **distraught**, but I had to meet Eugene in fifteen minutes.

To *embrace* means to hug.

"I have a test to study for, Mama. I will be home by eight."

"You are forgetting who you are, *Niña*. I have seen you staring down at that boy's house. You are heading for **humiliation** and pain." My mother said this in Spanish and in a resigned tone that surprised me, as if she had no **intention** of stopping me from "heading for humiliation and pain." I started for the door. She sat in front of the TV holding a white handkerchief to her face.

Niña means child. Here it is used like "dear."

I walked out to the street and around the chain-link fence that separated El Building from Eugene's house. The yard was neatly edged around the little walk that led to the door. It always amazed me how Paterson, the inner core of the city, had no apparent **logic** to its architecture. Small, neat, single **residences** like this one could be found right next to

---

reaction a response

utter total; complete

distraught terribly upset

humiliation shame

intention a plan

logic reasoning

residences places to live in

huge, **dilapidated** apartment buildings like El Building. My guess was that the little houses had been there first, then the immigrants had come in droves, and the **monstrosities** had been raised for them—the Italians, the Irish, the Jews, and now us, the Puerto Ricans and the blacks. The door was painted a deep green: *verde*, the color of hope, I had heard my mother say it: *Verde-Esperanza*.

I knocked softly. A few suspenseful moments later the door opened just a crack. The red, swollen face of a woman appeared. She had a halo of red hair floating over a delicate ivory face—the face of a doll—with freckles on the nose. Her **smudged** eye make-up made her look unreal to me, like a mannequin seen through a **warped** store window.

"What do you want?" Her voice was tiny and sweet-sounding, like a little girl's, but her tone was not friendly.

"I'm Eugene's friend. He asked me over. To study." I thrust out my books, a silly gesture that embarrassed me almost immediately.

"You live there?" She pointed up to El Building, which looked particularly ugly, like a gray prison with its many dirty windows and rusty fire escapes. The woman had stepped halfway out and I could see that she wore a white nurse's uniform with St. Joseph's Hospital on the name tag.

"Yes. I do."

She looked intently at me for a couple of heartbeats, then said as if to herself, "I don't know how you people do it." Then directly to me: "Listen. Honey. Eugene doesn't want to study with you. He is a smart boy. Doesn't need help. You understand me. I am truly sorry if he told you you could come over. He cannot study with you. It's nothing personal. You understand? We won't be in this place much longer, no need for him to get close to people—it'll just make it harder for him later. Run back home now."

---

dilapidated rundown, in poor condition

monstrosities things that are huge and ugly

smudged smeared

warped curved; out of focus

I couldn't move. I just stood there in shock at hearing these things said to me in such a honey-drenched voice. I had never heard an accent like hers, except for Eugene's softer **version**. It was as if she were singing me a little song.

"What's wrong? Didn't you hear what I said?" She seemed very angry, and I finally snapped out of my **trance**. I turned away from the green door, and heard her close it gently.

Our apartment was empty when I got home. My mother was in someone else's kitchen, seeking the **solace** she needed. Father would come in from his late shift at midnight. I would hear them talking softly in the kitchen for hours that night. They would not discuss their dreams for the future, or life in Puerto Rico, as they often did; that night they would talk sadly about the young widow and her two children, as if they were family. For the next few days, we would observe *luto* in our apartment; that is, we would practice **restraint** and silence—no loud music or laughter. Some of the women of El Building would wear black for weeks.

That night, I lay in my bed trying to feel the right thing for our dead President. But the tears that came up from a deep source inside me were strictly for me. When my mother came to the door, I pretended to be sleeping. Sometime during the night, I saw from my bed the streetlight come on. It had a pink halo around it. I went to my window and pressed my face to the cool glass. Looking up at the light I could see the white snow falling like a lace veil over its face. I did not look down to see it turning gray as it touched the ground below.

> The narrator has an epiphany here— she recognizes an important truth. What is the truth she sees?

> *Luto* means mourning or sorrow.

> The narrator ends with a visual image—that is, a word picture that appeals to our sense of sight. What does the image suggest about the narrator's feelings?

version a form or type	**trance** a condition in which one can't seem to move	**solace** comfort
		restraint control

AFTER READING THE SELECTION

American History *by Judith Ortiz-Cofer*

Directions Choose the letter of the best answer or write the answer using complete sentences.

Comprehension: Identifying Facts

1. On what day does this story take place?
   - A the day Eugene moves in
   - B the first day of school
   - C the day the president was shot
   - D an August day in Paterson, New Jersey

2. Where is Elena when she hears that Kennedy was shot?
   - A in El Building
   - B the playground of P.S. 13
   - C at the corner of Straight and Narrow
   - D in the classroom

3. What does Elena hate about her life?

4. How can Elena see Eugene's house?

5. Why does Elena like Eugene?

6. Why are honors classes not open to Elena?

7. Where do Elena's parents want to move when they retire?

8. Why does Elena get out of school early?

9. What has Elena planned on doing after school that day?

10. Who stops Elena from studying with Eugene?

Comprehension: Putting Ideas Together

11. How is El Building different on the day Kennedy is shot?
    - A There are jukeboxes blasting.
    - B There are children screeching.
    - C There is profound silence.
    - D There are women shouting.

12. How do Elena's parents feel about Paterson?
    - A Her mother is unhappy there.
    - B Her father wants a house.
    - C They want to move away.
    - D all of the above

13. Does Elena get along with her classmates? Explain.

14. What did Elena do to meet Eugene?

15. Why doesn't Elena tell Eugene that she can see inside his kitchen?

16. In what ways are Elena and Eugene similar?

17. Why does Elena think of her parents' dreams as "fairy tales"?

18. Why does Elena say that meeting Eugene made her think more about the present than the future?

19. Why does Elena feel happy even though the president has been shot?

20. Describe the way Eugene's mother treats Elena.

Understanding Literature: Epiphany

In fiction, an epiphany is a moment when a character recognizes or realizes an important truth. The epiphany deeply affects the person and sometimes changes him or her forever.

In "American History," the narrator, Elena, has an epiphany that reveals a hard truth about her life. The image at the end of the story—of Elena looking at the snow through the streetlight, rather than watching it fall to the ground— suggests the understanding she has reached from her epiphany on Eugene's doorstep.

21. In your own words, what is an epiphany?

22. What does Elena learn from what Eugene's mother says to her? What makes this moment an epiphany?

23. The narrator says the tears she shed that night "were strictly for me." What does she mean?

24. The day Elena realizes an important truth was also a day of epiphany for the entire country. What truth did America realize that day?

25. Have you ever had a moment that you might call an epiphany? What did you realize about yourself or about life?

Critical Thinking

26. Why do you think this story is called "American History"?

27. Compare Mr. DePalma's reaction to Kennedy's murder with his words to the students. Compare Eugene's mother's reaction with her treatment of Elena. What conclusions can you draw? How are people's feelings about the president different from their feelings about each other?

28. Why do you think Elena's mother does not stop her from going to Eugene's house, even though she knows she is "heading for humiliation and pain"?

29. What details does the narrator give that suggest how Puerto Ricans were treated in Elena's neighborhood?

Thinking Creatively

30. Why do you think Elena chooses to see the snow looking white, "falling like a lace veil," rather than gray as it touches the ground?

After Reading **continued on next page**

American History by Judith Ortiz-Cofer

 ### Grammar Check

Sometimes, writers create sentences by combining clauses. Clauses are word groups that contain both a subject and a verb. However, clauses are linked together in one sentence. Here is an example:

"The father was gone before I got up in the morning." The two clauses are: The father (subject) was gone (verb) before I (subject) got up (verb) in the morning. The first clause is the most important clause. It is called an independent clause. The second clause is the dependent clause. It tells us more information to help us understand the first clause. Look for other sentences in this story that use words like *before, after,* or *although.* These kinds of words subordinate (make less important) the words that follow them.

 ### Writing on Your Own

Think of a moment when you were very happy, but everyone else around you was sad. Write a brief description of the way you were feeling inside and the way you appeared on the outside.

 ### Speaking and Listening

Work in teams to make a group presentation to your class about any of the characters, settings, or plot events—especially Elena's epiphany—in the story. Prepare a chart with your main ideas. Give this chart to listeners after your presentation. Ask them to put a check mark by any of the main ideas they remembered from your presentation. Review these charts. Together, decide what you could have done to make your presentation more memorable to the audience.

 ### Technology and Viewing

Create a Web quest to help other students understand more about the setting of "American History." Locate links to Web sites that have information about culture (songs, movies, clothing, etc.) of the early 1960s, as well as information about current events. Create a list with the URLs you found.

BEFORE READING THE SELECTION

Thank You, M'am   by Langston Hughes

Langston Hughes
1902–1967

About the Author

In the 1920s, a section of New York City called Harlem became the center of a great explosion of African-American art. Today, we call this movement the Harlem Renaissance. Langston Hughes became one of the best-known writers of the Harlem Renaissance.

Langston Hughes was born in Joplin, Missouri. He always knew he loved to write. While Hughes was working in a Washington D.C. hotel, the well-known poet Vachel Lindsay took an interest in his writing. Lindsay helped bring attention to Hughes's work. By age 27, Hughes was making a living with his writing. He once said of his work, "My writing has been largely concerned with the depicting of Negro life in America."

Langston Hughes wrote short stories, plays, essays, and novels, but he is perhaps best known for his poetry.

About the Selection

We know from his other books, plays, and poems that Langston Hughes believed in family. The family was a safe zone in a world often soiled by racism and greed. The family trusted you. They cared for you, even when others didn't.

It was with these ideas in mind that Hughes probably wrote "Thank You, M'am." The story tells about a young boy and an older woman who, together, form a family of sorts by caring for each other.

Hughes wrote this story more than 50 years ago. As you read, you will notice little details about the way life was during that time. But the story's message is as timeless as this old saying: "It takes a village to raise a child."

Objectives

■ To read and appreciate a short story

■ To define and list events in a story's rising action

■ To identify and give examples of conflict, protagonist, and antagonist

Before Reading **continued on next page**

BEFORE READING THE SELECTION *(continued)*

Thank You, M'am by Langston Hughes

conflict the struggle of the main character against himself or herself, another person, or nature

protagonist the main character; also called the hero

antagonist the person or thing in the story struggling against the main character

rising action the events of the plot that add to the conflict

Literary Terms Like most stories, "Thank You, M'am" revolves around **conflict**. Conflict is a struggle between two forces. In fiction, the main character struggles against himself or herself, another person, or nature. In this story, the **protagonist**, or main character, struggles against an **antagonist**, another person who tries to keep the protagonist from reaching his goal. The conflict begins early in the story. Roger (the protagonist) tries and fails to steal Mrs. Jones's (the antagonist) purse. While this problem is solved, the two continue to struggle until a true conclusion to the story happens. The events that lead to that conclusion are part of the **rising action** of the story.

Reading on Your Own As you read this story, use the Sequence Chain chart described in Appendix A to keep track of all the events and important things characters say. After you finish, review these points. Star the place where you think the story reached a climax. In a group, compare your chart with others in your class. Did you miss any details?

Writing on Your Own Think of something you have done that you regretted later. Write 2–3 paragraphs describing how you felt. Think about this feeling as you read the story.

Vocabulary Focus As you read, look at the dialogue: "Here I am trying to get home to cook me a bite to eat, and you snatch my pocketbook! Maybe you ain't been to your supper either, late as it be. Have you?" Can you understand what it means? Does it use the same words you would use when you talk? When you find this sentence in the story, think about how you would say the same thing.

Think Before You Read What can you tell about this story by looking at its title, "Thank You, M'am"?

Thank You, M'am

She was a large woman with a large purse that had
everything in it but a hammer and nails. It had a long strap,
and she carried it slung across her shoulder. It was about
eleven o'clock at night, dark, and she was walking alone,
when a boy ran up behind her and tried to snatch her purse.
The strap broke with the sudden single tug the boy gave it
from behind. But the boy's weight and the weight of the purse
combined caused him to lose his balance. Instead of taking
off full blast as he had hoped, the boy fell on his back on the
sidewalk and his legs flew up. The large woman simply turned
around and kicked him right square in his blue-jeaned sitter.
Then she reached down, picked the boy up by his shirt front,
and shook him until his teeth rattled.

After that the woman said, "Pick up my pocketbook, boy,
and give it here."

She still held him tightly. But she bent down enough to
permit him to stoop and pick up her purse. Then she said,
"Now ain't you ashamed of yourself?"

Firmly gripped by his shirt front, the boy said, "Yes'm."

The woman said, "What did you want to do it for?"

The boy said, "I didn't aim to."

She said, "You a lie!"

By that time two or three people passed, stopped, turned
to look, and some stood watching.

"If I turn you loose, will you run?" asked the woman.

"Yes'm," said the boy.

"Then I won't turn you loose," said the woman. She did
not release him.

"Lady, I'm sorry," whispered the boy.

> As you read, see
> if you can find all
> the elements of a
> short story: plot,
> characters, setting,
> point of view, and
> theme.

> This story has a
> clear protagonist
> and antagonist.
> Which is which?

Notice the rising action in the story.

"Um-hum! Your face is dirty. I got a great mind to wash your face for you. Ain't you got nobody home to tell you to wash your face?"

"No'm," said the boy.

"Then it will get washed this evening," said the large woman, starting up the street, dragging the frightened boy behind her.

He looked as if he were fourteen or fifteen, frail and willow-wild, in tennis shoes and blue jeans.

The woman said, "You ought to be my son. I would teach you right from wrong. Least I can do right now is to wash your face. Are you hungry?"

"No'm," said the being-dragged boy. "I just want you to turn me loose."

"Was I bothering *you* when I turned that corner?" asked the woman.

"No'm."

Notice that much of this very short story is dialogue between the two characters. What is the effect of telling the story through dialogue?

"But you put yourself in contact with *me*," said the woman. "If you think that that contact is not going to last awhile, you got another thought coming. When I get through with you, sir, you are going to remember Mrs. Luella Bates Washington Jones."

Sweat popped out on the boy's face and he began to struggle. Mrs. Jones stopped, jerked him around in front of her, put a half nelson about his neck, and continued to drag him up the street. When she got to her door, she dragged the boy inside, down a hall, and into a large kitchenette-furnished room at the rear of the house. She switched on the light and left the door open. The boy could hear other roomers laughing and talking in the large house. Some of their doors were open, too, so he knew he and the woman were not alone. The woman still had him by the neck in the middle of her room.

A *half nelson* is a wrestling hold.

She said, "What is your name?"

"Roger," answered the boy.

"Then, Roger, you go to that sink and wash your face," said the woman, whereupon she turned him loose—at last. Roger looked at the door—looked at the woman—looked at the door—*and went to the sink.*

"Let the water run until it gets warm," she said. "Here's a clean towel."

"You gonna take me to jail?" asked the boy, bending over the sink.

"Not with that face, I would not take you nowhere," said the woman. "Here I am trying to get home to cook me a bite to eat, and you snatch my pocketbook! Maybe you ain't been to your supper either, late as it be. Have you?"

"There's nobody home at my house," said the boy.

"Then we'll eat," said the woman. "I believe you're hungry—or been hungry—to try to snatch my pocketbook!"

"I want a pair of blue **suede** shoes," said the boy.

"Well, you didn't have to snatch *my* pocketbook to get some suede shoes," said Mrs. Luella Bates Washington Jones. "You could of asked me."

"M'am?"

The water dripping from his face, the boy looked at her. There was a long pause. A very long pause. After he had dried his face, and not knowing what else to do, dried it again, the boy turned around, wondering what next. The door was open. He could make a dash for it down the hall. He could run, run, run, *run!*

The woman was sitting on the daybed. After a while she said, "I were young once and I wanted things I could not get."

There was another long pause. The boy's mouth opened. Then he frowned, not knowing he frowned.

The woman said, "Um-hum! You thought I was going to say *but,* didn't you? You thought I was going to say *but I didn't snatch people's pocketbooks.* Well, I wasn't going to say that." Pause. Silence. "I have done things, too, which I would not tell you, son—neither tell God, if He didn't already know.

suede leather with a
soft, velvety surface

Everybody's got something in common. So you set down while I fix us something to eat. You might run that comb through your hair so you will look presentable."

In another corner of the room behind a screen was a gas plate and an icebox. Mrs. Jones got up and went behind the screen. The woman did not watch the boy to see if he was going to run now, nor did she watch her purse, which she left behind her on the daybed. But the boy took care to sit on the far side of the room, away from the purse, where he thought she could easily see him out of the corner of her eye if she wanted to. He did not trust the woman *not* to trust him. And he did not want to be mistrusted now.

"Do you need somebody to go to the store," asked the boy, "maybe to get some milk or something?"

"Don't believe I do," said the woman, "unless you just want sweet milk yourself. I was going to make cocoa out of this canned milk I got here."

"That will be fine," said the boy.

A *gas plate,* also called a hot plate, is a heated iron plate for cooking in small spaces. An *icebox* is a refrigerator.

She heated some lima beans and ham she had in the icebox, made the cocoa, and set the table. The woman did not ask the boy anything about where he lived, or his folks, or anything else that would embarrass him. Instead, as they ate, she told him about her job in a hotel beauty shop that stayed open late, what the work was like, and how all kinds of women came in and out, blonds, redheads, and Spanish. Then she cut him a half of her ten-cent cake.

"Eat some more, son," she said.

When they were finished eating, she got up and said, "Now here, take this ten dollars and buy yourself some blue suede shoes. And next time, do not make the mistake of latching onto *my* pocketbook *nor nobody else's*—because shoes got by devilish ways will burn your feet. I got to get my rest now. But from here on in, son, I hope you will behave yourself."

She led him down the hall to the front door and opened it. "Good night! Behave yourself, boy!" she said, looking out into the street as he went down the steps.

The boy wanted to say something other than, "Thank you, M'am," to Mrs. Luella Bates Washington Jones, but although his lips moved, he couldn't even say that as he turned at the foot of the barren stoop and looked up at the large woman in the door. Then she shut the door.

The protagonist in this story faces more than one conflict. What does Roger struggle against?

Directions Choose the letter of the best answer or write the answer using complete sentences.

Comprehension: Identifying Facts

1. What happens when Roger tries to grab Mrs. Jones's purse?
   A He falls because the purse is so heavy.
   B He kicks her and makes her fall.
   C No one stops to see what is happening.
   D He puts a half nelson hold on her.

2. What does Roger want to buy with the money from Mrs. Jones's purse?

3. What does Mrs. Jones give Roger after they eat?

Comprehension: Putting Ideas Together

4. What personal things do we find out about Roger from this story?
   A No one is home even though it's late.
   B He has no money.
   C His face is dirty.
   D all of the above

5. What do we find out about Mrs. Jones's life?

6. When Mrs. Jones goes behind the screen to prepare supper, why does Roger sit where Mrs. Jones can easily see him?

Understanding Literature: Rising Action

Short stories usually explore a conflict that the main character faces. For example, in this story, Roger at first wants Mrs. Jones's purse. But, when Mrs. Jones brings him home, their conflict continues. At first, Roger wants to leave. But gradually he realizes that Mrs. Jones trusts him and he likes that feeling. All of the events and dialogue that show the conflict between Mrs. Jones and Roger are part of the story's rising action.

7. Use the Plot Mountain diagram described in Appendix A to chart events that lead up to the climax of the story when Roger realizes fully that Mrs. Jones trusts him.

8. Why do you think rising action got that name?

Critical Thinking

9. What other things might Mrs. Jones have done after she caught Roger trying to steal her purse? Why do you think she decides to take him home?

Thinking Creatively

10. In the beginning of the story, Roger thinks it was all right for him to steal money to buy shoes. How do you think he feels at the end of the story? Why do you think so?

Grammar Check

Exclamatory sentences express strong feelings. They always end with an exclamation point. Langston Hughes used many exclamatory sentences in this story. When he wrote, "You a lie!" he captured the anger Mrs. Jones felt at that point. Look for other exclamatory sentences in this story. What do they tell you about the way the characters felt when they said these words?

 ## Writing on Your Own

What kind of e-mail messages might Roger and Mrs. Jones share after the night they met? Create this conversation, including three messages from each person.

 ## Speaking

Imagine that someone is making a movie based on this story today. If you were going to play the role of Roger, how would you dress? What kind of body language would you use? How would you speak your lines? Explain your choices.

 ## Listening

Listen to an audio recording of this story prepared by your teacher. How is listening to this story different than reading it? Does hearing the story make it easier or harder to understand the story? Explain.

 ## Media

Use pictures from magazines or ones you create yourself to make a book cover. The cover is for an anthology, a book that has many stories from different authors. The book contains this story and others about young people who find their way out of problems with the help of someone else.

 ## Research

Langston Hughes wrote this story more than 50 years ago. What other events were happening during that time, especially those important to African Americans? One of the ways you could find out more about that time is by looking at newspaper articles written during the 1950s and 1960s. Most newspapers have a library of old articles. Plan a trip to a local paper to complete your research.

BEFORE READING THE SELECTION

Unfinished Message   by Toshio Mori

Toshio Mori
1910–1980

- To identify mood and tone in a short story and explain how they are developed
- To understand the purpose for an epilogue

About the Author

Toshio Mori was born in Oakland, California, in 1910. Later, he and his family moved to San Leandro, where he attended public school. After the United States entered World War II against Germany and Japan, President Franklin Roosevelt signed an order. It said that all Japanese Americans living on the West Coast had to move to special camps. Mori and his family were forced to move to the Topaz Relocation Center in Utah. There, Mori became active in the affairs of the camp. He helped start a newspaper and served as camp historian.

Toshio Mori's first book, *Yokohama, California,* was published in 1949. The book was the first collection of short stories written by a Japanese American published in the United States. In all his writing, Mori shows what life was like for Japanese Americans in California during the late 1930s and early 1940s.

About the Selection

"Unfinished Message" is from *The Chauvinist and Other Stories,* originally published in 1979. The details of the story show how Toshio Mori used his experiences in the Topaz Relocation Center as a background for his work.

The story gives us a look inside the lives of the *Issei* and their children, called *Nisei. Issei* is the Japanese name for people who left Japan to become the first generation of their family to live in the United States. Mori often writes about the small details of their lives that represent the larger issues his characters face. In an interview in 1979, he explained his writing this way: "I try to depict human beings, no matter what, living out their days as best they can, facing their human problems."

Literary Terms A story's details contribute to the **mood** it creates. Mood is the feeling created by a story. A story's mood can be happy or sad, edgy or relaxed, scary or funny. "Unfinished Message" creates an edgy, uneasy mood right from the beginning. Readers immediately meet a mother who can't sleep because she keeps seeing her soldier son's face. This first impression sets the **tone** for the rest of the story. Tone is the attitude the author takes toward his or her subject. A writer's tone might be bitter, loving, angry, light-hearted, or matter-of-fact. "Unfinished Message" ends with an **epilogue,** which rounds out the story by telling us what happened to the narrator's brother.

Reading on Your Own As you read, use the Character Analysis Guide, described in Appendix A, to gather facts and impressions about the narrator in this story. List the events that you think give you the most clues about the kind of person this character is. Based on this, complete the character traits you think best describe the narrator.

Writing on Your Own Make a list of reactions you might have if the government ordered your family to leave your home and go to a special camp.

Vocabulary Focus This selection uses many words about World War II. It talks about "the front" which means an area where fighting is going on. It tells about a relocation center, which was a place where Japanese Americans were sent at the beginning of the war. The mother is treated as an "enemy alien" or a person who is from a country at war with the United States. She was treated this way even though her son is serving in the war.

Think Before You Read How does the title of this story make you feel?

mood the feeling created by a piece of writing

tone the attitude an author takes toward a subject

epilogue a section coming after the story's end

Unfinished Message

World War II ended with Japan's surrender on August 14, 1945. In May of that year, the fighting was still going on.

As you read, notice how the author creates the mood of the story. Compare the mood with the tone—the author's attitude toward his subject.

It was on a chilly May night in 1945 in the middle of the Utah desert when my mother sharply called me. "I can't sleep tonight," she said. True, she had been fretting the past few nights, and I knew she was worried over her son at the Italian front.

I reassured her that everything would be all right. Hadn't he, I reasoned with her, come through without a scratch with a full year's service at the front, even with the 442nd Infantry Regiment?

"But I keep seeing Kazuo's face tonight," she said. "Each time I'm about to fall asleep his face keeps coming back."

I tried to calm her fears as best as I could. Nevertheless, she did not sleep that night.

The next night and the night following she slept fitfully more or less. Beneath her outward calm, however, she was under an **ordeal** only a mother could understand. "No news is good news. He's all right," I assured her.

A few days later we received a wire from the War Department that Kazuo had been seriously wounded. The news almost killed her. In the full medical report following we learned that he had a **fractured** skull but was resting peacefully. What struck me as odd was the day my brother was wounded. It was on May 5, the very night my mother was unable to sleep.

When we received word again, it was more cheerful. Kazuo was coming back on the hospital ship destined for home, and we were to decide the hospital nearest our home.

---

ordeal a terrible experience

fractured broken

We were still living in Topaz, Utah Relocation Center at the time, and the nearest available army hospital was the Fitzsimmons in Colorado.

"Let's have him transferred there so we can visit him as soon as he comes home," I said to Mother.

My mother would have none of it. "Do you think this is our real home? Our home is back in San Leandro, California. We'll be moving from here again, and Kazuo too will have to transfer. No, we'll go back and Kazuo can go to a hospital in California."

The mother refuses to think of the prison camp as "home."

My mother couldn't get out of the camp soon enough. She counted the days when the next train to California would take us back home. In the meantime we learned that Kazuo was being transferred to DeWitt Army Hospital in Auburn, California.

On our trip home, our train stopped for a few minutes at Auburn, and our first urge was to get off the train and visit Kazuo. My mother stared toward the Auburn interiors. "It must be only a few miles from here. Here we are, so close to him and yet so far."

We heeded our good judgment and did not get off the train. "We must make ready our home. It must be in a mess. We must first go home and get busy cleaning the place. Our home must resemble our old home for Kazuo."

It took us two weeks to clean the house and settle down. My mother had to apply to the United States Attorney's office for a travel permit because she was an enemy alien and Japan and United States were still at war. Secure with a permit my mother accompanied me to Auburn. All the way on the bus to the hospital she nervously weighed the seriousness of Kazuo's **actual** condition. Are his legs all **intact**, are his hands there? she wondered. Can he see, is he normal mentally? It wasn't until she saw him in person did she feel relieved. He could see, his hands were usable, but his legs? Mother talked constantly on everything she could think of but his condition. Before long, she became aware of his actual condition.

Notice that although Kazuo has been wounded serving in the United States Army, his mother is still considered "an enemy alien." What is the author's tone here?

actual true; real   **intact** whole, together

These are Japanese American soldiers returning to the United States in 1944.

Kazuo's head/brain injury has made his legs useless.

In order to relieve ourselves of the hot valley air caught inside of the ward, my brother suggested sitting on the screened porch. It was when the ward boy saw my brother moving on the bed that he came to help him to his wheelchair. The ward boy bodily lifted him on the chair, and Mother saw my brother's spindly legs. He was unable to walk.

Afterwards, Mother asked me to inquire the doctor about Kazuo's condition. Will he ever walk? The doctor I talked to was not too hopeful, but I did not tell Mother.

"He says there's a fifty-fifty **possibility** that Kazuo will walk," I said to Mother.

Coming home, Mother said, "I'm worried over him. If I only could live long enough to see him fully recovered."

After another operation on his head, my brother was transferred to Letterman Hospital in San Francisco, making possible weekly visits for Mother and I. Each time we saw him, she would take me aside and ask, "Do you think he's much improved? Isn't he better?"

That Christmas my brother got a two week **furlough** and came home for the first time since the war had started. I had to help him with his bath and toilet. My brother was confined to his wheelchair.

Time and again, Mother would ask me, "Will he ever walk again? I can't tell him that I worry over him."

Before my brother was released from the hospital, Mother died in her sleep on August 5, 1946. Although she complained of pains in the neck, we were totally unprepared for her death. Her doctor had previously **diagnosed** her **symptoms** as arthritis, but her death was sudden.

After her death our house became dark and silent. Even when my brother returned home for good in a wheelchair, the

possibility chance

furlough a leave of absence

diagnosed named the disease of someone

symptoms signs of disease

atmosphere was unchanged. We seemed to be companions in the dark. However, it changed one day.

As I sat quietly in the living room I heard a slight tapping on the window just above the divan where my mother had slept her last. When the taps repeated again, I went outside to check, knowing well that a stiff wind could move a branch of our lemon tree with a lemon or two tapping the wall of our house. There was no wind, no lemon near enough to reach the window. I was puzzled but did not confide in my brother when he joined me in the living room.

A *divan* is a couch used for sleeping.

I had all but forgotten the incident when my brother and I were quietly sitting in the living room near the spot where our mother had passed away. For a while I was not conscious of the slight tapping on the window. When the repeated taps were loud enough to be heard clearly, I first looked at the window and then glanced at my brother. He too had heard the taps.

"Did you hear that?" I said.

My brother nodded. "Sure," he said. "Did you hear it too? I heard it the other day but I thought it was strange."

We looked at the window. There were no birds in sight, no lemons tapping. Then the taps repeated. After a few moments of silence I was about to comment when we heard the tapping again. This time I looked silently at my brother and on tiptoes approached the window. The tapping continued so I softly touched the window pane. The instant my fingers touched the glass, it stopped.

My brother and I looked at each other, silently aware that it must have been Mother calling our attention. At that instant I became conscious of the purpose of the mysterious taps. I couldn't help but recall Mother's words, "I can't stop worrying over you, my son."

The tappings stopped once and for all after that. We never heard it again after the message had reached us.

EPILOGUE *This story was written nearly thirty years ago. My brother is alive and well, raising a family in San Leandro, California. He is still **paralyzed** to this day.*

Why do you think the author has included an epilogue?

paralyzed unable to move

Directions Choose the letter of the best answer or write the answer using complete sentences.

Comprehension: Identifying Facts

1. Why can't the mother sleep?
   - **A** She didn't want to leave Topaz.
   - **B** She was worried about her son.
   - **C** She had received a wire.
   - **D** Kazuo was coming home.

2. What does the wire from the War Department say has happened to Kazuo?

3. What do the brothers hear while sitting in the living room?

Comprehension: Putting Ideas Together

4. Why does the narrator not tell his mother how badly Kazuo is hurt?
   - **A** He doesn't know.
   - **B** The doctor asks him not to tell her.
   - **C** He wants to protect her.
   - **D** He thought Kazuo would get better.

5. Why does the mother insist that Kazuo go to a hospital in California?

6. How does the mother's death affect her sons?

Understanding Literature: Mood and Tone

The mood in a short story is the feeling it creates. A writer develops a mood by events in the plot, by descriptions of setting, by the use of images, and by what characters say and do. Mood can also be affected by point of view and word choice.

A story's mood and its tone can be very different. For example, if a different author had written this story, his or her tone may have been angry. The mood of the story might be the same, but the tone, or the author's attitude toward the story, would have been very different.

7. How would you describe the mood of "Unfinished Message"?

8. Mori wrote in a matter-of-fact way. How did this tone affect the mood of the story?

Critical Thinking

9. Why do you think the window tapping stops after the brothers realize that it might be their mother?

Thinking Creatively

10. What is the "Unfinished Message" in this story?

Grammar Check

Compound sentences are sentences that contain more than one subject and more than one verb. This sentence is a compound sentence: "No, we'll go back and Kazuo can go to a hospital in California." The two subjects are *we* and *Kazuo*. The two verbs are *will go* and *can go*. You can look at this sentence as two smaller (simple) sentences combined together. (We'll go back. Kazuo can go to a hospital in California.) Find four examples of compound sentences in the story. Write them down, underlining their subjects and verbs.

 Writing on Your Own

Select a paragraph or two from the story. Rewrite your selection to give more details or to make it more eerie (strange, spooky).

 Speaking and Listening

In small groups, pick one person to play the part of Kazuo. That person should spend some time researching World War II. The others in the group should imagine that they are reporters. They will interview Kazuo about the war, the battles he fought, and how he feels coming back to America.

Those interviewing Kazuo will make a list of questions to ask him. Take turns asking the questions. Conclude the activity by writing a short article about Kazuo and the war. The people who played the part of Kazuo should review the articles. Were the articles true to what they said?

 Media

Use instruments, including your voice or music software, to create a song based on the mood or tone of this story. You may want to listen to music popular during World War II or traditional Japanese music to find ideas.

 Technology

Create a blog where writers can assume the roles of the characters in "Unfinished Message." Post messages about events in the story as well as other events that may have happened to them. Writers should make sure that they write in character, speaking as if these events were happening to them.

SKILLS LESSON

Conflict is at the heart of a story's plot. Conflict results when something stands in the way of what the protagonist wants or needs to do.

We can think about conflict as the two sides of a struggle. There are three basic kinds of conflicts in fiction.

- *Person versus (against) person.* Here, the protagonist is stopped from doing something by another character. For example, in "Thank You, M'am" Roger wants money. Mrs. Jones stops him.

- *Person versus environment.* In this, there is a conflict between people and their environment, or the conditions under which they live. In "American History," Elena struggles against what people think of her because she is Puerto Rican and lives in El Building.

- *Person versus self.* This conflict puts a person against his or her own mind. In "Everyday Use," the mother struggles to understand and respond to both her daughters.

Review

1. What are two examples of conflict within the mind of a character in "Everyday Use"?

2. Give an example of a story in which the conflict is between a character and his or her environment.

3. The very short story "Thank You, M'am" manages to include all three kinds of conflict. What is an example of each?

4. Which kind of conflict do you enjoy most in a short story? Why?

5. Do you think a story has to have some kind of conflict? Why or why not?

Writing on Your Own

Choose one type of conflict. Use the Plot Mountain diagram described in Appendix A. Outline the plot of a short story you would like to tell, based on that conflict. Write an opening paragraph that sets up the conflict. Exchange the paragraph with a partner for review. Rewrite the paragraph based on the review.

Short stories are among the most popular forms of fiction. Like all fiction, short stories have plot, setting, characters, point of view, and theme. Unlike longer forms, however, short stories tend to feature a brief time period and only one main setting. Writers tend to include only the most important descriptive details. Everything in a short story works to set a mood and to develop one or more themes.

Short stories are part of the kind of literature called prose. Prose—all writing that is not poetry—also includes the fables, myths, tall tales, and legends like those you have studied in other units.

This unit has presented five short stories with very different styles, moods, and effects. From the group, you get a sense of the wide range offered by this literary form.

Selections

- "The Celebrated Jumping Frog of Calaveras County," by Mark Twain, describes the funny adventures of a gambling man.

- "Everyday Use," by Alice Walker, is about an African American mother and her two daughters. One of the daughters has come home for a visit.

- "American History," by Judith Ortiz-Cofer, tells of an important day in American history. The day becomes important in another way for a Puerto Rican girl living in New Jersey.

- "Thank You, M'am," by Langston Hughes, is the story of an attempted purse-snatching that does not go at all the way a young man intended.

- "Unfinished Message," by Toshio Mori, concerns a Japanese American mother, her two sons, and a strange event that happens after her death.

Directions Choose the letter of the best answer or write the answer using complete sentences.

Comprehension: Identifying Facts

1. What does Andrew Jackson do after he loses the fight with a dog that has no hind legs?
   A He chewed on a bone.
   B He limped off and died.
   C He wagged his tail.
   D He hid under the table.

2. Describe the dress Dee wears when she comes to visit her mother.

3. How does Elena's mother react to President Kennedy's death?

4. Why didn't Mrs. Jones turn Roger loose at first?

5. Why did the mother in "Unfinished Message" have to apply for a travel permit?

Comprehension: Putting Ideas Together

6. In "Everyday Use," how does Mama show she is proud of her home and her heritage?
   A She keeps her yard clean.
   B She names Dee after her aunt.
   C She makes sure Maggie gets the quilts.
   D all of the above

7. In Mark Twain's story, what does the narrator think of Simon Wheeler?

8. Describe the setting and mood at the beginning of "American History."

9. How does Mrs. Jones show that she cares about Roger?

10. Do you think the events in "Unfinished Message" are just coincidences? Explain.

Understanding Literature: Point of View

Stories are usually told from one of two different points of view:

■ *First person.* The story is narrated by one of the characters in the story. The narrator uses the pronouns *I* and *we*.

■ *Third person.* The story is narrated by someone outside the story. A third-person narrator knows the thoughts and feelings of some of the characters in a story.

11. Which stories in this unit are written from a first-person point of view?

12. Which stories in this unit are written from a third-person point of view?

13. Which stories in this unit have two different points of view?

14. In your opinion, which kind of narrator presents the most powerful story?

15. Which point of view was used to narrate your favorite story in this unit? Why do you think the author chose to tell the story through this point of view?

Critical Thinking

16. Compare the way Mark Twain told his tale of the jumping frog with the way Alice Walker told her story "Everyday Use." How are they the same? How are they different?

17. Which protagonist, or main character, in these short stories do you like the best? Why?

18. In your opinion, what is the main theme, or message, of "Thank You, M'am"?

19. How would "Unfinished Message" be different if it had been told more like a ghost story?

Thinking Creatively

20. Which story would you choose as the basis of a play or a movie? Explain how you made this decision.

Speak and Listen

Mark Twain is one of America's finest storytellers. Create your own version of the story he tells in "The Celebrated Jumping Frog of Calaveras County" and tell it to your class.

Writing on Your Own

Write step-by-step directions that will help other students discover the point of view through which a story is told. Check your work to make sure it is understandable and free of grammar and spelling errors. Give your list to another student. Was the student able to follow your directions to identify the point of view? Together, look over your directions. Where could they be improved?

Beyond Words

Create a series of drawings that might be used to illustrate one of the short stories in this unit.

Test-Taking Tip

Before you begin an exam, skim through the whole test to find out what is expected of you. Try to set aside enough time to complete each section.

Sherlock Holmes and Professor Moriarty
Sidney Paget, 1893

S hort stories of suspense are among the most popular forms of literature. In this kind of fiction, as readers become involved in the story, they are not certain what will happen or what some events in the plot mean. This doubt keeps readers interested. Writers of suspense stories like to take what is expected and turn it into something new—and sometimes something scary. In suspense stories, the line between what is real and what is not can often be blurred.

In this unit, you will read four stories that will surprise you, play with what you expect, and keep your imagination working even after you've reached a story's end.

"There is no terror in a bang, only in the anticipation of it."

—Alfred Hitchcock, quoted in *Halliwell's Filmgoer's Companion*, 1984

Unit 5

About Suspense in the Short Story

Readers everywhere enjoy stories of suspense. They tell each other ghost stories. They line up to see scary movies. Many people enjoy being frightened. They walk through graveyards at night. They visit haunted houses at amusement parks. They suspect that everything will be all right. However, they do not know what will actually happen. People enjoy a little hint of danger and the unexpected.

Suspense in a story keeps readers on edge. As they read, they cannot predict what will happen next. They may think they know, but they can't be sure. Writers of suspense stories play with what readers expect. They do this by controlling how much readers and characters know about what is happening and what it means.

In some stories, readers know much more than the characters do. Alfred Hitchcock, a filmmaker who is considered a master of suspense, describes this technique with a simple example. He tells of four characters sitting around a table. The audience sees from the start that there is a bomb under the table. They expect that the bomb will go off. However, they do not know for sure, nor do they know when. They have to wait and see. Waiting creates suspense.

In other stories, characters know more than the readers know. In this kind of suspense story, authors may hint that something strange is about to happen. Yet readers do not know exactly what it is, or when or how it will happen. Characters may know, but readers have to finish the story before they uncover this secret.

In placing these hints or clues in a short story, authors are using the technique of *foreshadowing*. Foreshadowing may consist of things characters say or do. Authors can also foreshadow events by using a setting that captures the suspenseful nature of the story. For example, in "The Fall of the House of Usher," Edgar Allan Poe foreshadows the events that will occur. He opens his classic short story with these words:

"During the whole of the chill, dark and soundless day in the autumn of the year, when the clouds hung oppressively low in the heavens, I had been passing alone, on horseback through a singularly dreary tract of country, and at length found myself, as the shadow of the evening drew on, within view of the melancholy house of Usher."

Poe: House of Usher; Woodcut by Constant le Breton for a 20th century edition of Edgar Allan Poe's "The Fall of the House of Usher"

From the beginning, then, readers know that they are in a place of great mystery. They know they must expect the unexpected.

Of course, authors sometimes do just the opposite. They bring readers into a setting that seems completely normal. Nothing seems out of the ordinary. Just as readers become comfortable in this place, writers make the unexpected happen.

As a reader, you just never know. That is what makes short stories with suspense so much fun to read.

The short stories in this unit all have an element of suspense. In "The Lady, or the Tiger?" Frank Stockton keeps his readers involved by leaving them hanging on the edge of that question. In "The Lottery," Shirley Jackson creates a world that only *seems* ordinary, where the characters know much more than readers do until the horrifying end of the tale. In W. W. Jacobs's "The Monkey's Paw," readers watch as an elderly couple makes a wish that seems harmless but turns into a disaster. Finally, in Susan Power's "Red Moccasins" readers enter a shadowy world where no one can be sure what is real.

The Lady, or the Tiger? *by Frank Stockton*

Frank Stockton
1834–1902

About the Author

Frank Stockton was born in Philadelphia in 1834. He began his storytelling career when he was just a boy, creating tales for his brothers and sisters. As an adult, he wrote in many different forms, including short stories, novels, fairy tales, humor, and science fiction. *Science fiction* stories are imaginary tales based on real or invented happenings in science.

Stockton did some of his writing for popular children's magazines. He and the famous children's author Mary Mapes Dodge started *St. Nicholas* magazine in 1873. Sometimes, Stockton wrote so many stories for an issue that some of them had to be published under another name, called a *pen name.*

In 1878, his health failing, Stockton retired to a small farm and continued to write. He died in 1902. Today he is remembered for his novels such as *Rudder Grange,* his science fiction works such as *The Great War Syndicate,* and his collections of children's stories.

About the Selection

Frank Stockton wrote "The Lady, or the Tiger?" in 1882 for a reading at a literary club. The members loved the story. He expanded it for *The Century* magazine. It was published in the November 1882 issue. It quickly became one of the world's most famous short stories. People everywhere talked about its strange ending. For example, the famous poet Robert Browning believed the man chose the door with the tiger behind it.

But Stockton never said. Instead, he wrote and published another story called "The Discourager of Hesitancy." It began where this story left off. But, by the end, readers were still confused. To this day, when people say, "the lady, or the tiger?" they are talking about a problem that has no logical solution.

Literary Terms This story begins by using humor and **satire** to describe a "semibarbaric" king's system of justice. Then the author presents a problem and begins the **rising action** that makes the problem hard to solve. Just when the problem comes to a **climax**, the story ends. The climax is the highest point of excitement or suspense in a story's plot. Readers expect that after the climax, the story will show how the problem is solved. This story does something else. "The Lady, or the Tiger?" is a story of **suspense**, and readers have to expect the unexpected.

Reading on Your Own During a story's **exposition**, or introduction, readers gather some background information, such as the setting and the main characters. After that point, the main problems of the story are revealed and the conflict begins. As you read, use the Plot Mountain chart described in Appendix A. Keep track of the story's exposition and its rising action. Note important information you learn during these parts of the story.

Writing on Your Own Write a paragraph about a time you had to make a choice between two things and you could not figure out what to do.

Vocabulary Focus Adding prefixes to root words is one of the most common ways to make new words. For example, by adding the prefix *un-* (not) to the root word *trammeled,* you come up with a word *untrammeled,* that means free, or not bound. Look for other words in the story that use the prefix *un-, in-,* or *im-*. These prefixes mean "not"—so *impartial* means fair, or not favoring one over another; and *incorruptible* means honorable, or not able to bribe or corrupt.

Think Before You Read What do you think about when you read the title of this story?

satire humorous writing that makes fun of foolishness or evil

rising action the events of the plot that add to the conflict

climax the high point of interest or suspense in a story or play

suspense a quality in a story that makes the reader uncertain or nervous about what will happen next

exposition the part of short stories that introduces setting, characters, and the situation

The *Lady,* or the Tiger?

Semibarbaric means that the king was somewhat civilized and somewhat savage.

Self-communing means thinking deeply about oneself.

This king has absolute power—he does whatever he wants. As you read, notice how the fancy, difficult language pokes fun at a king so sure of himself.

In the very olden time there lived a semibarbaric king, whose ideas, though somewhat polished and sharpened by the **progressiveness** of distant Latin neighbors, were still large, **florid**, and **untrammeled**, as became the half of him which was **barbaric**. He was a man of **exuberant** fancy, and, withal, of an authority so irresistible that, at his will, he turned his varied fancies into facts. He was greatly given to self-communing; and when he and himself agreed upon any thing, the thing was done. When every member of his domestic and political systems moved smoothly in its appointed course, his nature was **bland** and **genial**; but whenever there was a little hitch, and some of his orbs got out of their orbits, he was blander and more genial still, for nothing pleased him so much as to make the crooked straight, and crush down uneven places.

progressiveness the state of being advanced, or accepting of new ideas

florid healthy

untrammeled not bound; free

barbaric uncivilized; savage

exuberant high-spirited

bland dull, unexciting

genial friendly

Among the borrowed notions by which his barbarism had become semified was that of the public arena, in which, by exhibitions of manly and beastly valor, the minds of his subjects were refined and cultured.

But even here the exuberant and barbaric fancy **asserted** itself. The arena of the king was built not to give the people an opportunity of hearing the **rhapsodies** of dying gladiators, nor to enable them to view the **inevitable** conclusion of a conflict between religious opinions and hungry jaws, but for purposes far better adapted to widen and develop the mental energies of the people. This vast amphitheatre, with its encircling galleries, its mysterious vaults, and its unseen passages, was an agent of poetic justice, in which crime was punished, or virtue rewarded, by the decrees of an **impartial** and **incorruptible** chance.

When a subject was accused of a crime of sufficient importance to interest the king, public notice was given that on an appointed day the fate of the accused person would be decided in the king's arena—a structure which well deserved its name; for, although its form and plan were borrowed from afar, its purpose **emanated** solely from the brain of this man, who, every barleycorn a king, knew no tradition to which he owed more allegiance than pleased his fancy, and who ingrafted on every adopted form of human thought and action the rich growth of his barbaric **idealism**.

When all the people had assembled in the galleries, and the king, surrounded by his court, sat high up on his throne of royal state on one side of the arena, he gave a signal, a door beneath him opened, and the accused subject stepped out into the amphitheatre. Directly opposite him, on the other side of the enclosed space, were two doors, exactly alike and side by

Semified, a made-up word, shows how the author creates humor and satire. The king's idea of holding public events in arenas has helped make him only *semibarbaric*—only half uncivilized and savage.

The ancient Romans also watched battles to the death between *gladiators* (slaves trained as fighters) in large public arenas or *amphitheatres.* They too claimed that such public spectacles taught people valuable lessons.

The king did whatever pleased him, no matter where the original idea came from.

asserted put oneself or one's ideas forward	**inevitable** impossible to avoid	**emanated** came forth
rhapsodies joyful songs	**impartial** fair	**idealism** a belief in the highest standards
	incorruptible honorable	

side. It was the duty and the privilege of the person on trial to walk directly to these doors and open one of them. He could open either door he pleased: he was subject to no **guidance** or influence but that of the afore-mentioned impartial and incorruptible chance. If he opened the one, there came out of it a hungry tiger, the fiercest and most cruel that could be **procured**, which immediately sprang upon him and tore him to pieces, as a punishment for his guilt. The moment that the case of the criminal was thus decided, **doleful** iron bells were clanged, great wails went up from the hired mourners posted on the outer rim of the arena, and the vast audience, with bowed heads and downcast hearts, **wended** slowly their homeward way, mourning greatly that one so young and fair, or so old and respected, should have **merited** so **dire** a fate.

But if the accused person opened the other door, there came forth from it a lady, the most suitable to his years and station that his Majesty could select among his fair subjects; and to this lady he was immediately married, as a reward of his innocence. It mattered not that he might already possess a wife and family, or that his affections might be engaged upon an object of his own selection: the

> Why do you think the king hires mourners?

guidance direction; instruction	**doleful** sad; mournful	**dire** severe; terrible
procured gotten or obtained	**wended** traveled	
	merited deserved	

king allowed no such **subordinate** arrangements to interfere with his great scheme of **retribution** and reward. The exercises, as in the other instance, took place immediately, and in the arena. Another door opened beneath the king, and a priest, followed by a band of choristers, and dancing maidens blowing joyous airs on golden horns and treading an epithalamic measure, advanced to where the pair stood side by side; and the wedding was promptly and cheerily solemnized. Then the gay brass bells rang forth their merry peals, the people shouted glad hurrahs, and the innocent man, **preceded** by children strewing flowers on his path, led his bride to his home.

A *chorister* is a singer. An *epithalamium*, from the Greek word for bridal chamber, is a song or poem in honor of a bride and bridegroom.

This was the king's semibarbaric method of **administering** justice. Its perfect fairness is obvious. The criminal could not know out of which door would come the lady: he opened either he pleased, without having the slightest idea whether, in the next instant, he was to be devoured or married. On some occasions the tiger came out of one door, and on some out of the other. The decisions of this **tribunal** were not only fair, they were positively determinate: the accused person was instantly punished if he found himself guilty; and if innocent, he was rewarded on the spot, whether he liked it or not. There was no escape from the judgments of the king's arena.

All of this description is the exposition of this short story.

The **institution** was a very popular one. When the people gathered together on one of the great trial-days, they never knew whether they were to witness a bloody slaughter or a **hilarious** wedding. This element of uncertainty lent an interest to the occasion which it could not otherwise have attained. Thus the masses were entertained and pleased, and the thinking part of the community could bring no charge of unfairness against this plan; for did not the accused person have the whole matter in his own hands?

The king considers his system fair because the accused person himself chooses the door to open. What is wrong with this reasoning? What do you think about the king's "justice"?

subordinate lower class	**administering** managing; directing	**institution** an important custom
retribution revenge; return for wrongdoing	**tribunal** a court of justice	**hilarious** very funny
preceded came before		

Many stories, especially fairy tales, are about *romance*, or love affairs, between poor young men and royal women.

This semibarbaric king had a daughter as blooming as his most florid fancies, and with a soul as **fervent** and **imperious** as his own. As is usual in such cases, she was the apple of his eye, and was loved by him above all humanity. Among his courtiers was a young man of that fineness of blood and lowness of station common to the conventional heroes of romance who love royal maidens. This royal maiden was well satisfied with her lover, for he was handsome and brave to a degree **unsurpassed** in all this kingdom; and she loved him with an **ardor** that had enough of barbarism in it to make it exceedingly warm and strong. This love affair moved on happily for many months, until one day the king happened to discover its existence. He did not hesitate nor **waver** in regard to his duty in the premises. The youth was immediately cast into prison, and a day was appointed for his trial in the king's arena. This, of course, was an especially important occasion; and his Majesty, as well as all the people, were greatly interested in the workings and development of this trial. Never before had such a case occurred; never before had a subject dared to love the daughter of a king. In afteryears such things became commonplace enough; but then they were, in no slight degree, novel and startling.

Here, the rising action of the story begins.

The tiger-cages of the kingdom were searched for the most savage and **relentless** beasts, from which the fiercest monster might be selected for the arena; and the ranks of maiden youth and beauty throughout the land were carefully surveyed by **competent** judges, in order that the young man might have a fitting bride in case fate did not determine for him a different destiny. Of course everybody knew that the deed with which the accused was charged had been done. He had loved the princess, and neither he, she, nor any one else thought of denying the fact; but the king would not think of allowing any fact of this kind to interfere with the workings

fervent having strong feelings	**unsurpassed** best; highest	**relentless** without pity
imperious bossy	**ardor** deep feeling	**competent** able to do something
	waver to back down	

of the tribunal, in which he took such great delight and satisfaction. No matter how the affair turned out, the youth would be disposed of; and the king would take an **aesthetic** pleasure in watching the course of events, which would determine whether or not the young man had done wrong in allowing himself to love the princess.

Why does the king use the arena even when everyone agrees the accused is guilty?

The appointed day arrived. From far and near the people gathered, and thronged the great galleries of the arena; and crowds, unable to gain **admittance**, massed themselves against its outside walls. The king and his court were in their places, opposite the twin doors—those fateful **portals**, so terrible in their similarity.

All was ready. The signal was given. A door beneath the royal party opened, and the lover of the princess walked into the arena. Tall, beautiful, fair, his appearance was greeted with a low hum of admiration and anxiety. Half the audience had not known so grand a youth had lived among them. No wonder the princess loved him! What a terrible thing for him to be there!

As the youth advanced into the arena, he turned, as the custom was, to bow to the king: but he did not think at all of that royal personage; his eyes were fixed upon the princess, who sat to the right of her father. Had it not been for the **moiety** of barbarism in her nature it is **probable** that lady would not have been there; but her intense and **fervid** soul would not allow her to be absent on an occasion in which she was so terribly interested. From the moment that the decree had gone forth that her lover should decide his fate in the king's arena, she had thought of nothing, night or day, but this great event and the various subjects connected with it. Possessed of more power, influence, and force of character than any one who had ever before been interested in such a case, she had done what no other person had done—she had possessed herself of the secret of the doors. She knew in

aesthetic artistic	**portals** doors	**probable** likely
admittance entrance	**moiety** half	**fervid** full of strong feeling

which of the two rooms that lay behind those doors stood the cage of the tiger, with its open front, and in which waited the lady. Through these thick doors, heavily curtained with skins on the inside, it was impossible that any noise or suggestion should come from within to the person who should approach to raise the latch of one of them; but gold, and the power of a woman's will, had brought the secret to the princess.

And not only did she know in which room stood the lady ready to emerge, all blushing and **radiant**, should her door be opened, but she knew who the lady was. It was one of the fairest and loveliest of the damsels of the court who had been selected as the reward of the accused youth, should he be proved innocent of the crime of **aspiring** to one so far above him; and the princess hated her. Often had she seen, or imagined that she had seen, this fair creature throwing glances of admiration upon the person of her lover, and sometimes she thought these glances were **perceived** and even returned. Now and then she had seen them talking together; it was but for a moment or two, but much can be said in a brief space; it may have been on most unimportant topics, but how could she know that? The girl was lovely, but she had dared to raise her eyes to the loved one of the princess; and, with all the **intensity** of the savage blood **transmitted** to her through long lines of wholly barbaric ancestors, she hated the woman who blushed and trembled behind that silent door.

When her lover turned and looked at her, and his eye met hers as she sat there paler and whiter than any one in the vast ocean of anxious faces about her, he saw, by that power of quick **perception** which is given to those whose souls are one, that she knew behind which door crouched the tiger, and behind which stood the lady. He had expected her to know it. He understood her nature, and his soul was assured that she would never rest until she had made plain to herself this thing, hidden to all other lookers-on, even to the king. The

radiant glowing	**perceived** understood	**transmitted** sent
aspiring seeking	**intensity** strength	**perception** an understanding

only hope for the youth in which there was any element of certainty was based upon the success of the princess in discovering this mystery; and the moment he looked upon her, he saw she had succeeded, as in his soul he knew she would succeed.

Then it was that his quick and anxious glance asked the question, "Which?" It was as plain to her as if he shouted it from where he stood. There was not an instant to be lost. The question was asked in a flash; it must be answered in another.

Her right arm lay on the cushioned parapet before her. She raised her hand, and made a slight, quick movement toward the right. No one but her lover saw her. Every eye but his was fixed on the man in the arena.

He turned, and with a firm and rapid step he walked across the empty space. Every heart stopped beating, every breath was held, every eye was fixed immovably upon that man. Without the slightest hesitation, he went to the door on the right, and opened it.

Now, the point of the story is this: Did the tiger come out of that door, or did the lady?

The more we reflect upon this question, the harder it is to answer. It involves a study of the human heart which leads us through **devious mazes** of **passion**, out of which it is difficult to find our way. Think of it, fair reader, not as if the decision of the question depended upon yourself, but upon that hot-blooded, semibarbaric princess, her soul at a white heat beneath the combined fires of despair and jealousy. She had lost him, but who should have him?

How often, in her waking hours and in her dreams, had she started in wild horror and covered her face with her hands as she thought of her lover opening the door on the other side of which waited the cruel fangs of the tiger!

But how much oftener had she seen him at the other door! How in her grievous reveries had she gnashed her teeth and torn her hair when she saw his start of **rapturous** delight as he opened the door of the lady! How her soul had burned in **agony** when she had seen him rush to meet that woman, with her flushing cheek and sparkling eye of triumph; when she had seen him lead her forth, his whole frame kindled with the joy of recovered life; when she had heard the glad shouts from the **multitude**, and the wild ringing of the happy bells; when she had seen the priest, with his joyous followers, advance to the couple, and make them man and wife before her very eyes; and when she had seen them walk away together upon their path of flowers, followed by the tremendous shouts of the

Here is the climax of the story. Suspense is at its highest point. Readers expect the rest of the story to show how the problem is resolved.

A *grievous reverie* is a daydream causing sorrow.

devious crooked; sly	**passion** very strong feelings	**agony** great pain
mazes webs; puzzles		**multitude** crowd
	rapturous extremely happy	

hilarious multitude, in which her one despairing shriek was lost and drowned!

Would it not be better for him to die at once, and go to wait for her in the blessed regions of semibarbaric **futurity**?

And yet, that awful tiger, those shrieks, that blood!

Her decision had been indicated in an instant, but it had been made after days and nights of **anguished deliberation**. She had known she would be asked, she had decided what she would answer, and, without the slightest hesitation, she had moved her hand to the right.

The question of her decision is one not to be lightly considered, and it is not for me to presume to set myself up as the one person able to answer it. And so I leave it with all of you: Which came out of the opened door—the lady, or the tiger?

> Which do you think came out of the opened door? Why do you suppose the author chose to end the story in this way?

---

futurity future event   **anguished** very great pain or grief   **deliberation** careful thought

AFTER READING THE SELECTION

The Lady, or the Tiger? *by Frank Stockton*

Directions Choose the letter of the best answer or write the answer using complete sentences.

Comprehension: Identifying Facts

1. What does the king use his arena for?
   A circuses
   B selling barleycorn
   C gladiator fights
   D a way of punishing crime

2. Who comes to the arena?
   A the town's people
   B the accused
   C the king and his court
   D all of the above

3. What is behind each of the two doors in the arena?

4. What did the two doors look like?

5. What happens if the tiger comes out of the door?

6. Why does the king throw his daughter's lover into prison?

7. Since her lover's arrest, what has the princess thought about?

8. What does the princess know that no one else had ever known?

9. What does the princess's lover expect the princess to know?

10. How does the princess feel about the lady behind the door?

Comprehension: Putting Ideas Together

11. What sort of a ruler is the king?
    A kind and gentle
    B easily swayed
    C demanding and stubborn
    D unhappy

12. Who decides which door to open?
    A the king   C the accused
    B the king's court   D the public

13. Why does the king think his system is fair?

14. What kind of a father is the king?

15. What preparations are made for the trial of the princess's lover?

16. Why does the king think he has found the perfect solution by putting the princess's lover on trial?

17. What are some things the princess does that might be considered "semibarbaric"?

18. Why is the princess's decision hard for her to make?

19. Why does her lover believe that the princess will tell him the right door to pick?

20. What things does the princess have to consider as she makes her decision about the trial?

Understanding Literature: Climax

The climax of a story—sometimes called the turning point—is the highest point of interest or suspense. The rising action of the plot builds to this point. At the climax, the main character either solves the problem of the story, or realizes that the problem will never be solved.

"The Lady, or the Tiger?" turns this notion around. Stockton provides a complete exposition of the people and the background of the story. He builds the rising action carefully. But, then he stops it. His readers are left trying to figure out what the climax of the story actually is.

21. What is another term for climax?

22. What does a story's climax reveal to readers?

23. In "The Lady, or the Tiger?" what events in the plot could be considered the rising action of the story?

24. Some people say that this story does reach its climax when it seems clear that the lover will open the door on the right. What do you think?

25. As a reader, how did you feel when the story ended without its problem being solved? Explain your answer.

Critical Thinking

26. Do you think the king's system of justice is fair? Why or why not?

27. Which character in this story seems to be the most logical thinker? Explain your response.

28. Besides its ending, are there any other elements of suspense in this story?

29. If you had to make the same decision as the princess, would you have told your lover to pick the door that hid the tiger, or the door that hid the lady? Explain your answer.

Thinking Creatively

30. How might you update this story to make it popular with readers today?

After Reading continued on next page

The Lady, or the Tiger? *by Frank Stockton*

 ### Grammar Check

Writers use semicolons (;) to connect two independent clauses. Independent clauses have a subject and a verb. For example, Stockton uses a semicolon in this sentence: "The question was asked in a flash; it must be answered in another." The semicolon joins two clauses that could stand on their own as sentences. What are the two sentences? Why do you think Stockton chose to write them that way? Semicolons are also used to connect two independent clauses that have many commas. Find four other examples where Stockton used a semicolon to connect two independent clauses.

 ### Writing on Your Own

How do you think this story really ended? Write a newspaper article that relates what actually happened that day at the arena.

 ### Speaking

Prepare a speech telling how you think the story ends. Support your view with facts and details from the story. Practice your speech using a plan to support your claim: stress important words, keep the tone consistent, and use proper body language.

 ### Listening

One way of showing speakers that you are paying attention is to paraphrase. When you paraphrase, you respond to the speaker by saying the same words they related—but in a different way. For example, if a person read the first paragraph of the story, you might respond with this paraphrase: "The king seems to have a strange mix of polished and unpolished characteristics." In pairs, practice reading parts of the story and paraphrasing in response.

 ### Technology

Work in teams of three or four to create an add-on story using one of the characters or the setting from this story. Each person on the team should write one paragraph. The first person should begin the story. Use word processing software to write; then save the file and e-mail it to the next person in the group. That person adds a paragraph. Each person might want to set their work apart from one another by changing the font or font color. After everyone has contributed, print the story and read it aloud to the team. How do you think you did?

BEFORE READING THE SELECTION

The Lottery   by Shirley Jackson

About the Author

Shirley Jackson was born in San Francisco in 1916. As a child, she liked to stay in her room, writing poetry and exploring what she called "other worlds." She married Stanley Edgar Hyman and had four children. Jackson once wrote that her family's "major exports" were "books and children, both of which we produce in abundance."

Jackson's work first came to the world's attention in 1948. Her story "The Lottery" was published in *The New Yorker* magazine. Other suspense thrillers soon followed, including her novels *The Haunting of Hill House, Hangsaman,* and *We Have Always Lived in the Castle.* Her fiction is about disturbed states of mind, ghosts, murder, and other dark subjects. However, Shirley Jackson also published two funny accounts of her life with her children, *Life Among the Savages* and *Raising Demons.*

About the Selection

Shirley Jackson's "The Lottery" brought in more mail from readers than any other story *The New Yorker* had ever published. People demanded to know what the story meant. When asked for her explanation, Jackson often refused. However, when she was pressed, she finally said that she based the story's setting on North Bennington, Vermont, the town in which she lived. She said she hoped that readers would be shocked by the story's "pointless violence and general inhumanity in their own lives."

A lottery is a game of chance. People pay to enter their names in a drawing. The one whose name is selected at random wins a prize. However, as you'll find out, sometimes the prize isn't worth winning.

Shirley Jackson
1916–1965

Objectives

■ To identify foreshadowing in a suspense story

■ To define and give examples of irony and archetypes in short stories

Before Reading **continued on next page**

The Lottery   *by Shirley Jackson*

foreshadowing
clues or hints that a
writer gives about
something that has
not yet happened

irony the
difference between
what is expected to
happen in a story
and what does
happen

archetype
a universal plot,
character element,
or theme

Literary Terms The true horror of this story doesn't begin until readers finally understand what is happening. It is almost as if Shirley Jackson has created a trap. When readers finally realize what is going on, they often look back at examples of **foreshadowing**—hints they didn't notice at the time about what was going to happen. One hint might be found in some of the characters' names. Old Man Warner does "warn" the townspeople about what will happen if they stop the lottery. This story is an excellent example of the use of **irony**. Irony is the difference between what is expected to happen and what does happen.

Reading on Your Own Many people think this story is an **archetype**, or an image or theme that occurs many times in literature. "The Lottery" is about a *scapegoat*, a person who takes the blame for something he or she did not do. Before you start to read, think about any stories you might have read or movies you have seen that featured a scapegoat. Based on that, what do you predict this story will be about?

Writing on Your Own Describe the strangest town you have ever visited. In your writing, use images that appeal to a reader's senses.

Vocabulary Focus Words have strict dictionary definitions. This is called their *denotation*. However, people also associate different things with words. These emotions or imaginative associations are called the *connotations* of a word. For example, when many people hear the word *lottery*, they usually have a pleasant reaction. After all, a lottery usually means winning a prize—a great deal of money, for example. The author relies on that connotation to build her story. As you read, notice how the connotation of the word *lottery* changes.

Think Before You Read Have you ever been punished for something you didn't do? How did you feel?

The Lottery

The morning of June 27th was clear and sunny, with the fresh warmth of a full-summer day; the flowers were blossoming **profusely** and the grass was richly green. The people of the village began to gather in the square, between the post office and the bank, around ten o'clock; in some towns there were so many people that the **lottery** took two days and had to be started on June 26th, but in this village, where there were only about three hundred people, the whole lottery took less than two hours, so it could begin at ten o'clock in the morning and still be through in time to allow the villagers to get home for noon dinner.

The children assembled first, of course. School was recently over for the summer, and the feeling of liberty sat uneasily on most of them; they tended to gather together quietly for a while before they broke into **boisterous** play, and their talk was still of the classroom and the teacher, of books and **reprimands**. Bobby Martin had already stuffed his pockets full of stones, and the other boys soon followed his example, selecting the smoothest and roundest stones; Bobby and Harry Jones and Dickie Delacroix—the villagers pronounced his name "Dellacroy"—eventually made a great pile of stones in one corner of the square and guarded it against the raids of the other boys. The girls stood aside, talking among themselves, looking over their shoulders at the boys, and the very small children rolled in the dust or clung to the hands of their older brothers and sisters.

As you read, ask yourself what each detail adds to what you expect will happen in this story.

Notice that this lottery happens in other villages too—not just in this one.

---

profusely generously; in large amounts

lottery a game of chance

boisterous noisy; wild

reprimands scoldings

Soon the men began to gather, surveying their own children, speaking of planting and rain, tractors and taxes. They stood together, away from the pile of stones in the corner, and their jokes were quiet and they smiled rather than laughed. The women, wearing faded house dresses and sweaters, came shortly after their menfolk. They greeted one another and exchanged bits of gossip as they went to join their husbands. Soon the women, standing by their husbands, began to call to their children, and the children came **reluctantly**, having to be called four or five times. Bobby Martin ducked under his mother's grasping hand and ran, laughing, back to the pile of stones. His father spoke up sharply, and Bobby came quickly and took his place between his father and his oldest brother.

The lottery was conducted—as were the square dances, the teen-age club, the Halloween program—by Mr. Summers, who had time and energy to devote to **civic** activities. He was a round-faced, **jovial** man and he ran the coal business, and people were sorry for him, because he had no children and his wife was a scold. When he arrived in the square, carrying the black wooden box, there was a murmur of conversation among the villagers, and he waved and called, "Little late today, folks." The postmaster, Mr. Graves, followed him, carrying a three-legged stool, and the stool was put in the center of the square and Mr. Summers set the black box down on it. The villagers kept their distance, leaving a space between themselves and the stool, and when Mr. Summers said, "Some of you fellows want to give me a hand?" there was a hesitation before two men, Mr. Martin and his oldest son, Baxter, came forward to hold the box steady on the stool while Mr. Summers stirred up the papers inside it.

The original **paraphernalia** for the lottery had been lost long ago, and the black box now resting on the stool had been put into use even before Old Man Warner, the oldest man in town, was born. Mr. Summers spoke frequently to

The suspense and, later, the horror of this story builds from matter-of-fact details. Notice that the boys have gathered stones.

reluctantly without wanting to	**civic** community	**paraphernalia** equipment
	jovial happy; friendly	

the villagers about making a new box, but no one liked to upset even as much **tradition** as was represented by the black box. There was a story that the present box had been made with some pieces of the box that had **preceded** it, the one that had been constructed when the first people settled down to make a village here. Every year, after the lottery, Mr. Summers began talking again about a new box, but every year the subject was allowed to fade off without anything's being done. The black box grew shabbier each year; by now it was no longer completely black but splintered badly along one side to show the original wood color, and in some places faded or stained.

Mr. Martin and his oldest son, Baxter, held the black box securely on the stool until Mr. Summers had stirred the papers thoroughly with his hand. Because so much of the **ritual** had been forgotten or **discarded**, Mr. Summers had been successful in having slips of paper substituted for the chips of wood that had been used for generations. Chips of wood, Mr. Summers had argued, had been all very well when the village was tiny, but now that the population was more than three hundred and likely to keep on growing, it was necessary to use something that would fit more easily into the black box. The night before the lottery, Mr. Summers and Mr. Graves made up the slips of paper and put them in the box, and it was then taken to the safe of Mr. Summers' coal company and locked up until Mr. Summers was ready to take it to the square next morning. The rest of the year, the box was put away, sometimes one place, sometimes another; it had spent one year in Mr. Graves's barn and another year underfoot in the post office, and sometimes it was set on a shelf in the Martin grocery and left there.

There was a great deal of fussing to be done before Mr. Summers declared the lottery open. There were the lists to make up—of heads of families, heads of households in each family, members of each household in each family. There was the proper swearing-in of Mr. Summers by the postmaster, as the official of the lottery; at one time, some people

At this point, what do we know about the lottery? How often is it held? How do the people feel about it? What do they know of its history?

tradition a custom	**ritual** the way a thing	**discarded** threw away
preceded came before	is regularly done	or cast off

Rainy Day Crowd,
Diana Ong, 1999

remembered, there had been a **recital** of some sort, performed by the official of the lottery, a **perfunctory**, tuneless chant that had been rattled off duly each year; some people believed that the official of the lottery used to stand just so when he said or sang it, others believed that he was supposed to walk among the people, but years and years ago this part of the ritual had been allowed to **lapse**. There had been, also, a ritual salute, which the official of the lottery had had to use in addressing each person who came up to draw from the box, but this also had changed with time, until now it was felt necessary only for the official to speak to each person approaching. Mr. Summers was very good at all this; in his clean white shirt and blue jeans, with one hand resting carelessly on the black box, he seemed very proper and important as he talked **interminably** to Mr. Graves and the Martins.

recital a performance of music

perfunctory done merely out of duty

lapse to end

interminably without end

Just as Mr. Summers finally left off talking and turned to the assembled villagers, Mrs. Hutchinson came hurriedly along the path to the square, her sweater thrown over her shoulders, and slid into place in the back of the crowd. "Clean forgot what day it was," she said to Mrs. Delacroix, who stood next to her, and they both laughed softly. "Thought my old man was out back stacking wood," Mrs. Hutchinson went on, "and then I looked out the window and the kids were gone, and then I remembered it was the twenty-seventh and came a-running." She dried her hands on her apron, and Mrs. Delacroix said, "You're in time, though. They're still talking away up there."

Mrs. Hutchinson craned her neck to see through the crowd and found her husband and children standing near the front. She tapped Mrs. Delacroix on the arm as a farewell and began to make her way through the crowd. The people separated good-humoredly to let her through; two or three people said, in voices just loud enough to be heard across the crowd, "Here comes your Missus, Hutchinson," and "Bill, she made it after all." Mrs. Hutchinson reached her husband, and Mr. Summers, who had been waiting, said cheerfully, "Thought we were going to have to get on without you, Tessie." Mrs. Hutchinson said, grinning, "Wouldn't have me leave m'dishes in the sink, now, would you, Joe?," and soft laughter ran through the crowd as the people stirred back into position after Mrs. Hutchinson's arrival.

"Well, now," Mr. Summers said soberly, "guess we better get started, get this over with, so's we can go back to work. Anybody ain't here?"

"Dunbar," several people said. "Dunbar, Dunbar."

Mr. Summers consulted his list. "Clyde Dunbar," he said. "That's right. He's broke his leg, hasn't he? Who's drawing for him?"

"Me, I guess," a woman said, and Mr. Summers turned to look at her. "Wife draws for her husband," Mr. Summers said. "Don't you have a grown boy to do it for you, Janey?" Although Mr. Summers and everyone else in the village knew the answer perfectly well, it was the business of the official of the lottery to ask such questions formally. Mr. Summers waited with an expression of polite interest while Mrs. Dunbar answered.

"Horace's not but sixteen yet," Mrs. Dunbar said regretfully. "Guess I gotta fill in for the old man this year."

"Right," Mr. Summers said. He made a note on the list he was holding. Then he asked, "Watson boy drawing this year?"

A tall boy in the crowd raised his hand. "Here," he said. "I'm drawing for m'mother and me." He blinked his eyes nervously and ducked his head as several voices in the crowd said things like "Good fellow, Jack," and "Glad to see your mother's got a man to do it."

"Well," Mr. Summers said, "guess that's everyone. Old Man Warner make it?"

"Here," a voice said, and Mr. Summers nodded.

A sudden hush fell on the crowd as Mr. Summers cleared his throat and looked at the list. "All ready?" he called. "Now, I'll read the names—heads of families first—and the men come up and take a paper out of the box. Keep the paper folded in your hand without looking at it until everyone has had a turn. Everything clear?"

The people had done it so many times that they only half listened to the directions; most of them were quiet, wetting their lips, not looking around. Then Mr. Summers raised one hand high and said, "Adams." A man **disengaged** himself from the crowd and came forward. "Hi, Steve," Mr. Summers said, and Mr. Adams said, "Hi, Joe." They grinned at one another humorlessly and nervously. Then Mr. Adams reached into the black box and took out a folded paper. He held it firmly by one corner as he turned and went hastily back to his place in the crowd, where he stood a little apart from his family, not looking down at his hand.

"Allen." Mr. Summers said. "Anderson. . . . Bentham."

"Seems like there's no time at all between lotteries any more," Mrs. Delacroix said to Mrs. Graves in the back row. "Seems like we got through with the last one only last week."

> Why do you think Mr. Adams is nervous?

disengaged pulled away from

"Time sure goes fast," Mrs. Graves said.

"Clark. . . . Delacroix."

"There goes my old man," Mrs. Delacroix said. She held her breath while her husband went forward.

"Dunbar," Mr. Summers said, and Mrs. Dunbar went steadily to the box while one of the women said, "Go on, Janey," and another said, "There she goes."

"We're next," Mrs. Graves said. She watched while Mr. Graves came around from the side of the box, greeted Mr. Summers gravely, and selected a slip of paper from the box. By now, all through the crowd there were men holding the small folded papers in their large hands, turning them over and over nervously. Mrs. Dunbar and her two sons stood together, Mrs. Dunbar holding the slip of paper.

"Harburt. . . . Hutchinson."

"Get up there, Bill," Mrs. Hutchinson said, and the people near her laughed.

"Jones."

"They do say," Mr. Adams said to Old Man Warner, who stood next to him, "that over in the north village they're talking of giving up the lottery."

Old Man Warner snorted. "Pack of crazy fools," he said. "Listening to the young folks, nothing's good enough for *them*. Next thing you know, they'll be wanting to go back to living in caves, nobody work any more, live *that* way for a while. Used to be a saying about 'Lottery in June, corn be heavy soon.' First thing you know, we'd all be eating stewed chickweed and acorns. There's *always* been a lottery," he added **petulantly**. "Bad enough to see young Joe Summers up there joking with everybody."

"Some places have already quit lotteries," Mrs. Adams said.

"Nothing but trouble in *that*," Old Man Warner said stoutly. "Pack of young fools."

"Martin." And Bobby Martin watched his father go forward. "Overdyke. . . . Percy."

> Why does Old Man Warner call the people over in the north village a "pack of crazy fools"?

petulantly in a grouchy, grumpy way

The Pretty Housewife,
Amedeo Modigliani, 1915

"I wish they'd hurry," Mrs. Dunbar said to her older son. "I wish they'd hurry."

"They're almost through," her son said.

"You get ready to run tell Dad," Mrs. Dunbar said.

Mr. Summers called his own name and then stepped forward **precisely** and selected a slip from the box. Then he called, "Warner."

"Seventy-seventh year I been in the lottery," Old Man Warner said as he went through the crowd. "Seventy-seventh time."

"Watson." The tall boy came awkwardly through the crowd. Someone said, "Don't be nervous, Jack." Mr. Summers said, "Take your time, son."

"Zanini."

After that, there was a long pause, a breathless pause, until Mr. Summers, holding his slip of paper in the air, said, "All right, fellows." For a minute, no one moved, and then all the slips of paper were opened. Suddenly, all the women began to speak at once, saying, "Who is it?," "Who's got it?," "Is it the Dunbars?," "Is it the Watsons?" Then the voices began to say, "It's Hutchinson. It's Bill," "Bill Hutchinson's got it."

"Go tell your father," Mrs. Dunbar said to her older son.

People began to look around to see the Hutchinsons. Bill Hutchinson was standing quiet, staring down at the paper in his hand. Suddenly, Tessie Hutchinson shouted to Mr. Summers, "You didn't give him time enough to take any paper he wanted. I saw you. It wasn't fair!"

precisely correctly

"Be a good sport, Tessie," Mrs. Delacroix called, and Mrs. Graves said, "All of us took the same chance."

"Shut up, Tessie," Bill Hutchinson said.

"Well, everyone," Mr. Summers said, "that was done pretty fast, and now we've got to be hurrying a little more to get it done in time." He consulted his next list. "Bill," he said, "you draw for the Hutchinson family. You got any other households in the Hutchinsons?"

"There's Don and Eva," Mrs. Hutchinson yelled. "Make *them* take their chance!"

"Daughters draw with their husbands' families, Tessie," Mr. Summers said gently. "You know that as well as anyone else."

"I guess not, Joe," Bill Hutchinson said regretfully. "My daughter draws with her husband's family, that's only fair. And I've got no other family except the kids."

"Then, as far as drawing for families is concerned, it's you," Mr. Summers said in explanation, "and as far as drawing for households is concerned, that's you, too. Right?"

"Right," Bill Hutchinson said.

"How many kids, Bill?" Mr. Summers asked formally.

"Three," Bill Hutchinson said. "There's Bill, Jr., and Nancy, and little Dave. And Tessie and me."

"All right, then," Mr. Summers said. "Harry, you got their tickets back?"

Mr. Graves nodded and held up the slips of paper. "Put them in the box, then," Mr. Summers directed. "Take Bill's and put it in."

"I think we ought to start over," Mrs. Hutchinson said, as quietly as she could. "I tell you it wasn't *fair*. You didn't give him time enough to choose. *Every*body saw that."

Mr. Graves had selected the five slips and put them in the box, and he dropped all the papers but those onto the ground, where the breeze caught them and lifted them off.

"Listen, everybody," Mrs. Hutchinson was saying to the people around her.

"Ready, Bill?" Mr. Summers asked, and Bill Hutchinson, with one quick glance around at his wife and children, nodded.

What do you think will happen next?

"Remember," Mr. Summers said, "take the slips and keep them folded until each person has taken one. Harry, you help little Dave." Mr. Graves took the hand of the little boy, who came willingly with him up to the box. "Take a paper out of the box, Davy," Mr. Summers said. Davy put his hand into the box and laughed. "Take just *one* paper," Mr. Summers said. "Harry, you hold it for him." Mr. Graves took the child's hand and removed the folded paper from the tight fist and held it while little Dave stood next to him and looked up at him wonderingly.

"Nancy next," Mr. Summers said. Nancy was twelve, and her school friends breathed heavily as she went forward, switching her skirt, and took a slip daintily from the box. "Bill, Jr.," Mr. Summers said, and Billy, his face red and his feet over-large, nearly knocked the box over as he got a paper out. "Tessie," Mr. Summers said. She hesitated for a minute, looking around **defiantly**, and then set her lips and went up to the box. She snatched a paper out and held it behind her.

Why does Mrs. Hutchinson hesitate?

"Bill," Mr. Summers said, and Bill Hutchinson reached into the box and felt around, bringing his hand out at last with the slip of paper in it.

The crowd was quiet. A girl whispered, "I hope it's not Nancy," and the sound of the whisper reached the edges of the crowd.

"It's not the way it used to be," Old Man Warner said clearly. "People ain't the way they used to be."

"All right," Mr. Summers said. "Open the papers. Harry, you open little Dave's."

Mr. Graves opened the slip of paper and there was a general sigh through the crowd as he held it up and everyone could see that it was blank. Nancy and Bill, Jr., opened theirs at the same time, and both beamed and laughed, turning around to the crowd and holding their slips of paper above their heads.

defiantly with bold resistance

"Tessie," Mr. Summers said. There was a pause, and then Mr. Summers looked at Bill Hutchinson, and Bill unfolded his paper and showed it. It was blank.

"It's Tessie," Mr. Summers said, and his voice was hushed. "Show us her paper, Bill."

Bill Hutchinson went over to his wife and forced the slip of paper out of her hand. It had a black spot on it, the black spot Mr. Summers had made the night before with the heavy pencil in the coal-company office. Bill Hutchinson held it up, and there was a stir in the crowd.

"All right, folks," Mr. Summers said. "Let's finish quickly."

Although the villagers had forgotten the ritual and lost the original black box, they still remembered to use stones. The pile of stones the boys had made earlier was ready; there were stones on the ground with the blowing scraps of paper that had come out of the box. Mrs. Delacroix selected a stone so large she had to pick it up with both hands and turned to Mrs. Dunbar. "Come on," she said. "Hurry up."

Mrs. Dunbar had small stones in both hands, and she said, gasping for breath, "I can't run at all. You'll have to go ahead and I'll catch up with you."

The children had stones already, and someone gave little Davy Hutchinson a few pebbles.

Tessie Hutchinson was in the center of a cleared space by now, and she held her hands out desperately as the villagers moved in on her. "It isn't fair," she said. A stone hit her on the side of the head.

Old Man Warner was saying, "Come on, come on, everyone." Steve Adams was in the front of the crowd of villagers, with Mrs. Graves beside him.

"It isn't fair, it isn't right," Mrs. Hutchinson screamed, and then they were upon her.

Go back and reread parts of the story. What details do you notice now that foreshadow the horror of this story?

Why is it ironic that Mrs. Hutchinson forgot about the lottery?

AFTER READING THE SELECTION

The Lottery   by Shirley Jackson

Directions Choose the letter of the best answer or write the answer using complete sentences.

Comprehension: Identifying Facts

1. What does Bobby Martin do while he waits for the lottery to begin?
   A rolls in the dust
   B looks over his shoulder
   C holds his brother's hand
   D collects stones

2. Who conducts the lottery?
   A Mr. Summers
   B Mr. Graves
   C Old Man Warner
   D Bobby Martin

3. How does the black box look?

4. What lists have to be made before the lottery can begin?

5. Why is Mrs. Hutchinson late?

6. Which villagers must draw a piece of paper from the black box?

7. Who draws the marked piece of paper?

8. What do the final five pieces of paper placed in the black box stand for?

9. What almost happens when Billy draws his slip of paper?

10. How do the people "finish" the lottery?

Comprehension: Putting Ideas Together

11. What is an ordinary happening at the beginning of the story?
    A Small children stood in lines.
    B The children played games.
    C Husbands worked.
    D People were silent.

12. What is an unusual happening in the beginning of the story?
    A Families all stood together.
    B The children became quiet.
    C Some boys gathered stones.
    D all of the above

13. Describe the story's setting—its time and place.

14. How and where is the lottery set up?

15. How have the lottery rituals changed over the years?

16. How does the way Mrs. Hutchinson acts at the start of the lottery compare with the way she acts when her family is chosen?

17. Why is Old Man Warner an important character in this story?

18. How would you describe Mr. Summers?

19. What do the townspeople think about the lottery?

20. How might all the small ordinary details of the lottery affect the way readers see this story's ending?

Understanding Literature: Irony

In a story, *verbal irony* happens when a character or the narrator says one thing, but, in the reader's mind, it means something else. Consider Old Man Warner's comment—"Nothing but trouble in *that*"—in response to people suggesting that the town stop holding lotteries. When readers finally see what the lottery is, this comment becomes ironic. The lottery—not the lack of it—is nothing but trouble. *Situational irony*— also used in "The Lottery"—happens when readers expect one outcome, and another one happens.

21. What is the difference between verbal irony and situational irony?

22. Mr. Warner says "Lottery in June, corn be heavy soon." Is this an example of verbal or situational irony?

23. Mrs. Hutchinson, late for the lottery, explains that she "clean forgot what day it was." How is this ironic?

24. What outcome might a reader expect if they read only the first part of "The Lottery"?

25. What is the actual outcome? How is this ironic?

Critical Thinking

26. What do you think this story means? Support your opinion with evidence from the story.

27. Why do you think the people refuse to give up the lottery?

28. What does Old Man Warner mean when he says, "It's not the way it used to be. People ain't the way they used to be"?

29. How would you feel if you were a Hutchinson and found that you had drawn a blank piece of paper?

Thinking Creatively

30. The lottery is described as a custom that the townspeople have been following so long that they no longer remember how or why it started. What is a custom you know about that people seem to follow just because they've "always done it that way"? How is this like the situation described in the story?

After Reading continued on next page

The Lottery   *by Shirley Jackson*

 Grammar Check

Tense is the form of a verb or action word that expresses time. Authors choose to use different verb tenses at different times. For example, Shirley Jackson tells this story using past tense verbs. From this, readers know that the events of the story already happened. Past tense verbs often end in *–d* or *–ed*. Choose one paragraph in the story. Change all the past tense verbs to present tense verbs, as if the action is happening as you watch. How does this change your impressions of the story?

 Writing on Your Own

Turn the tables on "The Lottery." Continue the story by writing several paragraphs that add a new and unexpected twist to the ending of the story.

 Speaking and Listening

Imagine that you live in the town where the lottery was held. A debate is scheduled to decide whether the lottery will continue. Decide whether you are for or against the lottery. Outline your reasons. Present them in a town meeting situation. Tell the group your opinion and the reasons you formed this opinion. After everyone has listened to the presentations, the class should vote: Which side made the best arguments? Will the lottery continue or not?

 Media

"The Lottery" has been made into a television program, a movie, and a ballet. How might you read the story differently if you first saw it in one of these forms?

 Research

Use the K-W-L chart, described in Appendix A, to explain what you know about "The Lottery" and what you still want to know. Enter **The Lottery literary criticism** on a search engine or in a library computer system. You can find magazines that have articles either online or in your library. After you have completed your research, finish the chart, detailing what you have learned.

BEFORE READING THE SELECTION

The Monkey's Paw by W. W. Jacobs

About the Author

W. W. (William Wymark) Jacobs was born in London in 1863. He grew up in an area near the docks of London. He saw ships and sailors from all over the world. He never forgot the stories he heard there. In fact, they gave him ideas for most of the stories and novels he went on to write.

Jacobs was in his 20s, working as a clerk, when he began to publish stories in magazines. His first collection of stories, *Many Cargoes,* in 1896, was a success. This led to Jacobs becoming a full-time writer. He wrote several novels, but he is mainly known for his short stories. Most of his stories are about sailors and the sea. Some are humorous and some, like "The Monkey's Paw," are tales of suspense and horror.

W. W. Jacobs
1863–1943

About the Selection

"The Monkey's Paw" is W. W. Jacobs's most famous story. No doubt he had heard tales like it as a boy on the London docks from sailors returning from ports of call. The story first appeared in *Harper's Monthly* in 1902. It was also included in a later collection of Jacobs's short stories called *The Lady of the Barge.* The story has been used as the basis of other stories and plays. It even inspired a Halloween episode of *The Simpsons.*

The story takes place at a time when England was a strong world power. At that point, it had many colonies. English soldiers, such as the one you'll meet in this story, were sent to many unusual places to protect England's interests. The story begins in an English home on a lonely road on a stormy night, the perfect setting for a story of suspense.

Objectives

■ To read and understand suspense in a short story

■ To identify and give examples of a story's falling action and denouement

■ To explore a story that pits person against fate

Before Reading continued on next page

The Monkey's Paw *by W. W. Jacobs*

falling action the parts of the story that follow the climax

denouement the story's resolution

Literary Terms People often trace the action of a short story using a graphic like the Plot Mountain chart described in Appendix A. Exposition generally starts the story, followed by rising action and a climax. After that, the story winds down. **Falling action** brings it toward a conclusion, followed by a **denouement**, or final outcome. Suspense writers often postpone the climax until the very last moment. They hope to keep their readers caught up in the story. They prefer that their readers linger over the details such as the power of the monkey's paw. This story features a conflict called "person versus fate." *Fate* is a power beyond any person's control. In this kind of conflict, people are powerless to solve the story's problem.

Reading on Your Own As you read this story, stop to ask yourself if the details you are reading might give you clues about what will happen next. Suspense stories often include foreshadowing, or hints to readers. Sometimes these clues are easily understood. For example, this story's setting—a rainy night in a lonely part of town—gives a hint of danger. Other clues are more difficult to find. One way to find these clues is by rereading sections of the story.

Writing on Your Own What do you think the phrase *be careful what you wish for* means? Write a brief explanation.

Vocabulary Focus The language used to create this story was the language of England in the early 1900s. There may be some words in it that may not make sense to you. For example, Mr. White says, "only two houses in the road are *let*." Americans would say that the homes are rented. *Pounds*, not dollars, are used in England. As you read, look for other words that are different from the words you use today.

Think Before You Read What do you think a monkey's paw is?

THE MONKEY'S PAW

Without, the night was cold and wet; but in the small parlor of Laburnam Villa the blinds were drawn and the fire burned brightly. Father and son were at chess, the former, who possessed ideas about the game involving **radical** changes, putting his king into such sharp and unnecessary perils that it even **provoked** comment from the white-haired old lady knitting **placidly** by the fire.

"Hark at the wind," said Mr. White, who, having seen a fatal mistake after it was too late, was **amiably desirous** of preventing his son from seeing it.

"I'm listening," said the latter, grimly surveying the board as he stretched out his hand. "Check."

"I should hardly think that he'd come tonight," said his father, with his hand **poised** over the board.

"Mate," replied the son.

"That's the worst of living so far out," bawled Mr. White, with sudden and unlooked-for violence; "of all the beastly, slushy, out-of-the-way places to live in, this is the worst. Pathway's a bog, and the road's a **torrent**. I don't know what people are thinking about. I suppose because only two houses in the road are let, they think it doesn't matter."

"Never mind, dear," said his wife, soothingly; "perhaps you'll win the next one."

As you read, notice how details of setting slowly increase the mood of horror and suspense.

Notice how Mr. White describes the setting of their house. Only two houses in the road are *let*, meaning rented—theirs and one other. Otherwise, they are alone.

radical extreme	**placidly** calmly	**poised** held without moving
provoked caused someone to take action	**amiably** kindly	
	desirous wishing	**torrent** a flood

Mr. White looked up sharply, just in time to **intercept** a knowing glance between mother and son. The words died away on his lips, and he hid a guilty grin in his thin gray beard.

"There he is," said Herbert White, as the gate banged to loudly and heavy footsteps came toward the door.

The old man rose with **hospitable haste**, and opening the door, was heard **condoling** with the new arrival. The new arrival also condoled with himself, so that Mrs. White said, "Tut, tut!" and coughed gently as her husband entered the room, followed by a tall, burly man, beady of eye and rubicund of visage.

"Sergeant-Major Morris," he said, introducing him.

The sergeant-major shook hands, and taking the proffered seat by the fire, watched contentedly while his host got out whiskey and tumblers and stood a small copper kettle on the fire.

At the third glass his eyes got brighter, and he began to talk, the little family circle regarding with eager interest this visitor from distant parts, as he squared his broad shoulders in the chair and spoke of wild scenes and **doughty** deeds; of wars and **plagues** and strange peoples.

"Twenty-one years of it," said Mr. White, nodding at his wife and son. "When he went away, he was a slip of a youth in the warehouse. Now look at him."

"He don't look to have taken much harm," said Mrs. White politely.

"I'd like to go to India myself," said the old man, "just to look round a bit, you know."

"Better where you are," said the sergeant-major, shaking his head. He put down the empty glass, and sighing softly, shook it again.

"I should like to see those old temples and fakirs and jugglers," said the old man. "What was that you started telling me the other day about a monkey's paw or something, Morris?"

"Nothing," said the soldier hastily. "Leastways nothing worth hearing."

intercept to catch	**haste** speed	**doughty** brave
hospitable welcoming	**condoling** expressing sorrow	**plagues** diseases

"Monkey's paw?" said Mrs. White curiously.

"Well, it's just a bit of what you might call magic, perhaps," said the sergeant-major offhandedly.

His three listeners leaned forward eagerly. The visitor absentmindedly put his empty glass to his lips and then set it down again. His host filled it for him.

"To look at," said the sergeant-major, fumbling in his pocket, "it's just an ordinary little paw, dried to a mummy."

He took something out of his pocket and proffered it. Mrs. White drew back with a **grimace**; but her son, taking it, examined it curiously.

"And what is there special about it?" inquired Mr. White as he took it from his son, and having examined it, placed it upon the table.

"It had a spell put on it by an old fakir," said the sergeant-major, "a very holy man. He wanted to show that fate ruled people's lives and that those who interfered with it did so to their sorrow. He put a spell on it so that three separate men could each have three wishes from it."

His manner was so **impressive** that his hearers were conscious that their light laughter jarred somewhat.

"Well, why don't you have three, sir?" said Herbert White, cleverly.

The soldier regarded him in the way that middle age is wont to regard **presumptuous** youth. "I have," he said quietly; and his blotchy face whitened.

"And did you really have the three wishes granted?" asked Mrs. White.

"I did," said the sergeant-major; and his glass tapped against his strong teeth.

"And has anybody else wished?" **persisted** the old lady.

"The first man had his three wishes. Yes," was the reply; "I don't know what the first two were, but the third was for death. That's how I got the paw."

> The fakir's spell is the first of several foreshadowings of evil connected with the monkey's paw.

---

grimace an expression of disgust

impressive grand

presumptuous too bold

persisted continued

His tones were so grave that a hush fell upon the group.

"If you've had your three wishes, it's no good to you now, then, Morris," said the old man at last. "What do you keep it for?"

The soldier shook his head. "Fancy, I suppose," he said slowly. "I did have some idea of selling it, but I don't think I will. It has caused enough mischief already. Besides, people won't buy. They think it's a fairy tale, some of them; and those who do think anything of it want to try it first and pay me afterward."

"If you could have another three wishes," said the old man, eyeing him keenly, "would you have them?"

"I don't know," said the other. "I don't know."

He took the paw, and dangling it between his forefinger and thumb, suddenly threw it upon the fire. White, with a slight cry, stooped down and snatched it off.

"Better let it burn," said the soldier solemnly.

"If you don't want it, Morris," said the other, "give it to me."

"I won't," said his friend **doggedly**. "I threw it on the fire. If you keep it, don't blame me for what happens. Pitch it on the fire again like a sensible man."

> Why does Sergeant-Major Morris want to destroy the monkey's paw?

doggedly stubbornly

The other shook his head and examined his new possession closely. "How do you do it?" he inquired.

"Hold it up in your right hand and wish aloud," said the sergeant-major, "but I warn you of the **consequences**."

"Sounds like the Arabian Nights," said Mrs. White as she rose and began to set the supper. "Don't you think you might wish for four pairs of hands for me?"

Her husband drew the talisman from his pocket; and then all three burst into laughter as the sergeant-major, with a look of alarm on his face, caught him by the arm.

A talisman is a charm, something with magical powers.

"If you must wish," he said, gruffly, "wish for something sensible."

Mr. White dropped it back in his pocket, and placing chairs, motioned his friend to the table. In the business of supper the talisman was partly forgotten, and afterward the three sat listening in an **enthralled** fashion to a second **installment** of the soldier's adventures in India.

"If the tale about the monkey's paw is not more truthful than those he has been telling us," said Herbert as the door closed behind their guest, just in time for him to catch the last train, "we shan't make much out of it."

"Did you give him anything for it, Father?" inquired Mrs. White, regarding her husband closely.

"A trifle," said he, coloring slightly. "He didn't want it, but I made him take it. And he pressed me again to throw it away."

"Likely," said Herbert with pretended horror. "Why, we're going to be rich and famous and happy. Wish to be an emperor, Father, to begin with: then you can't be henpecked."

Henpecked means nagged.

He darted round the table, **pursued** by the **maligned** Mrs. White armed with an antimacassar.

Mr. White took the paw from his pocket and eyed it **dubiously**. "I don't know what to wish for, and that's a fact," he said slowly. "It seems to me I've got all I want."

An antimacassar is a cover to protect the back of a chair.

consequences results or effects	**installment** one part	**maligned** unfairly accused
	pursued chased	
enthralled very interested		**dubiously** with doubt; suspiciously

Cleared the house means *paid for* the house.

"If you only cleared the house, you'd be quite happy, wouldn't you?" said Herbert with his hand on his father's shoulder. "Well, wish for two hundred pounds, then; that'll just do it."

His father, smiling shamefacedly at his own **credulity**, held up the talisman, as his son, with a solemn face, somewhat marred by a wink at his mother, sat down at the piano and struck a few impressive chords.

Pounds are English money. This is the amount Mr. White needs to pay the mortgage on his house.

"I wish for two hundred pounds," said the old man distinctly.

A fine crash from the piano greeted the words, interrupted by a shuddering cry from the old man. His wife and son ran toward him.

"It moved," he cried with a glance of disgust at the object as it lay on the floor.

"As I wished, it twisted in my hand like a snake."

"Well, I don't see the money," said his son as he picked it up and placed it on the table, "and I bet I never shall."

"It must have been your fancy, Father," said his wife, regarding him anxiously.

He shook his head. "Never mind, though; there's no harm, but it gave me a shock all the same."

They sat down by the fire again while the two men finished their pipes. Outside, the wind was higher than ever; and the old man started nervously at the sound of a door banging upstairs. A silence unusual and **depressing** settled upon all three, which lasted until the old couple rose to retire for the night.

How is the mood of the story changing?

"I expect you'll find the cash tied up in a big bag in the middle of your bed," said Herbert, as he bade them good night, "and something horrible squatting up on top of the wardrobe watching you as you pocket your ill-gotten gains."

He sat alone in the darkness, gazing at the dying fire and seeing faces in it. The last face was so horrible and so simian that he gazed at it in amazement. It got so vivid that, with a little uneasy laugh, he felt on the table for a glass containing

Simian means apelike.

credulity willingness to believe   **depressing** saddening

a little water to throw over it. His hand grasped the monkey's paw, and with a little shiver he wiped his hand on his coat and went up to bed.

In the brightness of the wintry sun next morning as it streamed over the breakfast table he laughed at his fears. There was an air of **prosaic** wholesomeness about the room which it had lacked on the previous night; and the dirty, shriveled little paw was pitched on the sideboard with a carelessness which betokened no great belief in its **virtues.**

"I suppose all old soldiers are the same," said Mrs. White. "The idea of our listening to such nonsense! How could wishes be granted in these days? And if they could, how could two hundred pounds hurt you, Father?"

"Might drop on his head from the sky," said the **frivolous** Herbert.

"Morris said the things happened so naturally," said his father, "that you might if you so wished **attribute** it to **coincidence**."

"Well, don't break into the money before I come back," said Herbert as he rose from the table. "I'm afraid it'll turn you into a mean, **avaricious** man; and we shall have to **disown** you."

His mother laughed, and following him to the door, watched him down the road, and returning to the breakfast table, was very happy at the expense of her husband's credulity. All of which did not prevent her from scurrying to the door at the postman's knock, nor prevent her from referring somewhat shortly to retired sergeants-major of bibulous habits when she found that the post brought a tailor's bill.

Bibulous habits means a fondness for drinking whiskey.

"Herbert will have some more of his funny remarks, I expect, when he comes home," she said as they sat at dinner.

prosaic everyday	**attribute** to credit something to	**avaricious** greedy
virtues good qualities		**disown** to refuse to recognize as your own
frivolous playful	**coincidence** chance	

"I dare say," said Mr. White, pouring himself out some beer; "but for all that, the thing moved in my hand; that I'll swear to."

"You thought it did," said the old lady soothingly.

"I say it did," replied the other. "There was no thought about it; I had just—What's the matter?"

His wife made no reply. She was watching the mysterious movements of a man outside, who, peering in an undecided fashion at the house, appeared to be trying to make up his mind to enter. In mental connection with the two hundred pounds, she noticed that the stranger was well dressed and wore a silk hat of glossy newness. Three times he passed at the gate, and then walked on again. The fourth time he stood with his hand upon it, and then with sudden resolution flung it open and walked up the path. Mrs. White at the same moment placed her hands behind her, and hurriedly unfastening the strings of her apron, put that article of **apparel** beneath the cushion of her chair.

She brought the stranger, who seemed ill at ease, into the room. He gazed at her **furtively** and listened in a **preoccupied** fashion as the old lady apologized for the appearance of the room, and her husband's coat, a garment which he usually reserved for the garden. She then waited as patiently

apparel	furtively	preoccupied
clothing	secretly, as if ashamed	thinking of something else

as her sex would permit, for him to **broach** his business; but he was at first strangely silent.

"I—was asked to call," he said at last and stooped and picked a piece of cotton from his trousers. "I come from Maw and Meggins."

The old lady started. "Is anything the matter?" she asked, breathlessly. "Has anything happened to Herbert? What is it? What is it?"

Her husband interposed. "There, there, Mother," he said. "Sit down, and don't jump to conclusions. You've not brought bad news, I'm sure, sir"; and he eyed the other **wistfully.**

"I'm sorry—," began the visitor.

"Is he hurt?" demanded the mother wildly.

The visitor bowed in **assent.** "Badly hurt," he said quietly, "but he is not in any pain."

"Oh, thank God!" said the old woman, clasping her hands. "Thank God for that! Thank—"

She broke off suddenly as the **sinister** meaning of the **assurance** dawned upon her and she saw the awful **confirmation** of her fears in the other's **averted** face. She caught her breath, and turning to her slower-witted husband, laid her trembling old hand upon his. There was a long silence.

"He was caught in the machinery," said the visitor at length in a low voice.

"Caught in the machinery," repeated Mr. White in a dazed fashion, "yes."

He sat staring blankly out at the window, and taking his wife's hand between his own, pressed it as he had been wont to do in their old courting-days nearly forty years before.

"He was the only one left to us," he said, turning gently to the visitor. "It is hard."

> To *interpose* is to come between. Mr. White steps in to reassure his wife.

broach to begin a topic	**assent** agreement	**confirmation** proof
wistfully sadly	**sinister** evil	**averted** turned away
	assurance a promise	

The other coughed and, rising, walked slowly to the window. "The firm wished me to **convey** their sincere sympathy with you in your great loss," he said, without looking round. "I beg that you will understand I am only their servant and merely obeying orders."

There was no reply; the old woman's face was white, her eyes staring, and her breath **inaudible**; on the husband's face was a look such as his friend the sergeant might have carried into his first action.

"I was to say that Maw and Meggins disclaim all responsibility," continued the other. "They admit no **liability** at all; but in consideration of your son's services, they wish to present you with a certain sum as **compensation**."

Mr. White dropped his wife's hand, and rising to his feet, gazed with a look of horror at his visitor. His dry lips shaped the words. "How much?"

"Two hundred pounds," was the answer.

Why does this question and its answer cause such horror?

Unconscious of his wife's shriek, the old man smiled faintly, put out his hands like a sightless man, and dropped, a senseless heap, to the floor.

In the huge new cemetery, some two miles distant, the old people buried their dead, and came back to a house steeped in shadow and silence. It was all over so quickly that at first they could hardly realize it and remained in a state of **expectation** as though of something else to happen—something else which was to lighten this load, too heavy for old hearts to bear.

Do you think the falling action has begun?

But the days passed, and expectation gave place to resignation—the hopeless resignation of the old, sometimes miscalled **apathy**. Sometimes they hardly exchanged a word, for now they had nothing to talk about and their days were long to weariness.

It was about a week after that the old man, waking suddenly in the night, stretched out his hand and found himself alone. The room was in darkness, and the sound of

convey to pass along	**liability** responsibility	**expectation** looking forward to
inaudible not loud enough to be heard	**compensation** a payment for damages	**apathy** a lack of feeling

subdued weeping came from the window. He raised himself in bed and listened.

"Come back," he said tenderly. "You will be cold."

"It is colder for my son," said the old woman, and wept afresh.

The sound of her sobs died away on his ears. The bed was warm, and his eyes heavy with sleep. He dozed fitfully and then slept until a sudden wild cry from his wife awoke him with a start.

"The paw!" she cried wildly. "The monkey's paw!"

He started up in alarm. "Where? Where is it? What's the matter?"

She came stumbling across the room toward him. "I want it," she said quietly. "You've not destroyed it?"

"It's in the parlor, on the **bracket**," he replied marveling. "Why?"

She cried and laughed together, and bending over, kissed his cheek.

"I only just thought of it," she said **hysterically**. "Why didn't I think of it before? Why didn't you think of it?"

"Think of what?" he questioned.

"The other two wishes," she replied rapidly. "We've only had one."

"Was not that enough?" he demanded fiercely.

"No," she cried triumphantly; "we'll have one more. Go down and get it quickly, and wish our boy alive again."

The man sat up in bed and flung the bedclothes from his **quaking** limbs. "Good God, you are mad!" he cried, **aghast**.

"Get it," she panted; "get it quickly, and wish—Oh, my boy, my boy!"

Her husband struck a match and lit the candle. "Get back to bed," he said unsteadily. "You don't know what you are saying."

"We had the first wish granted," said the old woman feverishly; "why not the second?"

"A coincidence," stammered the old man.

> Why do you think Mrs. White wants the monkey's paw?

subdued muffled	**hysterically** in wild excitement	**quaking** shaking, trembling
bracket shelf		**aghast** shocked

"Go and get it and wish," cried his wife, quivering with excitement.

The old man turned and regarded her, and his voice shook. "He has been dead ten days, and besides he—I would not tell you else, but—I could only recognize him by his clothing. If he was too terrible for you to see then, how now?"

"Bring him back," cried the old woman and dragged him toward the door. "Do you think I fear the child I have nursed?"

He went down in the darkness and felt his way to the parlor and then to the mantelpiece. The talisman was in its place, and a horrible fear that the unspoken wish might bring his **mutilated** son before him ere he could escape from the room seized upon him, and he caught his breath as he found that he had lost the direction of the door. His brow cold with sweat, he felt his way round the table and groped along the wall until he found himself in the small passage with the unwholesome thing in his hand.

Even his wife's face seemed changed as he entered the room. It was white and **expectant** and to his fears seemed to have an unnatural look upon it. He was afraid of her.

"Wish!" she cried in a strong voice.

"It is foolish and wicked," he **faltered**.

Why is Mr. White afraid to wish for his son's return?

"Wish!" repeated his wife.

He raised his hand. "I wish my son alive again."

The talisman fell to the floor, and he regarded it fearfully. Then he sank trembling into a chair as the old woman, with burning eyes, walked to the window and raised the blind.

He sat until he was chilled with the cold, glancing occasionally at the figure of the old woman peering through the window. The candle end, which had burned below the rim of the china candlestick, was throwing pulsating shadows on the ceiling and walls, until, with a flicker larger than the rest, it **expired**. The old man, with an unspeakable sense of relief at the failure of the talisman, crept back to his bed; and

mutilated damaged, destroyed

expectant waiting for something to happen

faltered spoken weakly

expired went out

a minute or two afterward the old woman came silently and **apathetically** beside him.

Neither spoke but lay silently listening to the ticking of the clock. A stair creaked, and a squeaky mouse scurried noisily through the wall. The darkness was **oppressive**; and after lying for some time screwing up his courage, he took the box of matches, and striking one, went downstairs for a candle.

At the foot of the stairs the match went out, and he paused to strike another; and at the same moment a knock, so quiet and **stealthy** as to be scarcely **audible**, sounded on the front door.

The matches fell from his hand and spilled in the passage. He stood motionless, his breath suspended until the knock was repeated. Then he turned and fled swiftly back to his room and closed the door behind him. A third knock sounded through the house.

"What's that?" cried the old woman, starting up.

"A rat," said the old man in shaking tones—"A rat. It passed me on the stairs."

His wife sat up in bed listening. A loud knock resounded through the house.

"It's Herbert!" she screamed. "It's Herbert!"

She ran to the door; but her husband was before her and, catching her by the arm, held her tightly.

"What are you going to do?" he whispered hoarsely.

"It's my boy; it's Herbert!" she cried, struggling mechanically. "I forgot it was two miles away. What are you holding me for? Let go. I must open the door."

"For God's sake, don't let it in," cried the old man, trembling.

"You're afraid of your own son," she cried, struggling. "Let me go. I'm coming, Herbert; I'm coming."

There was another knock, and another. The old woman with a sudden wrench broke free and ran from the room. Her husband followed to the landing and called after her appealingly as she hurried downstairs. He heard the chain

> Who do you think is at the door?

> The fakir wanted to show that fate rules people's lives and those who interfere do so to their sorrow. How have the Whites interfered with fate?

apathetically with little feeling

oppressive heavy

stealthy secretive

audible loud enough to be heard

rattle back and the bottom bolt drawn slowly and stiffly from the socket. Then the old woman's voice, strained and panting.

"The bolt," she cried loudly. "Come down. I can't reach it."

But her husband was on his hands and knees groping wildly on the floor in search of the paw. If he could only find it before the thing outside got in. A perfect fusillade of knocks **reverberated** through the house, and he heard the scraping of a chair as his wife put it down in the passage against the door. He heard the creaking of the bolt as it came slowly back; and at the same moment he found the monkey's paw and frantically breathed his third and last wish.

The knocking ceased suddenly, although the echoes of it were still in the house. He heard the chair drawn back, and the door opened. A cold wind rushed up the staircase, and a long loud wail of disappointment and **misery** from his wife gave him courage to run down to her side and then to the gate beyond. The street lamp flickering opposite shone on a quiet and deserted road.

> The knocks sound like bullets hitting the house.

> What do you think his third wish is?

> The falling action is combined with the denouement in this story.

---

reverberated echoed   **misery** suffering

Directions Choose the letter of the best answer or write the answer using complete sentences.

Comprehension: Identifying Facts

1. Where are the Whites as the story opens?
   A in their parlor C in the kitchen
   B outside   D in India

2. How does Mr. White feel about the place he lives?
   A He thinks it is charming.
   B He likes living in town.
   C He does not like living outside of town.
   D He thinks the area is crowded with homes.

3. Who comes to visit the Whites?

4. What does the visitor talk about at first?

5. According to Morris, what kind of a spell did a fakir put on the paw?

6. What is Mr. White's first wish?

7. What happens to the paw when he makes this wish?

8. What does Mrs. White beg her husband to wish for next?

9. What does Mr. White say is making the loud knocking sound?

10. Why can't Mrs. White open the door?

Comprehension: Putting Ideas Together

11. What details in the beginning of the story foreshadow the story's strange happenings?
    A the lonely location
    B the fact that it is night
    C the fact that it is raining
    D all of the above

12. How do the members of the White family seem to feel about each other?
    A They don't like each other.
    B They are always quarreling.
    C They love and respect each other.
    D They are suspicious of each other.

13. How does Mr. White coax the sergeant-major into talking about the monkey's paw?

14. How did the sergeant-major get the paw in the first place?

15. What reasons does the sergeant-major give for not getting rid of the paw?

16. Describe the face Herbert sees in the fire.

17. How does Mr. White get the money he wished for?

18. What kind of a plan does Mrs. White think of to get her son back?

After Reading **continued on next page**

19. How does the story's mood change after the visit from the company representative?

20. What is Mr. White's third wish?

Understanding Literature: Falling Action and Denouement

In "The Monkey's Paw," the climax of the story occurs when Mrs. White almost opens the door and Mr. White finally finds the monkey's paw. All of the exposition and rising action pushes toward this point, when the tension in the story is at its highest. The story action that follows the climax is called falling action.

Many short stories often end with a denouement. In French, denouement means *unknotting*. At this point, all the complications in the story are "unraveled." The problems raised in the story are solved. The story's loose ends are tied up. All the reader's questions have been answered. This point is also called the story's resolution. Some feel that "The Monkey's Paw" doesn't include a denouement. Readers, they say, are still left with many questions.

21. When does the climax of "The Monkey's Paw" occur?

22. What do you learn in the falling action of this story?

23. Are the story's problems resolved in the final part of "The Monkey's Paw"? Explain.

24. If you charted the action line of this story using the Plot Mountain graphic described in Appendix A, where would most of the events occur?

25. As a reader, do you feel that you need a denouement to be satisfied with the story? Explain your answer.

Critical Thinking

26. If you were Mr. White, would you have made the third wish? Why or why not?

27. At what point in the story did you feel that its suspense was at the highest? Why?

28. In what ways, if any, does the story prove the fakir's statement that fate rules people's lives?

29. How is this short story the same as and different from the others in this unit?

Thinking Creatively

30. What do you think were Sergeant-Major Morris's three wishes? Explain.

✔ Grammar Check

Much of this story is told through dialogue, or the words characters speak to one another. As you may have noticed, each time a character speaks, the exact words are surrounded by quotation marks. The first word of the quotation is always capitalized. For example, look at this sentence: *"The bolt," she cried loudly. "Come down. I can't reach it."* The exact words Mrs. White says are surrounded by quotation marks. They are also punctuated with either a comma or a period. In other lines of dialogue, an exclamation point or a question mark might also be used. Look for several examples of dialogue in this story, where the characters speak directly to each other. How are they the same? How are they different?

Writing on Your Own

What becomes of the monkey's paw? Three men made three wishes on it, so its magic is gone. Imagine that Mrs. White finds the paw one day as she is cleaning. Write a brief description of what she does with it.

Speaking and Listening

Prepare an oral presentation, stating your opinion on the success (or failure) of W. W. Jacobs to tell a suspenseful story. Find examples in this story to support your position. Organize your presentation by using an outline. Rehearse your speech before you present it to the class. After they listen to your presentation, ask for their feedback. Did they feel you gave an effective presentation?

Technology and Viewing

Use a digital camera to take a series of photos that you think capture the intensity of "The Monkey's Paw." Create an online scrapbook of images, entering captions taken directly from the story.

Research

Conduct a survey among students at your school. Ask the question, "If you could have three wishes, what would they be?" Collect their responses and review them. What were the most popular responses? Make a chart showing the results of your survey.

BEFORE READING THE SELECTION

Red Moccasins   *by Susan Power*

Susan Power
1961–

Objectives

- To read and understand suspense in a short story
- To explore the way an unreliable narrator affects a story
- To identify and describe image and flashback as literary devices

About the Author

Susan Power's life is strongly rooted in the culture of the Standing Rock Sioux people. She is a member of this Dakota group. Power has a Sioux name, Wanakcha Washtewin, which means *prairie flower*. Like her Indian name, Power's writing is grounded in her past. Her stories are about things that happened to her ancestors—the people in her family who were born before she was.

Susan Power was born in Chicago in 1961. She earned a law degree but then enrolled in the University of Iowa's Writers' Workshop. During her three years there she "lived, ate, slept, dreamed, [and] breathed fiction." At school she began to explore the things that united her to her people and their traditions.

Her first novel, *The Grass Dancer*, received the 1995 PEN/ Hemingway Award for the best first book of fiction. A second novel, *Strong Heart Society*, soon followed. Her short stories have been published in many magazines and were included in the 1993 and 1997 editions of *The Best American Short Stories*.

About the Selection

The Dakota Sioux people Power writes about live on a reservation. Reservations are parcels of land "reserved" for American Indians by the U.S. government. These areas were often places where people lost hope. They were forced to live far away from the land where their ancestors had lived and the way of life that was part of their culture.

However, the people in "Red Moccasins" live in two worlds: the natural and the supernatural. Their reality includes ordinary events, such as having fun and singing songs. It also includes extraordinary events, such as dream visits from ancestors.

The suspense in this story builds as horrible events in the natural world give way to increasingly frightening events in the supernatural world.

Literary Terms Susan Power builds her suspense story "Red Moccasins" carefully. Each detail of mood, plot, setting, and character contributes to a growing sense of terror. The author uses objects as symbols and events from the past as **flashbacks**. Even the words that are repeated are clues that enrich this frightening story. The story is told by a first-person narrator, Anna Thunder, who is also the main character. Anna is in a very emotional state. Because of this, she can be called an **unreliable narrator.** The way she relates events may not be the "true" or most complete way to see them. Readers must decide for themselves what really happens.

Reading on Your Own As you read "Red Moccasins," use the **images** the author creates to imagine what it would be like to actually be in the story. In your imagination, listen to the singing and other sounds. Imagine the brilliant colors you read about. Picture the heavy banks of snow. As you pay attention to these images, the story becomes a kind of movie you see in your mind.

Writing on Your Own Recall a time when you were very sad. Write a brief description of the way the world looked to you at that time. Use images that appeal to a readers' five senses.

Vocabulary Focus This story deals with a disease called *tuberculosis*. In the story it is called *consumption*. There were special rest homes called *sanatoriums* for people with tuberculosis. The disease makes people very ill, and can spread to others. The disease may cause people to have a fever, cough, and have trouble breathing. Without proper treatment, tuberculosis can kill people.

Think Before You Read Predict how a story about red moccasins could be suspenseful.

---

flashback a look into the past at some point in a story

unreliable narrator a first-person narrator whose views cannot be depended on to be completely true

image a picture in the reader's mind created by words

Red Moccasins

As you read, notice the point of view of this first-person narrator. In what ways might she be unreliable in her view of what happens and why?

My niece Bernardine Blue Kettle, the one I called Dina, was thirteen—too old to be sitting on my lap. But there she was, her long legs draped over mine and her feet scraping the ground. Our fingers were laced together, both sets of arms wrapped around her pole waist. My four-year-old son, Chaske, was sitting on the floor, drumming a pillow with my long wooden cooking spoon. He covered one ear with his hand and twisted his face to imitate the Sioux singers he worshipped, old men who **singed** their vocal cords on high notes. He pounded his song into the pillow, making the Sioux **lullaby** sound **energetic** as a powwow song.

This image of Dina dancing around Chaske foreshadows a later event in the story.

"Dance for me," I told Dina. I wanted her to play along with Chaske. Dina left my lap and danced around her cousin as if he were a drummer at the powwow grounds. She was serious, aware of her posture, light on her feet, tucking sharp elbows into her sides. Max, my son's pet **owlet**, watched Dina circle the room. He bobbed forward on the offbeat from his perch atop the mantel clock. My husband had discovered him wandering through a prairie dog town.

singed burned	**lullaby** a bedtime song	**energetic** lively
		owlet a baby owl

"Look at Max," I told the children. "You've got him dancing, too." But Max quickly tired of the game and used his long legs to turn himself around, so all we could see were his feathered back and hunched shoulders.

I clapped and clapped when the song ended, and Chaske gave up the spoon so I could stir his supper, another batch of the watery potato soup we'd been eating for weeks.

It was 1935 and a good portion of North Dakota had dried up and blown away. Grit peppered our food, coated our teeth, and silted our water. We heard that cities as distant as Chicago and New York were sprinkled with Plains topsoil. I thought it was fitting, somehow. I imagined angry ancestors fed up with Removal grabbing fistfuls of **parched** earth to fling toward Washington, making the president choke on dust and ashes. We prayed for rain, and when it did not come, when instead we were **strangled** by **consumption**, many people said the end of the world had come to the Standing Rock Sioux Reservation. I was not a doomsday **disciple**. I wouldn't let the world end while my son, Chaske, still had so much living to do.

"Bet you can't guess what's for supper," I teased Chaske, who was perched on Dina's shoulders.

parched dried out
strangled choked

consumption tuberculosis, a lung disease easily spread from person to person

disciple a follower

The *Removal* on page 269 refers to the forced movement of American Indians to reservations. The reservations were camps that became their homes. Many were removed to the Dust Bowl, areas of the prairie states that get dust storms. In these storms, strong winds remove the topsoil.

"Potato soup!" he shouted, delighted to be suddenly taller than me. Dina rolled her eyes but didn't say anything. She bounced Chaske up and down, stooped over and then lifted on her toes like a horse rearing on its hind legs.

They looked like two opposites, like people with blood running from separate rivers. Chaske, whose **baptism** name was Emery Bauer, Jr., after his German father, was sturdy and tall for his age, his powerful calf muscles bulging like little crab apples under the skin. His hair was creamy yellow, the color of beeswax, and his eyes were a silvery gray, so pale they were almost white.

I couldn't trace Chaske's Sioux blood or find evidence of his father in his features and coloring. It was as if he came from his own place, having sidestepped all the family tracks laid out before him. Dina, on the other hand, was a blueprint of the women in our family, long-legged and graceful, thick braids grazing her narrow hips. Her little heart-shaped face was dark brown, the color of a full-blood, and her eyes black as onyx studs. Dina had been with me when I delivered Chaske, holding my hand while old women assisted me. Dina was the one who placed him in my arms, and I remember thinking, as she held him, that he looked like a bundle of sunflowers, yellow against her dusky skin. I placed the children together in my mind, couldn't imagine one without the other.

After supper Dina washed the dishes. It was so easy it was like a game to her because in my modern house, fit for a white woman, she could pump water directly into my kitchen sink and watch it drain away. She didn't have to go outside and haul buckets. I pulled out my sewing basket and let Chaske play with a jar full of buttons.

"Have you finished my costume?" Dina called over her shoulder.

This close connection in the narrator's mind between her son and her niece is another important bit of foreshadowing.

baptism a Christian ceremony for naming and for coming into the faith

"You'll be the first to know," I said. I laughed because she was so impatient, more impatient every day. I was sewing Dina her first complete Sioux costume. Ordinarily a mother would do this, but Dina's was the next thing to useless. Joyce Blue Kettle had never gotten close enough to a needle to stick herself, let alone sew a costume. As a child she'd been restless and boy-crazy, so she never learned to tan hides or do beadwork. If her mother scolded her, saying, "Look at your little cousin. Look at her fine beadwork," Joyce would puff out her bottom lip and squeeze round tears onto her flat cheeks. She would say, "You know I can't see right," pointing to her left eye, which was crossed, permanently focused on her nose. Of course, she managed to see well enough to paint her face and read movie magazines she swiped from the Lugers' store. Joyce and I were first cousins, which in our tribe made us sisters, **despite** our differences.

> The relationship between Joyce and the narrator is important to the story. How would you describe their relationship as children?

When Dina finished stacking the clean plates, I called her into the sitting room. "I'm almost ready to start your moccasins," I said. I traced the outline of her foot onto a scrap of cardboard so that the soles would match perfectly her fine narrow feet.

"Will you make me rattlesnake hair ties?" Dina asked. I dropped the **paring** knife I was using to cut the pattern from cardboard.

"Where did you see hair ties like that?" I was careful to leave the blade in my lap because my hands were shaking.

"I've dreamt about the Red Dress woman," she whispered. "And she had rattlesnake rattles tied in her hair. She shook them at me. She told me I could wear my hair like that."

"You can't," I said. I knew I sounded too angry. "When she comes after you, you should turn the other way."

"Have you seen her?" asked Dina, staring at me.

"Yes. But I discouraged her from coming." I didn't tell my niece that at her age I had dreamt about Čuwígnaka Ša, Red Dress, my dead grandmother. I had heard her insistent voice, crackling with energy, whispering promises of a deadly

---

despite in spite of   **paring** peeling

power passed on through the bloodlines from one woman to the next. I had seen her kneeling beside a fire, feeding it with objects stolen from her victims: buttons, letters, twists of hair. She sang her spells, replacing the words of an ancient honor song with those of her own choosing. She **doused** the flames.

"Could she really control people?" Dina asked.

"That's what they say. But it didn't do her any good. She spelled one too many and he killed her."

My niece held her unfinished costume in her hands. She stroked the blue trade cloth material and pinched the cowrie shells sprinkled across the dress and leggings. I'd hidden the beaded belt and the flour-sack cape covered with inch-long bugle beads to surprise her with later.

There was a knock at the kitchen door. Dina's father, Clifford Blue Kettle, poked his head into the kitchen and waved at me.

"Come on in," I said. He shook his head and twisted the doorknob like he was trying to wring it loose. Black bangs hid his eyes.

"Dina here?" he asked me, so whispery he had to clear his throat and ask me again. Dina stepped into the doorway between the sitting room and kitchen. "Your ma says to get home now," he told her.

"He's so shy around you," Dina said, laughing softly.

I waved off her comment as if I disagreed, but she was right; my cousin's husband had feelings for me. When we were children, he had followed me everywhere, helping me with my chores and bringing me little treasures he'd discovered: seashells, fool's gold, ripe chokecherries. One time he brought me a round glass eye he'd poked from the socket of his sister's doll. It was too much for Joyce. She **intercepted** the gift, snatched it from the palm of my hand as I studied the green iris. She took Clifford over the same way, ordering him around, demanding his attention, and because I didn't love Clifford, I let her keep him. It never seemed to occur to him that he could protest. He was **amiable** and slow-minded.

What sort of person was Red Dress, the narrator's grandmother?

Why is Clifford Blue Kettle shy around the narrator?

| **doused** put out | **intercepted** caught, blocked, cut off | **amiable** friendly; good-natured |

He longed to please. Even now he brought me little gifts or fashioned toys for Chaske, like my son's first baby rattle, and I could see he had something for me. One hand was hidden behind his back.

"What have you got there?" I asked. I walked to the door and tried to peek over his shoulder, which made him grin.

"Got these in a giveaway. Know Joyce can't use them." He handed me a mason jar full of red beads tiny as poppy seeds. I poured a few of them into my hand and admired their rich color, scarlet as a fresh wound sliced into my palm. I spilled them back into the jar.

"Thank you. I can put these to good use."

Having given me the gift, Clifford relaxed. He kicked the back steps with the toe of his boot. "Come on now," he called to his daughter.

Dina kissed Chaske's plump cheek before she left, and he smiled at her, kissing his fist and popping it against her arm.

I meant to stay up late to finish sewing Dina's leggings, but Chaske started coughing. He clenched his hands over his chest as if he had captured something between them, a sawing cricket or fluttering moth. I knew the odd gesture was a way he dealt with pain, trying to hammer it down. I carried Chaske to my lumpy brass bed and curled beside him. His coughing finally tapered off and he murmured, "Max."

"Max is fine," I said. "Go to sleep." I rubbed Chaske's back, my hand moving in circles, unable to relax while I listened to his breathing. His hair smelled like sweet grass, and his little body, changing too quickly from plump to wiry, warmed the bed. I guarded his sleep, forcing my breath into a perfect rhythm as if I could breathe for him, and in the morning I was weary but triumphant, having kept the world in orbit.

> Chaske's coughing and breathing worry the narrator.

I had been a widow for two months, since the end of November. Dr. Kessler, a **notorious alcoholic** but the only doctor on the reservation, had **diagnosed** Emery as consumptive and told him he should go to the white **sanatorium** in Rapid City, South Dakota.

"I better not," my husband said, **terse** as always. But after seven years of marriage, I could practically read Emery's mind. He didn't want to split up our family. If I became ill, I would never be admitted to the hospital Dr. Kessler had suggested; I would be sent to the **inferior** Sioux sanatorium where few patients recovered. And our son Chaske wasn't really an appropriate candidate for either place. Who knew where he would end up?

"We'll take our chances," Emery said, and so we did. Emery remained at home where I was to keep him well fed and well rested. Consumption was **rampant** by this time,

> Emery has tuberculosis. There was no cure or drug to treat the disease. The hospital for white people was better than the one for the Sioux. Rather than go where his wife would not be admitted, Emery chooses to stay home.

notorious well known, especially for something bad	**diagnosed** determined the medical condition of someone	**terse** using few words
alcoholic a problem drinker	**sanatorium** a hospital for treating certain illnesses	**inferior** second-rate
		rampant widespread

hitting nearly every family on our reservation, and no attempts were made to **quarantine** the sick from the healthy. My husband was a successful rancher, in partnership with his two brothers, and I couldn't keep him from work for very long. In the end it wasn't consumption that killed him but a wild horse he called Lutheran. Emery's two brothers brought my husband's body to me, stumbling beneath his bear weight. They were crying, promising me they would shoot that devil horse who had thrown Emery and broken his neck.

"No!" I said, and they looked suddenly **wary**. They grabbed my arms as if they expected me to pitch forward. "That horse did him a kindness." I wanted them to leave so I could comb Emery's hair and wash his face. "He didn't waste away from the consumption. He went quickly."

Later that night I sat on the edge of Chaske's cot. I told him that his sleeping father, laid out in the next room on our brass bed, was having such good dreams he didn't want to wake up.

"Is he dreaming about Max?" Chaske asked me.

"Yes," I said. "He's dreaming about all of us."

I panicked that night when I realized I didn't own a single photograph of my husband. It wasn't my memory I worried about, but Chaske's. He was so young I couldn't trust that he would remember Emery, the shape of his black beard, his tremendous wingspan and silent laugh. As Chaske slept I told him about his father, chanting our history until it became a song-story I hoped he would follow in his dreams.

I told him about the day I met Emery Bauer. It was the winter of 1928, and I was eighteen years old. I had been snowbound for several days in my family's cabin and was desperate to be outdoors where I could work the cramps out of my legs and fill my lungs with fresh air. I went for a long walk, fighting through high drifts, pausing only to search for **landmarks**.

I wandered onto the **leased** land of the Bauer ranch, thinking I was heading toward town. I came to a shallow

Here the narrator provides a flashback to the time, seven years earlier, when she met her future husband.

quarantine to keep separate	**wary** careful or cautious	**landmarks** objects that show location
		leased rented

frozen pond. The ice was uneven, marred by tangled clumps of weeds, but I noticed a man skimming across it as if on a smooth pane of glass. He balanced on silver blades slim as butter knives, **propelling** his barrel body forward and then magically backward, skirting the weeds and chiseling the ice with his skates. I had heard about ice-skating, but I'd never seen it done. I'd never seen a man spin like a top. I hunched beside a frozen bush, hoping he wouldn't notice me. But I was framed in white and difficult to miss. The graceful man suddenly skated toward me, stopping so quickly his blades spit a spray of ice. He towered over me, smiling, alternately fingering his black beard and tapping the heavy workboots slung around his neck.

"You like to dance on water?" he asked me. I shook my head. I didn't know what else to do. "I'm Emery," he said. He waited, staring directly into my eyes, which made me uncomfortable.

"I'm Anna Thunder," I finally answered.

"Now *that's* a name to live up to." He clapped his large hands together. "Come here, this will be fun." Emery removed his skates, which I saw were metal blades screwed onto a pair of workboots. He donned the shoes he'd been carrying and knelt in the snow. Even down on one knee he was tall.

"Give me your foot," he said. He was the only white man other than the doctor and reservation priest I had ever spoken to, but I trusted him completely. **Ironically**, I think it was his size that calmed me. He was such a giant he seemed uncomfortable in his body; his posture, an **accommodating** stoop, and his gestures, apologetic. Off the ice he shambled awkwardly. So I did as he requested. I watched him stuff one of his mittens in the toe of each boot and then fit the skates on my feet. He held my hands and pulled me across the ice. At first I was rigid and tottered on the slippery surface, but eventually I relaxed and pushed off the blades, cutting the ice with confident strokes.

---

propelling pushing forward	**ironically** unlike what one would expect	**accommodating** making up for

"God made you to skate," Emery breathed in my ear.

Our **courtship** was an ice dance, and Emery's wedding present to me was my own set of silver blades he'd ordered from the Sears catalogue. He attached them to a new pair of ankle-high laced boots cut out of fancy thin leather.

Emery and I married despite **disapproval** from both sides. Joyce Blue Kettle protested the loudest, flapping her tongue so much I thought she might wear it thin as a hair ribbon. Joyce had been married for several years by that time and was already a mother, but she was jealous.

"People will say you're greedy," Joyce confided to me the night before my wedding.

"What do you mean?" I only half listened, distracted as I was by the last minute details of polishing my shoes and combing my damp hair with a clump of sage to scent it.

"They say you're marrying him to get things. What about the seven new dresses, one for each day of the week, he bought you? What about the horsehair sofa and the brass bed? Didn't he even build you a house?"

Earlier that day I had taken Joyce on a tour of the new house, a neat clapboard structure made of planed lumber. I felt guilty as we moved through the rooms, the number of my possessions suddenly **overwhelming** me. All my life I had been taught that material goods were **dispensable**, things to be shared with friends and family. We were not supposed to have more than we needed, so there were endless rounds of giveaways at our dances, where people unburdened themselves of **accumulated** objects. But Emery was not Sioux, and his affection for me resulted in **lavish** offerings.

Let them say what they want, I decided. I repeated this aloud to my cousin Joyce, who was pinching the ivory-colored velvet **fabric** of my wedding cap.

"They know Emery has different ways," I said.

Notice that the narrator again refers to dancing. Here, she describes the time before she and Emery married as "an ice dance." This image will take on importance later in the story.

Why does the narrator feel guilty about the number of possessions in her new house?

courtship the period before marriage	**overwhelming** taking over one's thoughts or feelings	**accumulated** collected
disapproval dislike	**dispensable** easily done without	**lavish** very free in giving
		fabric cloth

"Whatever you say." Joyce shrugged her shoulders, and the next day when I pinned the elegant cap to my newly bobbed black hair, I noticed sharp **creases** in the pile that no amount of smoothing could repair.

On our first wedding anniversary, Emery and I gave a feast for my Sioux relatives. I'd thought time would set things right for Joyce, but she remained bitter about the match. She trailed after me at the feast, pretending to help me in the kitchen where she sat idle, letting her mouth do all the work.

"Čuwígnaka Ša was really looking out for you," she said, fighting a sly smile. She was referring to our grandmother, Red Dress. Joyce liked to tell people that Emery hadn't fallen for me, but for the old magic I had used to spell him. I ignored her, knowing that I'd never tested these powers. If they really existed, I figured they must have **atrophied** like an unused muscle. Besides, I'd heard people say the same thing about Joyce and her conquest of Clifford. I struggled for something pleasant to say.

> The narrator has never tried to use the powers her grandmother said were passed on to all the women in the family.

"That Bernardine's getting smarter every day, and Clifford looks like he's doing real good."

"That's because I keep him happy." Joyce smoothed a narrow hand across her wiry hair.

"You know, it works differently in my house," I said. "Emery comes up with so many ways to please me." I ran my own narrow hand from my waist to the round edge of my hip.

Later, I forgave Joyce because when she heard about my husband's sudden death she sent Bernardine to the house to watch over Chaske. Clifford accompanied his daughter, offering to take Emery's personal stock of two horses and one cow to his own place where he could tend them. I was grateful to my cousin for letting her family assist me.

Before his brothers buried him, I bathed Emery's face and trimmed his beard. I filled his pockets with the lemon drop candies he favored and the deck of cards we used to play gin rummy. Then I packed both pairs of ice skates in the coffin

---

creases folds, wrinkles   **atrophied** wasted
                                away

so that he would be waiting for me by a shallow frozen pond, ready to strap skates on my feet and take me ice-dancing.

Here again, the narrator refers to dancing—this time, dancing after death.

The first day of February was mild, so I opened the windows to air out the house. I'd traded two of my dresses for a scrawny chicken, and I was relieved to be cooking something other than potato soup. Max pecked at the chicken's liver, winking at me from his perch beside the stove.

I overheard Chaske talking to Max. "Atéwaye," my father, he called the young owl. I understood then that this was Chaske's way of keeping his father alive. "Atéwaye, look at this," he said, holding up a blue-and-white-swirled marble. He chattered for a long time, disturbing Max's sleep, until he started coughing. I moved to hold him, murmuring, "You aren't sick," because his eyes looked afraid, round as the owlet's.

He was racked by coughing fits most of the day, and his cheeks were flushed. By the time we finished supper, I considered bundling him up and trying to get him to Dr. Kessler's place, three miles away. But the wind changed. The sky was suddenly a heavy gray, and it seemed to be lowering itself, ready to flatten our reservation. Without the horses, I was afraid to set out on foot.

"Close the windows!" I shouted and felt foolish. I was the only one who could heed the command. So I sealed our house against a kicking wind and a crushing mantle of snow. Chaske and I went to bed early. I slept through the night for the first time in many weeks.

Chaske was worse the next day. The pain in his chest made him cry. I gave him castor oil, which Dr. Kessler had recommended for my husband, but it didn't seem to help. No one I knew had a phone, so I put on several layers of clothes and started to walk the half mile to Dina's place, thinking someone there could contact the doctor. But I realized it would take a long time to make it through such deep snow. I couldn't leave Chaske alone for very long.

At the time the story takes place, telephones in homes were not common.

I told him stories to take his mind off the pain. I even unpacked the baby rattle he'd given up years before, the rattlesnake rattle Clifford had made for him. I shook it beside his ear, **punctuating** my singing with its sliding rasp. I sang him funny songs, even dirty songs, and when the pain had exhausted him, I sang the Sioux lullaby he had so recently performed. He was too weak to raise his own voice, but he **wielded** the wooden cooking spoon in his hand and banged it against the wall. The brass bed rocked with our desperate rhythm, we churned the air with our noise. For a moment, I wondered if I could save Chaske myself, summon a healing magic. But I remembered Joyce's **futile** attempts to cure her crossed eye, the hours she spent as a child pointing her finger at the offending organ while staring at her reflection in a cracked mirror. I knew we did not have the healing touch.

The house was dark and my voice was almost gone when I heard a knock at the front door.

"Coming!" I croaked.

It was my cousin Joyce, standing on my front porch. I could see Emery's sorrel mare at the gate and Dina seated on my slender palomino. I waved to her.

"I come about the costume," Joyce said. At first I didn't know what she was talking about. "There's that powwow tonight," she continued, "up at the hall. Dina was hoping her costume was ready so she could wear it."

"Chaske is real sick. He needs the doctor. Could you stop at Kessler's place and tell him to come?"

Joyce promised to fetch him. She patted my arm.

I returned to Chaske warm with confidence. "Everything will be okay," I crooned, my voice clear and strong again. I rocked Chaske in the brass bed, held his body against mine as if I could absorb the tearing coughs. At least an hour passed. I was sinking into the dark and feeling hope drain away. I could actually *feel* it, a trickle of heat on my hands.

All this time I had pictured Joyce driving the horse through wet snow as high as its chest. I could see the horse swimming across snowfields to reach Dr. Kessler. But the

> The grandmother, Red Dress, had evil powers. The narrator realizes that the family magic, if it exists, will not heal.

---

punctuating marking regularly   **wielded** held, used   **futile** useless

picture changed. I saw my cousin and her daughter break through snow walls, pound the flakes to slush beneath the horses' hooves, but only as far as the community hall. They were inside the flat building, their cheeks pink and fingers warming in their jacket pockets. They were dancing together around the drum, their feet moving in a perfect mother-daughter **symmetry**. Then it was Dina, dancing alone as her mother watched from the sidelines, tracking the girl with the eye she could control. Her lips were pinched with satisfaction, she held herself stiff and straight in the wooden folding chair, proud. The picture dazzled my eyes as I sat in the dark room, burned itself against the backs of my eyelids. I imagined I could even hear the song that moved Bernardine's

> The narrator is imagining that, instead of fetching the doctor, Joyce and her daughter are dancing at the powwow.

symmetry balance

feet. It swept across the snow and spilled its notes against the bedroom window. The glass shrieked.

Finally I lit the lamp. I saw my reflection in the windowpane and noticed new lines etched in my face, drawn from nose to chin. I lifted the lamp high to regard the rest of the room. I nearly dropped it. Patches of brilliant red speckled the walls beside my bed and the faded quilts. My own hands were covered with blood from Chaske's lungs. His eyes were truly white now, as if his spirit were the only thing that had given them **pigmentation**. I knew I had lost him. But before I moved to wash his body, I poked my finger in his mouth, deep in a pool of black blood. I swallowed the fluid because wherever he had gone I wanted to follow close behind.

Why does the narrator swallow her son's blood?

My son's coffin was carried to town and stored in an icehouse. The ground was frozen, so we couldn't bury him just yet. Joyce Blue Kettle showed up at my door with small pails of food and wet eyes. She said Dina was so upset she couldn't get out of bed. I didn't let her inside the house.

"Get away," I said. I refused to open the door wider than an inch.

"I'm just sick about it. I didn't know how bad he was."

"You were dancing, weren't you? You were dancing."

Why didn't Joyce tell the doctor to come?

Her eyes sparkled and lit like a flash fire. "Who do you think you are? If Dina was sick you know that doctor wouldn't lift a finger to make it over here. He'd tell me to bring her in. What makes you think he'd come for yours? Is yours better than mine?"

I left the door cracked open and went to my room. I removed every dress from the wardrobe, even stepped out of the blue calico I was wearing. I rushed down the stairs in my cotton slip.

"Here!" I said, throwing the dresses at my cousin who waited, curious, on my front porch. "You always wanted them. Take them! Take them!"

pigmentation color

Joyce backed down the steps and hurried away. She nearly tripped over the skirt of one dress, the one I wore at my wedding. I watched her run across the frozen yard, my five remaining dresses clutched to her chest.

I was as frozen as the ground, frost on my upper lip, my tongue a chunk of ice. My mind was numb, but my fingers still worked. I dug out the red beads Clifford had given me. Originally I'd planned to find dark blue beads as well, intending to decorate Dina's moccasins with the two contrasting colors. But now I just wanted to finish the slippers.

It took me three full days to bead the moccasins. I beaded the upper half, the sides, the leather tongue, even the soles, using all but a handful of beads. The moccasins were pure red. In those three days, I didn't eat a single **morsel** of food. I kept my stomach filled with water. The pump had frozen so I had to drink gritty, melted snow. I let Max pick at the meals the community had cooked for me.

> The moccasins are red, the color connected with Red Dress, the grandmother with evil powers.

I remember the night I finished beading Dina's moccasins the way I remember stories I have read in books—from a distance, from behind a **barrier**, perhaps a sheet of ice. I folded Dina's costume and placed the moccasins on top. Then I wrapped the bundle in a pillowcase. I dressed to go outdoors, wearing Emery's workboots, and I fastened Chaske's baby rattle to my braid with a leather thong. I tossed the braid over my shoulder and heard its warning rasp. It was after midnight, but I didn't take a lantern; the moon was a chilly night-light. I picked up the package and was about to set off when something stopped me, a sudden prick of heat deep inside my body. The snow attracted my gaze as I paused in the doorway. It looked clean, as though it could deaden the spark. So I covered my head and arms with snow, molding it to my thighs. I didn't feel the chill or the moisture. I moved on like a snow queen.

> What does this way of remembering suggest about the narrator's state of mind on this night?

I can still hear my footsteps crackling through the drifts. I stopped several feet from the door of the Blue Kettle place.

---

morsel a small piece   **barrier** something that blocks the way

The narrator calls upon her grandmother for help. What does this tell you about what she's planning to do?

"Čuwígnaka Ša, you help me now," I **implored**. I hunched in the snow.

Bernardine, I called with my mind. *Bernardine.* I didn't speak aloud, but my head buzzed with her name, the syllables filled my throat. My teeth clicked her name. *Bernardine.*

She was wearing the flannel nightdress I'd given her for Christmas, and she was barefoot. She came right up to me. *We must dress you,* I said, still silent. She was obedient, her eyes glazed and swollen from crying. She lifted her arms so I could remove the nightdress. Her skin **shriveled** in the cold, but she didn't shiver. I dressed her then, in the trade cloth dress and leggings. I tied the belt around her waist and slipped the cape over her head. I smoothed her thick braids. Finally I knelt before her and fit the beaded moccasins on her feet. I tied the laces.

"You dance," I hissed. The words were white smoke in the air.

No one will ever know how many hours Bernardine danced in the snow. She danced herself into another world. Clifford found her the next day about a mile from their house, at the edge of a circular track she'd worn through high snowdrifts. People said she was frozen to a young hackberry tree, **embracing** it as if she had given up on her powwow steps and commenced waltzing.

I heard Joyce wanted someone to remove the shreds of leather and beads, all that remained of Dina's red moccasins. But the pieces were fused to her daughter's skin. One old woman started to cut them off, slicing into flesh, which was the moment Joyce stumbled out of her mind. So they left them on Dina's feet.

Notice that the children are together again, as the narrator always thought of them.

For two months she and my son, Chaske, rested side by side in the icehouse. People avoided me and my cousin after

| **implored** begged | **shriveled** dried into wrinkles | **embracing** hugging |

an initial round of visits. But everyone turned out for the joint burial.

Joyce and Clifford and I stood near the open graves. I noticed everyone else had pulled back. I don't remember a single word **uttered** by the Catholic priest. I don't even remember walking to the tiny cemetery behind the church. But I can hear the sound of Joyce's laughter. She giggled into a white handkerchief, tears rolling down her flat cheeks. Her short hair was patchy, singed in several places, and I guessed that Clifford had tried to set her hair with a curling iron. She looked years younger, her face smooth and empty, so different

uttered said

What does the narrator mean by "magic let loose can take on a life of its own"?

from my own face, which I hardly recognized anymore. My skin was parched and lined as the bottom of a dry creek bed.

That spring, after the children were buried, I discovered that magic let loose can take on a life of its own. I had made my niece dance, and there was no one to tell her to stop. Bernardine Blue Kettle was still dancing, this time around my pretty clapboard house. I didn't actually see her; I was too afraid to look, afraid I would see Chaske riding on her shoulders. But I heard the stamp and shuffle of her steps. She never visited at the same time, teasing me with her **unpredictability**, and there were no footprints in the dirt. But each time the noise ended and I found the courage to step onto my porch, I saw the flash of red beads that had fallen on the ground. I didn't touch them. I kicked the dirt to hide their gleam.

I noticed that even the magpies, always greedy for shimmering objects, **scavenged** in some other yard. They did not **covet** the sparkling red beads scattered outside my house.

unpredictability impossible to tell in advance

scavenged searched

covet to want

Directions Choose the letter of the best answer or write the answer using complete sentences.

Comprehension: Identifying Facts

1. What kind of song is Chaske playing?
   A a Sioux lullaby
   B a Sioux powwow song
   C a Sioux fable
   D a dance tune

2. How is Anna Thunder related to Dina?
   A Dina is her sister.
   B They are not related.
   C Dina is her niece.
   D Dina is her daughter.

3. What is Anna sewing for Dina?

4. What does Clifford bring Anna as a gift?

5. What does Dina say that Red Dress, in a dream, told her she could do?

6. Who was Red Dress?

7. How did Anna's husband die?

8. When her son is sick, what favor does she ask Joyce to do?

9. How long did Dina dance?

10. When were the children buried?

Comprehension: Putting Ideas Together

11. Why are people saying the end of the world has come to the reservation?
    A Many people had consumption.
    B There was no rain.
    C The soil was very dry.
    D all of the above

12. How are Dina and Chaske different in the way they look?
    A Chaske looks older than Dina.
    B Chaske is blond, Dina has dark hair.
    C Dina is blond, Chaske has dark hair.
    D Chaske and Dina look alike.

13. Why is Anna frightened when she hears Dina talk about Red Dress?

14. Why does Anna think Joyce is jealous of her?

15. Why does Anna pack both her husband's and her ice skates in his coffin?

16. What event causes the narrator to seek revenge against her cousin?

17. What is the narrator wearing when she goes to the Blue Kettle house?

18. Name several times in the story when dancing is featured.

After Reading continued on next page

19. What happens to Dina?

20. Why are the red moccasins an important symbol in this story?

Understanding Literature: Unreliable Narrator

A story's narrator plays an important part in the way readers see a story. Readers see only the details that the narrator presents. "Red Moccasins" is told from the point of view of the main character, Anna Thunder. She has faced two terrible events. Two months before the story opens, her husband died. In the course of the story, she loses her son. These kinds of events strongly affect people. In their grief, they may not think clearly. Because of Anna's grief, readers do not know if she is presenting all the facts of the story. She is an unreliable narrator. Readers must decide for themselves what really happens in the story and what it means.

21. How does an unreliable first-person narrator affect the story?

22. Give some examples of the way Anna acts that shows her state of mind after the death of her son.

23. As an unreliable narrator, what details or events may Anna have invented or twisted in her mind?

24. Anna Thunder can be considered unreliable because of her emotional state. For what other reasons might a narrator be considered unreliable?

25. How might "Red Moccasins" be different if it had a third-person narrator?

Critical Thinking

26. Why do you think Anna Thunder gives her cousin all her dresses?

27. The narrator says she remembers the night she finished beading Dina's moccasins "the way I remember stories I have read in books—from a distance, from behind a barrier, perhaps a sheet of ice." What does she mean?

28. What role does Red Dress, the narrator's dead grandmother, play in Dina's death?

29. Why do you think Anna Thunder causes the death of her niece, a 13-year-old girl she loves?

Thinking Creatively

30. Anna says, "I discovered that magic let loose can take on a life of its own." What does she mean? Do you agree or disagree? Why?

✓ Grammar Check

In formal English, the subject of the sentence and its verb have to agree with each other. If the noun in the subject talks about one person, then the verb has to be written in the single form. For example, in "My four-year-old son, Chaske, was sitting on the floor," the subject is *Chaske. Chaske* is the name of one person. The verb has to be the form used for single nouns. If you changed the subject of the sentence to *Chaske and Dina*, you would also need to change the verb form. Since the subject refers to more than one person, you would have to use a plural verb form. The sentence would then read, "Chaske and Dina *were sitting* on the floor." Pick five sentences from the first page of the story. Do they have single or plural subjects? Do they use single or plural verbs?

Writing on Your Own

Imagine the scene as Bernardine Blue Kettle "danced herself into another world." Write a paragraph describing what happened, narrated by Dina herself.

Speaking and Listening

In small groups, create tableaux representing scenes from this story. *Tableaux* are still pictures created by people acting as statues. Adopt the body posture your character would have shown at that point in the story. Audience members can tap a character lightly and ask him or her to respond to a question they have about the story at that point. Afterward, talk about what the actors and the audience learned from this experience.

Media

Create a script for a radio show during which you and your team members present reviews of "Red Moccasins." Express your opinions about the setting, plot, narrator, characters, and other story elements. Rehearse the script and change parts that seem unclear or awkward. Record your script using a tape recorder or microphone with your computer.

The plot of a short story includes the events of the story. Authors can develop their plots in several different ways.

A *chronological* plot moves forward in time until the story ends. Fables, myths, tall tales, and legends are usually told in chronological order. Shirley Jackson's "The Lottery" also uses a chronological plot. The story starts as people gather for their town's annual lottery and ends as they "finish" the event. In fact, the story's movement from a calm beginning to a horrible end adds to its powerful effect.

Another way authors develop their plots is by using *flashbacks*. A flashback interrupts chronological order to tell readers something important that happened earlier. The narrator of "Red Moccasins" offers flashbacks several times in her story, especially when she describes meeting her husband.

Review

1. How do you think flashbacks got their name?

2. What other stories, novels, movies, or television programs have you read or seen that used flashbacks?

3. Why might flashbacks be especially useful tools for people who write suspense stories?

4. What important information would you not know if Susan Power hadn't included flashbacks in her story?

5. How might rewriting the plot of "The Lottery" as a flashback affect a reader's sense of this plot? Would the story be as powerful? Why or why not?

Writing on Your Own

Think about a suspense story you know. Use the Sequence Chain organizer described in Appendix A to outline the story's plot events in chronological (time) order. Reorder the events to give some information in a flashback. Write a brief version of the story using chronological order, and one using flashbacks. Which is more successful?

Short stories of suspense hold readers' interest by keeping them wondering what will happen, when, and why. In some stories, readers know more than the characters do. Suspense is created as readers wait to see when characters will realize the situation, or when the expected will happen. In other stories, the characters know more than readers do. Suspense rises as readers try to guess what is happening, what will happen, or what the events really mean.

To create a mood of suspense, writers depend on such techniques as foreshadowing and irony. Foreshadowing gives the reader clues or hints about something that hasn't happened yet. Irony is the difference between what is expected to happen and what does happen.

Many suspense writers also use details of setting to build suspense. Some stories are set in lonely, dark places where readers feel strange events are likely. Other stories are set in ordinary, everyday places that gradually become settings for the unexpected.

Readers everywhere enjoy the way writers of suspense stories play with what is expected. Not knowing what will happen, not being sure what events mean, waiting for something surprising or strange, feeling a bit scared—these are all reading experiences that make suspense stories so popular.

Selections

- "The Lady, or the Tiger?" by Frank Stockton builds to the climax suggested by the story's title and then ends without answering the question.

- "The Lottery" by Shirley Jackson sets a trap for readers. It describes what seems to be an ordinary small town with a little custom the townspeople enjoy—until shocked readers begin to understand what that custom really is.

- "The Monkey's Paw," by W. W. Jacobs, describes members of a loving family who allow an evil object into their home and then suffer the horrible results.

- "Red Moccasins," by Susan Power, builds to a scary climax as a grief-stricken woman calls on dark magic to help her take revenge.

Directions Choose the letter of the best answer or write the answer using complete sentences.

Comprehension: Identifying Facts

1. In "The Lady, or the Tiger?" to which door does the princess point?
   A the door on the left
   B the closed door
   C neither door
   D the door on the right

2. In "The Lottery," on what day does the lottery take place?

3. In "The Lottery," how do the people "finish" the event?

4. How is Herbert White killed?

5. What important items does Dina Blue Kettle want to wear in her hair?

Comprehension: Putting Ideas Together

6. In "The Lady, or the Tiger?" why is the princess's lover thrown into jail?
   A He lied to the king.
   B He loved the king's daughter.
   C He refused to bow to the king.
   D He stole a tiger.

7. In "The Lottery," how long has the town held this event?

8. Why do you think that Mr. White wants the monkey's paw?

9. What are some examples of red images that Susan Power uses in "Red Moccasins"?

10. In "Red Moccasins," why is Joyce jealous of Anna?

Understanding Literature: Foreshadowing and Character Names

In suspense stories, authors often try to prepare their readers for a surprising ending by including clues called foreshadowing in the story's plot. One of the ways they can do this is by giving their characters names that are meaningful to the story. For example, in "Red Moccasins" the narrator is called Anna Thunder. When Anna's husband first hears her name, he says, "Now *that's* a name to live up to." Anna does indeed behave as threatening as thunder sounds.

11. How is the character of Mr. Summers like a summer day?

12. Why is Mr. Graves an appropriate name for a character in "The Lottery"?

13. Of what does Old Man Warner "warn" the people in the town?

14. Use a dictionary to look up the word *maw*. Why is it appropriate that Herbert works for a firm called Maw and Meggins?

15. Why do you think Anna always refers to her son as Chaske instead of his baptized name?

Critical Thinking

16. Why are the stories in this unit suspenseful?

17. Do you prefer to read a suspense story where you know more than the characters do or one where the characters know more than you? Explain.

18. Why is it important for suspense stories to have details that seem very ordinary?

19. Which of these stories would make the best movie? Why?

Thinking Creatively

20. In what ways is "Unfinished Message," from Unit 4, a suspense story? Explain your reasoning.

Speak and Listen

Imagine that you are a television reporter. You have been asked to give a one-minute report about the events in "The Lottery."

Write the report and time yourself reading it to be sure it isn't longer than one minute. Present your report to the class.

Writing on Your Own

The myth of Prometheus could be considered a tale of suspense. Review the myth, using the Story Map organizer described in Appendix A to outline the plot. Using this as your guide, write a suspense story. Remember to use some of the techniques suspense writers rely on, such as foreshadowing, irony, and setting. Ask a partner to review your story for anything that is unclear. Edit your story with these comments in mind. Create a final draft of the story.

Beyond Words

Anna Thunder had a talent for beading. Learn more about this skill. Make a beading project and display it in your classroom.

Test-Taking Tip

If you are having trouble answering a question on a test, go on to the next question. Come back to any skipped questions once you finish your first pass.

Diversity Collage
Jane Sterrett

Unit 6 Nonfiction

Nonfiction is factual prose writing. Since all prose that isn't fiction is called nonfiction, nonfiction takes many forms. Four of the most important are essays, speeches, biographies, and autobiographies. Nonfiction writers may use many of the techniques of fiction. However, readers expect nonfiction to present facts. Readers also expect nonfiction to have one or more specific purposes: to describe, explain, persuade, entertain, tell, or do several of these.

In this unit, you will read about a real sea monster, a wise grandfather, and a dignified businessman. You will also read about an embarrassing experience, an awakening, and a dangerous adventure on the highest mountain in the world. Finally, you will read a persuasive speech that shows how nonfiction can affect your feelings.

"Character cannot be developed in ease and quiet. Only through experiences of trial and suffering can the soul be strengthened, vision cleared, ambition inspired and success achieved."

—Helen Keller, *Helen Keller's Journal*, 1938

Unit 6

About Nonfiction

Nonfiction is a very broad category of literature. In general, every form of prose writing that is not fiction is nonfiction. A work of fiction comes from the author's imagination. Nonfiction is writing about real people, facts, and true experiences.

Nonfiction writers use many of the writing tools used in fiction. Nonfiction works may have suspense, irony, imagery, conflict, symbols, repetition, and humor. Authors may interpret experiences in personal ways and give personal opinions. However, readers expect nonfiction to deal with real events that happened to real people.

Readers also expect that nonfiction literature will have one or more specific purposes. The purpose of a nonfiction work is its central idea: the author's reason for writing. Works may describe, tell a story, persuade, explain, entertain, or do several of these at once.

Biographies and autobiographies are forms of nonfiction. They are true accounts of people's lives. A biography is written by someone other than the person whose life is being described. An autobiography is written by the person.

From both, readers expect to learn about the actual events of a person's life, and how that person feels and thinks about what happened.

Essays are another kind of nonfiction literature. The form of the essay was developed by the French writer Michel de Montaigne in the 1500s. For his short, nonfiction works intended to explain his ideas, Montaigne used the French term *J'essai,* which means "I try." Like short stories, essays are brief. In essays, authors try to communicate an idea, explain information, express an opinion, or explore how they feel. Reflective essays explore many sides of a topic about which an author has deep feelings. Biographical essays select a few important events from a person's life that show the person's character.

A nonfiction narrative tells a true story, usually in chronological order. Personal accounts may be longer than essays. They are written by people who have had an experience they want to explain. Two people who have had the same experience may see that experience in very different ways. Sometimes, personal accounts are in the form of a diary.

Ellis Island,
oil over a photograph, c. 1920

Speeches are also included in the category of nonfiction literature, even though they are actually oral presentations. Through them, speakers seek to connect with an audience to inform, entertain, or persuade them.

The nonfiction literature in this unit shows how today's authors continue to use essays and other forms to communicate their own thoughts on many different subjects. A never-before-seen world of strange fish awaits readers of the excerpt from Thor Heyerdahl's book *Kon-Tiki*. Rudolfo Anaya, in "A Celebration of Grandfathers," presents a touching reflective essay about what his grandfather and all older people can teach us. Yoshiko Uchida's

"Of Dry Goods and Black Bow Ties" is a biographical essay about an unusual man with unusual dignity. An excerpt from Maya Angelou's autobiography, *Gather Together in My Name,* describes an embarrassing experience that proved important in her life. In the excerpt from Helen Keller's autobiography, *The Story of My Life,* readers learn how Anne Sullivan awoke young Helen's desire to learn about the world around her. An excerpt from Jon Krakauer's *Into Thin Air* is a personal account of one of the greatest disasters in the history of climbing Mount Everest. The final selection is a persuasive speech by Barack Obama, who was elected to the U.S. Senate in 2004.

from Kon-Tiki   by Thor Heyerdahl

Thor Heyerdahl
1914–2002

Objectives

- To read and understand a nonfiction narrative
- To understand the role of chronological order and sequence in a narrative
- To define and identify examples of excerpts

About the Author

Thor Heyerdahl was an explorer and an adventurer. Born in southern Norway in 1914, he studied zoology—animal science—and geography in college. In 1936, he traveled to the islands of Polynesia to study the wildlife there. As he worked, Heyerdahl wondered how people first came to these islands. At the time, people believed that the first settlers in Polynesia came from Asia. Heyerdahl noticed that the winds and water currents ran from east to west. Because of this, he decided the first settlers could have come from South America.

In 1947, he and five friends set out to test his theory. They built a balsa-wood raft, named the *Kon-Tiki,* that was like the rafts used by ancient South Americans. The crew set sail from Peru. After 101 days and more than 4,000 miles, they arrived in Polynesia. Heyerdahl had the proof he needed: South Americans might have settled Polynesia.

Heyerdahl led other voyages. In one he sailed a papyrus boat to prove that ancient Egyptians could have sailed to South America and may have founded the Aztec and Incan cultures there.

Heyerdahl wrote about these and other adventures in his books *Kon-Tiki; Aku-Aku, The Secret of Easter Island;* and *Ra Expeditions.* His death in 2002 ended his 50-plus year career as an adventurer and author.

About the Selection

In this selection, Heyerdahl talks about an interesting part of the voyage of the *Kon-Tiki,* when he and the crew members meet up with all kinds of strange sea creatures. The highlight of these encounters is a visit by a true sea monster, one that few sailors have ever seen.

Literary Terms This selection is an **excerpt**, or small part, from Heyerdahl's **nonfiction** account of the voyage of the *Kon-Tiki*. Heyerdahl's book is written as a **narrative**, or story. Like most narratives, its events are told in **chronological** order, or in the **sequence** in which they happened.

Reading on Your Own As you read the first few pages of this selection, use a Main Idea Graphic described in Appendix A to help you chart the information Heyerdahl presents. As you list an event that occurs, note any time reference that Heyerdahl might have given. For example, the first note you might include on the chart might be: "Daytime: many creatures "visited" the *Kon-Tiki*." How does the author's use of chronological order help you as a reader?

Writing on Your Own What kind of people might have sailed with Heyerdahl on the *Kon-Tiki*? What were they like? Make a list describing at least five character traits these adventurers might have shared.

Vocabulary Focus Since this is a nonfiction narrative about sailing, the author uses many *nautical* terms, or terms that relate to the sea and sailing. For example, he talks about "glowing pellets [that] were washed up round our feet at the raft's *stern*." In this case, Heyerdahl used the word stern to mean the back of the boat. However, stern has several other meanings. For example, if you describe someone as being stern, you might be saying that person is hard-hearted. The meaning of the word depends on the way it is being used, or its context. As you read, watch for other sailing terms, such as *bow* and *swell*, that might have other meanings if they were used in other contexts.

Think Before You Read Would you have joined Heyerdahl's crew on the voyage across the ocean? Explain.

excerpt a short passage from a longer piece of writing

nonfiction prose writing about real people and true experiences

narrative a story, usually told in the order that it happened

chronological arranged in the order in which things happened

sequence the order of events

FROM KON-TIKI

As you read this excerpt, notice how Heyerdahl shapes his nonfiction narrative.

Phosphorescence is glowing light coming from something that has absorbed heat or light. *Plankton* are the tiny animal and plant life found in the ocean. The *stern* is the back of the raft.

Not a day passed but we, as we sat floating on the surface of the sea, were visited by **inquisitive** guests which wriggled and waggled about us, and a few of them, such as dolphins and pilot fish, grew so familiar that they accompanied the raft across the sea and kept round us day and night.

When night had fallen and the stars were twinkling in the dark tropical sky, a phosphorescence flashed around us in **rivalry** with the stars, and single glowing plankton resembled round live coals so vividly that we involuntarily drew in our bare legs when the glowing pellets were washed up round our feet at the raft's stern. When we caught them, we saw that they were little brightly shining species of shrimp. On such nights we were sometimes scared when two round shining eyes suddenly rose out of the sea right alongside the raft and glared at us with an unblinking **hypnotic** stare. The visitors were often big squids which came up and floated on the surface with their devilish green eyes shining in the dark like phosphorus. But sometimes the shining eyes were those of deep-water fish which came up only at night and lay staring, fascinated by the glimmer of light before them. Several times, when the sea was calm, the black water round the raft was suddenly full of round heads two or three feet in diameter, lying motionless and staring at us with great glowing eyes. On other nights balls of light three feet and more in diameter would be visible down in the water, flashing at **irregular** intervals like electric lights turned on for a moment.

---

inquisitive curious

rivalry a struggle to win

hypnotic causing a dreamlike state

irregular uneven

We gradually grew accustomed to having these subterranean or submarine creatures under the floor, but nevertheless we were just as surprised every time a new species appeared. About two o'clock on a cloudy night, when the man at the helm had difficulty in distinguishing black water from black sky, he caught sight of a faint **illumination** down in the water which slowly took the shape of a large animal. It was impossible to say whether it was plankton shining on its body, or whether the animal itself had a phosphorescent surface, but the glimmer down in the black water gave the ghostly creature **obscure, wavering** outlines. Sometimes it was roundish, sometimes oval, or triangular, and suddenly it split into two parts which swam to and fro under the raft independently of each other. Finally there were three of these large shining phantoms wandering round in slow circles under us.

They were real monsters, for the visible parts alone were some five fathoms long, and we all quickly collected on deck and followed the ghost dance. It went on for hour after hour, following the course of the raft. Mysterious and noiseless, our shining companions kept a good way beneath the surface, mostly on the starboard side where the light was, but often they were right under the raft or appeared on the port side. The glimmer of light on their backs **revealed** that the beasts were bigger than elephants but they were not whales, for they never came up to breathe. Were they giant ray fish which changed shape when they turned over on their sides? They took no notice at all if we held the light right down on the surface to **lure** them up, so that we might see what kind of creatures they were. And, like all proper goblins and ghosts, they had sunk into the depths when the dawn began to break.

We never got a proper explanation of this **nocturnal** visit from the three shining monsters, unless the solution was afforded by another visit we received a day and a half later in the full midday sunshine. It was May 24, and we were lying drifting on a leisurely swell in exactly 95° west by 7° south.

Subterranean means being under the surface of the earth. In this case, the creatures were from deep in the ocean.

A *fathom* is equal to six feet. Five fathoms is 30 feet.

The *starboard* side is the right when looking forward, the *port* side is the left.

A *swell* is a long wave.

illumination a light	**wavering** fluttering	**lure** to attract
obscure unclear	**revealed** showed	**nocturnal** nighttime

Heyerdahl has just hauled this shark on deck by grabbing its rough tail fin. The shark is helpless once the tail fin is above the water.

The *bow* is the front of the raft.

It was about noon, and we had thrown overboard the guts of two big dolphins we had caught earlier in the morning. I was having a refreshing plunge overboard at the bow, lying in the water but keeping a good lookout and hanging on to a rope end, when I caught sight of a thick brown fish, six feet long, which came swimming inquisitively toward me through the crystal-clear sea water. I hopped quickly up on to the edge of the raft and sat in the hot sun looking at the fish as it passed quietly, when I heard a wild war whoop from Knut, who was sitting aft behind the bamboo cabin. He bellowed "Shark!" till his voice cracked in a falsetto, and, as we had sharks swimming alongside the raft almost daily without creating such excitement, we all realized that this must be something extra-special and flocked astern to Knut's assistance.

Aft is near the *stern*, or back, of the raft.

Knut had been squatting there, washing his pants in the swell, and when he looked up for a moment he was staring straight into the biggest and ugliest face any of us had ever seen in the whole of our lives. It was the head of a **veritable** sea monster, so huge and so hideous that, if the Old Man of the Sea himself had come up, he could not have made such an impression on us. The head was broad and flat like a frog's, with two small eyes right at the sides, and a toadlike jaw which was four or five feet wide and had long fringes drooping from the corners of the mouth. Behind the head was an enormous body ending in a long thin tail with a pointed tail fin which stood straight up and showed that this sea monster was not any kind of whale. The body looked brownish under the water, but both head and body were thickly covered with small white spots.

In mythology, the Old Man of the Sea is a god who rose out of his home at the bottom of the sea to give advice to sailors.

The monster came quietly, lazily swimming after us from astern. It grinned like a bulldog and lashed gently with its tail. The large round dorsal fin projected clear of the water and sometimes the tail fin as well, and, when the creature was in the trough of the swell, the water flowed about the broad back as though washing round a submerged reef. In front of the broad jaws swam a whole crowd of zebra-striped pilot fish in fan formation, and large remora fish and other **parasites** sat firmly attached to the huge body and traveled with it through the water, so that the whole thing looked like a curious zoological collection crowded round something that resembled a floating deep-water reef.

Notice how the author tells the events in the sequence that they happened.

veritable true

parasites animals that depend on others for their life, giving nothing in return

A *beggarly trifle* means a small bit.

A twenty-five-pound dolphin, attached to six of our largest fishhooks, was hanging behind the raft as bait for sharks, and a swarm of the pilot fish shot straight off, nosed the dolphin without touching it, and then hurried back to their lord and master, the sea king. Like a mechanical monster it set its machinery going and came gliding at leisure toward the dolphin which lay, a beggarly trifle, before its jaws. We tried to pull the dolphin in, and the sea monster followed slowly, right up to the side of the raft. It did not open its mouth but just let the dolphin bump against it, as if to throw open the whole door for such an **insignificant** scrap was not worth while. When the giant came close up to the raft, it rubbed its back against the heavy steering oar, which was just lifted up out of the water, and now we had **ample** opportunity of studying the monster at the closest quarters—at such close quarters that I thought we had all gone mad, for we roared stupidly with laughter and shouted overexcitedly at the completely fantastic sight we saw. Walt Disney himself, with all his powers of imagination, could not have created a more hair-raising sea monster than that which thus suddenly lay with its terrific jaws along the raft's side.

Why do the men laugh? Do you think they are afraid?

The monster was a whale shark, the largest shark and the largest fish known in the world today. It is exceedingly rare, but scattered specimens are observed here and there in the tropical oceans. The whale shark has an average length of fifty feet, and according to zoologists it weighs fifteen tons. It is said that large specimens can attain a length of sixty feet; one harpooned baby had a liver weighing six hundred pounds and a collection of three thousand teeth in each of its broad jaws.

Our monster was so large that, when it began to swim in circles round us and under the raft, its head was visible on one side while the whole of its tail stuck out on the other. And so **incredibly grotesque, inert**, and stupid did it appear when

insignificant unimportant	**incredibly** unbelievably	**inert** unmoving
ample more than enough	**grotesque** very ugly	

Kon-Tiki had an open bamboo cabin and two masts lashed together with a square sail between. The raft was named for the Peruvian sun-god, who vanished across the sea to the west.

seen fullface that we could not help shouting with laughter, although we realized that it had strength enough in its tail to smash both balsa logs and ropes to pieces if it attacked us. Again and again it described narrower and narrower circles just under the raft, while all we could do was to wait and see what might happen. When it appeared on the other side, it glided **amiably** under the steering oar and lifted it up in the air, while the oar blade slid along the creature's back.

We stood round the raft with hand harpoons ready for action, but they seemed to us like toothpicks in relation to the mammoth beast we had to deal with. There was no indication that the whale shark ever thought of leaving us again; it

amiably kindly

circled round us and followed like a faithful dog, close up to the raft. None of us had ever experienced or thought we should experience anything like it; the whole adventure, with the sea monster swimming behind and under the raft, seemed so completely unnatural that we could not really take it seriously.

In reality the whale shark went on **encircling** us for barely an hour, but to us the visit seemed to last a whole day. At last it became too exciting for Erik, who was standing at a corner of the raft with an eight-foot hand harpoon, and, encouraged by ill-considered shouts, he raised the harpoon above his head. As the whale shark came gliding slowly toward him and its broad head moved right under the corner of the raft, Erik thrust the harpoon with all his giant strength down between his legs and deep into the whale shark's gristly head. It was a second or two before the giant understood properly what was happening. Then in a flash the **placid** half-wit was **transformed** into a mountain of steel muscles.

We heard a swishing noise as the harpoon line rushed over the edge of the raft and saw a **cascade** of water as the giant stood on its head and plunged down into the depths. The three men who were standing nearest were flung about the place, head over heels, and two of them were flayed and burned by the line as it rushed through the air. The thick line, strong enough to hold a boat, was caught up on the side of the raft but snapped at once like a piece of twine, and a few seconds later a broken-off harpoon shaft came up to the surface two hundred yards away. A shoal of frightened pilot fish shot off through the water in a desperate attempt to keep up with their old lord and master. We waited a long time for the monster to come racing back like an **infuriated** submarine, but we never saw anything more of him.

> Why do you think the whale shark's visit seemed to last all day?

> A *shoal* is a large group or school of fish.

---

encircling going around in a circle

placid calm; peaceful

transformed greatly changed

cascade a waterfall

infuriated very angry

Directions Choose the letter of the best answer or write the answer using complete sentences.

Comprehension: Identifying Facts

1. What are two of the "inquisitive guests" that stay with the raft day and night?
   A dolphins and pilot fish
   B giant rays and squids
   C plankton and shrimp
   D frogs and toads

2. After dark, what glows in the water as brightly as the stars?
   A giant squid
   B pilot fish
   C shrimp and plankton
   D electric lights

3. What are the "shining eyes" that sometimes frighten the sailors at night?

4. What do the three "monsters" look like to the men on the raft?

5. How do the men know that the "monsters" are not whales?

6. At what time of day does the whale shark first appear?

7. How does Heyerdahl describe the whale shark?

8. What animals swim near the whale shark?

9. What does Erik do to the whale shark?

10. How does the whale shark's behavior change after it is attacked?

Comprehension: Putting Ideas Together

11. What are some details of everyday life for the crew of the *Kon-Tiki*?
    A They catch fish to eat.
    B They wash their clothes in the ocean.
    C They swim in the ocean.
    D all of the above

12. How do the three "monsters" the crew sees behave like "ghosts"?
    A They are attracted to light.
    B They are very large.
    C They moan.
    D They seem to change shape.

13. How does the *Kon-Tiki's* crew feel about the strange fish they see?

14. Describe the day on which the whale shark first visited the *Kon-Tiki*.

15. Why does the crew laugh at the sight of the "sea monster"?

16. How does the crew estimate how large the whale shark is?

17. What details make the whale shark come alive for you?

After Reading **continued on next page**

18. How does the whale shark behave during its encounter with the *Kon-Tiki*?

19. Why does Erik harpoon the whale shark?

20. What does the crew expect would happen after this incident?

Understanding Literature: Narrative

Forms of nonfiction writing can be grouped by looking at the way the author organizes the material. In this excerpt from his book, Heyerdahl describes events chronologically. He presents a narrative, or nonfiction story.

A nonfiction narrative is different from the narrative of a short story. In both cases, a narrative is a story. However, in writing nonfiction narratives, authors present a series of actual events, told from their own points of view. In writing short stories, authors use an imagined plot and characters. Each story's point of view is determined by the person who narrates the story.

21. In a few words, describe the story Heyerdahl told in this narrative.

22. How would the narrative be different if it were written by someone who wasn't part of the crew?

23. How would readers be affected if Heyerdahl had told the story using flashbacks instead of chronological order?

24. If you were writing a short story based on the events Heyerdahl describes, how would you organize the narrative? Explain your reasoning.

25. Would you rather read a nonfiction narrative or a short story on the same topic? Explain.

Critical Thinking

26. Why do people sometimes laugh when something scary happens, as the crew did when the whale shark appeared?

27. How might Heyerdahl have written this part of his book differently if the whale shark had seriously damaged the *Kon-Tiki*?

28. What does Heyerdahl think about Erik's attempt to harpoon the whale shark? Support your answer.

29. What would you say is the author's main purpose in writing this excerpt?

Thinking Creatively

30. How would you have felt about being part of the crew on this adventure? Explain your answer.

Grammar Check

In formal English, possessive pronouns and nouns are used to show ownership. For example, Heyerdahl uses a possessive pronoun in this sentence: "He bellowed 'Shark!' till *his* voice cracked." *His* refers to Knut, the crew member who shouted "Shark!" Heyerdahl chose to use a pronoun that showed a single male person was shouting. He might have also written a similar sentence using a possessive form of a noun. That sentence might read: "We all heard Knut's shouts." The noun *Knut* becomes possessive by adding an apostrophe and an *s*. Find five examples in the excerpt in which Heyerdahl used possessive pronouns like *hers*, *my*, or *their*. Rewrite the sentences using possessive nouns in place of the pronouns. You may have to change the sentence to make sure it makes sense to readers.

 ## Writing on Your Own

Imagine that you are on the *Kon-Tiki* and you just saw the whale shark. Write a letter to your best friend describing the experience.

 ## Speaking

Prepare a speech for your class, presenting three key facts that show how unusual the creatures the *Kon-Tiki* crew saw really were. You may want to write brief notes to refer to as you speak, listing each fact and outlining what you want to say about it.

 ## Listening

In small groups, brainstorm ways in which listeners can keep track of the main ideas and supporting details a speaker presents. You may want to look at some of the graphic organizers described in Appendix A for ideas.

 ## Media and Technology

Using clay, papier-mâché, or a computer-assisted three-dimensional computer program, create a model of what you think the whale shark in this excerpt looked like. Before you begin designing, review the section of the text that describes the shark and other resources about whale sharks.

A Celebration of Grandfathers   by Rudolfo A. Anaya

Rudolfo A. Anaya
1937–

Objectives

- To read and appreciate a reflective essay
- To identify the chief characteristics of an essay
- To identify the purpose for which this essay was written
- To define and describe imagery and repetition as important writing tools

About the Author

Rudolfo Anaya has been called the founder of modern Chicano, or Mexican-American, literature. He was born in Pastura, New Mexico, in 1937. Pastura is south of the Pecos River. The stories and customs of the Mexican-American community in this part of America's Southwest have been important in Anaya's work. He has said that he has always "used the technique of the *cuento* (story). I am an oral storyteller, but now I do it on the printed page." Like other families in the area, Anaya's family spoke Spanish. This author did not learn English until he went to school. At first, it was very difficult for him. But he continued on because he knew his mother felt that it was important.

Anaya is probably best known for his first novel, *Bless Me, Ultima.* Published in 1972, this work received several awards. In addition to his other novels, Anaya has also written poetry, plays, essays, short stories, and children's books. In 2001, Anaya received a National Medal of Arts from President George W. Bush.

About the Selection

In many of his works, Anaya reaches back to his family. His mother, father, uncles, and especially his grandfather brought special richness to his life. This author once told of the ways his grandfather encouraged him to learn. "Words are a way, he said, they hold joy and they are a deadly power if misused," Anaya recounts. In this selection, first published in 1983, Anaya explores the deep relationship he has with the person he called *abuelito*—"dear grandpa"—throughout his life.

Literary Terms "A Celebration of Grandfathers" is an **essay**. Essays are short nonfiction works on a subject. A writer's **purpose** in an essay may be to tell a story, to describe, to explain, to persuade, to entertain, or to do several of these at once. Essays do not require one particular kind of order, and they don't have to have a plot, as short stories do. Instead, authors can present events in the order that seems best to them. Anaya's writing is rich in **imagery**, word pictures that appeal to the five senses. He also draws attention to his Mexican-American background by the **repetition** of Spanish phrases. "A Celebration of Grandfathers" is a **reflective essay**. In such an essay, the author explores many sides of a topic about which he or she has deep personal feelings.

essay a short nonfiction work on any subject

purpose a nonfiction writer's main idea or goal

imagery a picture in the reader's mind created by words

repetition using a word, phrase, or image more than once, for emphasis

reflective essay a personal essay exploring an author's feelings

Reading on Your Own As you read this selection, you may want to pause from time to time to summarize what Anaya has written. Ask yourself, "What is he trying to tell me in this section?" Use your own words to describe what you have just read—to a partner or silently to yourself.

Writing on Your Own List the letters from the word *grandfather* in a column on a piece of paper. After each letter, write a word describing a grandfather that begins with that letter.

Vocabulary Focus Anaya uses New Mexico as a backdrop for this story. This southwestern part of the United States was once part of Mexico. The place names in New Mexico are often in Spanish, the language of the people who settled there. For example, the Rio Grande, which separates Texas from Mexico, is a Spanish term meaning *Grand River*. As you read, look for other Spanish place names.

Think Before You Read What does the word *grandfather* make you think about? How is it different from *granddad* or *gramps*, for example?

A Celebration of Grandfathers

As you read, try to decide what the author's main purpose is in this reflective essay.

"Buenos días le dé Dios, abuelo." God give you a good day, grandfather. This is how I was taught as a child to greet my grandfather, or any grown person. It was a greeting of respect, a **cultural** value to be passed on from generation to generation, this respect for the old ones.

The old people I remember from my childhood were strong in their beliefs, and as we lived daily with them we learned a wise path of life to follow. They had something important to share with the young, and when they spoke the young listened. These old abuelos and abuelitas had worked the earth all their lives, and so they knew the value of **nurturing**, they knew the **sensitivity** of the earth. The daily struggle called for cooperation, and so every person contributed to the social fabric, and each person was respected for his contribution.

Abuelos and *abuelitas* are grandfathers and grandmothers.

The old ones had looked deep into the web that connects all **animate** and **inanimate** forms of life, and they recognized the great design of the **creation**.

Anaya uses imagery to describe the *web* connecting everything in the world. As you read, look for other images.

These *ancianos* from the cultures of the Rio Grande, living side by side, sharing, growing together, they knew the rhythms and cycles of time, from the preparation of the earth in the spring to the digging of the acequias that brought the water to the dance of harvest in the fall. They shared good

Ancianos are old people. *Acequias* are irrigation ditches.

cultural relating to the beliefs and customs of a group	**sensitivity** able to be easily hurt	**inanimate** nonliving, unmoving
nurturing feeding or caring for	**animate** living, conscious	**creation** the world

times and hard times. They helped each other through the **epidemics** and the personal **tragedies**, and they shared what little they had when the hot winds burned the land and no rain came. They learned that to **survive** one had to share in the process of life.

Hard workers all, they tilled the earth and farmed, ran the herds and spun wool, and carved their saints and their kachinas from cottonwood late in the winter nights. All worked with a deep faith which perplexes the modern mind.

Kachinas are small wooden dolls that represent the spirits of ancestors or gods.

Their faith shone in their eyes; it was in the strength of their grip, in the **creases** time wove into their faces. When they spoke, they spoke plainly and with few words, and they meant what they said. When they prayed, they went straight to the source of life. When there were good times, they knew how to dance in celebration and how to prepare the foods of the fiestas. All this they passed on to the young, so that a new generation would know what they had known, so the string of life would not be broken.

Fiestas are feasts or parties.

Today we would say that the old abuelitos lived **authentic** lives.

Newcomers to New Mexico often say that time seems to move slowly here. I think they mean they have come in contact with the inner strength of the people, a strength so solid it causes time itself to pause. Think of it. Think of the high, northern New Mexico villages, or the lonely ranches on the open llano. Think of the Indian pueblo which lies as solid as rock in the face of time. Remember the old people whose eyes seem like windows that peer into a distant past that makes absurdity of our **contemporary** world. That is what one feels when one **encounters** the old ones and their land, a pausing of time.

The *llano* is a plain. A *pueblo* is an Indian village in the Southwest.

We have all felt time stand still. We have all been in the presence of power, the knowledge of the old ones, the majestic peace of a mountain stream or an aspen grove or red buttes

A *butte* is a steep hill with a flat top.

epidemics widespread diseases	**survive** to go on living	**contemporary** modern
	creases folds; wrinkles	
tragedies misfortunes, suffering	**authentic** genuine; real	**encounters** meets or comes upon

rising into blue sky. We have all felt the light of dusk **permeate** the earth and cause time to pause in its flow.

I felt this when first touched by the spirit of Ultima, the old *curandera* who appears in my first novel, *Bless Me, Ultima.* This is how the young Antonio describes what he feels:

> When she came the beauty of the llano
> unfolded before my eyes, and the gurgling waters
> of the river sang to the hum of the turning earth.
> The magical time of childhood stood still, and the
> pulse of the living earth pressed its mystery into
> my living blood. She took my hand, and the silent,
> magic powers she possessed made beauty from the
> raw, sun-baked llano, the green river valley, and
> the blue bowl which was the white sun's home. My
> bare feet felt the throbbing earth, and my body
> trembled with excitement. Time stood still . . .

At other times, in other places, when I have been privileged to be with the old ones, to learn, I have felt this inner reserve of strength upon which they draw. I have been held motionless and speechless by the power of curanderas. I have felt the same power when I hunted with Cruz, high on the Taos mountain, where it was more than the **incredible** beauty of the mountain bathed in morning light, more than the shining of the quivering aspen, but a connection with life, as if a shining strand of light connected the particular and the **cosmic**. That feeling is an epiphany of time, a standing still of time.

But not all of our old ones are curanderos or hunters on the mountain. My grandfather was a plain man, a farmer from Puerto de Luna on the Pecos River. He was probably a descendent of those people who spilled over the mountain from Taos, following the Pecos River in search of farmland. There in that river valley he settled and raised a large family.

Bearded and walrus-mustached, he stood five feet tall, but to me as a child he was a giant. I remember him most for his silence. In the summers my parents sent me to live with him

A *curandera* is a medicine woman.

An *epiphany* is a moment when a character discovers an important truth. Here, Anaya experiences "a standing still of time."

| permeate to enter; to soak into | incredible hard to believe | cosmic relating to the universe |

on his farm, for I was to learn the ways of a farmer. My uncles also lived in that valley, the valley called Puerto de Luna, there where only the flow of the river and the whispering of the wind marked time. For me it was a magical place.

Puerto de Luna means port of the moon.

I remember once, while out hoeing the fields, I came upon an anthill, and before I knew it I was badly bitten. After he had covered my **welts** with the cool mud from the irrigation ditch, my grandfather calmly said: "Know where you stand." That is the way he spoke, in short phrases, to the point.

One very dry summer, the river dried to a trickle, there was no water for the fields. The young plants withered and died. In my sadness and with the impulses of youth I said, "I wish it would rain!" My grandfather touched me, looked up in the sky and whispered, "Pray for rain."

At this point, Anaya moves from general reflections on the wisdom of old people to specific memories of his own grandfather.

In his language there was a difference. He felt connected to the cycles that brought the rain or kept it from us. His prayer was a meaningful action, because he was a **participant** with the forces that filled our world, he was not a bystander.

A young man died at the village one summer. A very **tragic** death. He was dragged by his horse. When he was found I cried, for the boy was my friend. I did not understand why death had come to one so young. My grandfather took me aside and said: "Think of the death of the trees and the fields in the fall. The leaves fall, and everything rests, as if dead. But they bloom again in the spring. Death is only this small **transformation** in life."

welts lumps

participant one who takes part in

tragic sad, unfortunate

transformation a change

These are the things I remember, these fleeting images, few words.

I remember him driving his horse-drawn wagon into Santa Rosa in the fall when he brought his harvest produce to sell in the town. What a tower of strength seemed to come in that small man huddled on the seat of the giant wagon. One click of his tongue and the horses obeyed, stopped or turned as he wished. He never raised his whip. How unlike today when so much teaching is done with loud words and threatening hands.

I would run to greet the wagon, and the wagon would stop. "Buenos días le dé Dios, abuelo," I would say. This was the **prescribed** greeting of **esteem** and respect. Only after the greeting was given could we approach these **venerable** old people. "Buenos días le dé Dios, mi hijo," he would answer and smile, and then I could jump up on the wagon and sit at his side. Then I, too, became a king as I rode next to the old man who smelled of earth and sweat and other deep **aromas** from the orchards and fields of Puerto de Luna.

Mi hijo means my son.

We were all sons and daughters to him. But today the sons and daughters are breaking with the past, putting aside los abuelitos. The old values are threatened, and threatened most where it comes to those relationships with the old people. If we don't take the time to watch and feel the years of their final transformation, a part of our **humanity** will be **lessened**.

I grew up speaking Spanish, and oh! how difficult it was to learn English. Sometimes I would give up and cry out that I couldn't learn. Then he would say, "Ten paciencia." Have patience. *Paciencia*, a word with the strength of centuries, a word that said that someday we would **overcome**. *Paciencia*, how soothing a word coming from this old man who could still sling hundred-pound bags over his shoulder, chop wood

---

prescribed a rule to be followed

esteem honor

venerable aged; respected

aromas pleasant smells

humanity human beings

lessened taken away

overcome to win or get the better of

for hours on end, and hitch up his own horses and ride to town and back in one day.

"You have to learn the language of the Americanos," he said. "Me, I will live my last days in my valley. You will live in a new time, the time of the gringos."

A new time did come, a new time is here. How will we form it so it is fruitful? We need to know where we stand. We need to speak softly and respect others, and to share what we have. We need to pray not for **material** gain, but for rain for the fields, for the sun to nurture growth, for nights in which we can sleep in peace, and for a harvest in which everyone can share. Simple lessons from a simple man. These lessons he learned from his past which was deep and strong as the currents of the river of life, a life which could be stronger than death.

He was a man; he died. Not in his valley, but nevertheless cared for by his sons and daughters and flocks of grandchildren. At the end, I would enter his room which carried the smell of medications and Vicks, the faint **pungent** odor of urine, and cigarette smoke. Gone were the aroma of the fields, the strength of his young manhood. Gone also was his patience in the face of crippling old age. Small things bothered him; he shouted or turned sour when his **expectations** were not met. It was because he could not care for himself, because he was returning to that state of childhood, and all those wishes and desires were now wrapped in a crumbling old body.

"Ten paciencia," I once said to him, and he smiled. "I didn't know I would grow this old," he said. "Now, I can't even roll my own cigarettes." I rolled a cigarette for him, placed it in his mouth and lit it. I asked him why he smoked, the doctor had said it was bad for him. "I like to see the smoke rise," he said. He would smoke and doze, and his quilt was spotted with little burns where the cigarettes dropped. One of us had to sit and watch to make sure a fire didn't start.

Gringos are foreigners— Americans.

Why does Anaya repeat the phrase, "Ten paciencia," to his grandfather?

material physical; real	**expectations** what is expected or looked forward to
pungent sharp	

I would sit and look at him and remember what was said of him when he was a young man. He could mount a wild horse and break it, and he could ride as far as any man. He could dance all night at a dance, then work the acequia the following day. He helped neighbors, they helped him. He married, raised children. Small legends, the kind that make up everyman's life.

He was 94 when he died. Family, neighbors, and friends gathered; they all agreed he had led a rich life. I remembered the last years, the years he spent in bed. And as I remember now, I am reminded that it is too easy to romanticize old age. Sometimes we forget the pain of the transformation into old age, we forget the natural breaking down of the body. Not all go gentle into the last years, some go crying and cursing, forgetting the names of those they loved the most, withdrawing into an **internal anguish** few of us can know. May we be granted the patience and care to deal with our ancianos.

For some time we haven't looked at these changes and needs of the old ones. The American image created by the mass media is an image of youth, not of old age. It is the beautiful and the young who are praised in this society. If **analyzed** carefully, we see that same damaging thought has crept into the way society views the old. In response to the old, the mass media have just created old people who act like the young. It is only the healthy, pink-cheeked, outgoing, older persons we are shown in the media. And they are always selling something, as if an entire generation of old people were salesmen in their lives. Commercials show very lively old men, who must always be in excellent health according to the new myth, selling insurance policies or real estate as they are out golfing; older women selling coffee or toilet paper to those just married. That image does not **illustrate** the real life of the old ones.

Do you agree with the author? Are the older people you see in magazines and on television like the older people you know?

internal inside; unspoken	**analyzed** studied in detail	**illustrate** to show; to picture
anguish great pain		

Real life takes into account the natural cycle of growth and change. My grandfather pointed to the leaves falling from the tree. So time brings with its transformation the often painful, wearing-down process. Vision blurs, health **wanes**; even the act of walking carries with it the painful reminder of the autumn of life. But this process is something to be faced, not something to be hidden away by false images. Yes, the old can be young at heart, but in their own way, with their own dignity. They do not have to copy the always-young image of the Hollywood star.

My grandfather wanted to return to his valley to die. But by then the families of the valley had left in search of a better future. It is only now that there seems to be a return to the valley, a **revival**. The new generation seeks its roots, that value

wanes fades   **revival** a renewed interest in

of love for the land moves us to return to the place where our ancianos formed the culture.

I returned to Puerto de Luna last summer, to join the community in celebration of the founding of the church. I drove by my grandfather's home, my uncles' ranches, the neglected adobe washing down into the earth from whence it came. And I wondered, how might the values of my grandfather's generation live in our own? What can we **retain** to see us through these hard times? I was to become a farmer, and I became a writer. As I plow and plant my words, do I nurture as my grandfather did in his fields and orchards? The answers are not simple.

"They don't make men like that anymore," is a phrase we hear when one does honor to a man. I am glad I knew my grandfather. I am glad there are still times when I can see him in my dreams, hear him in my **reverie**. Sometimes I think I catch a whiff of that earthy aroma that was his smell, just as in lonely times sometimes I catch the fragrance of Ultima's herbs. Then I smile. How strong these people were to leave such a lasting impression.

So, as I would greet my abuelo long ago, it would help us all to greet the old ones we know with this kind and respectful greeting: "Buenos días le dé Dios."

What is the effect of the repetition of this Spanish greeting at the beginning, middle, and end of the essay?

retain keep   **reverie** a daydream

Directions Choose the letter of the best answer or write the answer using complete sentences.

Comprehension: Identifying Facts

1. According to Anaya, what is the proper greeting for a young person to say to a grown-up?
   A Abuelitas
   B Buenos días le dé Dios
   C Llano
   D Ancianos

2. Where did the ancianos (old people) come from?
   A the Rio Grande culture
   B hijo
   C curandera
   D none of these responses

3. Who is Ultima?

4. Where was the grandfather from?

5. Why does the author spend his summers with his grandfather?

6. What does the author's grandfather say when he was badly bitten by ants?

7. What does the grandfather say was only a small transformation in life?

8. According to his grandfather, why does the author have to learn English?

9. How old is the grandfather when he dies?

10. Why does Anaya return to Puerto de Luna after his grandfather dies?

Comprehension: Putting Ideas Together

11. What do the ancianos (old ones) recognize about life?
    A that everyone is important
    B the great design of life
    C how to cooperate
    D all of the above

12. What does the author think people feel when they encounter an old person?
    A that they are out of touch
    B a pausing of time
    C a feeling of sadness
    D regret

13. Where does the author feel the strength of the ancianos (old people)?

14. How does Anaya describe his grandfather?

15. How does his grandfather help Anaya accept the death of his young friend?

16. How does Anaya feel when he rides beside his grandfather in his wagon?

17. How does the author use the phrase *ten paciencia* ("be patient") in this story?

After Reading continued on next page

A Celebration of Grandfathers   by Rudolfo A. Anaya

18. How does the author care for his grandfather when he is in the hospital?

19. How does the mass media present old people, according to the author?

20. What is the final message the author gives in this essay?

Understanding Literature: Reflective Essay

A reflective essay is one in which the author stops to reflect, or think about events that have happened in the past. In these kinds of essays, authors look at a situation in many different ways. They look for the way things are connected. They explore how they felt. They try to make sense of what has happened.

People who write reflective essays such as "A Celebration of Grandfathers" have one main purpose—they want to share with readers their personal thoughts and feelings about something. In general, essays can be grouped according to their purpose. Some tell a story, some describe, some explain, some persuade, some entertain. Many essays have more than one purpose. Although Anaya's essay is considered a reflective essay, readers may also find that it describes, explains, or entertains.

21. For what main purpose do authors write reflective essays?

22. What ideas did Anaya want to share in his essay?

23. In your opinion, does this essay also describe, explain, persuade, or entertain readers? Why or why not?

24. Do you agree with Anaya's opinions? Explain.

25. If you were going to write a reflective essay on the place of older people in your life, what would be the main idea you would want to tell your readers? Why?

Critical Thinking

26. What clues does the title of this essay give you about what to expect?

27. Through which event do you learn the most about Anaya's grandfather?

28. Anaya says that old people pass their knowledge to younger people. How is this like what he has done in his essay?

29. How does this essay compare with the essay about the *Kon-Tiki*? Use the Venn Diagram as described in Appendix A to outline the similarities and differences in mood, tone, characters, events, and theme.

Thinking Creatively

30. How do you want to be remembered by your grandchildren?

Grammar Check

A *clause* is a group of words. An *independent*, or main, clause is a group of words that has a noun that serves as a subject and a verb. A subordinate or *dependent* clause cannot stand alone. An independent clause is a complete thought. A dependent clause needs more details to make a complete thought. It depends on an independent clause.

For example, in this essay, Anaya chooses to use both kinds of clauses to create sentences of varying lengths. He says, for example, ". . . before I knew it I was badly bitten." The two clauses Anaya used here are "before I knew it" and "I was badly bitten." "Before I knew it" is the dependent clause because the reader needs more information to complete the thought. "I was badly bitten" is the independent clause because it is a complete thought. Write down five examples of sentences in this essay that contain both dependent and independent clauses. Identify the clauses.

 ## Writing on Your Own

Write a reflective essay about the lessons your grandparents or other older people have taught you. You can find writing tips to help you in Appendix C.

 ## Speaking

Speakers sometimes organize their presentations according to cause and effect. Look at this example, taken from Anaya's essay:

Cause: The grandfather was a farmer.
Effect: He often smelled of the earth.

Outline a speech that you might give to your class, showing how the details of Anaya's essay might be organized by cause and effect.

 ## Listening

List some examples from this essay that show that the grandfather really listened to his grandson.

 ## Research

Use an atlas to locate the Pecos River, the Rio Grande, the Taos Mountains, and Puerto de Luna. What can you determine about the geography and climate of this area, based on the maps you found?

BEFORE READING THE SELECTION

Of Dry Goods and Black Bow Ties   by Yoshiko Uchida

Yoshiko Uchida
1921–1992

About the Author

On December 7, 1941, the day Japan bombed Pearl Harbor, Yoshiko Uchida was a senior at the University of California, Berkeley. Even though she had been born in California, Uchida, her family, and more than 100,000 other Japanese Americans were considered a risk to the safety of the United States. They were all forced to move to and stay in internment camps in the desert Southwest.

At the camp, Yoshiko Uchida taught at a school for the children. She began gathering details of her experiences. These would inspire many of her fiction and nonfiction works. Uchida once said that she wrote to give young Japanese Americans a sense of their own history. Her first book, *The Dancing Kettle and Other Japanese Tales,* is a collection of stories she heard as a child. Traveling to Japan after the war, she gathered more stories. These became part of two other collections of folktales, *The Magic Listening Cap* and *The Sea of Gold, and Other Tales from Japan.*

In 1971, her book *Journey to Topaz* was published. It told about life in the internment camp through the eyes of an 11 year old. In it, she explores what it means to be both Japanese and American at a time the two countries were at war.

About the Selection

In "Of Dry Goods and Black Bow Ties," Yoshiko Uchida shows what she called "the strength of spirit and the sense of hope and purpose" in the Japanese Americans she knew. She said she hopes her Japanese American readers will read to see the meaning of their past and get a greater sense of self-esteem. She hopes all readers will go beyond their images of what it means to be Japanese American and celebrate what she calls "our common humanity."

Literary Terms A **biography** is the story of a person's life, written by someone other than that person. "Of Dry Goods and Black Bow Ties" is a **biographical essay**, which means it is a true story. In it, the author introduces us to Mr. Shozo Shimada. The essay explores the character of this old and honorable gentleman. Uchida does this in part by using an unusual **symbol**—a black bow tie. Biographers make their subjects come alive in many of the same ways fiction writers do. Writers of biographical essays choose events and details that reveal people's personalities and values. The characters in this essay are Japanese immigrants who came to this country believing in the promise of America.

Reading on Your Own As you read, use the Character Analysis Guide described in Appendix A to list events in the life of Mr. Shimada. Think about his reactions in each situation. What do they tell you about the kind of person he is?

Writing on Your Own What do you feel like when you disappoint people? Create an e-mail you might send to a friend explaining how you feel.

Vocabulary Focus Mr. Shimada was involved in selling and using dry goods, or clothing and fabric. Many of the vocabulary terms in this essay are related to that business. *Dry goods* are things that are not measured by liquid amounts, such as quarts or pints. Uchida talks her father into wearing a *four-in-hand tie*—a necktie rather than a bow tie. Mr. Shimada becomes a *dressmaker*, a person who designs and sews dresses. What other dry goods or clothing terms do you find as you read? You can use context clues or a dictionary to help you unlock their meanings.

Think Before You Read What do you think of when you see a man wearing a bow tie?

biography the story of a person's life, written by someone other than the person

biographical essay a written work about true events in a person's life

symbol something that represents something else

OF DRY GOODS
and Black Bow Ties

A *four-in-hand* tie is a necktie.

As you read, notice the details the author has chosen to describe Mr. Shimada, the subject of this biographical essay.

Long after reaching the age of sixty, when my father was persuaded at last to wear a **conservative** four-in-hand tie, it was not because of his family's urging, but because Mr. Shimada (I shall call him that) had died. Until then, for some forty years, my father had always worn a plain black bow tie, a formality which was required on his first job in America and which he had continued to observe as faithfully as his father before him had worn his samurai sword.

My father came to America in 1906 when he was not yet twenty-one. Sailing from Japan on a small six-thousand-ton ship which was buffeted all the way by rough seas, he landed in Seattle on a **bleak** January day. He revived himself with the first solid meal he had enjoyed in many days, and then allowed himself one day of rest to restore his sagging spirits. Early on the second morning, wearing a stiff new bowler, he went to see Mr. Shozo Shimada to whom he carried a letter of introduction.

A *bowler* is a derby hat.

At that time, Shozo Shimada was Seattle's most successful Japanese business man. He owned a chain of dry goods stores which extended not only from Vancouver to Portland, but to cities in Japan as well. He had come to America in 1880, penniless but enterprising, and sought work as a laborer. It wasn't long, however, before he saw the **futility** of trying to **compete** with American laborers whose bodies were twice

Dry goods include clothing, cloth, lace, thread, buttons, and so on.

---

conservative usual, typical

bleak gloomy

futility uselessness

compete to try hard to gain something

his in muscle and bulk. He knew he would never go far as a laborer, but he did possess another skill that could give him a start toward better things. He knew how to sew. It was a matter of **expediency** over masculine pride. He set aside his shovel, bought a second-hand sewing machine, and hung a dressmaker's sign in his window. He was in business.

In those days, there were some Japanese women in Seattle who had neither homes nor families nor sewing machines, and were delighted to find a friendly Japanese person to do some sewing for them. They flocked to Mr. Shimada with bolts of cloth, **elated** to discover a dressmaker who could speak their native tongue and, although a male, sew western-styled dresses for them.

Mr. Shimada acquainted himself with the fine points of turning a seam, fitting sleeves, and coping with the slippery folds of silk, and soon the women told their friends and gave him enough business to keep him thriving and able to establish a healthy bank account. He became a trusted friend and **confidant** to many of them and soon they began to bring him what money they earned for safekeeping.

"Keep our money for us, Shimada-san," they urged, refusing to go to American banks whose tellers spoke in a language they could not understand.

> The addition of -san to Japanese names and titles shows respect.

At first the money **accumulated** slowly and Mr. Shimada used a pair of old socks as a **repository**, stuffing them into a far corner of his drawer beneath his union suits. But after a time, Mr. Shimada's private bank began to overflow and he soon found it necessary to **replenish** his supply of socks.

> Union suits means underwear.

He went to a small dry goods store downtown, and as he glanced about at the buttons, threads, needles and laces, it occurred to him that he owed it to the women to **invest**

expediency self-interest	**confidant** someone trusted with your secrets	**replenish** to build up again
elated delighted; thrilled	**accumulated** piled up	**invest** to put money into something, hoping for a profit
	repository place for safekeeping	

their savings in a business venture with more future than the dark recesses of his bureau drawer. That night he called a group of them together.

"Think, ladies," he began. "What are the two basic needs of the Japanese living in Seattle? Clothes to wear and food to eat," he answered himself. "Is that not right? Every man must buy a shirt to put on his back and pickles and rice for his stomach."

The women marveled at Mr. Shimada's cleverness as he spread before them his fine plans for a Japanese dry goods store that would not only carry everything available in an American dry goods store, but Japanese foodstuff as well. That was the beginning of the first Shimada Dry Goods Store on State Street.

By the time my father appeared, Mr. Shimada had long since abandoned his sewing machine and was well on his way to becoming a business **tycoon**. Although he had opened cautiously with such stock items as ginghams, flannel, handkerchiefs, socks, shirts, overalls, umbrellas and ladies' silk and cotton stockings, he now carried tins of salt rice crackers, bottles of soy sauce, vinegar, ginger root, fish-paste cakes, bean paste, Japanese pickles, dried mushrooms, salt fish, red beans, and just about every item of canned food that could be shipped from Japan. In addition, his was the first Japanese store to install a U.S. Post Office Station, and he thereby attained the right to fly an American flag in front of the large sign that bore the name of his shop.

When my father first saw the big American flag fluttering in front of Mr. Shimada's shop, he was **overcome** with admiration and awe. He expected that Mr. Shozo Shimada

Why does Mr. Shimada call the women together?

---

tycoon a rich business person

overcome to make weak or helpless

would be the finest of Americanized Japanese gentlemen, and when he met him, he was not disappointed.

Although Mr. Shimada was not very tall, he gave the **illusion** of height because of his erect carriage. He wore a spotless black alpaca suit, an **immaculate** white shirt and a white collar so stiff it might have overcome a lesser man. He also wore a black bow tie, black shoes that buttoned up the side and a gold watch whose thick chain looped grandly on his vest. He was probably in his fifties then, a ruddy-faced man whose hair, already turning white, was parted carefully in the center. He was an imposing figure to **confront** a young man fresh from Japan with scarcely a future to look forward to. My father bowed, summoned as much dignity as he could muster, and presented the letter of introduction he carried to him.

An *alpaca* suit was made from the wool of the alpaca, an animal similar to a llama.

Mr. Shimada was quick to sense his need. "Do you know anything about bookkeeping?" he inquired.

"I intend to go to night school to learn this very skill," my father answered.

Mr. Shimada could **assess** a man's qualities in a very few minutes. He looked my father straight in the eye and said, "Consider yourself hired." Then he added, "I have a few basic rules. My employees must at all times wear a clean white shirt and a black bow tie. They must answer the telephone promptly with the words, 'Good morning or good afternoon, Shimada's Dry Goods,' and they must always treat each customer with respect. It never hurts to be polite," he said thoughtfully. "One never knows when one might be **indebted** to even the lowliest of beggars."

My father was impressed with these modest words from a man of such success. He accepted them with a sense of mission and from that day was committed to white shirts and black bow ties, and treated every customer, no matter how humble, with respect and courtesy. When, in later years, he

---

illusion something that appears different from what it is

immaculate very clean

confront to meet face to face

assess to determine the value of

indebted owing a favor

had his own home, he never failed to answer the phone before it could ring twice if at all possible.

My father worked with Mr. Shimada for ten years, becoming first the buyer for his Seattle store and later, manager of the Portland branch. During this time Mr. Shimada continued on a course of **exhilarated expansion**. He established two Japanese banks in Seattle, bought a fifteen-room house outside the dreary confines of the Japanese community and dressed his wife and daughter in velvets and ostrich feathers. When his daughter became eighteen, he sent her to study in Paris, and the party he gave on the eve of her departure, hiring musicians, as well as **caterers** to serve roast turkey, **venison**, baked ham and **champagne**, seemed to **verify** rumors that he had become one of the first Japanese **millionaires** of America.

---

exhilarated excited	**venison** deer meat	**verify** to prove that something is true
expansion growth	**champagne** a sparkling wine	
caterers people who supply prepared food		**millionaires** very rich people

In spite of his **phenomenal** success, however, Mr. Shimada never forgot his early friends nor lost any of his generosity, and this, **ironically** enough, was his undoing. Many of the women for whom he had once sewn dresses were now well established, and they came to him requesting loans with which they and their husbands might open grocery stores and laundries and shoe repair shops. Mr. Shimada helped them all and never demanded any **collateral**. He operated his banks on faith and trust and gave no thought to such common **prudence** as maintaining a reserve.

When my father was called to a new position with a large Japanese firm in San Francisco, Mr. Shimada came down to Portland to extend personally his good wishes. He took Father to a Chinese dinner and told him over the peanut duck and chow mein that he would like always to be considered a friend.

"If I can ever be of assistance to you," he said, "don't ever hesitate to call." And with a firm shake of the hand, he wished my father well.

That was in 1916. My father wrote regularly to Mr. Shimada telling him of his new job, of his bride, and later, of his two children. Mr. Shimada did not write often, but each Christmas he sent a box of Oregon apples and pears, and at New Year's a slab of heavy white rice paste from his Seattle shop.

In 1929 the letters and gifts stopped coming, and Father learned from friends in Seattle that both of Mr. Shimada's banks had failed. He immediately **dispatched** a letter to Mr. Shimada, but it was returned unopened. The next news he had was that Mr. Shimada had had to sell all of his shops. My father was now manager of the San Francisco branch of his firm. He wrote once more asking Mr. Shimada if there was anything he could do to help. The letter did not come back, but there was no reply, and my father did not write again. After all, how do you offer help to the head of a fallen empire? It seemed almost **irreverent**.

> Why was Mr. Shimada so loyal to his friends?

> In 1929 the stock market crashed and the Great Depression began. Many banks and businesses failed.

phenomenal amazing	**collateral** property as protection for payment	**dispatched** sent
ironically unlike what one would expect	**prudence** wisdom; common sense	**irreverent** not offering the proper respect

It was many years later that Mr. Shimada appeared one night at our home in Berkeley. In the dim light of the front porch my mother was startled to see an elderly gentleman wearing striped pants, a morning coat and a shabby black hat. In his hand he carried a small black **satchel**. When she invited him inside, she saw that the morning coat was faded, and his shoes badly in need of a shine.

A *morning coat* is a jacket with tails in back, worn for daytime formal events.

"I am Shimada," he announced with a courtly bow, and it was my mother who felt **inadequate** to the occasion. She hurriedly pulled off her apron and went to call my father. When he heard who was in the living room, he put on his coat and tie before going out to greet his old friend.

Mr. Shimada spoke to them about Father's friends in Seattle and about his daughter who was now married and living in Denver. He spoke of a **typhoon** that had recently swept over Japan, and he drank the tea my mother served and ate a piece of her chocolate cake. Only then did he open his black satchel.

"I thought your girls might enjoy these books," he said, as he drew out a brochure describing *The Book of Knowledge*.

"Fourteen volumes that will tell them of the wonders of this world." He spread his arms in a magnificent gesture that recalled his **eloquence** of the past. "I wish I could give them to your children as a personal gift," he added softly.

Without asking the price of the set, my father wrote a check for one hundred dollars and gave it to Mr. Shimada.

Mr. Shimada glanced at the check and said, "You have given me fifty dollars too much." He seemed troubled for only a moment, however, and quickly added, "Ah, the balance is for a deposit, is it? Very well, yours will be the first deposit in my next bank."

"Is your home still in Seattle then?" Father asked cautiously.

satchel a small suitcase

inadequate unable to do what is required

typhoon a powerful storm

eloquence ability to speak with great feeling and expression

"I am living there, yes," Mr. Shimada answered.

And then, suddenly overcome with memories of the past, he spoke in a voice so low he could scarcely be heard.

"I paid back every cent," he murmured. "It took ten years, but I paid it back. All of it. I owe nothing."

"You are a true gentleman, Shimada-san," Father said. "You always will be." Then he pointed to the black tie he wore, saying, "You see, I am still one of the Shimada men."

That was the last time my father saw Shozo Shimada. Some time later he heard that he had returned to Japan as penniless as the day he set out for America.

It wasn't until the Christmas after we heard of Mr. Shimada's death that I ventured to give my father a silk four-in-hand tie. It was charcoal gray and flecked with threads of silver. My father looked at it for a long time before he tried it on, and then fingering it gently, he said, "Well, perhaps it is time now that I put away my black bow ties."

How would you describe the character of Mr. Shimada?

How is the black bow tie used as a symbol in this story?

Directions Choose the letter of the best answer or write the answer using complete sentences.

Comprehension: Identifying Facts

1. What does Mr. Shimada do to earn money when he comes to America?
   A He opens a bank.
   B He returns to Japan.
   C He becomes a dressmaker.
   D He buys a store.

2. At first, what does Mr. Shimada do with the money people give him for safekeeping?
   A buys more fabric
   B keeps it in a sock
   C invests it in the stock market
   D sends it to Japan

3. What does Mr. Shimada say were the two basic needs of the Japanese living in Seattle?

4. What makes Mr. Shimada's store different?

5. What are some of the food items available in Mr. Shimada's store?

6. How does Mr. Shimada operate his banks?

7. What does Mr. Shimada send to the Uchidas each Christmas?

8. What happens to Mr. Shimada's banks in 1929?

9. What does Mr. Shimada say about his past business troubles?

10. When does Uchida's father finally put on a long necktie?

Comprehension: Putting Ideas Together

11. How does Mr. Shimada earn the confidence of the Japanese ladies in his neighborhood?
   A He speaks Japanese.
   B He is good at his job.
   C He could sew western-style dresses.
   D all of the above

12. How does Mr. Shimada suggest the women in his community invest their money?
   A in a Japanese store
   B in an American store
   C in the bank
   D in encyclopedias

13. What does the U.S. flag flying outside Mr. Shimada's store mean?

14. What are Mr. Shimada's rules for his employees?

15. How does Mr. Shimada use his wealth?

16. Why is generosity Mr. Shimada's downfall?

17. Why does Mr. Shimada come to visit the Uchida family years later?

18. What details in the essay show how Mr. Shimada feels about his business failure?

19. Which people in the essay call Mr. Shimada "Shimada-san"? What does that say about this man?

20. Why does Mr. Uchida continue wearing a black bow tie until well after Mr. Shimada dies?

Understanding Literature: Biographical Essay

In writing a biography, authors describe not only people's lives, but also the times in which they lived. These details help readers understand the person being written about.

"Of Dry Goods and Black Bow Ties" is set in Seattle, Washington. Many Japanese American immigrants settled there in the late 1800s and early 1900s, in a place they called Nihonmachi, or Japantown. People like the author's father and Mr. Shimada came to America looking for the opportunity to improve their lives. In her biographical essay, Uchida recreates this world through details and carefully selected events.

21. What did Japanese immigrants at this time think about America? What evidence can you find in the story?

22. What kind of dresses does Mr. Shimada sew? What does this say about Japanese American women of the time?

23. In his first store, Mr. Shimada sells Japanese food products. What does this tell you about Japanese American culture at this time?

24. How does Mr. Shimada's appearance show his character and values? What details does the author provide about the way he looks?

25. List two other details of early Japanese American culture that you learn in this essay.

Critical Thinking

26. How is a black bow tie used as a symbol in this story?

27. How does the Uchida family feel about Mr. Shimada? Give examples.

28. Why does the author's father finally decide "it is time" to put away his black bow ties?

29. How are Mr. Shimada and Rudolfo Anaya's grandfather similar? How are they different?

After Reading **continued on next page**

Of Dry Goods and Black Bow Ties by Yoshiko Uchida

Thinking Creatively

30. Uchida uses the black bow tie as a symbol of Japanese-American workers. What symbol might she use for American workers today? Explain.

 Grammar Check

Modifiers change, or modify the meanings of words around them. Modifiers that are not in the proper place in a sentence can confuse readers. In this sentence, "Only then did he open his black satchel," the modifying word is *only*. Uchida placed the modifier correctly. Since it relates to the word *then*, it is placed right next to it. Consider the different meaning Uchida would have created if she had written, "Then he opened his only black satchel." In a similar way, this sentence has a dangling or misplaced modifier: "Sailing from Japan, his business failed soon after." "Sailing from Japan" is a modifying phrase. People might read this sentence and think that the business sailed from Japan, which is impossible. Using the modifying group of words correctly would give you this sentence, "Sailing from Japan, the man landed in Seattle."

 Writing on Your Own

Create a poster or flyer that Mr. Shimada might have used to announce the opening of his first store.

 Speaking and Listening

Imagine that you are staying with the Uchida family when Mr. Shimada visits. Since you don't speak Japanese, you have to depend on other clues to understand what is happening. Describe how Mr. Shimada, the mother, and the father stand and gesture. Explore the tones they may use as they talk and listen to each other. Explain what these nonverbal signals tell you about these characters and their relationship to each other.

 Media and Technology

Japanese immigrants like Shozo Shimada faced many problems when they came to this country. To see what they faced, use the Internet to locate newspaper articles on this topic. Search San Francisco museums to find more information on the history of the city.

BEFORE READING THE SELECTION

from *Gather Together in My Name* by *Maya Angelou*

About the Author

On a clear, cold January day in 1993, Maya Angelou read her poem "On the Pulse of Morning" at the inauguration of President Bill Clinton. She was the first African American and the first woman to present her work at such an occasion.

Angelou was named Marguerite Johnson when she was born in 1928 in St. Louis. She spent most of her troubled childhood in Stamps, Arkansas. When she was still a teen she left home, determined to find her own way.

For a while, Angelou took any job she could find. She cooked. She served food in a restaurant. She was a dancer. She adopted her new name, the one by which people know her today. In the 1960s, she married a South African freedom fighter and moved to Cairo, Egypt. There she became the editor of the only English-language newspaper in the Middle East. Returning to the United States, she began to publish her writing.

Maya Angelou has written poetry, novels, short stories, plays, and articles. She is probably best known for the five volumes of her **autobiography**. In it, she tells of her life and times as an African American woman.

About the Selection

This excerpt comes from the second in Maya Angelou's series of autobiographical books, *Gather Together in My Name*, published in 1974. The book tells of her life from her late teens through her 20s, as she struggled to leave childhood behind and become her own person. At this point in the story, she calls herself Rita Johnson. She is living with her mother and young son. She dreams of a "knight in shining armor" who will lead her to a new life. Unfortunately, the man who shows up in this essay isn't quite that person.

Maya Angelou
1928–

Objectives

- To read and understand the form and content of an autobiography
- To describe and define humor and tone as tools a writer can use

autobiography
the story of a person's life, written by that person

Before Reading **continued on next page**

from Gather Together in My Name *by Maya Angelou*

humor writing intended to amuse

tone the attitude an author takes toward a subject

Literary Terms An *autobiography* is a true story that is written by the person that actually experienced it. This selection tells about an event in Angelou's life that could be considered both serious and silly. The reader sees the event through the author's eyes. Angelou tells her story with a great deal of **humor**. With this light touch, Angelou describes a highly embarrassing moment. She looks back on this event as an older person, using a kind **tone** that shows how much she respects the person she once was.

Reading on Your Own As you read this essay, look for vocabulary words or sentence structures that tell you how the author feels about her younger self and the embarrassing situation. For example, in the first paragraph, Angelou says that she *knew* her charming prince was going to come and give her many gifts. This language she chose suggests that an older Angelou feels that her younger self wasn't very realistic. However, she says it in a very gentle way.

Writing on Your Own When you were very young, did anything ever happen to you or your family that you felt was embarrassing? Write a journal entry about it. First, use the writer's voice you might have had when the event actually happened to you. Then rewrite the story using your current writer's voice.

Vocabulary Focus You may see some words in this essay that are unfamiliar to you. Words like *sophistication, notion,* and *smirk*, for example, are very challenging. In order to unlock their meanings, you might want to try using a reference book. A *thesaurus* contains words and their *synonyms*, or words that mean almost the same thing. One of the synonyms may be more familiar to you.

Think Before You Read How do you feel when you see something embarrassing happen to another person?

from Gather Together in My Name

My charming prince was going to appear out of the blue and offer me a cornucopia of goodies. I would only have to smile to have them brought to my feet.

R. L. Poole was to prove my dreams at least **partially prophetic**. When I opened the door to his ring and informed him that I was Rita Johnson, his already long face **depressed** another inch.

"The . . . uh . . . dancer?" His voice was slow and cloudy.

Dancer? Of course. I had been a cook, waitress, madam, bus girl—why not a dancer? After all, it was the only thing I had studied.

"Yes, I'm a dancer." I looked at him boldly. "Why?"

"I'm looking for a dancer, to work with me."

I thought he might be a talent scout for a chorus line or maybe the big stage show, featuring colored dancers, called "Change Your Luck."

"Come in."

We sat at the dining-room table and I offered a coffee. He looked me over, one feature at a time. My legs (long), my hips (spare), my breasts (nearly **nonexistent**). He drank the coffee slowly.

"I've studied since I was fourteen," I said. . . .

"I'm Poole. From Chicago." His announcement held no boast, and I was sure that represented sophistication rather than false modesty. "I do rhythm tap and I want a

> A *cornucopia* is also called a horn of plenty. The author uses this image and the "charming prince" to suggest that she was hoping for a better life.

> Poole doesn't brag, and Rita is sure this means he is polished and worldly, everything she wants to be.

---

partially partly

prophetic able to tell the future

depressed fell

nonexistent not there

To *flash* means to frame or highlight another dancer. A.G.V.A. stands for American Guild of Variety Artists, a performers' union.

Scale means the minimum union wage: $22.50 an hour. *Gigs* are jobs. The *Local* is the union office. *Ends* means money.

Notice the details in this autobiography.

girl partner. She doesn't have to do much but flash. Are you agva?" ("Flash" and "A.G.V.A." were words unknown to me.)

I sat quietly and looked at him. Let him figure it out for himself.

"I met the woman at the record shop and she told me about you. Said all you talked about was dancing. She gave me your address.

"Some cats from the Local, musicians, straightened me out with the contacts for a few gigs. Scale is twenty-two fifty, but I'll do a few under scale to get some ends together."

I hadn't the slightest notion of what he was talking about. Scale. Agva. Gigs. Local. Ends.

"More coffee?" I went into the kitchen, walking like a model, chin down and **sternum** up, and my tail bone tucked under like white women.

I put on a fresh pot of coffee and tried desperately to decide on a role for myself. Should I be mysterious and **sultry**, asking nothing, answering all questions with a knowing smirk, or should I be the open, friendly, palsy every-boy's-sister girl-next-door type? No decision came to my mind, so I went back into the dining room, my legs stuck together with fine **decorum**.

"What did you study?"

"Ballet. Modern Ballet and the Theory of Dance." I made it sound like Advanced Thermonuclear Propulsion.

His face fell again.

"Any tap-dancing?"

"No."

"**Jazz**?"

"No."

"Acrobatics?"

Rita mentions some of the popular dances of the time.

"No." I was losing him, so I jumped in the gap. "I used to win every jitterbug contest. I can do the Texas Hop. The Off Time. The boogie-woogie. The Camel Walk. The New Coup de Grâce. And I can do the split."

sternum the breastbone	**decorum** proper behavior	**jazz** popular dance with strong rhythms
sultry sexy		

With that I stood up, straddle-legged, and looked down into his sad face, then I began to slide down to the floor.

I was unprepared for the movement (I had on a straight skirt), but R.L. was less ready than I. As my legs slipped apart and down, I lifted my arms in the graceful ballet position number 1 and watched the **impresario's** face race from mild interest to **incredulous**. My hem caught mid-thigh and I felt my **equilibrium** teeter. With a quick slight of hand I jerked up my skirt and continued my downward glide. I hummed a little snatch of song during the last part of the slither, and kept my mind on Sonja Henie in her cute little tutus.

Unfortunately, I hadn't practiced the split in months, so my pelvic bones resisted with force. I was only two inches from the floor, and I gave a couple of little bounces. I accomplished more than I planned. My skirt seams gave before my bones surrendered. Then my left foot got caught between the legs of Mother's heavy oak table, and the other foot jumped at the gas heater and captured the pipe that ran from the jets into the wall. Pinned down at my **extremities** with the tendons in my legs screaming for ease, I felt as if I were being crucified to the floor, but in true "show must go on" fashion I kept my back straight and my arms uplifted in a position that would have made Pavlova proud. Then I looked at R.L. to see

Ballet is dance that combines different poses and steps with leaps and turns. There are five basic positions, or poses, in ballet—Rita has raised her arms in the correct pose for first position.

A *tutu* is a short skirt worn by ballet dancers.

Pavlova was a famous ballet dancer.

impresario someone who manages or directs a show

incredulous not believing

equilibrium balance

extremities hands or feet

How does the use of humor affect the tone of this story?

Avaricious means greedy. Here, the table didn't want to give up Rita's leg.

Do you think Rita got the job?

what impression I was making. Pity at my **predicament** was drawing him up from his chair, and **solicitude** was written over his face with a brush wider than a kitchen mop.

My independence and privacy would not allow me to accept help. I lowered my arms and balanced my hands on the floor and jerked my right foot. It held on to the pipe, so I jerked again. I must have been in excellent shape. The pipe came away from the stove, and gas hissed out steadily like ten fat men resting on a summer's day.

R.L. stepped over me and looked down into the gas jet. . . . He swiveled over to the window and opened it as wide as it would go, then back down to the stove. Near the wall at the end of the pipe, he found a tap and turned it. The hissing died and the thick sweetish odor **diluted**.

I had still to **extricate** my other leg from the avaricious table.

R.L. lifted an edge of the table, and my ankle was **miraculously** free. I could have gotten up, but my feelings were so hurt by the stupid clumsiness that I just rolled over on my stomach, beat my hands on the floor and cried like a baby.

There was no doubt that R. L. Poole had just witnessed his strangest **audition**. He could have walked down the hall and out the door, leaving me breathing in the dust of the ancient rug, but he didn't. I heard the chair creak, announcing that he had sat back down.

I was sure he was doing his best to hold in his laughter. I tried for more tears, to irritate him and force him to leave, but the tear ducts had closed and the sound I made was as false as a show girl's eyelashes. Nothing for it but to get up.

I dried my face with dusty hands and lifted my head. R.L. was sitting at the table in the same chair, his head propped up with his hand. The dark-brown face was **somber** and he said quietly, "Well, anyway, you've got nice legs."

predicament a problem	**diluted** watered down; made weak	**miraculously** magically
solicitude concern	**extricate** to untangle	**audition** a tryout
		somber grave, serious

AFTER READING THE SELECTION

from Gather Together in My Name by Maya Angelou

Directions Choose the letter of the best answer or write the answer using complete sentences.

Comprehension: Identifying Facts

1. Who does Rita think R. L. Poole is?
   - **A** a movie producer
   - **B** a musician
   - **C** a talent scout
   - **D** her brother

2. What does Rita tell Poole when he asks her what kind of dance she studied?

3. What dance move does Rita try to do for Poole?

Comprehension: Putting Ideas Together

4. Why does Rita feel confused when Poole starts talking?
   - **A** He speaks very softly.
   - **B** He uses a lot of terms she didn't know.
   - **C** There is a lot of noise in the apartment.
   - **D** She is not paying attention.

5. What happens when Rita tries to impress Poole with her dance move?

6. What are some of the funniest parts of this essay?

Understanding Literature: Autobiography

An autobiography is the story of a person's life, written by the person. The author tells about events and about his or her reactions to these events. An autobiography is a deeply personal work. Authors decide which experiences were most important in shaping their lives.

As writers look back on certain events, they may see them differently than they did at the time they happened. Readers need to decide what the author's tone is toward the material. An experience that seemed earthshaking at the time may be told using a humorous tone.

7. What do you think Angelou remembers most clearly about her first meeting with R. L. Poole? How does she show this in her writing?

8. How might the tone of this essay change if the adult Angelou was still depressed that her audition for Mr. Poole didn't go well?

Critical Thinking

9. How did Rita and R. L. Poole behave in a way that surprised you? That surprised themselves?

After Reading **continued on next page**

from *Gather Together in My Name* by *Maya Angelou*

Thinking Creatively

10. What do you think might have happened if Rita had actually gotten a job with Poole?

 Grammar Check

In formal English, the subjects and verbs in a sentence have to agree with each other. That means that they both have to be written in a single form, or they both have to be written in the plural form. Sometimes young writers get confused when the subject of the sentence is an indefinite pronoun like *anyone*, *no one*, or *everybody*. These pronouns are all singular and need the single form of a verb. So, it would be correct to say, "Everybody [single] in my classes knows [single] that Maya Angelou is a great writer." Some people might think that this sounds funny, because the word *classes* is plural and sits near the verb in the sentence. But *in my classes* is a phrase that changes the meaning of the subject, which is the single form of the indefinite pronoun *everybody*. Pick a two-paragraph section from the essay and look at the subjects and verbs in each sentence. Did Angelou follow the rule of having single subject nouns and pronouns with single verbs?

 Writing on Your Own

Write a brief description about an event that happened when you were younger. Ask someone who was there when the event happened to read it. Do they remember the event in the same way? Would they add or change any details? What does this tell you about autobiographies?

 Speaking and Listening

With two other people, take turns reading sections from this selection. One person could read the parts of the narrator, and the others could read Rita's and R. L. Poole's words. How can you change your tone of voice to make the events of the audition sound funny?

 Viewing

Maya Angelou has also written screenplays for movies and television series. Locate and view a video or DVD of one of these programs. How is her writing the same as and different from her writing in this essay?

BEFORE READING THE SELECTION

from *The Story of My Life*   by Helen Keller

About the Author

Helen Keller had a healthy life for her first 19 months. Then, before her second birthday, she got very sick. As a result, she lost her sight and hearing. It was as if someone had drawn a curtain between her and the life she was just beginning to know.

Helen Keller's teacher, Anne Sullivan, was the person who drew that curtain aside. The two remained together until Sullivan's death in 1936. Anne Sullivan was herself partially blind from a childhood infection. She taught Helen by spelling words into her hand using a system she had learned at the famous Perkins School for the Blind in Boston.

Helen Keller went on to graduate from Radcliffe College. She became a famous writer and speaker, raising money for the education of blind people and for other social causes. She published seven books, including *Out of the Dark* and *The Story of My Life*. Her meeting with Anne Sullivan and her triumph over great misfortune became the subject of a well-known play and movie called *The Miracle Worker*.

About the Selection

Helen Keller's autobiography, *The Story of My Life,* appeared first as a series of monthly selections in *Ladies Home Journal.* She began to write it when she was a student at Radcliffe. At first, she typed it on a regular typewriter. When she stopped, she had to remember the exact words she had ended with before she could begin again.

Keller's account of her own life was published as a book in 1902. Today, it is still her most popular work. In it, she dedicated her work to Alexander Graham Bell, "who has taught the deaf to speak." In this excerpt from her autobiography, Keller also celebrates another great teacher, Anne Sullivan.

Helen Keller
1880–1968

Objectives

- To read and appreciate an autobiographical essay
- To define and find examples of analogies and imagery

***Before Reading* continued on next page**

from The Story of My Life by Helen Keller

analogy a comparison between two otherwise different objects that share some of the same characteristics

Literary Terms In this excerpt, Keller describes how her love for learning grew from roots planted and cared for by her teacher. She uses **analogies**, or word comparisons, to make this part of her life clear for her readers. Analogies invite readers to create mental pictures comparing two things and finding the ways they might be connected. Keller's writing is also rich in *imagery*, or word pictures. Since she was blind and deaf, her images call on the other senses, especially touch and smell.

Reading on Your Own As you read, pay attention to the images Keller presents. Use your memories to recall the way a very soft object, like a chick, might feel. In your mind, listen to the snort that Keller's pony gives. Think of heavy perfume when you read about the scent of wild grapes. Like all writers, Keller depends on readers to recall these memories of something they have smelled, tasted, felt, seen, or heard to complete the story. By remembering a sensory image, readers make a text more real.

Writing on Your Own Locate a copy of the Braille alphabet that non-seeing readers use to read and write. Use its characters to write two sentences from this essay. Braille is actually a raised alphabet, created by a special machine or printer that punches dots in the paper so they can be felt. However, writing with the dots of this alphabet gives you an idea of the way it is constructed.

Vocabulary Focus With a partner, scan over the words that are defined on each page. Take turns finding the words that are defined on the page. Read the sentence where you find them, and use each term in a meaningful sentence.

Think Before You Read What challenges might face a writer who cannot see or hear? How might these challenges be overcome?

from
The Story of My Life

For a long time I had no regular lessons. Even when I studied most earnestly it seemed more like play than work. Everything Miss Sullivan taught me she **illustrated** by a beautiful story or a poem. Whenever anything delighted or interested me she talked it over with me just as if she were a little girl herself. What many children think of with dread, as a painful plodding through grammar, hard sums and harder definitions, is to-day one of my most precious memories. . . .

We read and studied out of doors, preferring the sunlit woods to the house. All my early lessons have in them the breath of the woods—the fine, **resinous** odour of pine needles, blended with the perfume of wild grapes. Seated in the gracious shade of a wild tulip tree, I learned to think that everything has a lesson and a suggestion. "The loveliness of things taught me all their use." Indeed, everything that could hum, or buzz, or sing, or bloom, had a part in my education—noisy-throated frogs, katydids and crickets held in my hand until, forgetting their **embarrassment**, they **trilled** their reedy note, little downy chickens and wildflowers, the dogwood

> As you read, notice how Helen Keller describes Anne Sullivan's teaching methods.

Anne Sullivan became Helen Keller's teacher in 1887, shortly before Helen was seven years old.

illustrated made clear

resinous relating to a sticky substance that flows from some trees

embarrassment an uneasy feeling

trilled sang

blossoms, meadow-violets and budding fruit trees. I felt the bursting cotton-bolls and fingered their soft fiber and fuzzy seeds; I felt the low **soughing** of the wind through the cornstalks, the silky rustling of the long leaves, and the indignant snort of my pony, as we caught him in the pasture and put the bit in his mouth—ah me! how well I remember the spicy, clovery smell of his breath! . . .

Our favourite walk was to Keller's Landing, an old tumble-down lumber-wharf on the Tennessee River, used during the Civil War to land soldiers. There we spent many happy hours and played at learning geography. I built dams of pebbles, made islands and lakes, and dug river-beds, all for fun, and never dreamed that I was learning a lesson. I listened with increasing wonder to Miss Sullivan's descriptions of the great round world with its burning mountains, buried cities, moving rivers of ice, and many other things as strange. She made raised maps in clay, so that I could feel the mountain ridges and valleys, and follow with my fingers the **devious** course of rivers. . . .

Arithmetic seems to have been the only study I did not like. From the first I was not interested in the science of numbers. Miss Sullivan tried to teach me to count by stringing beads in groups, and by arranging kindergarten straws I learned to add and subtract. I never had patience to arrange more than five or six groups at a time. When I had accomplished this my conscience was at rest for the day, and I went out quickly to find my playmates. . . .

Once there were eleven tadpoles in a glass globe set in a window full of plants. I remember the eagerness with which I made discoveries about them. It was great fun to plunge my hand into the bowl and feel the tadpoles frisk about, and to let them slip and slide between my fingers. One day a more **ambitious** fellow leaped beyond the edge of the bowl and fell on the floor, where I found him to all appearance more dead than alive. The only sign of life was a slight wriggling

Favourite is the British spelling of favorite. On the previous page, *odour* is the British spelling of odor.

Notice all the sensory images in this paragraph.

soughing sighing	**ambitious** determined
devious crooked; sly	

of his tail. But no sooner had he returned to his element than he darted to the bottom, swimming round and round in joyous activity. He had made his leap, he had seen the great world, and was content to stay in his pretty glass house under the big fuchsia tree until he attained the dignity of froghood. Then he went to live in the leafy pool at the end of the garden, where he made the summer nights musical with his quaint love-song.

Thus I learned from life itself. At the beginning I was only a little mass of possibilities. It was my teacher who unfolded and developed them. When she came, everything about me breathed of love and joy and was full of meaning. She has never since let pass an opportunity to point out the beauty that is in everything, nor has she ceased trying in thought and action and example to make my life sweet and useful.

Helen Keller, 1905

It was my teacher's genius, her quick sympathy, her loving **tact** which made the first years of my education so beautiful. It was because she seized the right moment to **impart** knowledge that made it so pleasant and acceptable to me. She realized that a child's mind is like a shallow brook which ripples and dances merrily over the stony course of its education and reflects here a flower, there a bush, yonder a fleecy cloud; and she attempted to guide my mind on its way, knowing that like a brook it should be fed by mountain streams and hidden springs, until it broadened out into a deep river, capable of reflecting in its **placid** surface, billowy hills, the **luminous** shadows of trees and the blue heavens, as well as the sweet face of a little flower.

> Trace this analogy between a shallow brook and a child's mind. What does each reflect? How do the reflections change when the brook becomes a deep river? How does a human mind change as it is educated?

tact skill and grace in dealing with others	**impart** to tell; to make known	**placid** calm; peaceful
		luminous filled with light

AFTER READING THE SELECTION

from The Story of My Life   by Helen Keller

Directions Choose the letter of the best answer or write the answer using complete sentences.

Comprehension: Identifying Facts

1. Where do Helen Keller and her teacher usually read and study?
   A in the library
   B outdoors
   C in the living room
   D sitting in a tree

2. What is the only subject Keller does not like?

3. What does her teacher take every opportunity to do?

Comprehension: Putting Ideas Together

4. What smells does Helen remember from her lessons?
   A downy chickens and wildflowers
   B rustling leaves and her pony's snort
   C resinous pine needles and the perfume of wild grapes
   D bursting cotton balls and their soft fibers

5. How does Keller learn geography?

6. What happens to the tadpole that jumped out of the bowl?

Understanding Literature: Analogies

An *analogy* is a comparison between two things. The two things are alike in some ways but are mainly different from each other. Writers use analogies to explain an unfamiliar thing by comparing it to something familiar.

Helen Keller uses the image of a shallow brook growing into a deep river as an analogy for a child's mind as it learns about the world. The brook and the child's mind are very different. However, the child's mind grows when new information is added. This education, Keller is saying, is like what happens to a brook when it is fed by "mountain streams and hidden springs."

7. In your own words, what is an analogy?

8. What other things do readers learn from Keller's analogy comparing a child's mind to a shallow brook?

Critical Thinking

9. In Keller's mind, what makes a great teacher?

Thinking Creatively

10. Not once in this selection does Keller mention being blind and deaf. Why do you think she leaves out that information?

✓ Grammar Check

Commas are a common form of punctuation. They are used to separate the parts of a sentence. Look at how Keller used them in this sentence: "I built dams of pebbles, made islands and lakes, and dug river-beds, all for fun, and never dreamed that I was learning a lesson." In it, she describes what she does at Keller's Landing. She builds dams. She makes islands and lakes. She digs river beds. She does it all for fun. She never dreams she was learning. Keller's sentence combines all those thoughts. It also tells them in a more flowing way. Look for other places in this essay where Keller used commas. If she didn't use this form of punctuation, what would she have had to say? How would it sound to readers?

Writing on Your Own

Helen Keller might not have described how things looked because she could not see. She could touch, smell, taste, and also feel vibrations. Select a paragraph from this selection and add details that Keller might have included if she had been able to see.

Speaking and Listening

Plan to interview a teacher about the reasons he or she chose to teach. Make a list of questions before the interview. Review the questions to make sure they are clear and help you get the information you need. Practice asking the questions with a partner. Then interview the teacher you chose. At the end of the activity, ask the teacher what worked well about your interview.

Media

In teams, use an audio recorder to capture the sounds of several locations in your school. Play the recording you made for other teams. Can they identify all the places in which you recorded? Discuss with a partner the benefits and disadvantages of only using your sense of hearing. How would it feel to have no sight and no hearing abilities?

from Into Thin Air by *Jon Krakauer*

About the Author

Jon Krakauer was born in 1954. He had an unusual childhood hero—Willi Unsoeld. Unsoeld, a friend of Jon's father, was part of the first American climbing expedition to Mount Everest. He helped Krakauer climb his first mountain when he was only eight years old.

After college, Jon Krakauer became, in his own words, a "climbing bum." He worked some of the time as a carpenter and climbed the rest of the time. He was often asked to write articles about his adventures.

In 1996, *Outside* magazine asked him to write a story about a new business. Companies had been set up to guide people to the top of Mount Everest, the highest mountain in the world. These people, some of whom were not experienced climbers, paid as much as $65,000 for this experience. Krakauer was hired to see what this alarming trend was all about. Near Mount Everest, Krakauer joined a group of Everest-bound climbers led by one of the best guides in the business.

Objectives

- To read and appreciate a personal account
- To define and give examples of diary, irony, suspense, and conflict as used in nonfiction

About the Selection

Krakauer wrote about this trip in *Outside* magazine and in his book *Into Thin Air*. This narrative is taken from his book. It talks about the ordeal of reaching the summit and the equally-challenging descent or climb down from Everest.

In this excerpt, the group confronts two of the life-threatening problems climbers know very well. One danger in climbing is the lack of oxygen or *hypoxia*. At high altitudes, the air contains less oxygen. Breathing becomes difficult. Climbers can lose awareness and judgment. Another major problem climbers face is the weather. Unfortunately, Krakauer's group had to cope with both problems. Just after "summiting," or reaching the top, a terrible storm hit the mountain. Before it was over, four of the climbers in his group were dead.

Literary Terms *Into Thin Air* is a **personal account** or true story. It tells about what turned out to be Everest's deadliest climbing season. During the climb, Krakauer wrote notes every day in his **diary**. His diary, or daily record, became the basis for his book. Krakauer uses writer's tools to tell his story. His writing is filled with **irony** and **suspense**. What you expect to happen does not, making you nervous as you read the story. The person-against-nature **conflict** makes this a great story of how he lived through the experience.

Reading on Your Own This excerpt is full of suspense. The question is, "Will these climbers get out of this experience alive?" As you read, think about the information the author gives you that relates to that question. Predict how the story will end, based on what you know at different points in your reading.

Writing on Your Own Imagine that you are in a dangerous situation. You want to send a text message to the police to let them know where you are, why you are in trouble, and that you need help. What is the clearest way you can say that, using the fewest words possible?

Vocabulary Focus Because of this narrative's setting, some of the terms Krakauer uses relate to the geography of the mountain. He talks about *outcroppings*, or pieces of rock that stick out of the mountain. A *col* is a mountain pass, or a place in a mountain range that allows people to move more easily through them. Climbers on Mount Everest sometimes use the North or South Cols in the region as their routes to the top.

Think Before You Read What does the phrase "into thin air" mean to you? Based on this title, do you think the author wrote this narrative in order to describe, explain, persuade, or entertain his readers?

personal account a true story about an experience, told by a person who lived through it

diary a daily record of events and feelings

irony the difference between what is expected to happen in a story and what does happen

suspense a quality in a story that makes the reader uncertain or nervous about what will happen next

conflict the struggle of the main character against himself or herself, another person, or nature

from

Into Thin Air

Mount Everest is on the border between Tibet and Nepal in the Himalayas. At over 29,000 feet, it is the highest mountain in the world.

from Chapter Thirteen

Southeast Ridge
May 10, 1996
27,600 feet

Bottled oxygen does not make the top of Everest feel like sea level. Climbing above the South Summit with my regulator delivering just under two liters of oxygen per minute, I had to stop and draw three or four lungfuls of air after each **ponderous** step. Then I'd take one more step and have to pause for another four heaving breaths—and this was the fastest pace I could manage. Because the oxygen systems we were using delivered a lean mix of **compressed** gas and **ambient** air, 29,000 feet with gas felt like **approximately** 26,000 feet without gas. But the bottled oxygen **conferred** other benefits that weren't so easily quantified.

Climbing along the blade of the summit ridge, sucking gas into my ragged lungs, I enjoyed a strange, **unwarranted** sense of calm. The world beyond the rubber mask was

Climbing Mount Everest is a classic conflict between human beings and nature. As you read, notice how Krakauer explains the two "sides" of the conflict.

ponderous heavy	**ambient** present on all sides	**conferred** supplied
compressed compact, under pressure	**approximately** nearly	**unwarranted** uncalled-for

stupendously vivid but seemed not quite real, as if a movie were being projected in slow motion across the front of my goggles. I felt drugged, **disengaged**, thoroughly **insulated** from **external stimuli**. I had to remind myself over and over that there was 7,000 feet of sky on either side, that everything was at stake here, that I would pay for a single bungled step with my life.

Half an hour above the South Summit I arrived at the foot of the Hillary Step. One of the most famous pitches in all of mountaineering, its forty feet of near-vertical rock and ice looked **daunting**, but—as any serious climber would—I'd wanted very badly to take the "sharp end" of the rope and lead the Step. It was clear, however, that Boukreev, Beidleman, and Harris all felt the same way, and it was hypoxic delusion on my part to think that any of them was going to let a client hog such a **coveted** lead.

In the end, Boukreev—as senior guide and the only one of us who had climbed Everest previously—claimed the honor; with Beidleman paying out the rope, he did a masterful job of leading the pitch. But it was a slow process, and as he painstakingly ascended toward the crest of the Step, I nervously studied my watch and wondered whether I might run out of oxygen. My first canister had expired at 7:00 A.M. on the Balcony, after lasting about seven hours. Using this as a benchmark, at the South Summit I'd calculated that my second canister would expire around 2:00 P.M., which I stupidly assumed would allow plenty of time to reach the summit and return to the South Summit to retrieve my third oxygen bottle. But now it was already after 1:00, and I was beginning to have serious doubts. . . .

The Hillary Step is named for Sir Edmund Hillary of New Zealand. In 1953, he and Tenzing Norgay of Nepal were the first to reach the summit of Everest. A *pitch* is a slope. The summit lies about 20 to 30 minutes beyond the Hillary Step.

Hypoxic delusion means a trick of the mind due to lack of oxygen.

Notice how Krakauer builds suspense.

stupendously amazingly

disengaged withdrawn

insulated protected from

external outside

stimuli something that makes you active

daunting frightening

coveted wanted

Plodding slowly up the last few steps to the summit, I had the sensation of being underwater, of life moving at quarter speed. And then I found myself atop a slender wedge of ice, **adorned** with a discarded oxygen cylinder and a battered aluminum survey pole, with nowhere higher to climb. A string of Buddhist prayer flags snapped furiously in the wind. Far below, down a side of the mountain I had never laid eyes on, the dry Tibetan plateau stretched to the horizon as a boundless **expanse** of dun-colored earth.

Reaching the top of Everest is supposed to trigger a **surge** of intense **elation**; against long odds, after all, I had just attained a goal I'd coveted since childhood. But the summit was really only the halfway point. Any impulse I might have felt toward self-congratulation was **extinguished** by **overwhelming apprehension** about the long, dangerous descent that lay ahead.

Everest Summit
29,028 feet

The Hillary Step

The South Summit

The Balcony
27,600 feet

Camp Four
26,000 feet

adorned decorated	**elation** great happiness	**overwhelming** too much
expanse something vast, spread out	**extinguished** put out	**apprehension** fear; dread
surge a rush or flow		

from Chapter Fourteen

Summit
1:12 P.M., May 10, 1996
29,028 feet

From the Balcony I descended a few hundred feet down a broad, gentle snow gully without incident, but then things began to get sketchy. The route **meandered** through outcroppings of broken shale blanketed with six inches of fresh snow. **Negotiating** the puzzling, **infirm** terrain demanded unceasing concentration, an all-but-impossible feat in my punch-drunk state. . . .

I sat down to rest on a broad, sloping ledge, but after a few minutes a deafening BOOM! frightened me back to my feet. Enough new snow had accumulated that I feared a massive slab avalanche had released on the slopes above, but when I spun around to look I saw nothing. Then there was another BOOM!, accompanied by a flash that momentarily lit up the sky, and I realized I was hearing the crash of thunder.

In the morning, on the way up, I'd made a point of continually studying the route on this part of the mountain, frequently looking down to pick out **landmarks** that would be helpful on the descent, **compulsively** memorizing the terrain: "Remember to turn left at the **buttress** that looks like a ship's prow. Then follow that skinny line of snow until it curves sharply to the right." This was something I'd trained myself to do many years earlier, a drill I forced myself to go through every time I climbed, and on Everest it may have saved my life. By 6:00 P.M., as the storm **escalated** into a full-scale blizzard with driving snow and winds gusting in excess of 60 knots, I came upon the rope that had been fixed by the Montenegrins on the snow slope 600 feet above the Col. Sobered by the force

> The personal account from his diary continues.

> Krakauer is dazed and confused— *punch drunk*— because of lack of oxygen.

> A storm has begun. The suspense builds as Krakauer fights his way back down to camp.

> Montenegro is part of the former Yugoslavia. A *col* is a mountain pass.

---

meandered followed a winding course

negotiating managing

infirm not solid or stable

landmarks objects that show location

compulsively unable to stop

buttress part of a mountain that sticks out

escalated got stronger

of the rising **tempest**, I realized that I'd gotten down the trickiest ground just in the nick of time.

Wrapping the fixed line around my arms to rappel, I continued down through the blizzard. Some minutes later I was overwhelmed by a disturbingly familiar feeling of **suffocation**, and I realized that my oxygen had once again run out. Three hours earlier when I'd attached my regulator to my third and last oxygen canister, I'd noticed that the **gauge** indicated that the bottle was only half full. I'd figured that would be enough to get me most of the way down, though, so I hadn't bothered exchanging it for a full one. And now the gas was gone.

I pulled the mask from my face, left it hanging around my neck, and pressed onward, surprisingly unconcerned. However, without **supplemental** oxygen, I moved more slowly, and I had to stop and rest more often. . . .

I was so far beyond ordinary exhaustion that I experienced a queer **detachment** from my body, as if I were observing my descent from a few feet overhead. I imagined that I was dressed in a green cardigan and wingtips. And although the gale was generating a windchill in excess of seventy below zero Fahrenheit, I felt strangely, disturbingly warm.

At 6:30, as the last of the daylight seeped from the sky, I'd descended to within 200 vertical feet of Camp Four. Only one obstacle now stood between me and safety: a bulging incline of hard, glassy ice that I would have to descend without a rope. Snow pellets borne by 70-knot gusts stung my face; any exposed flesh was instantly frozen. The tents, no more than 650 horizontal feet away, were only **intermittently** visible through the whiteout. There was no margin for error. Worried about making a critical blunder, I sat down to **marshal** my energy before descending further.

To *rappel* is to descend by sliding down a rope passed under one thigh, across the body, and over the opposite shoulder.

Wingtips are fancy, dress shoes. Krakauer's mind is playing tricks on him.

Climbers begin their summit attempt at midnight, hoping to reach the summit by noon. It takes four to six hours to descend from the summit back to Camp Four.

tempest a bad storm	**supplemental** additional, extra	**intermittently** off and on
suffocation not being able to breathe	**detachment** separation from	**marshal** to gather
gauge a tool for measuring		

Once I was off my feet, **inertia** took hold. It was so much easier to remain at rest than to summon the **initiative** to tackle the dangerous ice slope; so I just sat there as the storm roared around me, letting my mind drift, doing nothing for perhaps forty-five minutes.

I'd tightened the drawstrings on my hood until only a tiny opening remained around my eyes, and I was removing the useless, frozen oxygen mask from beneath my chin when Andy Harris suddenly appeared out of the gloom beside me. Shining my headlamp in his direction, I reflectively **recoiled** when I saw the **appalling** condition of his face. His cheeks were coated with an armor of frost, one eye was frozen shut, and he was **slurring** his words badly. He looked in serious trouble. "Which way to the tents?" Andy blurted, frantic to reach shelter.

I pointed in the direction of Camp Four, then warned him about the ice just below us. "It's steeper than it looks!" I yelled, straining to make myself heard over the tempest. "Maybe I should go down first and get a rope from camp—" As I was in midsentence, Andy **abruptly** turned away and moved over the lip of the ice slope, leaving me sitting there dumbfounded.

Scooting on his butt, he started down the steepest part of the incline. "Andy," I shouted after him, "it's crazy to try it like that! You're going to blow it for sure!" He yelled something back, but his words were carried off by the screaming wind. A second later he lost his purchase, flipped . . . and was suddenly rocketing headfirst down the ice.

Two hundred feet below, I could just make out Andy's motionless form slumped at the foot of the incline. I was sure he'd broken at least a leg, maybe his neck. But then, incredibly, he stood up, waved that he was O.K., and started lurching toward Camp Four, which, at the moment was in plain sight, 500 feet beyond.

Krakauer does not discover until later that this climber was not Andy Harris, his guide. Andy Harris died on the mountain.

inertia not able to move	**recoiled** drew back in horror	**slurring** leaving out or blurring sounds
initiative drive; energy	**appalling** dreadful	**abruptly** suddenly, without warning

Camp Four, at 26,000 feet, is in a windy, lonely pass the size of a football field. The air above this altitude is dangerously thin.

Crampons are climbing irons—steel spikes attached to the climber's boots.

I could see the shadowy forms of three or four people standing outside the tents; their headlamps flickered through curtains of blowing snow. I watched Harris walk toward them across the flats, a distance he covered in less than ten minutes. When the clouds closed in a moment later, cutting off my view, he was within sixty feet of the tents, maybe closer. I didn't see him again after that, but I was certain that he'd reached the **security** of camp, where Chuldum and Arita would doubtless be waiting with hot tea. Sitting out in the storm, with the ice bulge still standing between me and the tents, I felt a pang of envy. I was angry that my guide hadn't waited for me.

My backpack held little more than three empty oxygen canisters and a pint of frozen lemonade; it probably weighed no more than sixteen or eighteen pounds. But I was tired, and worried about getting down the incline without breaking a leg, so I tossed the pack over the edge and hoped it would come to rest where I could retrieve it. Then I stood up and started down the ice, which was as smooth and hard as the surface of a bowling ball.

Fifteen minutes of **dicey**, fatiguing crampon work brought me safely to the bottom of the incline, where I easily located my pack, and another ten minutes after that I was in camp myself. I lunged into my tent with my crampons still on, zipped the door tight, and sprawled across the frost-covered floor too tired to even sit upright. For the first time I had a sense of how wasted I really was: I was more exhausted than I'd ever been in my life. But I was safe. Andy was safe. The others would be coming into camp soon. We'd . . . done it. We'd climbed Everest. It had been a little sketchy there for a while, but in the end everything had turned out great.

It would be many hours before I learned that everything had not in fact turned out great—that nineteen men and women were stranded up on the mountain by the storm, caught in a desperate struggle for their lives.

security safety   **dicey** risky

AFTER READING THE SELECTION

from Into Thin Air by Jon Krakauer

Directions Choose the letter of the best answer or write the answer using complete sentences.

Comprehension: Identifying Facts

1. Climbing above the South Summit, Krakauer has to use _____ in order to breathe.
   - **A** bottled water **C** rappels
   - **B** crampons **D** bottled oxygen

2. Half an hour above the South Summit, what landmark does Krakauer reach?
   - **A** Mount Everest's summit
   - **B** the Hillary Step
   - **C** base camp
   - **D** the pitch

3. Who leads the pitch at the Hillary Step?

4. When did Krakauer predict his second oxygen tank would run out?

5. How high is the summit of Mount Everest?

6. As he moves slowly toward the summit, how does Krakauer feel?

7. What had Krakauer done as he climbed up the mountain in the morning?

8. Without supplemental oxygen, how does Krakauer move?

9. By 6:30 in the evening, what point had Krakauer reached in his descent toward Camp Four?

10. How does Krakauer safely reach the bottom of the ice slope?

Comprehension: Putting Ideas Together

11. Why does Krakauer climb so slowly above the South Summit of Everest?
    - **A** He isn't getting enough oxygen.
    - **B** It's snowing.
    - **C** He is sick.
    - **D** He gave his oxygen tanks to others.

12. How does the world around Krakauer seem as he climbs the blade of the summit ridge?
    - **A** noisy and hectic
    - **B** calm and safe
    - **C** like a carnival
    - **D** frightening

13. What is the Hillary Step?

14. How does Krakauer's concern about time build suspense?

15. What is ironic about Krakauer's feelings when he reaches the summit?

16. After Krakauer uses all his oxygen, how does he feel?

After Reading **continued on next page**

17. What is Krakauer's final obstacle in his attempt to return to camp?

18. When Krakauer sees the person he thinks is Andy Harris, how does he react?

19. Compare how Krakauer and the person he thinks was Andy Harris descend the ice slope.

20. What is ironic about Krakauer's thoughts when he reaches his tent?

Understanding Literature: Personal Account

A *personal account* is a narrative, or story, about an event told by a person who lived through it. Personal accounts are nonfiction, but authors shape events as they remember them. When more than one person has an experience, each may see the event in a different way.

After Jon Krakauer's story first came out, several other survivors of the expedition complained that Krakauer had not been entirely truthful. He had not written the story in exactly the way they remembered it. He had, however, written it as well and as truthfully as he could.

21. How is a personal account like a story?

22. Why might two people who shared an experience tell different stories of what happened?

23. How do you think Andy Harris might have told this story?

24. What are some ways readers can tell this selection is a personal account?

25. Why do you think people like to read personal accounts about dangerous adventures like this one?

Critical Thinking

26. Climbing mountains like Everest is made even more dangerous by the thin air at such high altitudes. How does Krakauer make his readers aware of this danger?

27. How did the appearance of "Andy Harris" help save Krakauer's life?

28. Krakauer makes his way back from the summit alone. What does this say about him as a person?

29. What else would you like to know about this part of the expedition, other than what Krakauer tells you?

Thinking Creatively

30. There have been thousands of attempts to climb Mount Everest. More than 1,000 climbers have succeeded. Hundreds have died trying. Why do you think people are driven to climb Mount Everest? If you had a chance to climb Everest, would you? Why or why not?

Grammar Check

Look at these two quotes from this narrative:

"Reaching the top of Everest is supposed to trigger a surge of intense elation . . ."

"Plodding slowly up the last few steps to the summit, I had the sensation of being underwater . . . "

The words ending in *–ing* are used in two different ways. *Reaching* is a verb form that is used as a noun. It is called a gerund. *Plodding* is a participle that begins a phrase that describes *I* (the author). Review the text to find more words that end in *–ing*. Are they verbs, or verb forms such as gerunds or participles?

 ## Writing on Your Own

Imagine that you are a weather observer at the foot of Mount Everest. Write a weather bulletin advising climbers that you have just spotted a large storm approaching. Use details from Krakauer's account to describe the weather climbers might expect.

 ## Speaking

Imagine that you are a salesperson trying to make wealthy people sign up for an Everest-climbing expedition. What might you tell them to convince them that this is an adventure of a lifetime? Prepare a presentation by outlining your main points. Practice your speech several times until you feel comfortable with its content and message. Ask a classmate to help you by listening to what you say and giving you tips about ways you might improve.

 ## Listening

On the internet, you can find Jon Krakauer narrating sections of *Into Thin Air*. Ask your teacher to help you find a Web site so you may listen to it. How does listening to this author affect the way you think about his work?

  ## Media and Technology

Use a digital camera and an audio recorder to create a sound and light experience based on *Into Thin Air*. Make sure that your presentation represents the struggle Krakauer faced in summiting and returning to camp.

BEFORE READING THE SELECTION

Barack Obama
1961–

Objectives

■ To read and understand a persuasive speech

■ To define and give examples of diction and style as they relate to speeches

About the Author

As Barack Obama explains in this selection, he is living what many people would call the American dream. His family valued a good education and made sure he had one. He attended a private high school in Hawaii, where he lived. Later he graduated from Columbia University. He moved to Illinois and became a community organizer for Chicago's South Side. There he worked to improve living conditions in poor neighborhoods.

After three years in Chicago, he returned to school. He attended Harvard Law School. There, he became the first African American president of the *Harvard Law Review.* This position is a great honor. He then returned to Chicago as a lawyer, concentrating on cases involving civil rights. In 1996, he was elected to the Illinois Senate. In 2005, he became a United States senator representing Illinois.

Many people have been impressed by Senator Obama's ability to work well with all kinds of people. They predict he has an even brighter future ahead of him.

About the Selection

This selection presents a portion of a speech Senator Obama gave in 2004 while running for the U.S. Senate. In the first part of the speech, he tells about his family history. His grandfather worked in the oil fields during the Great Depression in the 1930s. This was a time in America when there was a severe slowdown of business activity. People lost all their savings. Many were out of work. When the Japanese bombed Pearl Harbor in 1941, Obama's grandfather joined the army to fight in World War II.

As he closes this speech, Obama also recalls another event in American history. He talks about America's young men and women fighting in the Mekong Delta during the Vietnam War in the 1960s.

Literary Terms Many people classify this speech as a **persuasive speech** because it encourages people to consider all Americans as one people. This genre, or kind of nonfiction, is meant to be listened to as well as read. Sometimes, speeches like these follow all the rules of formal English. Sometimes they don't. That choice depends on the word choice or **diction** and **style** of the author and speaker. Speakers usually try to plan what their audience will expect and write their speeches to meet what their audience wants to hear.

Reading on Your Own Sometimes, as you read a speech, you need to *hear* parts of it in order to fully appreciate the author/speaker's style and diction. As you read, speak the words softly to yourself, or read them aloud to a partner. You may also want to find an expert reader to read or record this speech for you. Recordings of the full speech are also available on the Internet.

Writing on Your Own Have you ever heard a truly great speech, one that made you take action or realize something about life? Write a description of that speech. State the reasons why the speech was memorable and the effect it had on your thoughts or behavior.

Vocabulary Focus This selection is an excerpt from a speech Barack Obama delivered to the Democratic National Convention in 2004. His speech was a *keynote address*, which is a major speech. A keynote address sets the tone and tells the message on which a group wants to focus. A *convention* is a meeting of members of a political party to choose a candidate. A *declaration* is a statement.

Think Before You Read How might a speech be different from an essay? How might it be the same?

persuasive speech a spoken work designed to make people act a certain way or believe one thing

diction the proper choice of words; speaking clearly, saying each word so that it is clearly understood

style an author's way of writing

FROM

KEYNOTE ★ ADDRESS

As you read this persuasive speech, think about how it might have sounded as it was spoken.

Kenya is in Africa. A *domestic servant* is hired help.

The *G.I. Bill* is a government program that helps pay for college. *F.H.A.* is a government program that helps people get home loans.

On behalf of the great state of Illinois, crossroads of a nation, Land of Lincoln, let me express my deepest gratitude for the privilege of addressing this convention.

Tonight is a particular honor for me because—let's face it—my presence on this stage is pretty unlikely. My father was a foreign student, born and raised in a small village in Kenya. He grew up herding goats, went to school in a tin-roof shack. His father—my grandfather—was a cook, a domestic servant to the British.

But my grandfather had larger dreams for his son. Through hard work and **perseverance**, my father got a scholarship to study in a magical place, America, that shone as a beacon of freedom and opportunity to so many who had come before.

While studying here, my father met my mother. She was born in a town on the other side of the world, in Kansas. Her father worked on oil rigs and farms through most of the Depression. The day after Pearl Harbor, my grandfather signed up for duty; joined Patton's army, marched across Europe. Back home, my grandmother raised their baby and went to work on a bomber assembly line. After the war, they studied on the G.I. Bill, bought a house through F.H.A., and later moved west, all the way to Hawaii in search of opportunity.

perseverance sticking to a purpose

And they, too, had big dreams for their daughter.

A common dream, born of two continents. My parents shared not only an **improbable** love, they shared an abiding faith in the possibilities of this nation. They would give me an African name, Barack, or "blessed," believing that in a **tolerant** America your name is no barrier to success. They imagined me going to the best schools in the land, even though they weren't rich, because in a generous America you don't have to be rich to achieve your potential.

They are both passed away now. And yet, I know that, on this night, they look down on me with great pride.

I stand here today, grateful for the **diversity** of my **heritage**, aware that my parents' dreams live on in my two

Keynote speaker Barack Obama, 2004

precious daughters. I stand here knowing that my story is part of the larger American story, that I owe a debt to all of those who came before me, and that in no other country on earth is my story even possible.

> If you *achieve your potential,* you are the best you can be.

Tonight, we gather to affirm the greatness of our nation—not because of the height of our skyscrapers, or the power of our military, or the size of our economy. Our pride is based on a very simple premise, summed up in a declaration made over two hundred years ago: "We hold these truths to be self-evident, that all men are created equal, that they are **endowed** by their Creator with certain **unalienable** rights, that among these are life, liberty, and the **pursuit** of happiness."

> This is a quote from The Declaration of Independence.

---

improbable not likely to happen

tolerant willing to let people do what they wish

diversity variety

heritage background of a person's family

endowed provided

unalienable cannot be taken away

pursuit the act of seeking

That is the true genius of America—a faith in simple dreams, an **insistence** on small miracles. That we can tuck in our children at night and know that they are fed and clothed and safe from harm. That we can say what we think, write what we think, without hearing a sudden knock on the door. That we can have an idea and start our own business without paying a bribe. That we can participate in the political process without fear of **retribution**, and that our votes will be counted—at least, most of the time.

This year, in this election, we are called to reaffirm our values and our commitments, to hold them against a hard reality and see how we are measuring up, to the legacy of our forebearers, and the promise of future generations. . . .

If there is a child on the South Side of Chicago who can't read, that matters to me, even if it's not my child. If there's a senior citizen somewhere who can't pay for their prescription drugs and has to choose between medicine and the rent, that makes my life poorer, even if it's not my grandparent. If there's an Arab American family being rounded up without benefit of an attorney or due process, that threatens my civil liberties.

It is that **fundamental** belief—that I am my brother's keeper, I am my sister's keeper—that makes this country work. It's what allows us to **pursue** our individual dreams and yet still come together as one American family.

E pluribus unum. Out of many, one.

Now even as we speak, there are those who are preparing to divide us, the spin masters and negative ad peddlers who embrace the politics of anything goes. Well, I say to them tonight, there is not a liberal America and a conservative America—there is the United States of America. There is not a Black America and White America and Latino America and Asian America—there's the United States of America. . . .

We are one people, all of us pledging allegiance to the Stars and Stripes, all of us defending the United States of

| **insistence** demand | **retribution** return for wrongdoing | **fundamental** basic |
| | | **pursue** seek |

U.S. President
George W. Bush,
First Lady Laura
Bush, and U.S.
Senator Barack
Obama, 2005

America. In the end, that's what this election is about. Do we participate in a politics of **cynicism**, or do we participate in a politics of hope? . . .

I'm not talking about blind **optimism** here—the almost willful ignorance that thinks unemployment will go away if we just don't think about it, or the health care crisis will solve itself if we just ignore it. I'm talking about something more **substantial**. It's the hope of slaves sitting around a fire singing freedom songs. The hope of immigrants setting out for distant shores. The hope of a young naval lieutenant bravely patrolling the Mekong Delta. The hope of a millworker's son who dares to defy the odds. The hope of a skinny kid with a funny name who believes that America has a place for him, too.

Hope in the face of difficulty. Hope in the face of uncertainty.

The **audacity** of hope! In the end, that is God's greatest gift to us, the bedrock of this nation. A belief in things not seen. A belief that there are better days ahead.

Willful ignorance means to pretend something is not there.

How would you describe the speaker's diction and style? How would you feel as you listened to these words?

cynicism doubting	**substantial** important
optimism hopefulness	**audacity** boldness

from Keynote Address   by Barack Obama

Directions Choose the letter of the best answer or write the answer using complete sentences.

Comprehension: Identifying Facts

1. Senator Obama's father was born and raised in_____.
   - **A** Chicago
   - **B** Oklahoma
   - **C** Kenya
   - **D** Washington, D.C.

2. Why did the author's parents give him the name *Barack*?

3. According to the author, what is the fundamental belief that makes this country work?

Comprehension: Putting Ideas Together

4. What did Obama's parents have in common?
   - **A** They believed in the promise of America.
   - **B** They were born in America.
   - **C** They went to college.
   - **D** nothing

5. Why does it matter to Obama if there is a child in Chicago who can't read?

6. How does Obama think we should deal with the people who want to divide America?

Understanding Literature: Diction

All authors consider the needs and expectations of their audiences as they choose the words through which they will express their ideas. This process is sometimes called *determining diction*. For authors who present their writings orally and publicly, these choices are even more critical. They can tell immediately if they have made the right choices by the way their audience reacts. If the audience expects formal diction and the speaker delivers a speech using informal diction, the audience will not listen carefully.

7. How does diction influence an audience?

8. How would you describe the style of diction Obama used in creating his speech?

Critical Thinking

9. What was Obama's purpose in writing and delivering this speech? Do you think he was successful?

Thinking Creatively

10. How would you have felt if you were in the audience when Obama delivered his speech? Describe your response.

Grammar Check

Semicolons and colons are two kinds of useful punctuation marks. A *semicolon* joins two clauses that could be independent sentences. A *colon* is used before a list, an explanation, or a definition. Locate at least one example where Obama uses a colon or semicolon in his speech. For what purpose does he use it? How does it affect your sense of what the author is saying?

Writing on Your Own

Write a one-minute report for a television news program explaining Obama's speech and its importance.

Speaking

Practice presenting portions of this speech to your class. Think about what the words say, the speaker, and the occasion for which the speech was given. Use this knowledge to power your presentation.

Listening

Rhetoric is the art of making people believe something by using language. Included in this art are several tools. One of these is called *asyndeton.*

It involves leaving out conjunctions between words, phrases, or clauses. Consider this part of Obama's speech that begins, "It's *the hope of* slaves sitting around a fire singing freedom songs. *The hope of* immigrants setting out for distant shores . . ." How does the repetition of this key phrase and the lack of conjunctions help the audience understand his point?

Media and Technology

Create a computer presentation that might have been projected behind Senator Obama as he gave his speech. Select color and images that enhance what he was saying. Consider using music to create a mood that echoes the mood Senator Obama created with his speech. You may also want to add key words from the speech to emphasize their impact.

Research

In your library or on the Internet, find out all you can about the person that represents you in Congress. Everyone in America is represented by both a member of the Senate and a member of the House of Representatives. On the Internet, many of these sites have URL addresses that end in **.gov.**

Authors use imagery to appeal to readers' five senses. Images in literature are most often visual—creating mental pictures that help us see an essay, story, or poem more completely. For example, in the excerpt from *Into Thin Air,* Jon Krakauer presents the visual image he himself had while suffering from altitude sickness. He pictured himself looking ridiculous, climbing the mountain in a sweater and wingtip shoes. Sharing this image helps readers understand his mental state. In "Of Dry Goods and Black Bow Ties," the visual image of Mr. Shimada is important. We need to see him in his "spotless black alpaca suit, an immaculate white shirt and a white collar so stiff it might have overcome a lesser man."

Authors also create images appealing to the other senses. Rudolfo Anaya remembers the powerful smells of earth and sweat when he describes his grandfather. Helen Keller writes of the "spicy, clovery smell" of her pony's breath. In the excerpt from Maya Angelou's *Gather Together in My Name,* the only sound readers hear after Rita's attempt to impress Mr. Poole is the gas "hiss[ing] out steadily like ten fat men resting on a summer's day." The image shows how ridiculous Rita felt at that point.

In appealing to the five senses, writers add realistic details that help readers become involved on more than one level.

Review

1. In your own words, explain what imagery in literature is.

2. Why do authors use imagery?

3. To which sense does this image appeal? "I felt the bursting cotton-bolls and fingered their soft fiber and fuzzy seeds."

4. Senator Obama presented many visual images in his speech. List three of them.

5. List three other images used in the selections in this unit. Explain to which sense each appeals.

Writing on Your Own

Write a paragraph describing a baby. Use images that appeal to each of the five senses.

Nonfiction includes every form of prose writing that concerns real people, facts, and true experiences. Unlike fiction, nonfiction doesn't have to have a plot, character development, setting, or theme. Writers present and shape real events as their memory and understanding demand.

The purpose of a nonfiction work may be to explain, persuade, tell, describe, entertain, or to do several of these at once. Writers use many of the techniques of fiction—suspense, irony, imagery, symbols, conflict, repetition, humor—but readers expect nonfiction to be about real events that happened to real people.

Biographies and autobiographies, true accounts of people's lives, are popular forms of nonfiction. Another popular form is the essay, a short nonfiction work on any subject. Nonfiction narratives tell true stories, usually in chronological order. People who have had experiences they want to explain write personal accounts, which can be longer than essays.

Nonfiction books and essays are as popular as fiction. Readers turn to nonfiction for many reasons. One is the desire to understand human experience and the world through facts and how they view them.

Selections

■ The excerpt from Thor Heyerdahl's book *Kon-Tiki,* the story of a 4,000-mile trip across the Pacific by raft, describes an encounter with a real-life sea monster.

■ In his reflective essay "A Celebration of Grandfathers," Rudolfo Anaya honors his grandfather, his Mexican American traditions, and all old people.

■ Yoshiko Uchida's biographical essay, "Of Dry Goods and Black Bow Ties," gives readers a glimpse into the life of Japanese immigrants in the United States.

■ In the excerpt from Maya Angelou's autobiography, *Gather Together in My Name,* the author looks back with humor at an embarrassing moment.

■ Helen Keller, in the excerpt from *The Story of My Life,* describes how her teacher, Anne Sullivan, awakened her to the joys of learning about the world.

■ In the excerpt from *Into Thin Air,* Jon Krakauer tells of his Mount Everest expedition that turned deadly.

■ Barack Obama's Keynote Address is an uplifting speech, recounting his family's past and looking forward to America's future.

Directions Choose the letter of the best answer or write the answer using complete sentences.

Comprehension: Identifying Facts

1. How does Heyerdahl's crew think the whale shark was going to behave after being harpooned?
   A calmly
   B like an infuriated submarine
   C like a clown
   D like a pilot fish

2. What does *ten paciencia* mean?

3. Who was, at one time, Seattle's most successful Japanese businessman?

4. What kind of dancing had Rita studied?

5. Why does Senator Obama say it was unlikely that he would be giving an important speech?

Comprehension: Putting Ideas Together

6. What do Thor Heyerdahl and Jon Krakauer have in common?
   A They are both adventurers.
   B nothing
   C They are both Norwegian.
   D They both climbed a mountain.

7. Describe the view of older people that Rudolfo Anaya says the media has created.

8. Why might Mr. Shimada be considered an honorable man?

9. How might Helen Keller describe the perfect teacher?

10. What American values does Barack Obama celebrate in his speech?

Understanding Literature: Essays

Many essays follow a pattern: introduction, body, and conclusion. In the introduction, usually the first paragraph, authors may announce or suggest their purpose for writing. The body of the essay includes paragraphs that support the purpose. The conclusion sums up the essay's major ideas. The conclusion may also include the author's opinion or view of the topic.

Although this order works for many authors, others have used different patterns. Their purposes for writing may not fit into a three-part pattern.

11. Which essays or excerpts in this unit have the basic three-part pattern: introduction, body, conclusion?

12. Which essays or excerpts use different patterns?

13. Other than their order, what else is similar about the pieces with introductions, bodies, and conclusions (for example—their subject matter, their purpose)?

14. What do you see that is similar in the other essays or excerpts?

15. Which is more important to you as a reader: the pattern or content? Why?

Critical Thinking

16. Some people say that calling nonfiction anything that is "not fiction" is like calling Shakespeare's plays "not novels." Do you think it is useful to call so many types of writing "nonfiction"? Explain.

17. Why do you think Rudolfo Anaya decided to write about his grandfather within a reflective essay, rather than writing a biographical essay about him, as Yoshiko Uchida does about Mr. Shimada?

18. Compare the setting, characters, and events of two selections in this unit.

19. Which selection in this unit did you enjoy reading the most? What makes this writing especially interesting to you?

Thinking Creatively

20. If someone were writing about your life, which form of nonfiction would be best? Why?

Speak and Listen

Choose one of the selections in this unit. Make a list of questions to ask people in your class about their reactions to this work. Interview several people. Present what you learn from this survey.

Writing on Your Own

Jon Krakauer created *Into Thin Air* by looking back over his diary, a journal he kept during the expedition to Mount Everest. Using his personal account as a reference, recreate that journal. Use time references Krakauer gives to organize your work. Describe what you imagine he is feeling and thinking, as well as the incredible sights he is observing. Include images about any sensory impressions he may have during the trek.

Beyond Words

Helen Keller learned geography from the clay maps that Anne Sullivan made for her. In this spirit, create a work of art that could be appreciated by a person who is blind.

Test-Taking Tip

Look for specifics in each test question that tell you in what form your answer is to be. For example, some questions ask for a paragraph, and others may require only a sentence.

The Poet
Salvator Rosa, 1600s

Poetry

Poets express ideas, share memories, create beautiful or startling images, or entertain. Poetry is a short form of literature that has its own forms and depends on certain rhythms. Poets must pay close attention to both the sound and the meaning of each word. They use writing tools that help them get the most out of every word. Poetry is known for creating powerful or beautiful impressions with words.

In this unit, you will meet poets from many parts of the world and from many life experiences.

"To read a poem is to hear it with our eyes; to hear it is to see it with our ears."

—Octavio Paz,
Alternating Current,
1967

Unit 7

About Poetry

The first thing readers notice about most poems is that they look different from short stories and other kinds of prose. Although one poem can look very different from another, in general we can say that poetry is literature in verse form. Poems have particular kinds of patterns and rhythm and are often divided into stanzas. A *stanza* is a group of lines that forms a unit of a poem. Poetry is also known for painting powerful or beautiful impressions with words. People sometimes try to understand what poetry is by comparing it to prose.

Like all writers, poets want to communicate ideas and impressions. They have a purpose, and they want to entertain readers or get them thinking. However, compared with most prose literature, poems are short. Each word poets select has to be exactly right.

Writers of both prose and poetry use many tools to communicate in words. Because poets try to get the most out of few words, they use these tools more often. As you'll see in the Writer's Tool Chest that follows, the poet's tools depend on the fact that each word has both sound and meaning. As babies, we learn about the sounds of words.

Then we learn that those sounds have meanings. We come to know that the sounds making up the word *light* mean a kind of energy that allows us to see. We also learn that we can use the same word in different ways to mean different things. For example:

The light of the lamp

Dragonflies light on the clothesline

Writers—especially poets—are very aware of both the sound and the meaning of words. Poets often use sound to create mood and meaning. They use tools such as alliteration—repeating beginning sounds—and onomatopoeia—words that sound like their meanings. They expand the meanings of words with tools such as imagery and figurative language.

Poetry takes a different form than prose. Short stories, novels, and other kinds of prose are written in sentences and paragraphs. Poets usually use lines instead of sentences and stanzas instead of paragraphs.

Poets often use patterns of rhyming words. Rhyming words are words that end in the same sound. *Bit* and *wit* are rhyming words. Both end with the *it* sound. Some kinds of poems have specific rules of rhyme and rhythm.

LaRoche Guyon,
Theodore Robinson,
1891

For example, limericks are five-line poems, usually humorous. They have a certain pattern of rhyming words at the end of each line. In a limerick, the first, second, and fifth lines rhyme. The third and fourth lines have a different rhyme. We show the pattern by giving rhyming lines the same letter. For example, the rhyming pattern of a limerick is shown by *a a b b a.*

There are many kinds of rhyme, but many poems don't rhyme at all. Poems can also have a special rhythm. Rhythm is the pattern created by the stressed and unstressed syllables in a line of poetry. However, poets do not have to use rhythm, either.

If all this is true, then what makes poetry *poetry*? People have been trying to answer that question for many years.

The American poet Robert Frost said that poetry is what gets lost in the translation. What he meant was that a poem is not just a string of words. It is a personal impression of what those words together mean to the poet and to each reader.

The poems in this unit have been grouped into four sections: ballads and songs, rhyme and rhythm, imagery, and voices. Within each section are poems with very different tones, purposes, forms, and techniques. You'll meet poets from many different backgrounds, writing from a wide range of life experiences.

A Writer's Tool Chest

Tools that Use the Meaning of Words

Imagery the use of word pictures that appeal to the five senses

Example: *December. Frost crackling*
Beneath my steps, my breath
Before me, then gone,

These words paint a word picture of winter. Readers *hear* the crackling frost, *see* a puff of breath, and *feel* the cold air. In this way, the poet allows readers to hear, see, and feel winter.

Figurative Language language that uses word pictures to compare or describe, and that is not meant to be taken literally

Example: *In the August grass*
Struck by the last rays of sun
The cracked teacup screams.

In this example, the poet has a cracked teacup screaming, an image that is not meant to be taken literally. The language gives readers a sense of strangeness, danger, and violence. It is hot *(August)*, and when the sun's last rays strike the cracked teacup, it *screams*. Figurative language usually includes metaphor, simile, personification, and hyperbole.

Metaphor a figure of speech that says one thing *is* another

Example: *Hold fast to dreams*
For if dreams die
Life is a broken-winged bird
That cannot fly.

In this example, life without dreams is compared to a bird with broken wings.

Personification giving characters such as animals and objects the characteristics of humans

Example: *Stormy, husky, brawling,*
City of the Big Shoulders:

In this example, the poet describes a city as if it were a person.

Simile a figure of speech in which two things are compared using a phrase that includes the word *like* or *as*

Example: *O, my luve's like a red, red rose,*
That's newly sprung in June,

In this example, the loved one is compared to a red rose that has just bloomed, using the word *like*.

Hyperbole using an overstatement to show that something is important

Example: *And I will luve thee still, my dear,*
Till a' the seas gang dry.

In this example, the lover says he will love his dear one until all the seas run dry. He overstates his case to prove his love.

Tools that Use the Sound of Words

Alliteration repeating sounds by using words whose beginning sounds are the same

Example: *Be the caller, the called,*
         The singer, the song, and the sung.

In this example, the beginning *c* sounds are repeated in the first line. The beginning *s* sounds are repeated in the second line.

Assonance repeating sounds by using words with the same vowel sounds

Example: *We real cool. We*
         Left school.

In this example, the *oo* vowel sound is repeated.

Onomatopoeia using words that sound like their meanings

Example: *How they tinkle, tinkle, tinkle,*
         In the icy air of night!

In this example, the word *tinkle* sounds like the small, silver bells being described. *Tinkle* also means a series of short, high sounds from a bell. Other words that sound like their meanings are *buzz* and *hiss*.

Repetition using a word, phrase, or image more than once, for emphasis

Example: *this morning*
         this morning
         i met myself

Using this technique in a poem about an amazing experience reflects the speaker's excitement as she begins to tell her story.

Rhyme words that end with the same or similar sounds

Example: *'Twas brillig, and the slithy toves*
         Did gyre and gimble in the wabe;
         All mimsy were the borogoves,
         And the mome raths outgrabe.

Despite the nonsense words, notice that the first and third lines and the second and fourth lines rhyme.

End rhyme a rhyming pattern in which the ends of lines contain the same sound

Example: *"Mother dear, may I go downtown*
         Instead of out to play,
         And march the streets of Birmingham
         In a Freedom March today?"

The second and fourth lines show end rhyme.

Internal rhyme rhyme that occurs within one line of a poem—*internal* means inside

Example: *He left it dead, and with its head*
         He went galumphing back.

Dead and *head* have the same ending sound. This means that they are rhyming words. Since both appear in the same line of the poem, they are an example of internal rhyme.

Rhyme scheme the pattern created by the ending sounds of the lines of a poem

Example: *Two roads diverged in a yellow wood,*   *a*
         And sorry I could not travel both   *b*
         And be one traveler, long I stood   *a*
         And looked down one as far as I could   *a*
         To where it bent in the undergrowth;   *b*

The rhyme scheme for this poem is: *a b a a b*. This is a way of showing that the first, third, and fourth lines rhyme, and the second and fifth lines rhyme.

Rhythm a pattern created by the stressed and unstressed syllables in a line of poetry

Example: *As I walked out in the streets of Laredo,*
         As I walked out in Laredo one day,

The rhythm pattern of these lines can be heard by breaking the words into syllables and reading the lines aloud, noticing which syllables you stress, or put the accent on:

As I walked OUT in the STREETS of La-RE-do,
(11 syllables)

As I walked OUT in La-RE-do one DAY,
(10 syllables)

BEFORE READING THE SELECTIONS

Robert Burns
1759–1796

Dudley Randall
1914–2000

Objectives

■ To appreciate ballads as a combination of poetry, song, and storytelling

■ To understand how rhyme, rhythm, and repetition add to the structure of a ballad

■ To describe and give examples of refrain and stanza

About the Authors and Selections

Ballads and songs have long been popular forms of **poetry**. In England during the 1800s, for example, people wrote and published individual ballads for people to read. For inspiration, these writers used stories, songs, and poems from folklore. They also made up ballads about modern-day events. Hundreds of thousands of copies of their ballads were sold— in a country where very few could read.

Some of the ballads and songs in this section grew out of a certain culture, passed from person to person. Robert Burns wrote the ballad "A Red, Red Rose" while he was gathering traditional Scottish songs for a book that he hoped would preserve this art form. His ballad was inspired by these songs. It was first published as a song in 1794. This famous poet also wrote "Auld Lang Syne," the song many people sing on New Year's Eve.

As you learned in Unit 3, traditional folk ballads tell simple stories and probably were sung as well as spoken. "The Streets of Laredo" tells a story about people and places in America's Old West. We don't know who first told this story of the death of a cowboy in Laredo, Texas. However, it continues to be an important part of American folklore.

Ballads are still used by poets to tell new stories. In "Ballad of Birmingham," Dudley Randall tells the tragic true story of the 1963 bombing of a church in Birmingham, Alabama. Four young African American girls were killed. Randall's poem was also set to music and recorded. Many people first heard this chilling ballad as a song. The bombing horrified the American people and focused attention on the sometimes-violent struggle for civil rights.

Literary Terms The ballads in this section tell stories. They use **rhythm** and **rhyming** words to create a pattern of sounds that is pleasing to readers. Rhythm is the beat behind the words. Rhyming words end with the same sounds. In many cases, the writers who created these ballads also use **repetition**, or repeated words and phrases, sometimes as a **refrain**. The repetition calls attention to these words and helps create the poem's effect. Many ballads are arranged in four-line **stanzas.** A stanza is a group of lines that forms a unit in a poem. They are similar to the paragraphs in a story.

Reading on Your Own When you first read these ballads, think about them as stories. Use a Prediction Guide, described in Appendix A, to help you chart each ballad's story elements, such as the story's setting and characters. Then, reread the ballads as songs or poems. How do the ballad's poetic elements, such as repeated words and rhymes, change the way you think of the story?

Writing on Your Own Most songs today use rhyming words and rhythm, just as these ballads do. Why do you think these writer's tools are still popular today? Write your ideas.

Vocabulary Focus The vocabulary poets use is often determined by the time and the place in which they live. For example, Robert Burns wrote his poem in his native Scottish *dialect*. The words he chose were familiar to him and the people of that time. *Bonnie lass* means a pretty girl, and *a'* means all. *Gang* means go, and *weel* means well. Predict what language choices the author of the "Ballad of Birmingham" might have made, based on the fact that he was writing about America in the 1960s.

Think Before You Read What one important event in your life would make a good topic for a ballad or song? Why?

ballad a form of poetry that tells a story, passed from person to person, often as a simple song with rhyming words and a refrain

poetry literature in verse form that usually has rhythm and paints powerful or beautiful impressions with words

rhythm a pattern created by the stressed and unstressed syllables in a line of poetry

rhyme words that end with the same sounds

repetition using a word, phrase, or image more than once, for emphasis

refrain repeated line in a poem or song that creates a mood or gives importance to something

stanza a group of lines that forms a unit in a poem

Innocent Youth,
Thomas Edwin Mostyn

A Red, Red Rose

O, my luve's like a red, red rose,
That's newly sprung in June,
O, my luve's like the melodie,
4 That's sweetly play'd in tune.

As fair art thou, my bonnie lass,
So deep in luve am I,
And I will luve thee still, my dear,
8 Till a' the seas gang dry.

Till a' the seas gang dry, my dear,
And the rocks melt wi' the sun!
And I will luve thee still, my dear,
12 While the sands o' life shall run.

And fare thee weel, my only luve,
And fare thee weel a while!
And I will come again, my luve,
16 Tho' it were ten thousand mile!

—*Robert Burns*

The Streets of Laredo

As I walked out in the streets of Laredo,
As I walked out in Laredo one day,
I spied a poor cowboy wrapped up in white linen,
4 Wrapped in white linen as cold as the clay.

Oh, beat the drums slowly, and play the **fife** lowly,
Play the dead march as you carry me along,
Take me to the green valley, there lay the sod o'er me,
8 For I'm a young cowboy, and I know I've done wrong.

Let sixteen **gamblers** come handle my **coffin**,
Let sixteen cowboys come sing me a song,
Take me to the graveyard, and lay the sod o'er me,
12 For I'm a poor cowboy, and I know I've done wrong.

It was once in the saddle I used to go dashing,
It was once in the saddle I used to go gay,
First to the dram house, and then to the card house,
16 Got shot in the breast, and I'm dying today.

Get six jolly cowboys to carry my coffin,
Get six pretty maidens to bear up my **pall**,
Put bunches of roses all over my coffin,
20 Put roses to deaden the sods as they fall.

Oh, bury me beside my knife and my six-shooter,
My spurs on my heel, my rifle by my side,
And over my coffin put a bottle of brandy,
24 That's the cowboy's drink, and carry me along.

We beat the drums slowly and played the fife lowly,
And bitterly wept as we bore him along,
For we all loved our comrade, so brave, young, and
    handsome,
28 We all loved our comrade, although he'd done wrong.

—*Traditional American Ballad*

There is a change of speakers between the first and second stanzas. Who is the speaker from the second until the last stanza?

A *dram house* (line 15) is a bar, or saloon. A *card house* is a place to gamble.

Notice the repeated words and rhythm in this poem.

---

fife a small flute

gamblers people who play games for money

coffin a box that holds a dead body

pall a cloth that covers a coffin

Ballad of Birmingham

(On the bombing of a church in Birmingham, Alabama, 1963)

In 1963, Dr. Martin Luther King, Jr., led nonviolent civil rights demonstrations— Freedom Marches— in Birmingham, Alabama. Demonstrators were met with attack dogs, tear gas, cattle prods, and fire hoses.

"Mother dear, may I go downtown
Instead of out to play,
And march the streets of Birmingham
4   In a Freedom March today?"

"No, baby, no, you may not go,
For the dogs are fierce and wild,
And clubs and hoses, guns and jails
8   Aren't good for a little child."

"But, mother, I won't be alone.
Other children will go with me,
And march the streets of Birmingham
12 To make our country free."

"No, baby, no, you may not go,
For I fear those guns will fire.
But you may go to church instead
16 And sing in the children's choir."

She has combed and brushed her night-dark hair,
And bathed rose petal sweet,
And drawn white gloves on her small brown hands,
20 And white shoes on her feet.

The mother smiled to know her child
Was in the sacred place,
But that smile was the last smile
24 To come upon her face.

For when she heard the explosion,
Her eyes grew wet and wild.
She raced through the streets of Birmingham
28 Calling for her child.

She clawed through bits of glass and brick,
Then lifted out a shoe.
"O, here's the shoe my baby wore,
32 But, baby, where are you?"

—*Dudley Randall*

What is the irony in this poem?

Funeral services were held for the bombing victims in 1963.

AFTER READING THE SELECTIONS

Ballads and Songs

Directions Choose the letter of the best answer or write the answer using complete sentences.

Comprehension: Identifying Facts

1. To what two things does the lover compare his love in Burns's poem?
   A a rose and June
   B the sea and rocks
   C a red rose and a melodie
   D a mile and the sea

2. How long does the person narrating the Burns's poem say he will love his "dear"?
   A until the seas go dry
   B until the rocks melt
   C until the sands of life run out
   D all of the above

3. How long will the lover be gone?

4. What is the setting for "The Streets of Laredo"?

5. How is the "poor cowboy" dressed?

6. Where does the cowboy want to be buried?

7. What musical instruments does the crowd play?

8. What does the child ask to do at the beginning of "Ballad of Birmingham"?

9. Why won't her mother let her do this?

10. Where did the young girl go instead?

Comprehension: Putting Ideas Together

11. How do you know the Burns's narrator is leaving?
    A He says he will return.
    B He waves.
    C The seas are dry.
    D It's June.

12. Why does the poet use the image of the sea running dry?
    A to remind him of yesterday
    B to explain his journey
    C to state he will never leave his love, because this will never happen
    D because it rhymes

13. How does the "poor cowboy" want his funeral to be handled?

14. What does the young cowboy regret?

15. Do the townspeople like the cowboy? Explain.

16. What information does the subtitle of "Ballad of Birmingham" give you?

17. How does Randall describe Birmingham at that time?

After Reading **continued on next page**

Ballads and Songs

18. Why does the mother want her daughter to go to church?

19. How does the mother feel when she hears the explosion?

20. How is the ending of "Ballad of Birmingham" unexpected?

Understanding Literature: Rhythm

Rhythm in poetry is similar to rhythm in music. It is the beat behind the words. The rhythm of poetry is built on the syllables—the individual sounds—of words. For example, *Laredo* has three syllables, or beats: *La, re,* and *do.* The second syllable—*re*—is stressed, or accented. The first and third syllables are unstressed, or unaccented. We say *La-RE-do,* not *La-re-DO.* Another three-syllable word in the same ballad, *bitterly,* shows a different pattern. Its first syllable is stressed. We pronounce the word *BIT-ter-ly.* Poets often use special patterns of rhythm in their poetry to achieve certain effects.

21. How many syllables are in each line of the first stanza of "The Streets of Laredo"?

22. Which syllables are stressed?

23. Does this pattern of syllables continue throughout the ballad? Explain.

24. How does this pattern of syllables compare with the pattern of syllables in "Ballad of Birmingham"?

25. How does the rhythm—the pattern of syllables—in "Ballad of Birmingham" compare with the pattern of syllables in a song you like?

Critical Thinking

26. From clues in the ballad, what do you think the cowboy did wrong?

27. Why do you think Randall didn't give names to the characters in his ballad? What effect might this have on readers?

28. Use the Semantic Table described in Appendix A to compare the way the word *rose* is used in all three ballads. You might use characteristics such as "beautiful," "practical," and "aromatic" in the left column.

29. How do all of these poems tell a story? Explain your thinking.

Thinking Creatively

30. If you were going to write a ballad about a real event that was as important and terrible as the Birmingham church bombing, which event would you select? Why?

Grammar Check

Poets use end punctuation much as any author does. They use periods at the end of a sentence containing a complete thought. They use question marks to ask questions and exclamation points to state things very strongly. Review the end punctuation used in the three ballads in this section. Some people are tempted to read each line of a poem as a sentence. However, this is not what the poet intended. Reread the poems, stopping only for an end punctuation mark. How does this review help you better understand the poet's message?

 Writing on Your Own

Write a ballad telling a story you think should be told. Include at least four stanzas. Use the poems in this section as models. Look at the writing tips in Appendix C to help you think about and complete this assignment.

 Speaking

In groups, talk about the reasons these authors may have had in writing these ballads. Create a list that shows the ideas you considered and the one you finally chose as each author's purpose. Present your main idea to the entire class, giving the reasons for your selections.

 Listening

Hold a contest to see who can present one of these ballads most effectively. As a group, decide on a list of standards that students will have to meet. Give the list to all the judges. Rate each student based on how well he or she did in meeting the standards.

 Media

Find a song chart that tells you the way one of these ballads has been traditionally sung. You can use online resources or those in your public library. Learn how to play or sing the song, using the version you locate or making up your own tune. Record your version of the ballad using a tape recorder or computer.

Rhyme and Rhythm

David McCord
1897–1997

Gwendolyn Brooks
1917–2000

Objectives

■ To explore how rhythm and rhyme affect readers' experiences with poetry

■ To identify the limerick as a form of poetry that uses a specific pattern

■ To define and give examples of alliteration, assonance, and onomatopoeia

About the Authors and Selections

The poems in this section show you how poets create patterns of rhyme and rhythm in their works.

David McCord was a poet, essayist, and artist. He published 550 poems. Most of them were written for young readers. McCord once defined poetry as "the best dream from which one ever [woke] too soon." McCord's poem, "Bléssed Lord, what it is to be young," celebrates the joys of being a young person. It was first published in the 1960s as part of McCord's book *One at a Time*. McCord's work as a poet was honored by many people, including Harvard University and the National Council of Teachers of English.

In 1950, Gwendolyn Brooks became the first African American to win a Pulitzer Prize—for *Annie Allen,* a verse narrative. She grew up in Chicago and most of her poetry is about African American life. "WE REAL COOL" captures the rhythms of Chicago's pool halls and city streets, and of the young African American men who make this world their own. In interviews, Brooks said the pool players she had in mind when she wrote the poem were not sure about their place in the world. She told interviewers that she always said the "we" very softly, because she wanted to show how uncertain the boys were. Brooks loved to create poems. Her first poem was published in a magazine in 1930, when she was only 13 years old. She continued to write poetry and to open the world of poetry to everyone.

Lewis Carroll, the pen name of Charles Lutwidge Dodgson, was a British mathematician and writer in the 1800s. He gave the world *Alice's Adventures in Wonderland* and *Through the Looking-Glass,* two classic books of fantasy. The poem "Jabberwocky," from *Through the Looking-Glass,* was written in part as a gift for Carroll's brothers and sisters.

To help them understand the nonsense words of "Jabberwocky," Carroll gave them a few definitions:

brillig the time for broiling dinner; the end of the afternoon

slithy a word that combines the words *slimy* and *lithe*, and means smooth and active

toves a kind of badger

gyre to scratch like a dog

gimble to make holes in everything

wabe a side of a hill

Lewis Carroll
1832–1898

Edgar Allan Poe
1809–1849

Using these definitions, the first stanza of "Jabberwocky" means: "It was late afternoon, and the smooth, active badgers were scratching themselves and making holes in the side of the hill."

The readers of the world owe a great deal to Edgar Allan Poe. He was a unique American author who lived during the 1800s. During his short career, he created the detective story and perfected the American short story. He created tales of horror and suspense that continue to thrill readers. Along with others, he also started science fiction writing, a genre of literature that continues to be popular today. However, Poe chose to describe himself as a poet. "The Raven," "Annabel Lee," and "The Bells" are three of his most famous poems. "The Bells" shows how poets can use sound to create different moods. This poem grew from a short poem of 19 lines. A friend of Poe's suggested the first line, and Poe completed the poem. From that, it grew into an incredibly detailed look at different kinds of bells and the role they play in everyone's lives. The longer poem was first published in 1849 in a magazine.

Before Reading **continued on next page**

BEFORE READING THE SELECTIONS *(continued)*

Rhyme and Rhythm

alliteration
repeating sounds by using words whose beginning sounds are the same

assonance
repeating sounds by using words with the same vowel sounds

onomatopoeia
using words that sound like their meanings

limerick a five-line poem in which the first, second, and fifth lines, and the third and fourth lines, rhyme

Literary Terms All the poems in this section are built on the sound and meaning of words. This is especially true in "Jabberwocky," where Lewis Carroll's nonsense words are turned into poetry using these tools. Gwendolyn Brooks relies on **alliteration** in the lines, "We/lurk late" by using words that begin with the *l* sound. David McCord uses **assonance** by repeating the short *o* sound in his poem. Poe's "The Bells" is truly built on sounds. In it, Poe used **onomatopoeia**, alliteration, and assonance to create the mood of four different kinds of bells. Onomatopoeia uses words that sound like their meaning. These poems differ, however, in their patterns. McCord's poem "Blesséd Lord, what it is to be young" uses a poetry pattern called the **limerick**. On the other hand, "WE REAL COOL" is made up of eight rhyming, three-word sentences.

Reading on Your Own Poetry is not meant to be read quickly, even though some poems look very short. Read the poems in this section three times. First, understand the meaning of the words. Second, listen to the way the words sound. Third, see how the meanings and sounds come together.

Writing on Your Own Make a list of adjectives you could use to describe yourself. All of them should use alliteration, or have the same first sound as the first sound in your name.

Vocabulary Focus In "The Bells," Poe repeats the phrase "Runic rhyme." *Runes* are a type of very old letters used in ancient writing systems in northern Europe. These letters were used to write. However, they were also used as symbols to cast spells and tell fortunes. By using the phrase *Runic rhyme*, Poe is saying that the bells might have a secret message for the people who listen to them.

Think Before You Read What word patterns do you use when you talk to your friends that show rhythm and rhyme?

Blessèd Lord, what it is to be young

Blessèd Lord, what it is to be young:
To be of, to be for, be among—
    Be enchanted, **enthralled**,
    Be the caller, the called,
The singer, the song, and the sung.

— *David McCord*

The rhyme scheme here is the same as in all limericks: *a a b b a*. Here, however, the poet has a serious message.

WE REAL COOL

The Pool Players.
Seven at the Golden Shovel.

We real cool. We
Left school. We

Lurk late. We
Strike straight. We

Sing sin. We
Thin gin. We

Jazz June. We
Die soon.

— *Gwendolyn Brooks*

Brooks uses both alliteration and assonance. *Lurk late* and *strike straight* are examples of alliteration. *Cool* and *school* are examples of assonance.

enthralled charmed

JABBERWOCKY

'Twas means it was.

How does the poet help us understand what all these nonsense words might mean?

The Jabberwock, after the design by Sir John Tenniel, for the first edition, 1872, of "Through the Looking Glass."

'Twas brillig, and the slithy toves
    Did gyre and gimble in the wabe;
All mimsy were the borogoves,
4   And the mome raths outgrabe.

"Beware the Jabberwock, my son!
    The jaws that bite, the claws that catch!
Beware the Jubjub bird, and **shun**
8   The frumious Bandersnatch!"

He took his vorpal sword in hand:
    Long time the manxome foe he sought—
So rested he by the Tumtum tree,
12   And stood awhile in thought.

And as in uffish thought he stood,
    The Jabberwock, with eyes of flame,
Came whiffling through the tulgey wood,
16   And burbled as it came!

One, two! One, two! And through and through
    The vorpal blade went snicker-snack!
He left it dead, and with its head
20   He went galumphing back.

"And hast thou slain the Jabberwock?
    Come to my arms, my beamish boy!
O frabjous day! Callooh! Callay!"
24   He chortled in his joy.

'Twas brillig, and the slithy toves
    Did gyre and gimble in the wabe;
All mimsy were the borogoves,
28   And the mome raths outgrabe.

—*Lewis Carroll*

shun to avoid

The Bells

I

Hear the sledges with the bells—
    Silver bells!
What a world of merriment their melody **foretells**!
    How they tinkle, tinkle, tinkle,
      In the icy air of night!
6   While the stars that oversprinkle
    All the heavens, seem to twinkle
       With a crystalline delight;
    Keeping time, time, time,
    In a sort of Runic rhyme,
To the tintinnabulation that so musically wells
12   From the bells, bells, bells, bells,
      Bells, bells, bells—
From the jingling and the tinkling of the bells.

Sledges are sleighs, or sleds.

Runic means songlike, or poem-like. *Tintinnabulation* is the ringing of bells.

II

Hear the mellow wedding bells—
    Golden bells!
What a world of happiness their **harmony** foretells!
    Through the **balmy** air of night
18   How they ring out their delight!—
    From the **molten**-golden notes,
      And all in tune,
    What a liquid ditty floats
To the turtle-dove that listens, while she **gloats**
24   On the moon!

Poe uses onomatopoeia, imitating the sound of silvery sleigh bells with words like *tinkle, oversprinkle, twinkle.* In what other ways does he use sound to create the music of these bells?

foretells tells the future

harmony melody

balmy mild

molten heated until liquid

gloats delights in

Oh, from out the sounding cells,
What a gush of **euphony voluminously** wells!
How it swells!
How it dwells
On the Future!—how it tells
30   Of the **rapture** that impels
To the swinging and the ringing
Of the bells, bells, bells—
Of the bells, bells, bells, bells,
Bells, bells, bells—
To the rhyming and the chiming of the bells!

III

36   Hear the loud alarum bells!
Brazen bells!
What a tale of terror, now their turbulency tells!
In the startled ear of night
How they scream out their affright!
Too much horrified to speak,
42   They can only shriek, shriek,
Out of tune,
In a clamorous appealing to the mercy of the fire,
In a mad **expostulation** with the deaf and frantic fire,
Leaping higher, higher, higher,
With a desperate desire,
48   And a **resolute endeavor**
Now—now to sit or never,
By the side of the pale-faced moon.
Oh, the bells, bells, bells!

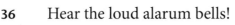

euphony a pleasing sound

voluminously hugely

rapture great happiness

brazen made of brass; bold

expostulation objection; complaint

resolute determined, firm

endeavor attempt; effort

What a tale their terror tells
        Of Despair!
54   How they clang, and clash, and roar!
    What a horror they outpour
On the **bosom** of the **palpitating** air!
        Yet the ear, it fully knows,
            By the twanging
            And the clanging,
60   How the danger **ebbs** and flows;
        Yet the ear distinctly tells,
            In the jangling,
            And the wrangling,
        How the danger sinks and swells,
By the sinking or the swelling in the anger of the bells—
66   Of the bells—
    Of the bells, bells, bells, bells,
            Bells, bells, bells—
In the clamor and the clanging of the bells!

Poe uses sounds like the *ang* in *twanging, clanging, jangling,* and *wrangling* to give a sense of these alarm bells.

IV

        Hear the tolling of the bells—
            Iron bells!
72 What a world of solemn thought their monody **compels**!
        In the silence of the night,
        How we shiver with affright
    At the **melancholy** menace of their tone!
        For every sound that floats
        From the rust within their throats
78   Is a groan.
        And the people—ah, the people—
        They that dwell up in the **steeple**,
            All alone,

A *monody* is a poem of grief; it is also a steady sound of one instrument or voice in music.

bosom a breast; a heart	**ebbs** slows down; gets lower	**melancholy** sad
palpitating beating rapidly and strongly	**compels** makes happen	**steeple** a church tower

And who, tolling, tolling, tolling,
  In that muffled **monotone**,
84   Feel a glory in so rolling
    On the human heart a stone—
They are neither man nor woman—
They are neither **brute** nor human—
    They are Ghouls:—
And their king it is who tolls:—
90   And he rolls, rolls, rolls,
    Rolls
      A pæan from the bells!
And his merry bosom swells
    With the pæan of the bells!
And he dances, and he yells;
96   Keeping time, time, time,
In a sort of Runic rhyme,
    To the pæan of the bells:—
      Of the bells:
    Keeping time, time, time,
In a sort of Runic rhyme,
102   To the throbbing of the bells—
    Of the bells, bells, bells—
To the sobbing of the bells:—
Keeping time, time, time,
    As he **knells**, knells, knells,
In a happy Runic rhyme,
108   To the rolling of the bells—
Of the bells, bells, bells:—
    To the tolling of the bells—
Of the bells, bells, bells, bells,
    Bells, bells, bells—
To the moaning and the groaning of the bells.

—*Edgar Allan Poe*

Ghouls are evil spirits that rob graves.

A *pæan* is a song of triumph or thanksgiving; the king of the ghouls is happy to grieve human beings with his bells.

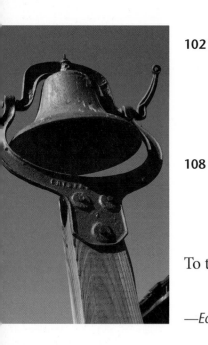

monotone sameness; on one note   **brute** an animal   **knells** rings for a death, funeral, or disaster

Rhyme and Rhythm

Directions Choose the letter of the best answer or write the answer using complete sentences.

Comprehension: Identifying Facts

1. What is the topic of McCord's poem?
   A being sad   C being young
   B hearing songs D asking questions

2. Who is "we" in "WE REAL COOL"?
   A the pool players
   B school dropouts
   C people who die young
   D all of the above

3. According to Brooks's poem, what do the speakers sing?

4. Of what does the father warn his son in "Jabberwocky"?

5. What two other creatures is the boy warned about?

6. How does the boy slay the Jabberwock?

7. In Poe's poem, what do the sledge bells foretell?

8. What color are the wedding bells in Poe's poem?

9. Which word describes the sounds of the alarum bells?

10. In Poe's poem, who sounds the church bells at night?

Comprehension: Putting Ideas Together

11. What line in McCord's poem shows the completeness of being young?
    A "Blesséd Lord"
    B "We real cool. We"
    C "The singer, the song, and the sung."
    D "Jazz June. We"

12. In her poem, Gwendolyn Brooks thinks the future of the pool players is _____.
    A rosy   C angry
    B dismal   D thoughtful

13. Retell the story of "Jabberwocky" in your own words.

14. How does the son feel when he kills the Jabberwock?

15. How does the father feel when his son comes back with the head of the Jabberwock?

16. What kind of a mood is created by the stanza of "The Bells" that talks about sleigh bells?

17. Why would people being married like to hear the harmony of the golden bells?

18. According to Poe, what effect do the alarum bells have on the people who hear them?

After Reading **continued on next page**

Rhyme and Rhythm

19. What is the difference between the mood in the second and third stanzas of Poe's poem?

20. What are the characteristics of the world the iron bells create as they toll?

Understanding Literature: Alliteration, Consonance, and Assonance

Using words with similar sounds helps create rhyme, rhythm, and "music" in a poem. The sounds can be matched in several ways.

When poets use words whose first sound matches, as in David McCord's "The singer, the song, and the sung," they are using a tool called alliteration. This kind of alliteration can also be called *consonance*. Gwendolyn Brooks uses alliteration and consonance in "We/Lurk late. We/strike straight." Notice the matching sounds at the beginning and ending of the words.

When poets use words that have the same vowel sounds, they are using a tool called *assonance*. In Brooks's poem, "cool" and "school" have the same vowel sound.

21. In *Jack and Jill went up a hill*, which words show alliteration?

22. In *Jack and Jill went up a hill*, which words show assonance?

23. Find two examples of alliteration in "Jabberwocky."

24. Find two examples of both alliteration and assonance in "The Bells."

25. Why do you think poets use tools like alliteration and assonance? What are some of their effects on poems?

Critical Thinking

26. Use a Venn Diagram, described in Appendix A, to compare McCord's poem and Brooks's poem. Both give word pictures about being young.

27. What is the effect of the short, rhymed lines of "WE REAL COOL"?

28. What are some words Poe repeats throughout "The Bells"? What do the repetitions add to the poem?

29. Which stanza of "The Bells" do you think is most similar to the climax of a story?

Thinking Creatively

30. Would you say that your life is more like the youth described in "Blesséd Lord, what it is to be young," or more like the pool players' lives in "WE REAL COOL"? Explain.

Grammar Check

Adjectives are words that describe nouns or pronouns. Poets use them to create a stronger and more detailed image in the reader's mind. For example, Poe talks about the "icy air." *Icy* is an adjective telling readers how the air feels or looks. Adjectives can also help writers compare two nouns or pronouns. For example, if someone says Brooks's poem is easier to understand than Carroll's, they are using a *comparative* form of the adjective *easy*. Comparative adjectives usually end in *–er* or *–ier*. They are used to compare two things. If writers want to compare more than two things, they use the *superlative* form of the adjective. They would say, for example, that McCord's poem was the easiest to understand in this section. Superlative adjectives usually end in *–est* or *–iest*.

 Writing on Your Own

What pictures did you see in your mind as you read each of the four stanzas of "The Bells"? Write a two-sentence description of the images you see for each stanza.

 Speaking

Practice presenting "Jabberwocky" as a choral reading. One person could take the role of the father. The others in the group could become the chorus, reading all the other lines. Practice reading all together, with pacing that helps the audience understand the words of the poem.

 Listening

In groups, brainstorm some things you should pay attention to when you listen to poems that are read aloud. Think about questions like these: Should you listen to the meaning of the words? Should you listen to the way they sound? Should you combine these two purposes? How might you do that? How can you best remember what you hear?

 Viewing

Is the illustration of *The Jabberwock* on page 394 different from the way you thought about the Jabberwock? How is it the same? Think about an illustration you might create to show a reader what the father looked like.

Victor Hugo
1802–1885

Langston Hughes
1902–1967

Objectives

- To explore how imagery helps readers understand poems
- To define and give examples of figurative language, metaphor, simile, tanka, and haiku

About the Authors and Selections

Sometimes poets use a writing tool called **imagery**. They create word pictures that appeal to the five senses—sight, smell, taste, touch, hearing. Through imagery, poets ask readers to remember the sweetness of a ripe pear or the mournful sound of a train whistle in the night. Imagery helps readers to see, hear, taste, touch, and smell a poem—rather than just think about it. All the poems in this section include striking images.

Victor Hugo was the leading literary figure in France during the 1800s. He is considered a master of French poetry. He published many books of poetry and wrote many plays. He is best known in the United States for his two great novels, *The Hunchback of Notre Dame* and *Les Misérables.* The six short lines of his poem "Be Like the Bird" give readers a clear image of a bird singing in spite of danger.

Langston Hughes wrote short stories, plays, and novels, but he is best known for his poetry. He wrote several poems about dreams. These poems all have clear images that describe how important it is to keep dreams and goals alive. "Dreams" uses two powerful images to describe what happens when dreams die.

The poet Gary Soto was born in Fresno, California. He draws many of his images from his Mexican heritage. His poem "Oranges" comes from his 1985 collection *Black Hair.* He uses images that help us see, hear, touch, smell, and taste his memory of a first girlfriend.

Lance Henson grew up in the Southern Cheyenne culture near Calumet, Oklahoma. He has published 17 volumes of poetry. Much of his work is about American Indian experiences. In "flock," he creates a sharp image drawn directly from his life on a farm in Oklahoma.

William Carlos Williams lived most of his life in Rutherford, New Jersey. He was a pediatrician as well as one of America's most important poets. "The Red Wheelbarrow," first published in 1938, is one of his most famous poems. In it, he asks readers to see a truth about life by looking clearly with their eyes, recalling their memories of the images in the poem.

In "Haiku," Etheridge Knight uses a series of nine short poems that present very clear and often startling images. Knight wrote this poem during his term in prison. Later, the poem became part of Knight's first book, *Poems from Prison,* published in 1968.

Lady Sei Shonagon was a lady-in-waiting in the court of Japan in the 900s. "The rooster's crowing" was included in an anthology of Japanese poetry collected in the 1200s. The image in the poem uses mainly the sense of hearing.

Natasha Trethewey's poem "Gathering" centers on images of harvesting fruit. An award-winning poet, Trethewey shares her love of poetry with college students, helping them develop their own writers' voices. She was born in Gulfport, Mississippi, in 1966.

Before Reading continued on next page

imagery a picture in the reader's mind created by words

William Carlos Williams
1883–1963

Etheridge Knight
1931–1991

Gary Soto
1952–

Lance Henson
1944–

Natasha Trethewey
1966–

BEFORE READING THE SELECTIONS *(continued)*

Imagery

figurative language
language that uses word pictures to compare or describe, and that is not meant to be taken as the truth

simile a figure of speech in which two things are compared using a phrase that includes the word *like* or *as*

metaphor a figure of speech that says one thing *is* another

tanka a form of Japanese poetry having five lines with five syllables in the first, seven in the second, five in the third, and seven in the fourth and fifth

haiku a form of Japanese poetry having three lines with five syllables in the first, seven in the second, and five in the third

Literary Terms One of the most important tools any writer can use is **figurative language**, or creating word pictures that help readers see a text in their minds. For example, Henson's poem "flock" ends with a powerful **simile** of snow moving "like an ancient herd." **Metaphor** is also a technique of figurative language. Hughes uses this writer's tool when he says, "Life is a barren field."

Reading on Your Own Two of the poems in this section follow specific and centuries-old word patterns. "The rooster's crowing" is a traditional form of Japanese poetry called **tanka**. Tanka usually contains 31 syllables, divided into five lines, each containing an image that flows into the next. **Haiku** is another form of traditional Japanese poetry. This form of poetry contains 17 syllables in three lines, built around one particular image. As you read the tanka and haiku in this section, look to see how these patterns carry the images the poets want readers to experience. See the images in your mind.

Writing on Your Own Sit quietly in a favorite place for a few minutes. Notice all the information that comes from your senses, such as sounds, smells, and images. Make a list of them as you notice them. Later, use one image to create a short poem.

Vocabulary Focus Poets depend on readers to call on all they have done and all they remember to add meaning to the poem itself. For example, in Lance Henson's poem, he talks about snow. The word *snow* has a specific meaning, or *denotation*. When Lance Henson asks the reader to see the snow as a moving herd, he is building a *connotation* in the reader's mind. Readers still know what *snow* means. Now they can see it as an image connected with past feelings and impressions.

Think Before You Read How might these poems compare to the others in this unit?

Be Like the Bird

Be like the bird, who
Halting in his flight
On limb too slight
Feels it give way beneath him,
Yet sings
Knowing he hath wings.

—*Victor Hugo*

Which senses does Hugo appeal to in this image of a bird? Why should we "be like the bird"?

Dreams

Hold fast to dreams
For if dreams die
Life is a broken-winged bird
That cannot fly.

Hold fast to dreams
For when dreams go
Life is a **barren** field
Frozen with snow.

—*Langston Hughes*

Hughes uses two images to describe life without dreams. What is he saying about the importance of holding on to your dreams?

What are the metaphors Hughes uses?

barren without life

Oranges

The first time I walked
With a girl, I was twelve,
Cold, and weighted down
With two oranges in my jacket.
December. Frost crackling
6 Beneath my steps, my breath
Before me, then gone,
As I walked toward
Her house, the one whose
Porch light burned yellow
Night and day, in any weather.
12 A dog barked at me, until
She came out pulling
At her gloves, face bright
With rouge. I smiled,
Touched her shoulder, and led
Her down the street, across
18 A used car lot and a line
Of newly planted trees,
Until we were breathing
Before a drugstore. We
Entered, the tiny bell
Bringing a saleslady
24 Down a narrow aisle of goods.
I turned to the candies
Tiered like bleachers,
And asked what she wanted—
Light in her eyes, a smile
Starting at the corners

Color is important in this poem. Notice the oranges, the yellow porch light, the girl's face "bright with rouge"—reddish makeup on her cheeks. Where else does color stand out?

tiered arranged in rows, one above the other

30 Of her mouth. I fingered
A nickel in my pocket,
And when she lifted a chocolate
That cost a dime,
I didn't say anything.
I took the nickel from
36 My pocket, then an orange,
And set them quietly on
The counter. When I looked up,
The lady's eyes met mine,
And held them, knowing
Very well what it was all
42 About.

       Outside,
A few cars hissing past,
Fog hanging like old
Coats between the trees.
I took my girl's hand
48 In mine for two blocks,
Then released it to let
Her unwrap the chocolate.
I peeled my orange
That was so bright against
The gray of December
54 That, from some distance,
Someone might have thought
I was making a fire in my hands.

—*Gary Soto*

Which images help you see, hear, touch, smell, and taste the poet's memory?

Notice the simile here.

flock

across the road
ice huddles against the trees

there is only a whisper of
leaves among the cottonwoods

and over the joyless valley

snow moves
like an ancient herd

—*Lance Henson*

The images in "flock" create a cold, empty feeling as the land and animals pass through winter. What picture do you get in your mind from the last two lines?

The Red Wheelbarrow

so much depends
upon

a red wheel
barrow

glazed with rain
water

beside the white
chickens.

—*William Carlos Williams*

Williams paints a kind of "picture" with words. His imagery depends on color and on the shininess of a wheelbarrow covered with rain water.

glazed glassy; smooth and shiny

Haiku

–1–

Eastern guard tower
glints in sunset; **convicts** rest
like lizards on rocks.

–2–

The piano man
is sitting at 3 am
his songs drop like plum.

–3–

Morning sun slants cell.
Drunks stagger like cripple flies
On the Jailhouse floor.

–4–

To write a blues song
Is to regiment **riots**
and pluck gems from graves.

–5–

A bare pecan tree
slips a pencil shadow down
a moonlit snow slope.

–6–

The falling snow flakes
Can not **blunt** the hard aches nor
Match the steel stillness.

–7–

Under moon shadows
A tall boy flashes knife and
Slices star bright ice.

–8–

In the August grass
Struck by the last rays of sun
The cracked teacup screams.

–9–

Making **jazz** swing in
Seventeen syllables AIN'T
No square poet's job.

—*Etheridge Knight*

The rooster's crowing

The rooster's crowing
In the middle of the night
Deceived the hearers;
But at Osaka's gateway
The guards are never fooled.

—*Lady Sei Shonagon*

In this tanka, Osaka is a major Japanese city. The rooster may fool some people into thinking it is morning. The guards at the gate think it may mean something else.

Blues (haiku #4) are a form of jazz. Blues songs are about the dark, sad parts of life. In this haiku, Knight compares writing a blues song to giving order to chaos and to taking something bright and beautiful from a dead place—something from nothing. What would "the blues" have to do with prison life?

What sense does Knight mainly appeal to with his images? What similes did he use?

glints gleams

convicts people in prison

riots public disorder

blunt to soften

jazz popular dance music with strong rhythms

Gathering

—for Sugar

Through tall grass, heavy
from rain, my aunt and I wade
into cool, fruit trees.

Near us, dragonflies
light on the clothesline, each touch
6   rippling to the next.

Green-black beetles swarm
the fruit, wings **droning** motion,
wet figs glistening.

We sigh, click our tongues,
our fingers reaching in, then
12   plucking what is left.

Under-ripe figs, green,
hard as jewels—these we save,
hold in deep white bowls.

She puts them to light
on the windowsill, tells me
18   to *wait, learn patience.*

I touch them each day,
watch them turn gold, grow sweet,
and give sweetness back.

I begin to see
our lives are like this—we take
24   what we need of light.

We glisten, preserve
handpicked days in memory,
our minds' dark pantry.

—*Natasha Trethewey*

As you read this
poem, can you
imagine yourself
in this poem's
setting?

How does
Trethewey use
figurative language
in her poem?

droning buzzing
sound

Imagery

Directions Choose the letter of the best answer or write the answer using complete sentences.

Comprehension: Identifying Facts

1. Why does the bird in Victor Hugo's poem sing?
   - **A** He likes to sing.
   - **B** He wants to sing.
   - **C** He knows he has wings.
   - **D** He is frightened.

2. In "Dreams" what does the poet say happens if dreams die?
   - **A** life is a broken-winged bird
   - **B** life is a blazing field
   - **C** dreams cannot fly
   - **D** life is fields with snow

3. What does the boy in Gary Soto's poem carry in his jacket?

4. How does the boy in "Oranges" pay for the ten-cent candy?

5. In "flock," how does the snow move, according to the poet?

6. In "The Red Wheelbarrow," what covers the wheelbarrow?

7. In Knight's first haiku, what are the resting convicts compared to?

8. According to Knight, what "AIN'T no square poet's job"?

9. In Lady Sei Shonagon's poem, what noise deceives the hearers?

10. In "Gathering," what kind of figs do the gatherers save?

Comprehension: Putting Ideas Together

11. What is Hugo saying about life in his poem?
    - **A** We cannot rise above danger.
    - **B** Sing when you are in trouble.
    - **C** Trust in yourself.
    - **D** Do not rest on a weak limb.

12. In "Dreams," how are the images of a barren field and a broken-winged bird the same?
    - **A** Both can sing songs.
    - **B** They are both red.
    - **C** Both cannot do what they are supposed to do.
    - **D** Neither can fly.

13. How does the young boy feel at the beginning of "Oranges"?

14. What does the saleslady realize when the boy pays for the chocolate?

15. What images in "flock" make you feel cold?

16. Describe the image Williams creates in "The Red Wheelbarrow."

After Reading **continued on next page**

AFTER READING THE SELECTIONS *(continued)*

Imagery

17. What is the setting for many of Knight's haiku? Explain.

18. Why does the rooster's crowing fool the people who are sleeping?

19. Why does the aunt tell the narrator of "Gathering" to have patience?

20. According to Trethewey, how is life like gathering figs?

Understanding Literature: Tanka and Haiku

Tanka and haiku are old forms of poetry that began in Japan. They are both brief. Both have a special pattern of rhythm. Tanka has five lines: five syllables in the first line, seven in the second, five in the third, and seven in the fourth and fifth. The pattern is 5–7–5–7–7.

Haiku has three lines: five syllables in the first line, seven in the second, and five in the third. The pattern is 5–7–5. The lines of haiku and tanka do not usually rhyme.

Tanka and haiku from old Japan were mainly about nature. Poets created images of the mountains, rivers, and trees they saw around them. Poets today use these forms to express many different thoughts and emotions.

21. How are tanka and haiku alike? How are they different?

22. Count the syllables in each of Knight's haiku. What syllable pattern does each stanza have?

23. What subjects does Etheridge Knight explore in his haiku?

24. Why do you think a modern writer like Knight would be interested in the haiku form? What does such a short form, with such strict rules for line and syllable count, ask of a poet?

25. In your opinion, why do tanka and haiku poets use images to express their thoughts?

Critical Thinking

26. Compare the image of a bird in Hugo's poem and in Hughes's poem. What does each mean? What picture does each create in your mind?

27. Why do you think Lance Henson calls his poem "flock"?

28. In what ways is "The Red Wheelbarrow" like haiku in its subject matter and effect?

Thinking Creatively

29. How might the poem "Oranges" have changed if the saleslady hadn't accepted the orange as payment?

30. What image in these poems was the most clear in your mind? Why?

Grammar Check

In writing, some poets always follow the rules of formal English writing. Their verbs and nouns always agree. They use participial phrases correctly. Words are always spelled correctly and used in the right form. Etheridge Knight, like many other modern poets, prefers to use language in a way that sometimes is not formal English. For example, he says that "making jazz swing in seventeen syllables ain't no square poet's job." If he had used formal English to say the same thing, he might have written, "making sense in seventeen syllables is a job for the professional poet." Why do you think Knight chooses to ignore the rules of formal English writing in his haiku? Do you think he would have ignored the rules of formal English if he wrote a letter of recommendation for one of his students? Explain your opinion.

 ## Writing on Your Own

Write a haiku about nature and a more modern haiku about the future.

 ## Speaking and Listening

Memorize one of these poems or prepare a presentation. In your presentation, use the words of a poem to build other word pictures. Practice your poem or presentation with a partner. Take turns performing your poem or presentation for the class. The audience should first tell the performers three things they liked about the presentation. Then they should add one comment about a specific way the speaker could improve.

 ## Media and Technology

Many modern poets have made recorded or written presentations of their most recent works available through the Internet. Use a search engine to locate other works or readings by poets in this section. After reading them, build your own presentation about one of these authors. Use computers and presentation software.

 ## Viewing

Locate a book or online source that presents pictures of modern art. Find drawings that match the mood, theme, or your feelings about the poems in this section.

Jane Hirshfield
1953–

Robert Frost
1874–1963

Objectives

- To understand how a poet's voice grows from tone and word choices
- To define and give examples of figurative language, mood, personification, repetition, hyperbole, and tone

About the Authors and Selections

In this section, you'll meet poets from a wide range of backgrounds and life experiences. Each has a special way of seeing the world. Each uses the tools of poetry in individual ways. In short, each poet has a clear, individual **voice**.

In "The Poet," Jane Hirshfield explores the quiet, rather lonely world of poets. She writes especially about women poets, whose life and work remain unknown to the wider world. Hirshfield first published this poem in *The Atlantic Monthly* in 1997. She has published six collections of her poems and written many essays about poets and poetry. In 2004, the Academy of American Poets gave her the 70th Academy Fellowship for her work.

Robert Frost is one of the most important and honored poets in recent times. "The Road Not Taken," first published in 1916, is one of Frost's best-known poems. In it, the poet tells how the course of his life was set when he was forced to choose between two roads in the woods. This choice becomes an image of the hard decisions people have to make.

Luis Omar Salinas is a noted poet whose main subject is the experience of Hispanic people in the United States. He was among the poets who founded the Chicano poetry movement in America. Chicano poets are people born in America whose parents and ancestors are Mexican. His 1973 poem "In a Farmhouse" is about a little boy who has worked all day in the cotton fields for $2.30. Salinas shows how poets can bring the world's attention to those who might otherwise be forgotten.

One of Lucille Clifton's main subjects for poetry is African American girls and women. Clifton's poem "this morning" describes an experience many adults have: seeing themselves as they used to be. The poem, which was first published in

1987, shows Clifton's love for the sounds of words. Clifton served as Maryland's Poet Laureate from 1979–1982.

Lan Nguyen was born in Vietnam in 1960. She spent her childhood in a country torn apart by war. "My Life Story" describes what it is like to be a young person surrounded by war and death. In simple terms, she tells how difficult it is to feel powerless—"only a sand in the big desert."

Gu Cheng, author of "A Headstrong Boy," was born in China in 1956. In 1974, he helped start a magazine to publish poetry and fiction, but the Chinese government did not approve. In his poem, Gu Cheng speaks in the voice of a "headstrong" boy, meaning a willful person who doesn't listen to others.

Carl Sandburg first earned national attention as a poet when *Poetry* magazine published "Chicago" in 1914. In all his work, Sandburg tries to capture the special ways of talking and thinking found in America's Midwest.

Nikki Giovanni has devoted much of her career to helping other African American writers find their way into the spotlight. In her poem "Nikki-Rosa," Giovanni comments on how the white culture tends to view the childhoods of African Americans who become famous. She makes it clear that "all the while I was quite happy."

Before Reading continued on next page

voice the way a writer expresses ideas through style, form, content, and purpose

Carl Sandburg
1878–1967

Nikki Giovanni
1943–

Luis Omar Salinas
1937–

Lucille Clifton
1936–

Voices

tone the attitude an author takes toward a subject

personification giving characters such as animals or objects the characteristics or qualities of humans

hyperbole an overstatement to show something is important

mood the feeling created by a piece of writing

Literary Terms Poets use tools to express a specific **tone**, or attitude, in their poems. For example, Gu Cheng uses *figurative language* to create images such as "an autumn coat the color of candle flame." Clifton uses *repetition*, repeating the phrase "this morning" to express joyful excitement. Sandburg builds his poem about Chicago by using **personification**, giving the city human characteristics. He also uses **hyperbole**, or makes things seem more than they are. Together these writer's tools and the poet's words create the poem's **mood** or feeling.

Reading on Your Own In some poetry, such as "The Road Not Taken," all the lines begin with a capital letter. This does not mean that you need to pause at the end of each line. Instead, you need to look for punctuation that tells you to pause: commas, semicolons, periods, exclamation points, colons, or dashes. This punctuation tells you how to read the poem. Other poems, such as "this morning," have no punctuation. In a poem like this, you need to look at where the poet ends lines and where she puts space to indicate a new stanza. Stanzas are like the paragraphs of a poem.

Writing on Your Own Write a humorous want ad that a poet might place in the newspaper. Advertise for things that the poet needs to create poems, such as a voice or figurative language. Before you begin, review want ads in the newspaper to get some ideas.

Vocabulary Focus Poets choose their words carefully. Look at the phrases "a *headstrong* boy," "two roads *diverged*," and "a *fathomless* sea." There are several other words the poets could have used. Use a thesaurus or dictionary to find other words the poets could have used.

Think Before You Read If a poet wrote about the lives of you and your friends, what kind of a voice would you want the poet to use? What kind of mood should the poem have?

The Poet

She is working now, in a room
not unlike this one,
the one where I write, or you read.
Her table is covered with paper.
The light of the lamp would be
6   tempered by a shade, where the bulb's
single harshness might dissolve,
but it is not; she has taken it off.
Her poems? I will never know them,
though they are the ones I most need.
Even the alphabet she writes in
12   I cannot **decipher**. Her chair—
let us imagine whether it is leather
or canvas, vinyl or wicker. Let her
have a chair, her shadeless lamp,
the table. Let one or two she loves
be in the next room. Let the door
18   be closed, the sleeping ones healthy.
Let her have time, and silence,
enough paper to make mistakes and go on.

—*Jane Hirshfield*

> The poet has taken the shade off her lamp, so nothing "tempers" the "harshness" of the light. Why do you think she has done this?

decipher to make clear; to explain

The Road Not Taken

Notice the rhyme scheme in every stanza: *a b a a b*. Frost uses end rhyme throughout the poem.

Two roads **diverged** in a yellow wood,
And sorry I could not travel both
And be one traveler, long I stood
And looked down one as far as I could
To where it bent in the undergrowth;

6 Then took the other, as just as fair,
And having perhaps a better claim,
Because it was grassy and wanted wear;
Though as for that the passing there
Had worn them really about the same.

And both that morning equally lay
12 In leaves no step had trodden black.
Oh, I kept the first for another day!
Yet knowing how way leads on to way,
I doubted if I should ever come back.

I shall be telling this with a sigh
Somewhere ages and ages **hence**:
18 Two roads diverged in a wood, and I—
I took the one less traveled by,
And that has made all the difference.

—*Robert Frost*

The speaker made a choice of path that "made all the difference" in his life. What important choices have you made in your life?

diverged branched off   **hence** in the future

In a Farmhouse

Fifteen miles
out of Robstown
with the Texas sun
4   fading in the distance
I sit in the bedroom
profoundly,
animated by the day's work
8   in the cottonfields.

I made two dollars and
thirty cents today
I am eight years old
12   and I wonder
how the rest of the Mestizos
do not go hungry
and if one were to die
16   of hunger
what an odd way
to leave for heaven.

—*Luis Omar Salinas*

Are you surprised to learn that the speaker is eight years old? How does this fact change the tone of the poem?

Mestizos are persons of mixed Spanish and American ancestry.

profoundly strongly   **animated** made lively, happy

this morning

(for the girls of eastern high school)

    this morning
    this morning
       i met myself

    coming in

5 a bright
    jungle girl
    shining
    quick as a snake
    a tall
10 tree girl a
    me girl

       i met myself

    this morning
    coming in

15 and all day
    i have been
    a black bell
    ringing
    i **survive**

20   survive
    survive

    —*Lucille Clifton*

Notice the tone of Clifton's poem. How do the sounds, short lines, and simple words help the reader see the young, lively girl being described?

survive to go on living

My Life Story

What shall I tell about my life?

a life of changes
a life of losing
remembering
eighteen years ago
6 a little child was born
surrounded by the love of family
so warm and tender
surrounded by mountains and rivers
so free and beautiful

But life was not
12 the dearest father passed away
and left a big scar in the child's head

She grew up with something missing in her
She had seen the people born and dying
  born from the war
    dying from guns and bombs

18 Sometimes she wished
she could do something
for herself and her people

But what could she do?

Nothing but watch and watch
for she is too small
24 only a sand in the big desert
no power
nothing at all

She is only herself
an ordinary person
carrying a dream
30 that seems so far, far, far away

The only thing she can do
is keep hoping
one day her dream will come true

God cannot be mean to her forever.

—*Lan Nguyen*

The poet describes very simply the horrors of growing up in a country at war.

In a metaphor, the poet compares herself to "a sand in the big desert"—one of millions, with no power.

A Headstrong Boy

Headstrong means willful—not willing to listen to anyone.

The boy wants to draw "eyes that never wept." Then, he wants to draw a love "who's never seen a mournful cloud." What do these two images have in common?

Furze is a shrub.

I guess my mother spoiled me—
I'm a headstrong boy. I want every instant
to be lovely as crayons.

4 I'd like to draw—on **chaste** white paper—
a clumsy freedom, eyes that never wept,
a piece of sky, a feather, a leaf,
a pale green evening, and an apple.

8 I'd like to draw dawn, the smile dew sees,
the earliest, tenderest love—an imaginary love
who's never seen a mournful cloud,
whose eyes the color of sky will gaze at me

12 forever, and never turn away.
I'd like to draw distance, a bright horizon,
carefree, rippling rivers, hills **sheathed** in green furze.
I want the lovers to stand together in silence,

16 I want each breathless moment to **beget** a flower.

| **chaste** pure | **sheathed** covered with something that protects | **beget** to produce |

I want to draw a future I've never seen—
nor ever can—though I'm sure she'll be beautiful.
I'll draw her an autumn coat the color of candle flame,
20 and maple leaves, and all the hearts that ever loved her.
I'll draw her a wedding, an early morning garden party,
swathed in candy-wrappers decked with winter scenes.

I'm a headstrong boy. I want to paint out every sorrow,
24 to cover the world with colored windows,
let all the eyes accustomed to darkness
be accustomed to light. I want to draw wind,
mountains, each one bigger than the last.
28 I want to draw the dream of the East,
a **fathomless** sea, a joyful voice.

Finally, I'd like to draw myself in one corner—
a panda, huddled in a dark Victorian forest,
32 hunkering in the quiet branches, homeless, lost,
not even a heart left behind me, far away,
only teeming dreams of berries
and great, wide eyes.

36 This pining's pointless.
I haven't any crayons,
any breathless moments.
All I have are fingers and pain.

40 I think I'll tear the paper to bits
and let them drift away,
hunting for butterflies.

—*Gu Cheng*
Translated by Donald Finkel

> Notice how the poet personifies the future as a woman. How is this woman described?

> From this stanza on, the poem's mood and tone change. What is the change?

> *Pining* means grieving, or weeping over something.

---

swathed wrapped   **fathomless** without bottom

Chicago

As you read, what jobs does Sandburg say Chicago can do? He is using personification.

Hog Butcher for the World,
Tool Maker, Stacker of Wheat,
Player with Railroads and the Nation's Freight Handler;

4   Stormy, husky, **brawling**,
City of the Big Shoulders:

They tell me you are wicked and I believe them, for I have seen
    your painted women under the gas lamps **luring** the farm boys.

8   And they tell me you are crooked and I answer: Yes, it is true
    I have seen the gunman kill and go free to kill again.
And they tell me you are **brutal** and my reply is: On the faces of
    women and children I have seen the marks of **wanton** hunger.

12   And having answered so I turn once more to those who sneer at
    this my city, and I give them back the sneer and say to them:
Come and show me another city with lifted head singing so proud
    to be alive and coarse and strong and cunning.

16   Flinging magnetic curses **amid** the toil of piling job on job,
    here is a tall bold slugger set vivid against the little soft cities;
Fierce as a dog with tongue lapping for action, cunning as a savage
    pitted against the wilderness,

Where does Sandburg use hyperbole?

brawling fighting	**brutal** cruel	**amid** within; between
luring attracting	**wanton** without mercy	

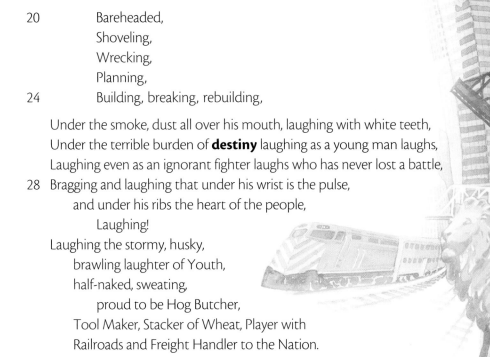

20   Bareheaded,
                Shoveling,
                Wrecking,
                Planning,
24   Building, breaking, rebuilding,

Under the smoke, dust all over his mouth, laughing with white teeth,
Under the terrible burden of **destiny** laughing as a young man laughs,
Laughing even as an ignorant fighter laughs who has never lost a battle,
28 Bragging and laughing that under his wrist is the pulse,
        and under his ribs the heart of the people,
            Laughing!
Laughing the stormy, husky,
      brawling laughter of Youth,
      half-naked, sweating,
        proud to be Hog Butcher,
      Tool Maker, Stacker of Wheat, Player with
      Railroads and Freight Handler to the Nation.

—*Carl Sandburg*

destiny what becomes
of someone or
something

425

NIKKI-ROSA

Woodlawn is a mainly African American suburb of Cincinnati, Ohio.

childhood **remembrances** are always a drag
if you're Black
3   you always remember things like living in Woodlawn
with no inside toilet
and if you become famous or something
6   they never talk about how happy you were to have your mother
all to yourself and
how good the water felt when you got your bath from one of those
9   big tubs that folk in chicago **barbecue** in
and somehow when you talk about home
it never gets across how much you
12 understood their feelings
as the whole family attended meetings about Hollydale
and even though you remember
15 your **biographers** never understand
your father's pain as he sells his stock
and another dream goes
18 and though you're poor it isn't poverty that
concerns you
and though they fought a lot
21 it isn't your father's drinking that makes any difference
but only that everybody is together and you
and your sister have happy birthdays and very good Christmasses
24 and I really hope no white person ever has cause to write about me
because they never understand Black love is Black wealth and they'll
probably talk about my hard childhood and never understand that
27 all the while I was quite happy

—*Nikki Giovanni*

The poet says that white people "never understand" that "Black love is Black wealth." What does she mean?

remembrances memories	**barbecue** to grill food outdoors	**biographers** people who write life stories of other persons

Directions Choose the letter of the best answer or write the answer using complete sentences.

Comprehension: Identifying Facts

1. In "The Poet," what has the poet done to her lamp?
   - A taken off the shade
   - B turned it off
   - C given it away
   - D decorated it

2. In "The Road Not Taken," which path does the narrator take?
   - A the path to the left
   - B the one less traveled by
   - C the grassy path
   - D the path to the right

3. How does the boy in "In a Farmhouse" make his money?

4. To whom does Lucille Clifton dedicate her poem "this morning"?

5. In "My Life Story," what event "left a big scar in the child's head"?

6. What is the only thing the child in "My Life Story" can keep hoping for?

7. What does the headstrong boy want every instant to be?

8. What does Carl Sandburg call the city of Chicago?

9. According to Nikki-Rosa, what are childhood remembrances?

10. What is the only thing that concerns the young African American girl who narrates "Nikki-Rosa"?

Comprehension: Putting Ideas Together

11. According to Hirshfield's poem, what does a poet need?
    - A a closed door C silence
    - B time   D all of these

12. Why does Frost's narrator doubt he would ever try the other path?
    - A He had miles to go.
    - B The other path was messy.
    - C The branching roads would take him far away.
    - D He wouldn't remember it.

13. Why does the little boy in "In a Farmhouse" worry about money?

14. When Lucille Clifton says "i met myself/coming in," what does she mean?

15. Why can't the narrator in "My Life Story" do anything to change her life?

16. What does the last line of "My Life Story" mean?

17. What kinds of images does the headstrong boy want to draw?

18. What does Sandburg like about Chicago?

After Reading continued on next page

19. What things about Chicago does he excuse?

20. Why doesn't the narrator in "Nikki-Rosa" want a white biographer to write about her life?

Understanding Literature: Patterns of Rhythm

Every poem has a special rhythm, created by the pattern of stressed and unstressed syllables in the words. When a word has more than one syllable, we stress one syllable more than the others. For example, the word *rhythm* has two syllables. We say *RHY-thm*, stressing the first syllable. In a poem, the rhythm is created by the way words are arranged in a single line of the poem.

The most common rhythm poets writing in English use is called *iamb*. It is a pattern of two syllables, the first one unstressed, the second stressed.

> Example: *They tell me you are wicked* would be read: *They TELL me YOU are WICK-ed*

Trochee is the opposite of iamb. It also is a two-syllable pattern. The first syllable is stressed. The second one is unstressed.

> Example: *Twinkle, twinkle little star* would be read: *TWIN-kle, TWIN-kle, LIT-tle STAR*

21. Which pattern is more like your heartbeat: an iamb or a trochee?

22. Is your first or last name iambic, trochaic, or something else?

23. How many syllables are there in the first line of "The Road Not Taken"?

24. Is the first line of Frost's poem mostly iambic or mostly trochaic?

25. What rhythm patterns do you hear in the lyrics (words) of your favorite songs? Are any iambic or trochaic?

Critical Thinking

26. Why might a poet need the kind of quiet space Hirshfield describes in her poem?

27. Compare the young man in Salinas's poem with the girls Lucille Clifton writes about.

28. Do you think Sandburg considers Chicago to be a strong or weak city? Why?

Thinking Creatively

29. What positive and negative qualities would you include in a poem about your hometown? Why?

30. Lucille Clifton thinks of herself as a bell ringing "i survive." Describe yourself coming in the door of your school. How would you act?

Grammar Check

In formal English, word structures within sentences have to be the same, or parallel. Here is an example. "I love *writing* [gerund] poetry, *singing* [gerund], and *watching* [gerund] the sun rise." This sentence has parallel structure because all the italicized words are gerunds. However, if you wrote, "I love *to watch* [infinitive] the sun rise, *singing* [gerund], and *poetry* [noun]," your sentence would not be parallel. Poets use parallel structure as well. Look at lines 4, 8, 13, 17, 23, and 30 in "A Headstrong Boy." What structure is the same in all these lines? How does this help the poet's message and the poem's structure?

 ## Writing on Your Own

With traditional Japanese tanka and haiku, one poet wrote a few lines of a poem and challenged another to add to it. Write a few lines of a poem. E-mail it to others and ask them to add to your poem and return it to you.

 ## Speaking

Plan a group presentation on a poet whose work is included in this section. Meet in your group to assign tasks. Decide how you will present the information. Complete your research and outline what you want to say. Practice your presentation before inviting an audience to observe it.

 ## Listening

Poetry slams are competitions where poets perform their own work. There are places throughout the country where you can either watch or take part in slams. Find and attend a competition near you, or start one of your own.

 ## Research

When writing research papers, it is often necessary to list online sources and the books and articles you use in a *bibliography*. There are several different formats for creating these lists. Look in Appendix C to see samples of bibliography items. List three sources you might use for a research paper about Robert Frost.

Blank Verse and Iambic Pentameter

One important pattern used in poetry is called *blank verse*. In blank verse, each line contains ten syllables. Each set of two syllables is iambic. Remember that an *iamb* is a pattern of two syllables, the first one unstressed, the second stressed. The rhythm of blank verse is called *iambic pentameter*. *Penta* means five. In each line of ten syllables, five are stressed—the second syllables in each pattern.

For example, *today* is an iambic word, because it has the stress, or accent, on the second syllable: *to-DAY*. When you read blank verse, you should hear this pattern:

> ta-DUM, ta-DUM, ta-DUM,
> ta-DUM, ta-DUM.

William Shakespeare used iambic pentameter in many of his plays. For example, read the following excerpt from *Romeo and Juliet*:

> Come, gentle night; come, loving, black-browed night;
>
> Give me my Romeo; and, when he shall die,
>
> Take him and cut him out in little stars,
>
> And he will make the face of heaven so fine
>
> That all the world will be in love with night
>
> And pay no worship to the garish sun.

Juliet tells how much she loves Romeo. "That all the world will be in love with night" contains ten syllables, so it is an example of pentameter. The stress pattern is:

> That ALL / the WORLD / will BE / in LOVE / with NIGHT

This is an iambic pattern—the second syllables are stressed. Therefore, this part of the play is written in iambic pentameter. It is an example of blank verse.

Review

1. How many syllables are in this line from Juliet's speech: "Take him and cut him out in little stars"?

2. Based on this syllable count, what do we call this rhythm?

3. Which syllables are stressed, or accented, in this line?

4. What do we call this pattern of stressed syllables?

5. Are all the lines in this speech examples of iambic pentameter? Give any examples of lines with a different pattern.

Writing on Your Own

Write two lines of poetry in iambic pentameter.

Poetry is different from prose in its form and language. Most poems are written in lines and stanzas. Some poems rhyme, and many have patterns of rhythm. Poets, even more than prose writers, use word "tools" that expand the sounds and add to the meanings of words.

Compared with most prose literature, poems are short. Using few words, poets create word pictures that tap into readers' senses, memories, and personal experiences. Some poets use patterns of rhyming words. They use stressed and unstressed syllables to help readers read and understand some poems. Other poets use no rhyme or regular rhythms. This is especially true of modern poets. The meaning of their poems comes mainly through word choice and word arrangement.

Like prose literature, poetry is as old as human expression. All cultures have poets and enjoy poetry. The range of subjects, forms, and language possible for poetry is vast.

Selections

- "Ballads and Songs" includes an old love poem, a cowboy ballad, and a modern ballad about a terrible bombing during the civil rights struggles of the 1960s.

- The poems in "Rhyme and Rhythm" show different uses of the writer's tools of sound. This section includes a serious limerick, a nonsense poem that makes perfect sense, and a poem that imitates the sounds and creates the mood of bells. Simple rhymes capture the jazzy, sometimes hopeless lives of young people.

- "Imagery" includes skillful uses of the tools of meaning. Two poems use a bird as a very different image. Other poems use images featuring colors, sounds, textures, smells, and tastes. Two poems show the power of the Japanese forms tanka and haiku. Another tells about lessons drawn from gathering fruit.

- In "Voices," there are poems from authors representing many different groups and a wide range of experiences. Poetry is used to help readers understand people they might never meet in life: unpublished poets, girls at a city high school, a young cotton-picker, a girl growing up in war-torn Vietnam. An experience as simple as choosing one path over another suggests other important choices people must make. Other poems tell about a happy childhood and a city made almost human by a poet's skillful use of language.

Directions Choose the letter of the best answer or write the answer using complete sentences.

Comprehension: Identifying Facts

1. In preparing her child for church, the mother in "Ballad of Birmingham" _____.
   A took her downtown
   B helped her put on white shoes
   C cut her hair
   D gave her some money

2. In "The Bells," how do the iron bells toll?

3. In "Oranges," when was the first time the narrator walked with a girl?

4. In "The Poet," who should be in the room next to the poet?

5. Why is the headstrong boy's pining pointless?

Comprehension: Putting Ideas Together

6. What words does Poe use that imitate the sounds they make (onomatopoeia)?
   A *Ghoul* and *endeavor*
   B *Tinkle* and *jingling*
   C *Liquid ditty floats*
   D *All* and *tune*

7. What kind of exaggeration, or hyperbole, does Burns use in his poem?

8. What is the tone of "The Road Not Taken"? Use evidence from the poem to explain your answer.

9. How does the narrator in "this morning" see her future?

10. Why does the headstrong boy want to imagine himself as a panda?

Understanding Literature: Form in Poetry

As you saw in the poetry included in this unit, poets use more than words to communicate. Some poets also use the *form* of the poem. This is a specific pattern of syllables and lines that becomes the backbone of the poem.

Some poems have punctuation, like prose does. In these poems, you need to look for punctuation that tells you where to pause. Commas, semicolons, periods, exclamation points, colons, or dashes may be used. The punctuation tells you how to read the poem.

Other poems, such as "this morning," have no punctuation. In a poem like this, you need to look at where Clifton ends lines and where she puts space to indicate a new stanza. Stanzas are like the paragraphs of a poem.

11. How does punctuation tell you where to pause in a poem?

12. How should you read a poem that has no punctuation?

13. Why should you pay attention to lines and stanzas in poems?

14. In the first two lines of Poe's "The Bells," where should you pause?

15. How many stanzas are in Poe's poem?

Critical Thinking

16. Which poem in this unit has the most optimistic or happiest mood? Explain your selection.

17. Compare the tone in two poems that focus on being young: "this morning" and "My Life Story."

18. Why does the narrator in "Nikki-Rosa" feel like her life has been happy—despite what other people might say?

Thinking Creatively

19. Do you think the traveler in "The Road Not Taken" regrets his choice? Explain your opinion.

20. If you were a poet, what kinds of poems would you write? Which subjects would you explore?

Speak and Listen

Some poems are meant to be read aloud. Look over Edgar Allan Poe's "The Bells." Pick one stanza and practice reading it aloud with expression and understanding. Make sure the tone of your voice matches the tone of the stanza. When you are satisfied with your work, record the stanza.

Writing on Your Own

Write a poem about a subject in one of the poems in this unit. Pick a topic and use a Concept Map, described in Appendix A, to brainstorm ideas about the topic. Consider whether you want the poem to rhyme or not, or be in specific form. Write and edit a draft. Ask a partner to review it, then rewrite the draft.

Beyond Words

Create a painting, drawing, or sculpture that represents one of the images from a poem in this unit.

Test-Taking Tip

When a test question asks you to write a paragraph, make a plan first. Jot down the main idea for your paragraph. List the supporting details you can include. Then write the paragraph.

Tkts on Broadway
Patti Mollica, 2001

Unit 8 Drama

D rama is a form of storytelling meant to be performed by actors on a stage. In the Western world, the kinds of drama we see today began in ancient Greece. Then and now, playwrights—writers of plays—tell their stories completely through the words and actions of characters. Plays are often grouped as either tragedies or comedies according to the outcome of their plots.

In this unit, you will read the last act of a classic tragedy of young love, the first scene from a powerful realistic drama about African American life after World War II, and a short television comedy.

"There was never yet an uninteresting life. Such a thing is an impossibility. Inside of the dullest exterior there is a drama, a comedy, and a tragedy."

—Mark Twain, 1905

Unit 8

About Drama

Drama is a special form of literature. Drama is meant to be performed as well as read. The word *drama* comes from the Greek word *dran*, meaning to do, or to act. The ancient Greeks were the first people in the Western world to set the form for the activity that we call drama.

Like other forms of literature in this text, plays are written to tell a story. However, when a play is performed, the story is told completely through the words—called dialogue—and actions of characters. Characters in a play are very similar to the characters in short stories, fables, legends, and tall tales. The play's main character is called the protagonist. There is usually an antagonist who tries to make things difficult for the protagonist. As in all literature, characters in a play can be flat or round, unchanging or changing. Playwrights, or writers of plays, cannot present characters' thoughts, as can writers of fiction. They have to let the characters speak for themselves or be revealed through the words of other characters.

Plays are divided into two groups according to the outcome of their plots: tragedies and comedies.

A tragedy is a serious play that ends unhappily, with the suffering or death of the main character. Tragedies usually explore serious subjects, such as the meaning of life and the importance of relationships. Comedies, on the other hand, have happy endings and are written to amuse people. In the comedies of ancient Greece, protagonists accomplished their goals, or got what they wanted. Today, people define comedy more broadly. Today's comedies are expected to make people laugh.

The action of a play is divided into acts and scenes. An act is a major unit of action. Acts are divided into smaller parts, called scenes. Each scene takes place in one setting only. This division into acts and scenes gives a play an order of events and allows settings to change. In Shakespeare's time, the five-act play was standard. Today's plays tend to be in three acts. Many plays have only one act.

Whether or not readers have seen a play on stage, most have seen another form of drama: plays written for television, film, and video. Like all plays, dramas written for these medias can be comedies or tragedies. They can tell stories about ordinary people or about unusual people.

At the Theatre,
Pierre Auguste Renoir, circa 1876

The main difference between plays and other forms of storytelling is that plays are meant to be performed by actors on a stage. The meaning of a play is found not only on the page, but also in the relationship between the play and its audience. Each time a play is performed, it becomes a new experience in some ways for both actors and audience. The dialogue stays the same, as do the costumes and sets. But the way the actors speak the lines and the way they move can change in small, yet important ways. That is why readers of a play need to imagine how lines would be spoken by actors, and how actions would be performed.

In this unit, you will sample three different forms of drama. William Shakespeare's *Romeo and Juliet* is the tragic story of two unlucky young lovers. This tale has gripped audiences around the world for centuries. Lorraine Hansberry's *A Raisin in the Sun* is a realistic modern drama. The play was written about 50 years ago and continues to be performed often. "Writer's Realm" is a script written for a television series by Anne Jarrell-France. It shows how today's television writers still use the basics of dramatic form.

**William Shakespeare
1564–1616**

Objectives

- To define elements in a drama that make it a tragedy
- To explore how a writer uses dialogue and monologue to tell a story
- To explain how a play is constructed using acts and scenes
- To define and give examples of climax, dramatic irony, and foreshadowing

About the Author

William Shakespeare is perhaps the best-known writer in the history of Western **drama**. A drama is a play, or a work written to be performed. People throughout the world have enjoyed his poems and dramas for centuries. Given this fame, it is surprising that so little is known of the actual man.

We know that Shakespeare was born in 1564 in Stratford-upon-Avon, England. He was the son of a businessman and probably attended the local school, where he would have read the classic plays of ancient Greece and Rome. He married Anne Hathaway in 1582, and they had three children. Little else is known of his life until 1592, when he is mentioned in records of the time as writing plays in London. In 1594, he became involved in the Lord Chamberlain's Men, a group that later performed in the Globe Theater. He acted with this group, wrote some of their plays, and eventually became a part owner of the company. Shakespeare retired from the theater and London around 1611. He returned to Stratford, where he died in 1616.

Shakespeare wrote many kinds of plays. Most were performed by his theater company, and he acted in several himself. His works are usually divided into four periods. *Romeo and Juliet* is from Shakespeare's second period. It was probably first performed in 1596.

About the Selection

Romeo and Juliet is a **tragedy**, meaning a play that ends with the suffering or death of one or more of the main characters. It tells the story of two young people whom Shakespeare describes as "star-crossed lovers." This means that they are unlucky, as if their sad future has been written in the stars. The play takes place in the northern Italian city of Verona. Juliet is part of the Capulet family. Romeo is a Montague. The Capulets and Montagues have been enemies for many years. Romeo and Juliet meet and fall in love before they realize that each is the other's sworn enemy. But their love is very strong, and they secretly marry. Then, in a street fight, Juliet's cousin, Tybalt, threatens Romeo's best friend, Mercutio. Romeo tries to break up the fight, but Tybalt kills Mercutio. In revenge, Romeo kills Tybalt. Angry, the Prince of Verona orders Romeo banished from the city. He must go to Mantua, a nearby town.

In the meantime, Juliet's parents have arranged for her to marry another man, Paris. Rather than do this, Juliet seeks the advice of Friar Lawrence. He is the Catholic brother who performed Juliet's secret wedding to Romeo. The friar gives her medicine that will make it appear as if she has died. The plan is that Friar Lawrence will write to Romeo, tell him what they have done, and have Romeo rescue Juliet from the Capulet family's tomb.

This selection is the fifth, and final, act of the play. As Act V begins, Juliet has taken the medicine. Others believe she is dead and lying in her tomb. Friar Lawrence has given his letter for Romeo to a messenger. Unfortunately, the messenger is delayed and Balthasar, Romeo's servant, gets to Romeo first. Balthasar doesn't know about Juliet's plan. He tells Romeo that Juliet is dead. The stage is set for the dramatic ending of the play.

drama a story told through the words and actions of characters, written to be performed as well as read; a play

tragedy a play that ends with the suffering or death of one or more of the main characters

Characters in *Romeo and Juliet,* Act V

The Montague Family	**Friends of the Montagues**	**Montague Family Servants**	**Others**
Romeo	Mercutio, *Romeo's friend and a relative of the Prince of Verona*	Balthasar, *Romeo's servant*	The Prince of Verona
Montague, *Romeo's father*			Friar Lawrence
Lady Montague, *Romeo's mother*			Friar John
			The apothecary
			Paris's page *(servant)*
The Capulet Family	**Friends of the Capulets**	**Capulet Family Servants**	Chief watchman
Juliet	Paris, *chosen by Juliet's parents to marry her and a relative of the Prince of Verona*	Juliet's nurse	Second watchman
Capulet, *Juliet's father*			Third watchman
Lady Capulet, *Juliet's mother*			
Tybalt, *Juliet's cousin*			

Before Reading **continued on next page**

Romeo and Juliet by *William Shakespeare*

act a major unit of action in a play

climax the high point of interest or suspense in a story or play

dialogue the conversation among characters in a story or play

monologue a speech by one person

foreshadowing clues or hints that a writer gives about something that has not yet happened

dramatic irony when the audience or reader knows more than the characters know

scene a unit of action in a play that takes place in one setting

Literary Terms In this selection, the final **act** of *Romeo and Juliet*, Shakespeare creates an emotional and heartbreaking **climax** for his "star-crossed" lovers. The climax of a play is its high point of interest. Through the **dialogue** and **monologues**—conversations and speeches—this famous author created, he gives his audience clues about what is going to happen. These clues, called **foreshadowing**, prepare the audience for this act's terrible events. The act includes a famous example of **dramatic irony**, when the audience realizes what Romeo does not. Only the audience knows that his Juliet is not dead. She has taken medicine that makes it look as if she is dead. By giving his audiences this knowledge, Shakespeare brings them directly into this tragedy.

Reading on Your Own Shakespeare's plays were written over 500 years ago, using the language and customs that were common in England at that time. You may want to read the notes in the margins first, to get an idea of what is happening in the play. Then, read the play that Shakespeare wrote. As you read, look for words and experiences in the play that foreshadow the tragic climax of this world-famous play.

Writing on Your Own Do you think people are really "star-crossed"—that their fate is already determined when they are born? Write a paragraph explaining your opinion on this topic.

Vocabulary Focus In writing this play, Shakespeare used stage directions in each **scene**, or setting, to tell the actors what to do. For example, *Enter* is a direction for the actor to come on stage. *Exit* or *Retires* is a direction for the actor to leave the stage. Shakespeare used the direction *Exeunt* when more than one actor was supposed to leave the stage. *Aside* is a direction for the actor to say his words, or lines, directly to the audience and not to the other actors on stage.

Think Before You Read Why do you think *Romeo and Juliet* might be one of Shakespeare's most famous plays?

Romeo & Juliet

Act V
Scene I. Mantua. A street.

Enter Romeo.

Romeo If I may trust the **flattering** truth of sleep,
My dreams presage some joyful news at hand.
My bosom's lord sits lightly in his throne,
And all this day an unaccustomed spirit
5   Lifts me above the ground with cheerful thoughts.
I dreamt my lady came and found me dead
(Strange dream that gives a dead man leave to think!)
And breathed such life with kisses in my lips
That I revived and was an emperor.
10   Ah me! How sweet is love itself possessed,
When but love's shadows are so rich in joy!

Enter Romeo's Man [Balthasar, booted].

News from Verona! How now, Balthasar?
Dost thou not bring me letters from the friar?
How doth my lady? Is my father well?
15   How fares my Juliet? That I ask again.
For nothing can be ill if she be well.

flattering pleasing or soothing to oneself

Man Then she is well, and nothing can be ill.
Her body sleeps in Capel's monument,
And her **immortal** part with angels lives.
20 I saw her laid low in her **kindred's** vault
And presently took post to tell it you.
O, pardon me for bringing these ill news,
Since you did leave it for my office, sir.

Romeo Is it e'en so? Then I defy you, stars!
25 Thou knowest my lodging. Get me ink and paper
And hire post horses. I will hence tonight.

Man I do **beseech** you, sir, have patience.
Your looks are pale and wild and do import
Some misadventure.

Romeo   Tush, thou art deceived.
30 Leave me and do the thing I bid thee do.
Hast thou no letters to me from the friar?

Man No, my good lord.

Romeo   No matter. Get thee gone.
And hire those horses. I'll be with thee straight.

Exit [Balthasar].

Well, Juliet, I will lie with thee tonight.
35 Let's see for means. O mischief, thou art swift
To enter in the thoughts of desperate men!
I do remember an apothecary,
And hereabouts 'a dwells, which late I noted,
In tatt'red weeds, with overwhelming brows,
40 **Culling** of simples. **Meager** were his looks,

Capel's monument is the Capulet family tomb.

Office means duty.

Romeo reacts to the news of Juliet's supposed death by announcing that he will return to Verona that night. Notice how Balthasar's words help us understand Romeo's feelings. Romeo's *pale* and *wild* appearance suggests some misfortune to come.

Romeo recalls seeing a druggist *(apothecary)* nearby, in torn clothing and with a frowning expression. The man was collecting herbs *(simples)* used as medicine.

immortal free from death	**beseech** to beg	**meager** thin
kindred relatives	**culling** collecting or sorting	

Sharp **misery** had worn him to the bones;
And in his needy shop a tortoise hung,
An alligator stuffed, and other skins
Of ill-shaped fishes; and about his shelves
45 A beggarly account of empty boxes,
Green earthen pots, bladders, and musty seeds,
Remnants of packthread, and old cakes of roses
Were thinly scatterèd, to make up a show.
Noting this **penury**, to myself I said,
50 "And if a man did need a poison now
Whose sale is present death in Mantua,
Here lives a caitiff **wretch** would sell it him."
O, this same thought did but forerun my need,
And this same needy man must sell it me.
55 As I remember, this should be the house.
Being holiday, the beggar's shop is shut.
What, ho! Apothecary!

[Enter Apothecary.]

Apothecary   Who calls so loud?

Romeo Come hither, man. I see that thou art poor.
Hold, there is forty ducats. Let me have
60 A dram of poison, such soon-speeding gear
As will **disperse** itself through all the veins
That the life-weary taker may fall dead,
And that the trunk may be **discharged** of breath
As **violently** as hasty powder fired
65 Doth hurry from the fatal cannon's womb.

Apothecary Such mortal drugs I have; but Mantua's law
Is death to any he that utters them.

The druggist,
Romeo recalls,
was very poor and
looked shabby.
Such a miserable
(caitiff) man, he
thinks, would sell
him poison, which
is illegal in Mantua.

Romeo asks for
fast-working *(soon-speeding)* poison.
The *trunk* is the
body.

Mortal means
deadly. *Utters*
means sells.

misery suffering	**wretch** a miserable creature	**discharged** let out
remnants traces	**disperse** to scatter	**violently** done with strong, rough force
penury poverty		

Romeo Art thou so bare and full of wretchedness
And fearest to die? **Famine** is in thy cheeks,
70 Need and **oppression** starveth in thy eyes,
Contempt and beggary hangs upon thy back:
The world is not thy friend, nor the world's law;
The world affords no law to make thee rich;
Then be not poor, but break it and take this.

75 **Apothecary** My poverty but not my will consents.

Romeo I pay thy poverty and not thy will.

Apothecary Put this in any liquid thing you will
And drink it off, and if you had the strength
Of twenty men, it would **dispatch** you straight.

80 **Romeo** There is thy gold—worse poison to men's souls,
Doing more murder in this **loathsome** world,
Than these poor compounds that thou mayst not sell.
I sell thee poison; thou hast sold me none.
Farewell. Buy food and get thyself in flesh.
85 Come, **cordial** and not poison, go with me
To Juliet's grave; for there must I use thee.

Exeunt.

Romeo urges the druggist to sell him the poison. He points out how poor and starving the man is. Since "the world's law," Romeo says, has not helped him, the druggist does not need to obey the law. The druggist gives in, but only because he needs the money.

Romeo notes that *gold*—money—has destroyed more people than poison has. For him, the poison is life-giving because it will take him where he thinks Juliet has gone: into death.

famine hunger	**contempt** scorn	**cordial** life-giving liquid
oppression unjust or cruel	**dispatch** to kill	
	loathsome hateful	

Friar Lawrence's *cell* is his small room. Friar John is the messenger who was to have brought the letter to Romeo in Mantua.

Scene II. Friar Lawrence's cell.

Enter Friar John to Friar Lawrence.

John Holy Franciscan friar, brother, ho!

Enter [Friar] Lawrence.

Lawrence This same should be the voice of Friar John.
Welcome from Mantua. What says Romeo?
Or, if his mind be writ, give me his letter.

5 **John** Going to find a barefoot brother out,
One of our order, to **associate** me
Here in this city visiting the sick,
And finding him, the searchers of the town,
Suspecting that we both were in a house
10 Where the **infectious pestilence** did **reign**,
Sealed up the doors, and would not let us forth,
So that my speed to Mantua there was stayed.

Lawrence Who bare my letter, then, to Romeo?

John I could not send it—here it is again—
15 Nor get a messenger to bring it thee,
So fearful were they of infection.

Lawrence Unhappy fortune! By my brotherhood,
The letter was not nice, but full of charge,
Of dear import; and the neglecting it
20 May do much danger. Friar John, go **hence**,
Get me an iron crow and bring it straight
Unto my cell.

Friar John was looking for another religious brother to go with him to Mantua. The other man was visiting sick people. Health officers, thinking that both had been with sick people and might spread disease, wouldn't let either leave. Friar John was unable to go to Mantua.

Friar Lawrence remarks that his letter was urgently important. *Nice* means unimportant.

An *iron crow* is a crowbar, a tool used to pry something open.

associate to accompany	**infectious** catching	**reign** rule
	pestilence disease	**hence** away

John   Brother, I'll go and bring it thee.

Exit.

Lawrence Now must I to the monument alone.
Within this three hours will fair Juliet wake.
25 She will beshrew me much that Romeo
Hath had no notice of these accidents;
But I will write again to Mantua,
And keep her at my cell till Romeo come —
Poor living corse, closed in a dead man's tomb!

Exit.

Friar Lawrence hurries off to the tomb where, in three hours, Juliet will wake up. He plans to write to Romeo again, keeping Juliet with him until Romeo arrives. *Corse* is another word for *corpse*, or dead body. Juliet is alive, but she appears dead.

Scene III. A churchyard; in it a monument belonging to the Capulets.

Enter Paris and his Page [with flowers and sweet water].

Paris Give me thy torch, boy. Hence, and stand **aloof**.
Yet put it out, for I would not be seen.
Under yond yew trees lay thee all along,
Holding thy ear close to the hollow ground.
5 So shall no foot upon the churchyard tread
(Being loose, unfirm, with digging up of graves)
But thou shalt hear it. Whistle then to me,
As signal that thou hearest something approach.
Give me those flowers. Do as I bid thee, go.

10 **Page** *[Aside]* I am almost afraid to stand alone
Here in the churchyard; yet I will adventure.

[Retires.]

Paris is the man Juliet's parents chose for her to marry. His young servant is with him.

Lay thee all along means lie flat on the ground. Paris asks the page to listen for the footsteps of anyone coming.

aloof apart

Paris Sweet flower, with flowers thy bridal bed I **strew**
　　(O woe! thy canopy is dust and stones)
　Which with sweet water nightly I will dew;
15　　Or, wanting that, with tears distilled by moans.
　The obsequies that I for thee will keep
　Nightly shall be to strew thy grave and weep.

Whistle Boy.

　The boy gives warning something doth approach.
　What cursèd foot wanders this way tonight
20　To cross my obsequies and true love's **rite**?
　What, with a torch? Muffle me, night, awhile.

[Retires.]

Enter Romeo, [and Balthasar with a torch,
a mattock, and a crow of iron].

Romeo Give me that mattock and the wrenching iron
　Hold, take this letter. Early in the morning
　See thou deliver it to my lord and father.
25　Give me the light. Upon thy life I charge thee,
　Whate'er thou hearest or seest, stand all aloof
　And do not interrupt me in my course.
　Why I descend into this bed of death
　Is partly to behold my lady's face,
30　But chiefly to take thence from her dead finger
　A precious ring—a ring that I must use
　In dear employment. Therefore hence, be gone.
　But if thou, jealous, dost return to **pry**
　In what I farther shall intend to do,
35　By heaven, I will tear thee joint by joint

Paris has come to Juliet's tomb to scatter perfumed flowers. Obsequies are funeral ceremonies.

Romeo and Balthasar have a torch (for light), an axe (mattock), and a crowbar (also called a wrenching iron). The tools are for opening Juliet's tomb.

Romeo plans to take a ring from Juliet's finger and use it for an important purpose (dear employment).

strew to scatter widely　**rite** a ceremony　**pry** to snoop; to spy

And strew this hungry churchyard with thy limbs.
The time and my intents are savage-wild,
More fierce and more **inexorable** far
Than empty tigers or the roaring sea.

40 **Balthasar** I will be gone, sir, and not trouble ye.

Romeo So shalt thou show me friendship. Take thou that
Live, and be prosperous; and farewell, good fellow.

Balthasar *[Aside]* For all this same, I'll hide me here-about
His looks I fear, and his intents I doubt. *[Retires.]*

45 **Romeo** Thou **detestable** maw, thou womb of death,
Gorged with the dearest **morsel** of the earth,
Thus I enforce thy rotten jaws to open,
And in despite I'll cram thee with more food.

[Romeo opens the tomb.]

Paris This is that banished **haughty** Montague
50 That murd'red my love's cousin—with which grief
It is supposed the fair creature died—
And here is come to do some villainous shame
To the dead bodies. I will **apprehend** him.
Stop thy **unhallowèd** toil, vile Montague!
55 Can **vengeance** be pursued further than death?
Condemnèd villain, I do apprehend thee.
Obey, and go with me; for thou must die.

Romeo I must indeed; and therefore came I hither.
Good gentle youth, tempt not a desp'rate man.
60 Fly hence and leave me. Think upon these gone;
Let them affright thee. I beseech thee, youth,

> Romeo curses the tomb as a *maw*, or stomach, that is stuffed with the *dearest morsel of the earth*—Juliet. He vows to add more food to the tomb—himself.

> Paris thinks Romeo, having killed Juliet's cousin, Tybalt, has come to take further revenge on the Capulet family. The family assumes that Juliet died from grief over Tybalt's death.

---

inexorable unable to be changed

detestable hateful

morsel a small piece

haughty feeling superior to others

apprehend to catch; to arrest

unhallowed unholy

vengeance harm done in return for a wrong

Romeo begs Paris, whom he does not recognize, not to anger him into more violence.

Conjurations are appeals. Paris ignores Romeo's plea.

Put not another sin upon my head
By urging me to fury. O, be gone!
By heaven, I love thee better than myself,
65 For I come hither armed against myself.
Stay not, be gone. Live, and hereafter say
A madman's mercy bid thee run away.

Paris I do defy thy conjurations.
And apprehend thee for a **felon** here.

70 **Romeo** Wilt thou **provoke** me? Then have at thee, boy!

[They fight.]

Page O Lord, they fight! I will go call the watch.

[Exit. Paris falls.]

Paris O, I am slain! If thou be merciful,
Open the tomb, lay me with Juliet.

[Dies.]

Here is the beginning of a monologue by Romeo. Romeo now recognizes Paris, who was a relative of Mercutio, Romeo's best friend. He bitterly regrets having killed him. *County* is a title, like Count. *Betossed* means upset. *To attend* means to pay attention to. *Writ* means wrote or written. *Lanthorn* is a dome with windows; it is also another word for lantern.

Romeo In faith, I will. Let me **peruse** this face.
75 Mercutio's **kinsman**, noble County Paris!
What said my man when my betossèd soul
Did not attend him as we rode? I think
He told me Paris should have married Juliet.
Said he not so, or did I dream it so?
80 Or am I mad, hearing him talk of Juliet,
To think it was so? O, give me thy hand,
One writ with me in sour misfortune's book!
I'll bury thee in a triumphant grave.
A grave? O, no, a lanthorn, slaught'red youth,

felon a person who has committed a crime

provoke to cause someone to take action

peruse to look at

kinsman a relative

85 For here lies Juliet, and her beauty makes
This vault a feasting presence full of light.
Death, lie thou there, by a dead man interred.

[Lays him in the tomb.]

How oft when men are at the point of death
Have they been merry! Which their keepers call
90 A lightning before death. O, how may I
Call this a lightning? O my love, my wife!
Death, that hath sucked the honey of thy breath,
Hath had no power yet upon thy beauty.
Thou art not conquered. Beauty's ensign yet
95 Is **crimson** in thy lips and in thy cheeks,
And death's pale flag is not advancèd there.
Tybalt, liest thou there in thy bloody sheet?
O, what more favor can I do thee
Then with that hand that cut thy youth in twain
100 To sunder his that was thine enemy?
Forgive me, cousin! Ah, dear Juliet,
Why art thou yet so fair? Shall I believe
That **unsubstantial** Death is amorous,
And that the lean **abhorrèd** monster keeps
105 Thee here in dark to be his paramour?
For fear of that I still will stay with thee
And never from this pallet of dim night
Depart again. Here, here will I remain
With worms that are thy chambermaids. O, here
110 Will I set up my everlasting rest
And shake the yoke of **inauspicious** stars
From this world-wearied flesh. Eyes, look your last!
Arms, take your last embrace! And lips, O you

Juliet's beauty makes the tomb seem like a hall lit for a celebration. *Interred* means buried. The dead man is Paris.

It used to be thought that people feel happy just before dying. Romeo does not feel this *lightning*. *Keepers* are jailers.

Juliet, whom the audience knows is not really dead, has color in her lips and cheeks. An *ensign* is a flag, or banner.

Romeo, seeing Tybalt's body, promises to kill himself with the same hand—his own—that murdered Tybalt.

Since Juliet remains so beautiful, Romeo wonders if Death has fallen in love with her. To protect her from her lover Death, Romeo will stay with her forever in the tomb (by killing himself).

crimson red	**unsubstantial** not physical, of the spirit	**abhorred** hated
		inauspicious unlucky

A *conduct* is a guide. The poison is Romeo's *bitter conduct* and *unsavory guide.* The *desperate pilot* is Romeo himself, running his *seasick weary bark* (his body—a *bark* is a boat) onto the rocks—into death.

Stumbling was considered a sign of bad luck to come.

The doors of breath, seal with a **righteous** kiss
115 A dateless bargain to **engrossing** death!
Come, bitter conduct; come, **unsavory** guide!
Thou desperate pilot, now at once run on
The dashing rocks thy seasick weary bark!
Here's to my love! *[Drinks.]* O true apothecary!
120 Thy drugs are quick. Thus with a kiss I die.   *[Falls.]*

Enter Friar [Lawrence], with lanthorn, crow, and spade.

Friar Saint Francis be my speed! How oft tonight
Have my old feet stumbled at graves! Who's there?

Balthasar Here's one, a friend, and one that knows you well.

righteous good; right   **engrossing** taking in everything   **unsavory** unpleasant; bad-tasting

Friar **Bliss** be upon you! Tell me, good my friend,
125 What torch is yond that vainly lends his light
To grubs and eyeless skulls? As I **discern**,
It burneth in the Capels' monument.

Balthasar It doth so, holy sir; and there's my master,
One that you love.

Friar   Who is it?

Balthasar   Romeo.

Friar How long hath he been there?

130 **Balthasar**   Full half an hour.

Friar Go with me to the vault.

Balthasar   I dare not, sir.
My master knows not but I am gone hence,
And fearfully did menace me with death
If I did stay to look on his intents.

135 **Friar** Stay then; I'll go alone. Fear comes upon me.
O, much I fear some ill unthrifty thing.

Balthasar As I did sleep under this yew tree here,
I dreamt my master and another fought,
And that my master slew him.

Friar   Romeo!
140 Alack, alack, what blood is this which stains
The stony entrance of this sepulcher?
What mean these masterless and gory swords
To lie discolored by this place of peace?

Friar Lawrence sees Romeo's light shining from the Capulets' tomb. He remarks that light is wasted on *grubs*—worms—and dead bodies. Since Romeo is now dead, the friar's words are truer than he knows.

Here you are reading a dialogue between Friar and Balthasar.

Ill means bad; *unthrifty* means unfortunate.

A *sepulcher* is a tomb. The friar sees Romeo's swords. They are *masterless* (abandoned) and bloody. The swords were used to kill Paris.

---

bliss great happiness   **discern** to recognize;
to make out

[Enters the tomb.]

Romeo! O, pale! Who else? What, Paris too?
145 And steeped in blood? Ah, what an unkind hour
Is guilty of this **lamentable** chance!
The lady stirs.

[Juliet rises.]

Juliet O comfortable friar! Where is my lord?
I do remember well where I should be,
150 And there I am. Where is my Romeo?

Friar I hear some noise. Lady, come from that nest
Of death, **contagion**, and unnatural sleep.
A greater power than we can **contradict**
Hath **thwarted** our intents. Come, come away.
155 Thy husband in thy **bosom** there lies dead;
And Paris too. Come, I'll dispose of thee
Among a sisterhood of holy **nuns**.
Stay not to question, for the watch is coming.
Come, go, good Juliet. I dare no longer stay.

160 **Juliet** Go, get thee hence, for I will not away.

Exit [Friar].

What's here? A cup, closed in my truelove's hand?
Poison, I see, hath been his timeless end.
O churl! Drunk all, and left no friendly drop
To help me after? I will kiss thy lips.
165 Haply some poison yet doth hang on them
To make me die with a restorative.   *[Kisses him.]*
Thy lips are warm!

Thwarted our intents means ruined our plans.

The friar has heard the watchman coming. Frightened of being discovered, he leaves.

A *churl* is a selfish person. Juliet calls Romeo selfish for leaving no *friendly drop* of poison for her. A *restorative* is medicine. She kisses Romeo in hopes of getting some poison from his lips.

lamentable causing sorrow

contagion a spreading disease

contradict to deny

thwarted blocked or stopped

bosom a breast; a heart

nuns women belonging to a religious order

Chief Watchman *[Within]* Lead, boy. Which way?

Juliet Yea, noise? Then I'll be brief. O happy dagger!

> *[Snatches Romeo's dagger.]*

This is thy **sheath**; there rust, and let me die.

> *[She stabs herself and falls.]*

> *Enter [Paris'] Boy and Watch.*

170 **Boy** This is the place. There, where the torch doth burn.

Chief Watchman The ground is bloody. Search about the churchyard.
Go, some of you; whoe'er you find attach.

Happy means convenient. Juliet thinks that Romeo's dagger is a good thing, because it will allow her to kill herself and join Romeo in death.

Do you think this may be the climax of the play?

Attach means arrest.

sheath a cover or case

[Exeunt some of the Watch.]

Pitiful sight! Here lies the County slain;
And Juliet bleeding, warm, and newly dead,
175 Who here hath lain this two days burièd.
Go, tell the Prince; run to the Capulets;
Raise up the Montagues; some others search.

[Exeunt others of the Watch.]

We see the ground whereon these woes do lie,
But the true ground of all these **piteous** woes

> The chief watchman says that they cannot understand the cause of these *woes* (misery, sorrows) without knowing the facts.

180 We cannot without **circumstance** descry.

Enter [some of the Watch, with] Romeo's Man [Balthasar].

Second Watchman Here's Romeo's man. We found
him in the churchyard.

Chief Watchman Hold him in safety till the Prince
come hither.

Enter Friar [Lawrence] and another Watchman.

Third Watchman Here is a friar that trembles, sighs,
  and weeps.
We took this mattock and this spade from him
185 As he was coming from this churchyard's side.

> *Stay* means keep or hold. They think that the friar may have something to do with these deaths.

Chief Watchman A great **suspicion**! Stay the friar too.

Enter the Prince [and Attendants].

Prince What misadventure is so early up,
That calls our person from our morning rest?

---

pitiful full of sadness   **piteous** miserable; sad   **suspicion** mistrust; doubt
circumstance details

Enter Capulet and his Wife [with others].

Capulet   What should it be, that is so shrieked abroad?

190 **Lady Capulet**   O, the people in the street cry "Romeo,"
Some "Juliet," and some "Paris"; and all run
With open outcry toward our monument.

Prince   What fear is this which startles in your ears?

Chief Watchman   **Sovereign**, here lies the County
   Paris slain;
195 And Romeo dead; and Juliet, dead before,
Warm and new killed.

Prince   Search, seek, and know how this foul murder comes.

Chief Watchman   Here is a friar, and slaughtered
   Romeo's man,
With instruments upon them fit to open
200 These dead men's tombs.

Capulet   O heavens! O wife, look how our daughter
   bleeds!
This dagger hath mista'en, for, lo, his house
Is empty on the back of Montague,
And it missheathèd in my daughter's bosom!

205 **Lady Capulet**   O me, this sight of death is as a bell
That warns my old age to a sepulcher.

Enter Montague [and others].

Prince   Come, Montague; for thou art early up
To see thy son and heir more early down.

Juliet's father says that the knife *(dagger)* in Juliet's body has lost its way. It should be in Romeo's back, not in his daughter's breast. His *house* is the knife's case.

sovereign a king

Montague Alas, my liege, my wife is dead tonight!
210 Grief of my son's **exile** hath stopped her breath.
What further woe **conspires** against mine age?

Prince Look, and thou shalt see.

Montague Oh thou untaught! What manners is in this,
To press before thy father to a grave?

215 **Prince** Seal up the mouth of outrage for a while,
Till we can clear these **ambiguities**
And know their spring, their head, their true descent;
And then will I be general of your woes
And lead you even to death. Meantime forbear,
220 And let mischance be slave to patience.
Bring forth the parties of suspicion.

Friar I am the greatest, able to do least,
Yet most suspected, as the time and place
Doth make against me, of this direful murder;
225 And here I stand, both to **impeach** and **purge**
Myself condemnèd and myself excused.

Prince Then say at once what thou dost know in this.

Friar I will be brief, for my short date of breath
Is not so long as is a **tedious** tale.
230 Romeo, there dead, was husband to that Juliet;
And she, there dead, that's Romeo's faithful wife.
I married them; and their stol'n marriage day
Was Tybalt's doomsday, whose **untimely** death
Banished the new-made bridegroom from this city;
235 For whom, and not for Tybalt, Juliet pined.

exile separation from homeland

conspires plots against

ambiguities mysteries

impeach to accuse

purge to free from blame

tedious tiring; boring

untimely before it should happen

You, to remove that **siege** of grief from her,
Betrothed and would have married her perforce
To County Paris. Then comes she to me
And with wild looks bid me **devise** some mean
240 To rid her from this second marriage,
Or in my cell there would she kill herself.
Then gave I her (so tutored by my art)
A sleeping **potion**; which so took effect
As I intended, for it wrought on her
245 The form of death. Meantime I writ to Romeo
That he should hither come as this **dire** night
To help to take her from her borrowed grave,
Being the time the potion's force should cease.
But he which bore my letter, Friar John,
250 Was stayed by accident, and yesternight
Returned my letter back. Then all alone
At the prefixèd hour of her waking
Came I to take her from her kindred's vault;
Meaning to keep her closely at my cell
255 Till I conveniently could send to Romeo.
But when I came, some minute ere the time
Of her awakening, here untimely lay
The noble Paris and true Romeo dead.
She wakes; and I **entreated** her come forth
260 And bear this work of heaven with patience;
But then a noise did scare me from the tomb,
And she, too desperate, would not go with me,
But, as it seems, did violence on herself.
All this I know, and to the marriage
265 Her nurse is privy; and if aught in this
Miscarried by my fault, let my old life

Wrought (line 244) means brought about. Friar Lawrence had given Juliet a drink that made her look as if she were dead.

The friar had written to Romeo, telling him to come to the tomb on this night, when the drink's effects would wear off.

When Friar John came back with Romeo's letter, undelivered, Friar Lawrence came alone to the tomb at the *prefixed*—set in advance—hour of Juliet's waking up. He planned to hide her in his room until he could contact Romeo. The friar found Romeo and Paris dead. He heard the watchmen, but Juliet would not go away with him. Instead, she *did violence on herself*—killed herself. The friar notes that Juliet's nurse is *privy*—shares the secret—to Juliet's marriage.

siege a serious attack

betrothed promised in marriage; engaged

devise to think up

potion a drink with special powers

dire severe; terrible

entreated begged

Be sacrificed some hour before his time
Unto the **rigor** of severest law.

Prince We still have known thee for a holy man.
270 Where's Romeo's man? What can he say to this?

Balthasar I brought my master news of Juliet's death;
And then in post he came from Mantua
To this same place, to this same monument.
This letter he early bid me give his father,
275 And threat'ned me with death, going in the vault,
If I departed not and left him there.

Prince Give me the letter. I will look on it.
Where is the County's page that raised the watch?
Sirrah, what made your master in this place?

280 **Boy** He came with flowers to strew his lady's grave;
And bid me stand aloof, and so I did.
Anon comes one with light to ope the tomb;
And by and by my master drew on him;
And then I ran away to call the watch.

285 **Prince** This letter doth make good the friar's words,
Their course of love, the tidings of her death;
And here he writes that he did buy a poison
Of a poor pothecary and therewithal
Came to this vault to die and lie with Juliet.
290 Where be these enemies? Capulet, Montague,
See what a **scourge** is laid upon your hate,
That heaven finds means to kill your joys with love.
And I, for winking at your **discords** too,
Have lost a brace of kinsmen. All are punished.

rigor strictness   **scourge** a punishment   **discords** quarrels

295 **Capulet** O brother Montague, give me thy hand.
This is my daughter's jointure, for no more
Can I demand.

    Montague   But I can give thee more;
For I will raise her statue in pure gold,
That whiles Verona by that name is known,
300 There shall no figure at such rate be set
As that of true and faithful Juliet.

    Capulet As rich shall Romeo's by his lady's lie—
Poor sacrifices of our **enmity**!

    Prince A glooming peace this morning with it brings.
305 The sun for sorrow will not show his head.
Go hence, to have more talk of these sad things;
Some shall be pardoned, and some punishèd;
For never was a story of more woe
Than this of Juliet and her Romeo.

                         [Exeunt omnes.]

FINIS

A *jointure* is a wedding gift. As his gift to his dead daughter, Juliet's father shakes hands with his former enemy, Romeo's father.

Montague will build a golden statue to Juliet. *Rate* means value. As long as their city is called Verona, no one will be as valued as *true and faithful Juliet*.

Capulet promises to build a similar statue to Romeo. The two young people were the *poor sacrifices* to their families' quarrels.

Glooming (line 304) means cloudy, gloomy.

enmity hatred

AFTER READING THE SELECTION

Romeo and Juliet *by William Shakespeare*

Directions Choose the letter of the best answer or write the answer using complete sentences.

Comprehension: Identifying Facts

1. What does Romeo say he dreamed about?
   - **A** Balthasar, Romeo's man
   - **B** news from Verona
   - **C** being asleep
   - **D** Juliet brings him back to life

2. What does Balthasar, Romeo's servant, tell him about Juliet?
   - **A** She is coming to see Romeo.
   - **B** Her body lies in the Capulet's family tomb.
   - **C** She is ill and needs help.
   - **D** Juliet has married Paris.

3. What does Romeo ask the apothecary (druggist) to give him?

4. Why is Friar John not able to deliver the letter to Romeo?

5. Who does Romeo fight with inside Juliet's tomb?

6. How does Romeo kill himself?

7. What happens to Juliet when Friar Lawrence enters the tomb?

8. What does Juliet do when she realizes that Romeo is dead?

9. Who explains the plan Romeo and Juliet had made in order to be married?

10. How does Romeo's father plan to honor Juliet?

Comprehension: Putting Ideas Together

11. Why is Romeo happy when the fifth act begins?
    - **A** He is going to get news about Juliet.
    - **B** He had a dream about Juliet.
    - **C** He is in love.
    - **D** all of the above

12. Why does Romeo decide he must kill himself?
    - **A** His cousin is dead.
    - **B** His family will no longer give him money.
    - **C** Juliet doesn't love him anymore.
    - **D** none of the above

13. How does Romeo convince the apothecary (druggist) to sell him the illegal poison?

14. Why is Friar Lawrence upset when he finds out Romeo never got his letter?

15. How does Paris feel as he enters Juliet's tomb?

16. Why does Romeo beg Paris not to fight with him?

17. Why does Romeo call the poison an "unsavory guide"?

18. Why have Friars Lawrence and John come to Juliet's tomb?

19. How does Juliet feel when she awakens?

20. Why does the Prince say "all are punished" at the end of this act?

Understanding Literature: Tragedy

A tragedy is a play with serious themes in which one or more main characters suffers or dies. The Greek philosopher Aristotle said that tragedies make an audience feel both pity and fear. The audience feels pity for the characters' suffering. They feel fear as they watch characters being destroyed. As they become involved in the play's events, however, they are *purged*—washed clean—of these strong emotions.

Shakespeare's tragedies followed the Greek model in some ways but also showed his own creative genius. *Romeo and Juliet* is Shakespeare's first romantic tragedy. He based it on a story that was already well known. His play made the tale of these tragic young lovers popular for centuries.

21. List four characteristics of a tragedy.

22. What events in this act might cause audiences to feel pity for Romeo and Juliet?

23. Why might audiences feel fear for the characters?

24. Why is this play called a romantic tragedy?

25. How does the conclusion of this play help the audience become purged of their strong emotions?

Critical Thinking

26. Do you think Romeo is justified in killing Paris? Why or why not?

27. In your own words, describe Juliet's feelings when she wakes up to find Romeo dead. How would you have felt? What would you have done?

28. At the end of the play, the prince says, "Some shall be pardoned, and some punished." Who do you think should be punished? Who should be pardoned? Why?

Thinking Creatively

29. How would this play have been different if Juliet had awakened from her drugged sleep just a few moments earlier?

After Reading continued on next page

30. If you were a friend of Romeo or Juliet, what would you have said or done when they told you they wanted to be married?

 Grammar Check

In formal English, writers use *parentheses* to set aside certain information in a sentence. Shakespeare uses parentheses in this act when the friar says: "Then gave I her (so tutored by my art)/ A sleeping potion." The sentence is complete without the information in the parentheses. Shakespeare also used brackets [like this] to set stage directions apart from the rest of the play. People who write plays today still use brackets around their stage directions. How are brackets and parentheses the same? How are they different? Find four places in this act when Shakespeare uses either parentheses or brackets.

 Writing on Your Own

When Romeo goes to Juliet's tomb, he gives Balthasar a letter to give to his father. Draft, revise, and write the letter that Romeo might have written. You may use Appendix C for help.

 Speaking

Dialogue is the conversation two or more people share in a story or play. With a partner, create a dialogue between Romeo and Juliet's parents, meeting to talk about the way their children feel about one another. Practice the dialogue and ask a classmate to review the presentation. Consider making changes based on the review before presenting the dialogue to your class.

 Listening

Imagine that you are going to see a performance of *Romeo and Juliet*. Think about the way you will listen to the dialogue as you watch the actors. What are you going to listen for? How can you best be prepared for listening to the words of this play? Create a listening strategy to address these questions.

 Research

In addition to being an outstanding writer, Shakespeare also coined, or first used, many words that we use today. Use a dictionary to learn the definitions and *etymology*, or word origin, of these words that Shakespeare first used:

birthplace   gloomy
bump   mountaineer
eyeball

BEFORE READING THE SELECTION

A Raisin in the Sun by Lorraine Hansberry

About the Author

Lorraine Hansberry was the first African American woman to have a play produced on Broadway: *A Raisin in the Sun,* in 1959. Born in Chicago in 1930, she was the child of well-respected parents. Famous African Americans, such as poet Langston Hughes, often came to their home. Her parents also fought against laws that kept African Americans from moving to certain neighborhoods and attending certain schools.

At first, Hansberry planned to be an artist. However, when she moved to New York in 1950, she discovered her true gift, writing. She followed *A Raisin in the Sun* with another play, *The Sign in Sidney Brustein's Window.* This play was less successful. Lorraine Hansberry died of cancer when she was 34.

About the Selection

A Raisin in the Sun is a play that marked many "firsts." It opened on Broadway on March 11, 1959, and won the New York Drama Critics Circle Award for Best Play. It was the first time an African American was awarded this prize. The play's director was the first African American to direct a play on Broadway. The play also helped the career of noted actor and director Sidney Poitier. The first cast also featured famous actors such as Ruby Dee, Louis Gossett Jr., and Ivan Dixon.

This play is set in Chicago in the early 1950s. It is based on Hansberry's family struggles in moving into a neighborhood where no other African Americans lived. The family challenged laws that discriminated against African Americans. The play features members of the Younger family, an extended African American family, as they struggle to find a better way to live their lives.

The selection you will read is Act I, Scene One, the very beginning of the play. The entire Younger family is waiting for an insurance check that they feel will solve all their problems.

Before Reading continued on next page

Lorraine Hansberry
1930–1965

Objectives

- To read and understand a drama
- To identify character traits and conflicts a playwright uses to drive the plot of a realistic drama
- To define and give examples of allusion and stage directions

realistic drama
a play that tells
a story just as it
might happen in
real life

stage directions
notes by the writer
of a play describing
such things as
setting, lighting,
sound effects, and
how the actors are
to look, behave,
move, and speak

character trait
a character's way of
thinking, behaving,
or speaking

conflict the
struggle of the
main character
against himself or
herself, another
person, or nature

playwright
a writer of plays

allusion
a reference to
characters or
themes in another
piece of literature

Literary Terms *A Raisin in the Sun* is a **realistic drama** about an African American family living in Chicago. It is a story about a family in the 1950s, shortly after World War II. Through her dialogue and **stage directions**, Hansberry creates a complex picture of the family's everyday world. The stage directions tell how the characters look and act and the way the stage looks. As the play begins, Hansberry is careful to present the **character traits** and **conflicts** that will become more developed as the play goes on. To set the tone of her drama, this **playwright** also includes an **allusion** or reference to Langston Hughes's poem "Dream Deferred" in the preface, or introduction to the play.

Reading on Your Own Look at the way the playwright, or writer of the drama, reveals the characters to you. As the play begins, what do they say to each other? What do their words show about their relationships? Predict what might happen to these characters later on in the play, based on the way they behave at the beginning of the play.

Writing on Your Own Think about a dream you may have had that you couldn't follow. Use that experience to write your thoughts about the question Hughes asks in his poem: "What happens to a dream deferred?" *Deferred* means put off.

Vocabulary Focus This play's dialogue reflects the way real people speak in real situations. Sometimes the dialect does not follow the rules of formal English. For example, when her husband asks if Travis is out of the bathroom, Ruth responds: "He ain't hardly got in there good yet." The audience knows what she means, even though she hasn't used formal English. Find three more examples of dialogue that use this kind of language. Rewrite them in formal English.

Think Before You Read From the way the play begins, do you think it will have a happy or sad ending?

What happens to a dream **deferred**?
Does it dry up
Like a raisin in the sun?
Or **fester** like a sore—
And then run?
Does it stink like rotten meat
Or crust and sugar over—
Like a syrupy sweet?

Maybe it just sags
Like a heavy load.

Or does it explode?

— *Langston Hughes*

A Raisin in the Sun

Act I

Scene One

The YOUNGER *living room would be a comfortable and well-ordered room if it were not for a number of indestructible contradictions to this state of being. Its furnishings are typical and undistinguished and their primary feature now is that they have clearly had to accommodate the living of too many people for too many years—and they are tired. Still, we can see that at some time, a time probably no longer remembered by the family (except perhaps for* MAMA*) the furnishings of this room were actually selected with care and love and even hope—and brought to this apartment and arranged with taste and pride.*

That was a long time ago. Now the once loved pattern of the couch upholstery has to fight to show itself from under acres of crocheted doilies and couch covers which have themselves finally come to be more important than the upholstery. And here a table or a chair has been moved to disguise the worn places in the carpet; but the carpet has fought back by showing its weariness, with depressing uniformity, elsewhere on its surface.

deferred put off   **fester** get infected

Weariness has, in fact, won in this room. Everything has been polished, washed, sat on, used, scrubbed too often. All pretenses but living itself have long since vanished from the very atmosphere of this room.

Moreover, a section of this room, for it is not really a room unto itself, though the landlord's lease would make it seem so, slopes backward to provide a small kitchen area, where the family prepares the meals that are eaten in the living room proper, which must also serve as dining room. The single window that has been provided for these "two" rooms is located in this kitchen area. The sole natural light the family may enjoy in the course of a day is only that which fights its way through this little window.

At left, a door leads to a bedroom which is shared by MAMA *and her daughter,* BENEATHA. *At right, opposite, is a second room (which in the beginning of the life of this apartment was probably a breakfast room) which serves as a bedroom for* WALTER *and his wife,* RUTH.

Time: Sometime between World War II and the present.

Place: Chicago's Southside.

At Rise: It is morning dark in the living room. TRAVIS *is asleep on the make-down bed at center. An alarm clock sounds from within the bedroom at right, and presently* RUTH *enters from that room and closes the door behind her. She crosses sleepily toward the window. As she passes her sleeping son she reaches down and shakes him a little. At the window she raises the shade and a dusky Southside morning light comes in feebly. She fills a pot with water and puts it on to boil. She calls to the boy, between yawns, in a slightly muffled voice.*

RUTH *is about thirty. We can see that she was a pretty girl, even* **exceptionally** *so, but now it is apparent that life has been little that she expected, and disappointment has already begun to hang in her face. In a few years, before thirty-five even, she will be known among her people as a "settled woman."*

She crosses to her son and gives him a good, final, rousing shake.

> "The present" is the 1950s.

> Notice all we learn about the setting and about Ruth in these stage directions. Stage directions in this drama (after the introduction) are in parentheses and printed in italics.

exceptionally more than usual

Ruth Come on now, boy, it's seven thirty! *(Her son sits up at last, in a stupor of sleepiness)* I say hurry up, Travis! You ain't the only person in the world got to use a bathroom! *(The child, a sturdy, handsome little boy of ten or eleven, drags himself out of the bed and almost blindly takes his towels and "today's clothes" from drawers and a closet and goes out to the bathroom, which is in an outside hall and which is shared by another family or families on the same floor.* RUTH *crosses to the bedroom door at right and opens it and calls in to her husband)* Walter Lee! . . . It's after seven thirty! Lemme see you do some waking up in there now! *(She waits)* You better get up from there, man! It's after seven thirty I tell you. *(She waits again)* All right, you just go ahead and lay there and next thing you know Travis be finished and Mr. Johnson'll be in there and you'll be fussing and cussing round here like a mad man! And be late too! *(She waits, at the end of patience)* Walter Lee—it's time for you to get up!

*(She waits another second and then starts to go into the bedroom, but is apparently satisfied that her husband has begun to get up. She stops, pulls the door to, and returns to the kitchen area. She wipes her face with a moist cloth and runs her fingers through her sleep-**disheveled** hair in a vain effort and ties an apron around her housecoat. The bedroom door at right opens and her husband stands in the doorway in his pajamas, which are rumpled and mismated. He is a lean, intense young man in his middle thirties, inclined to quick nervous movements and **erratic** speech habits— and always in his voice there is a quality of **indictment**)*

Walter Is he out yet?

Ruth What you mean *out*? He ain't hardly got in there good yet.

Walter *(Wandering in, still more **oriented** to sleep than to a new day)* Well, what was you doing all that yelling for if I can't even get in there yet? *(Stopping and thinking)* Check coming today?

Ruth They *said* Saturday and this is just Friday and I hopes to God you ain't going to get up here first thing this morning

As you read, decide what the most important conflict in this play is.

Notice how the dialogue helps make this play a realistic drama.

stupor a daze	**erratic** not ordinary; unexpected	**oriented** turned toward
disheveled not neat	**indictment** finding fault	

Drama Unit 8 **469**

and start talking to me 'bout no money—'cause I 'bout don't want to hear it.

Walter Something the matter with you this morning?

Ruth No—I'm just sleepy as the devil. What kind of eggs you want?

Walter Not scrambled. (RUTH *starts to scramble eggs*) Paper come? (RUTH *points impatiently to the rolled up* Tribune *on the table, and he gets it and spreads it out and vaguely reads the front page*) Set off another bomb yesterday.

Ruth (***Maximum indifference***) Did they?

Walter (*Looking up*) What's the matter with you?

Ruth Ain't nothing the matter with me. And don't keep asking me that this morning.

Walter Ain't nobody bothering you. (*Reading the news of the day absently again*) Say Colonel McCormick is sick.

Ruth (*Affecting tea-party interest*) Is he now? Poor thing.

Walter (*Sighing and looking at his watch*) Oh, me. (*He waits*) Now what is that boy doing in that bathroom all this time? He just going to have to start getting up earlier. I can't be being late to work on account of him fooling around in there.

Ruth (*Turning on him*) Oh, no he ain't going to be getting up no earlier no such thing! It ain't his fault that he can't get to bed no earlier nights 'cause he got a bunch of crazy good-for-nothing clowns sitting up running their mouths in what is supposed to be his bedroom after ten o'clock at night . . .

> Travis sleeps on a fold-out couch in the living room.

Walter That's what you mad about, ain't it? The things I want to talk about with my friends just couldn't be important in your mind, could they?

(*He rises and finds a cigarette in her handbag on the table and crosses to the little window and looks out, smoking and deeply enjoying this first one*)

---

maximum the most   **indifference** a lack of concern

Ruth *(Almost matter of factly, a complaint too automatic to deserve **emphasis**)* Why you always got to smoke before you eat in the morning?

Walter *(At the window)* Just look at 'em down there . . . Running and racing to work . . . *(He turns and faces his wife and watches her a moment at the stove, and then, suddenly)* You look young this morning, baby.

Ruth *(Indifferently)* Yeah?

Walter Just for a second—stirring them eggs. It's gone now— just for a second it was—you looked real young again. *(Then, **drily**)* It's gone now—you look like yourself again.

Ruth Man, if you don't shut up and leave me alone.

Walter *(Looking out to the street again)* First thing a man ought to learn in life is not to make love to no colored woman first thing in the morning. You all some evil people at eight o'clock in the morning.

(TRAVIS appears in the hall doorway, almost fully dressed and quite wide awake now, his towels and pajamas across his shoulders. He opens the door and signals for his father to make the bathroom in a hurry)

Travis *(Watching the bathroom)* Daddy, come on! *(WALTER gets his bathroom utensils and flies out to the bathroom)*

Ruth Sit down and have your breakfast, Travis.

Travis Mama, this is Friday. *(Gleefully)* Check coming tomorrow, huh?

Ruth You get your mind off money and eat your breakfast.

Travis *(Eating)* This is the morning we supposed to bring the fifty cents to school.

Ruth Well, I ain't got no fifty cents this morning.

Travis Teacher say we have to.

Since the Younger family shares the bathroom in the hall with another family, they must hurry to get in first.

---

emphasis importance   **drily** in a sharp, bitter way

Ruth I don't care what teacher say. I ain't got it. Eat your breakfast, Travis.

Travis I *am* eating.

Ruth Hush up now and just eat!

*(The boy gives her an **exasperated** look for her lack of understanding, and eats **grudgingly**)*

Travis You think Grandmama would have it?

What makes this dialogue sound like real life?

Ruth No! And I want you to stop asking your grandmother for money, you hear me?

Travis *(Outraged)* Gaaaleee! I don't ask her, she just gimme it sometimes!

Ruth Travis Willard Younger—I got too much on me this morning to be—

Travis Maybe Daddy—

Ruth *Travis!*

*(The boy hushes **abruptly**. They are both quiet and tense for several seconds)*

What are we learning about each person's character traits? How are the characters alike? How are they different?

Travis *(Presently)* Could I maybe go carry some groceries in front of the supermarket for a little while after school then?

Ruth Just hush, I said. (TRAVIS jabs his spoon into his cereal bowl viciously, and rests his head in anger upon his fists) If you through eating, you can get over there and make up your bed.

(The boy obeys stiffly and crosses the room, almost mechanically, to the bed and more or less carefully folds the covering. He carries the bedding into his mother's room and returns with his books and cap)

Travis *(Sulking and standing apart from her unnaturally)* I'm gone.

---

exasperated annoyed or bothered	**grudgingly** unwillingly	**abruptly** suddenly, without warning

Ruth (*Looking up from the stove to inspect him automatically*) Come here. (*He crosses to her and she studies his head*) If you don't take this comb and fix this here head, you better! (*TRAVIS puts down his books with a great sigh of **oppression**, and crosses to the mirror. His mother mutters under her breath about his "slubbornness"*) 'Bout to march out of here with that head looking just like chickens slept in it! I just don't know where you get your slubborn ways . . . And get your jacket, too. Looks chilly out this morning.

Travis (*With **conspicuously** brushed hair and jacket*) I'm gone.

Ruth Get carfare and milk money—(*Waving one finger*)—and not a single penny for no caps, you hear me?

Travis (*With **sullen** politeness*) Yes'm.

(*He turns in outrage to leave. His mother watches after him as in his **frustration** he approaches the door almost comically. When she speaks to him, her voice has become a very gentle tease*)

Ruth (*Mocking; as she thinks he would say it*) Oh, Mama makes me so mad sometimes, I don't know what to do! (*She waits and continues to his back as he stands stock-still in front of the door*) I wouldn't kiss that woman good-bye for nothing in this world this morning! (*The boy finally turns around and rolls his eyes at her, knowing the mood has changed and he is **vindicated**; he does not, however, move toward her yet*) Not for nothing in this world! (*She finally laughs aloud at him and holds out her arms to him and we see that it is a way between them, very old and practiced. He crosses to her and allows her to **embrace** him warmly but keeps his face fixed with **masculine** rigidity. She holds him back from her presently and looks at him and runs her fingers over the features of his face. With utter gentleness—*) Now—whose little old angry man are you?

Travis (*The masculinity and gruffness start to fade at last*) Aw gaalee—Mama . . .

oppression unjust treatment	**sullen** bad-tempered	**vindicated** forgiven
conspicuously obviously	**frustration** anger at defeat	**embrace** to hug
		masculine male

Ruth (*Mimicking*) Aw—gaaaaalleeeee, Mama! (*She pushes him, with rough playfulness and finality, toward the door*) Get on out of here or you going to be late.

Travis (*In the face of love, new* **aggressiveness**) Mama, could I *please* go carry groceries?

Ruth Honey, it's starting to get so cold evenings.

Walter (*Coming in from the bathroom and drawing a make-believe gun from a make-believe holster and shooting at his son*) What is it he wants to do?

Ruth Go carry groceries after school at the supermarket.

Walter Well, let him go . . .

Travis (*Quickly, to the ally*) I *have* to—she won't gimme the fifty cents . . .

Walter (*To his wife only*) Why not?

How would you describe Ruth's relationship with her son? With her husband? Between father and son?

Ruth (*Simply, and with flavor*) 'Cause we don't have it.

Walter (*To* RUTH *only*) What you tell the boy things like that for? (*Reaching down into his pants with a rather important gesture*) Here, son—

(*He hands the boy the coin, but his eyes are directed to his wife's.* TRAVIS *takes the money happily*)

Travis Thanks, Daddy.

(*He starts out.* RUTH *watches both of them with murder in her eyes.* WALTER *stands and stares back at her with* **defiance**, *and suddenly reaches into his pocket again on an afterthought*)

Walter (*Without even looking at his son, still staring hard at his wife*) In fact, here's another fifty cents . . . Buy yourself some fruit today—or take a taxicab to school or something!

Travis Whoopee—

(*He leaps up and clasps his father around the middle with his legs, and they face each other in* **mutual** *appreciation; slowly*

mimicking imitating	**aggressiveness** forceful energy	**defiance** to disobey boldly
		mutual shared

WALTER LEE *peeks around the boy to catch the **violent** rays from his wife's eyes and draws his head back as if shot)*

Walter You better get down now—and get to school, man.

Travis *(At the door)* O.K. Good-bye.

 (He exits)

Walter *(After him, pointing with pride)* That's *my* boy. *(She looks at him in disgust and turns back to her work)* You know what I was thinking 'bout in the bathroom this morning?

Ruth No.

Walter How come you always try to be so pleasant!

Ruth What is there to be pleasant 'bout!

Walter You want to know what I was thinking 'bout in the bathroom or not!

Ruth I know what you thinking 'bout.

Walter *(Ignoring her)* 'Bout what me and Willy Harris was talking about last night.

Ruth *(Immediately—a **refrain**)* Willy Harris is a good-for-nothing loud mouth.

Walter Anybody who talks to me has got to be a good-for-nothing loud mouth, ain't he? And what you know about who is just a good-for-nothing loud mouth? Charlie Atkins was just a "good-for-nothing loud mouth" too, wasn't he! When he wanted me to go in the dry-cleaning business with him. And now—he's grossing a hundred thousand a year. A hundred thousand dollars a year! You still call *him* a loud mouth!

Ruth *(Bitterly)* Oh, Walter Lee . . .

(She folds her head on her arms over the table)

> Why is Ruth so short with Walter?

violent furious	**refrain** repeated words

Walter *(Rising and coming to her and standing over her)* You tired, ain't you? Tired of everything. Me, the boy, the way we live—this beat-up hole—everything. Ain't you? *(She doesn't look up, doesn't answer)* So tired—moaning and groaning all the time, but you wouldn't do nothing to help, would you? You couldn't be on my side that long for nothing, could you?

Ruth Walter, please leave me alone.

Walter A man needs for a woman to back him up . . .

Ruth Walter—

Walter Mama would listen to you. You know she listen to you more than she do me and Bennie. She think more of you. All you have to do is just sit down with her when you drinking your coffee one morning and talking 'bout things like you do and—*(He sits down beside her and demonstrates **graphically** what he thinks her methods and tone should be)*—you just sip your coffee, see, and say easy like that you been thinking 'bout that deal Walter Lee is so interested in, 'bout the store and all, and sip some more coffee, like what you saying ain't really that important to you— And the next thing you know, she be listening good and asking you questions and when I come home—I can tell her the details. This ain't no fly-by-night **proposition**, baby. I mean we figured it out, me and Willy and Bobo.

Ruth *(With a frown)* Bobo?

Walter Yeah. You see, this little liquor store we got in mind cost seventy-five thousand and we figured the initial **investment** on the place be 'bout thirty thousand, see. That be ten thousand each. Course, there's a couple of hundred you got to pay so's you don't spend your life just waiting for them clowns to let your license get approved—

Ruth You mean **graft**?

Walter wants Ruth's help in getting his mother to lend him money to buy a liquor store with his friends.

---

graphically in a visual way

proposition a plan

investment money put into something, in hopes of a profit

graft getting something in a way that is against the law

Walter *(Frowning impatiently)* Don't call it that. See there, that just goes to show you what women understand about the world. Baby, don't *nothing* happen for you in this world 'less you pay *somebody* off!

Ruth Walter, leave me alone! *(She raises her head and stares at him **vigorously**—then says, more quietly) Eat* your eggs, they gonna be cold.

Walter *(Straightening up from her and looking off)* That's it. There you are. Man say to his woman: I got me a dream. His woman say: Eat your eggs. *(Sadly, but gaining in power)* Man say: I got to take hold of this here world, baby! And a woman will say: Eat your eggs and go to work. *(**Passionately** now)* Man say: I got to change my life, I'm choking to death, baby! And his woman say—*(In **utter anguish** as he brings his fists down on his thighs)*—Your eggs is getting cold!

Ruth *(Softly)* Walter, that ain't none of our money.

Walter *(Not listening at all or even looking at her)* This morning, I was lookin' in the mirror and thinking about it . . . I'm thirty-five years old; I been married eleven years and I got a boy who sleeps in the living room—*(Very, very quietly)*—and all I got to give him is stories about how rich white people live . . .

Ruth Eat your eggs, Walter.

Walter *Damn my eggs . . . damn all the eggs that ever was!*

Ruth Then go to work.

Walter *(Looking up at her)* See—I'm trying to talk to you 'bout myself—*(Shaking his head with the **repetition**)*—and all you can say is eat them eggs and go to work.

Ruth *(Wearily)* Honey, you never say nothing new. I listen to you every day, every night and every morning, and you never say nothing new. *(Shrugging)* So you would rather *be* Mr. Arnold than be his **chauffeur**. So—I would *rather* be living in Buckingham Palace.

> With the allusion to Langston Hughes's poem in mind, notice the dreams of each character. What is Walter's dream? Why is he angry about his wife's reaction to his dream?

vigorously with energy	**utter** total; complete	**repetition** repeating
passionately with great feeling	**anguish** great pain	**chauffeur** a hired driver

Walter That is just what is wrong with the colored woman in this world . . . Don't understand about building their men up and making 'em feel like they somebody. Like they can do something.

Ruth (*Drily, but to hurt*) There *are* colored men who do things.

Walter No thanks to the colored woman.

Ruth Well, being a colored woman, I guess I can't help myself none.

(*She rises and gets the ironing board and sets it up and attacks a huge pile of rough-dried clothes, sprinkling them in preparation for the ironing and then rolling them into tight fat balls*)

Walter (*Mumbling*) We one group of men tied to a race of women with small minds.

(*His sister* BENEATHA *enters. She is about twenty, as slim and intense as her brother. She is not as pretty as her sister-in-law, but her lean, almost **intellectual** face has a handsomeness of its own. She wears a bright-red flannel nightie, and her thick hair stands wildly about her head. Her speech is a mixture of many things; it is different from the rest of the family's insofar as education has **permeated** her sense of English—and perhaps the Midwest rather than the South has finally—at last—won out in her **inflection**; but not altogether, because over all of it is a soft **slurring** and **transformed** use of vowels which is the decided influence of the Southside. She passes through the room without looking at either* RUTH *or* WALTER *and goes to the outside door and looks, a little blindly, out to the bathroom. She sees that it has been lost to the Johnsons. She closes the door with a sleepy **vengeance** and crosses to the table and sits down a little defeated*)

Beneatha I am going to start timing those people.

Walter You should get up earlier.

What do we learn about Beneatha from these stage directions?

intellectual brainy	**inflection** pronunciation	**transformed** greatly changed
permeated entered	**slurring** sliding together	**vengeance** force

Beneatha *(Her face in her hands. She is still fighting the urge to go back to bed)* Really—would you suggest dawn? Where's the paper?

Walter *(Pushing the paper across the table to her as he studies her almost **clinically**, as though he has never seen her before)* You a horrible-looking chick at this hour.

Beneatha *(Drily)* Good morning, everybody.

Walter *(Senselessly)* How is school coming?

Beneatha *(In the same spirit)* Lovely. Lovely. And you know, **biology** is the greatest. *(Looking up at him)* I **dissected** something that looked just like you yesterday.

Walter I just wondered if you've made up your mind and everything.

Beneatha *(Gaining in sharpness and impatience)* And what did I answer yesterday morning—and the day before that?

Ruth *(From the ironing board, like someone disinterested and old)* Don't be so nasty, Bennie.

Beneatha *(Still to her brother)* And the day before that and the day before that!

Walter *(**Defensively**)* I'm interested in you. Something wrong with that? Ain't many girls who decide—

Walter and Beneatha *(In **unison**)*—"to be a doctor." *(Silence)*

Walter Have we figured out yet just exactly how much medical school is going to cost?

Ruth Walter Lee, why don't you leave that girl alone and get out of here to work?

Beneatha *(Exits to the bathroom and bangs on the door)* Come on out of there, please!

clinically as a scientist would	**dissected** cut up and examined	**unison** all together
biology the science of living things	**defensively** protecting oneself	

(She comes back into the room)

Walter *(Looking at his sister intently)* You know the check is coming tomorrow.

Beneatha *(Turning on him with a sharpness all her own)* That money belongs to Mama, Walter, and it's for her to decide how she wants to use it. I don't care if she wants to buy a house or a rocket ship or just nail it up somewhere and look at it. It's hers. Not ours—*hers.*

Walter *(Bitterly)* Now ain't that fine! You just got your mother's interest at heart, ain't you, girl? You such a nice girl—but if Mama got that money she can always take a few thousand and help you through school too—can't she?

Beneatha I have never asked anyone around here to do anything for me!

Walter No! And the line between asking and just accepting when the time comes is big and wide—ain't it!

Beneatha *(With fury)* What do you want from me, Brother—that I quit school or just drop dead, which!

Walter I don't want nothing but for you to stop acting holy 'round here. Me and Ruth done made some sacrifices for you—why can't you do something for the family?

Ruth Walter, don't be dragging me in it.

Walter You are in it—Don't you get up and go work in somebody's kitchen for the last three years to help put clothes on her back?

Ruth Oh, Walter—that's not fair . . .

Walter It ain't that nobody expects you to get on your knees and say thank you, Brother; thank you, Ruth; thank you, Mama—and thank you, Travis, for wearing the same pair of shoes for two semesters—

Beneatha *(Dropping to her knees)* Well—I *do*—all right?— thank everybody . . . and forgive me for ever wanting to be anything at all . . . forgive me, forgive me!

Ruth Please stop it! Your mama'll hear you.

Why do you think everyone is so interested in Mama's money?

Based on his remarks to his wife and sister, how would you describe Walter's view of women?

Walter Who the hell told you you had to be a doctor? If you so crazy 'bout messing 'round with sick people—then go be a nurse like other women—or just get married and be quiet . . .

Beneatha Well—you finally got it said . . . It took you three years but you finally got it said. Walter, give up; leave me alone—it's Mama's money.

Walter *He was my father, too!*

Beneatha So what? He was mine, too—and Travis' grandfather—but the **insurance** money belongs to Mama. Picking on me is not going to make her give it to you to **invest** in any **liquor** stores—*(Underbreath, dropping into a chair)*— and I for one say, God bless Mama for that!

Walter *(To* RUTH*)* See—did you hear? Did you hear!

Ruth Honey, please go to work.

Walter Nobody in this house is ever going to understand me.

Beneatha Because you're a nut.

Walter Who's a nut?

Beneatha You—you are a nut. Thee is mad, boy.

Walter *(Looking at his wife and his sister from the door, very sadly)* The world's most backward race of people, and that's a fact.

Beneatha *(Turning slowly in her chair)* And then there are all those **prophets** who would lead us out of the wilderness— *(*WALTER *slams out of the house)*—into the swamps!

Ruth Bennie, why you always gotta be pickin' on your brother? Can't you be a little sweeter sometimes? *(Door opens.* WALTER *walks in)*

Walter *(To* RUTH*)* I need some money for carfare.

> Beneatha and Walter's mother is expecting a check tomorrow from the life insurance policy of their father, who has died.

insurance coverage against loss	**invest** to put money into something, hoping for a profit	**liquor** drinks containing alcohol
		prophets people who see the future

The value of 50 cents in 1950 was great—worth many dollars now.

Ruth *(Looks at him, then warms; teasing, but tenderly)* Fifty cents? *(She goes to her bag and gets money)* Here, take a taxi.

*(WALTER exits. MAMA enters. She is a woman in her early sixties, full-bodied and strong. She is one of those women of a certain grace and beauty who wear it so unobtrusively that it takes a while to notice. Her dark-brown face is surrounded by the total whiteness of her hair, and, being a woman who has adjusted to many things in life and overcome many more, her face is full of strength. She has, we can see, wit and faith of a kind that keep her eyes lit and full of interest and **expectancy**. She is, in a word, a beautiful woman. Her bearing is perhaps most like the noble bearing of the women of the Hereros of Southwest Africa—rather as if she imagines that as she walks she still bears a basket or a vessel upon her head. Her speech, on the other hand, is as careless as her carriage is **precise**—she is inclined to slur everything—but her voice is perhaps not so much quiet as simply soft)*

What do we learn about Mama from these stage directions?

Mama Who that 'round here slamming doors at this hour?

*(She crosses through the room, goes to the window, opens it, and brings in a feeble little plant growing **doggedly** in a small pot on the windowsill. She feels the dirt and puts it back out)*

Ruth That was Walter Lee. He and Bennie was at it again.

Mama My children and they tempers. Lord, if this little old plant don't get more sun than it's been getting it ain't never going to see spring again. *(She turns from the window)* What's the matter with you this morning, Ruth? You looks right peaked. You aiming to iron all them things? Leave some for me. I'll get to 'em this afternoon. Bennie honey, it's too drafty for you to be sitting 'round half dressed. Where's your robe?

Beneatha In the cleaners.

Mama Well, go get mine and put it on.

Beneatha I'm not cold, Mama, honest.

---

expectancy looking forward to something   **precise** correct; exact   **doggedly** stubbornly

Mama I know—but you so thin . . .

Beneatha (*Irritably*) Mama, I'm not cold.

Mama (*Seeing the make-down bed as* TRAVIS *has left it*) Lord have mercy, look at that poor bed. Bless his heart—he tries, don't he?

(*She moves to the bed* TRAVIS *has sloppily made up*)

Ruth No—he don't half try at all 'cause he knows you going to come along behind him and fix everything. That's just how come he don't know how to do nothing right now—you done spoiled that boy so.

Mama Well—he's a little boy. Ain't supposed to know 'bout housekeeping. My baby, that's what he is. What you fix for his breakfast this morning?

Ruth (*Angrily*) I feed my son, Lena!

Mama I ain't meddling—(*Underbreath; busy-bodyish*) I just noticed all last week he had cold cereal, and when it starts getting this chilly in the fall a child ought to have some hot grits or something when he goes out in the cold—

Ruth (*Furious*) I gave him hot oats—is that all right!

Mama I ain't meddling. (*Pause*) Put a lot of nice butter on it? (RUTH *shoots her an angry look and does not reply*) He likes lots of butter.

Ruth (*Exasperated*) Lena—

Mama (*To* BENEATHA. MAMA *is inclined to wander conversationally sometimes*) What was you and your brother fussing 'bout this morning?

Beneatha It's not important, Mama.

(*She gets up and goes to look out at the bathroom, which is apparently free, and she picks up her towels and rushes out*)

Mama What was they fighting about?

> Notice how the dialogue sounds like everyday speech.

irritably in an annoyed way

Ruth Now you know as well as I do.

Mama (*Shaking her head*) Brother still worrying hisself sick about that money?

Ruth You know he is.

Mama You had breakfast?

Ruth Some coffee.

Mama Girl, you better start eating and looking after yourself better. You almost thin as Travis.

Ruth Lena—

Mama Un-hunh?

Ruth What are you going to do with it?

Mama Now don't you start, child. It's too early in the morning to be talking about money. It ain't Christian.

Ruth It's just that he got his heart set on that store—

Mama You mean that liquor store that Willy Harris want him to invest in?

Ruth Yes—

Mama We ain't no business people, Ruth. We just plain working folks.

Ruth Ain't nobody business people till they go into business. Walter Lee say colored people ain't never going to start getting ahead till they start **gambling** on some different kinds of things in the world—investments and things.

Mama What done got into you, girl? Walter Lee done finally sold you on investing.

Ruth No. Mama, something is happening between Walter and me. I don't know what it is—but he needs something— something I can't give him any more. He needs this chance, Lena.

> **gambling** betting money on; risking

Notice the way Mama describes Ruth. Apparently, Ruth looks thin and tired. As readers, we wouldn't know this unless a character or the stage directions described Ruth.

Mama *(Frowning deeply)* But liquor, honey—

Ruth Well—like Walter say—I spec people going to always be drinking themselves some liquor.

Mama Well—whether they drinks it or not ain't none of my business. But whether I go into business selling it to 'em *is*, and I don't want that on my **ledger** this late in life. *(Stopping suddenly and studying her daughter-in-law)* Ruth Younger, what's the matter with you today? You look like you could fall over right there.

Ruth I'm tired.

Mama Then you better stay home from work today.

Ruth I can't stay home. She'd be calling up the agency and screaming at them, "My girl didn't come in today—send me somebody! My girl didn't come in!" Oh, she just have a fit . . .

Mama Well, let her have it. I'll just call her up and say you got the flu—

Ruth *(Laughing)* Why the flu?

Mama 'Cause it sounds **respectable** to 'em. Something white people get, too. They know 'bout the flu. Otherwise they think you been cut up or something when you tell 'em you sick.

Ruth I got to go in. We need the money.

Mama Somebody would of thought my children done all but starved to death the way they talk about money here late. Child, we got a great big old check coming tomorrow.

Ruth *(Sincerely, but also **self-righteously**)* Now that's your money. It ain't got nothing to do with me. We all feel like that—Walter and Bennie and me—even Travis.

Why do you think Ruth has decided to support Walter's plan after all?

What does this talk between Ruth and Mama tell you about the family's attitudes toward white people? What does it reveal about the way white people treat the Youngers and other African Americans?

---

ledger an account book

respectable decent; proper

self-righteously convinced of one's own goodness

Mama *(Thoughtfully, and suddenly very far away)* Ten thousand dollars—

Ruth Sure is wonderful.

Mama Ten thousand dollars.

Ruth You know what you should do, Miss Lena? You should take yourself a trip somewhere. To Europe or South America or someplace—

Mama *(Throwing up her hands at the thought)* Oh, child!

Ruth I'm serious. Just pack up and leave! Go on away and enjoy yourself some. Forget about the family and have yourself a ball for once in your life—

Mama *(Drily)* You sound like I'm just about ready to die. Who'd go with me? What I look like wandering 'round Europe by myself?

Ruth Shoot—these here rich white women do it all the time. They don't think nothing of packing up they suitcases and piling on one of them big steamships and—swoosh!—they gone, child.

Mama Something always told me I wasn't no rich white woman.

Ruth Well—what are you going to do with it then?

Mama I ain't rightly decided. *(Thinking. She speaks now with emphasis)* Some of it got to be put away for Beneatha and her schoolin'—and ain't nothing going to touch that part of it. Nothing. *(She waits several seconds, trying to make up her mind about something, and looks at* RUTH *a little **tentatively** before going on)* Been thinking that we maybe could meet the notes on a little old two-story somewhere, with a yard where Travis could play in the summertime, if we use part of the insurance for a down payment and everybody kind of pitch in. I could maybe take on a little day work again, few days a week—

Ruth *(Studying her mother-in-law **furtively** and concentrating on her ironing, anxious to encourage without seeming to)* Well,

What are Mama's plans for the insurance money?

tentatively unsurely	**furtively** secretly, as if ashamed

Lord knows, we've put enough rent into this here rat trap to pay for four houses by now . . .

Mama *(Looking up at the words "rat trap" and then looking around and leaning back and sighing—in a suddenly reflective mood—)* "Rat trap"—yes, that's all it is. *(Smiling)* I remember just as well the day me and Big Walter moved in here. Hadn't been married but two weeks and wasn't planning on living here no more than a year. *(She shakes her head at the dissolved dream)* We was going to set away, little by little, don't you know, and buy a little place out in Morgan Park. We had even picked out the house. *(Chuckling a little)* Looks right dumpy today. But Lord, child, you should know all the dreams I had 'bout buying that house and fixing it up and making me a little garden in the back—*(She waits and stops smiling)* And didn't none of it happen.

*(Dropping her hands in a **futile** gesture)*

> What were Mama's dreams when she was young?

Ruth *(Keeps her head down, ironing)* Yes, life can be a barrel of disappointments, sometimes.

Mama Honey, Big Walter would come in here some nights back then and slump down on that couch there and just look at the rug, and look at me and look at the rug and then back at me—and I'd know he was down then . . . really down. *(After a second very long and thoughtful pause; she is seeing back to times that only she can see)* And then, Lord, when I lost that baby—little Claude—I almost thought I was going to lose Big Walter too. Oh, that man grieved hisself! He was one man to love his children.

Ruth Ain't nothin' can tear at you like losin' your baby.

Mama I guess that's how come that man finally worked hisself to death like he done. Like he was fighting his own war with this here world that took his baby from him.

Ruth He sure was a fine man, all right. I always liked Mr. Younger.

futile useless

Mama Crazy 'bout his children! God knows there was plenty wrong with Walter Younger—hard-headed, mean, kind of wild with women—plenty wrong with him. But he sure loved his children. Always wanted them to have something—be something. That's where Brother gets all these notions, I reckon. Big Walter used to say, he'd get right wet in the eyes sometimes, lean his head back with the water standing in his eyes and say, "Seem like God didn't see fit to give the black man nothing but dreams—but He did give us children to make them dreams seem worth while." *(She smiles)* He could talk like that, don't you know.

What do we learn about Walter and Beneatha's father in this dialogue between Ruth and Mama?

Ruth Yes, he sure could. He was a good man, Mr. Younger.

Mama Yes, a fine man—just couldn't never catch up with his dreams, that's all.

(BENEATHA *comes in, brushing her hair and looking up to the ceiling, where the sound of a vacuum cleaner has started up)*

Beneatha What could be so dirty on that woman's rugs that she has to vacuum them every single day?

Ruth I wish certain young women 'round here who I could name would take **inspiration** about certain rugs in a certain apartment I could also mention.

Beneatha *(Shrugging)* How much cleaning can a house need, for Christ's sakes.

Mama *(Not liking the Lord's name used thus)* Bennie!

Ruth Just listen to her—just listen!

Beneatha Oh, God!

Mama If you use the Lord's name just one more time—

Beneatha *(A bit of a whine)* Oh, Mama—

Ruth Fresh—just fresh as salt, this girl!

Beneatha *(Drily)* Well—if the salt loses its **savor**—

Mama Now that will do. I just ain't going to have you 'round here reciting the **scriptures** in vain—you hear me?

inspiration encouragement	**savor** special flavor or smell	**scriptures** Bible verses

Beneatha How did I manage to get on everybody's wrong side by just walking into a room?

Ruth If you weren't so fresh—

Beneatha Ruth, I'm twenty years old.

Mama What time you be home from school today?

Beneatha Kind of late. *(With enthusiasm)* Madeline is going to start my guitar lessons today.

(MAMA *and* RUTH *look up with the same expression*)

Mama Your *what* kind of lessons?

Beneatha Guitar.

Ruth Oh, Father!

Mama How come you done taken it in your mind to learn to play the guitar?

Beneatha I just want to, that's all.

Mama *(Smiling)* Lord, child, don't you know what to do with yourself? How long it going to be before you get tired of this now—like you got tired of that little play-acting group you joined last year? *(Looking at* RUTH*)* And what was it the year before that?

Why does Mama smile at Beneatha's latest interest?

Ruth The horseback-riding club for which she bought that fifty-five-dollar riding habit that's been hanging in the closet ever since!

Mama *(To* BENEATHA*)* Why you got to flit so from one thing to another, baby?

Beneatha *(Sharply)* I just want to learn to play the guitar. Is there anything wrong with that?

Mama Ain't nobody trying to stop you. I just wonders sometimes why you has to flit so from one thing to another all the time. You ain't never done nothing with all that camera equipment you brought home—

Beneatha I don't flit! I—I experiment with different forms of expression—

How is Beneatha different from Mama and Ruth? What are her dreams?

Ruth Like riding a horse?

Beneatha —People have to express themselves one way or another.

Mama What is it you want to express?

Beneatha *(Angrily)* Me! (MAMA *and* RUTH *look at each other and burst into* **raucous** *laughter*) Don't worry—I don't expect you to understand.

Mama *(To change the subject)* Who you going out with tomorrow night?

Beneatha *(With displeasure)* George Murchison again.

Mama *(Pleased)* Oh—you getting a little sweet on him?

Ruth You ask me, this child ain't sweet on nobody but herself—*(Underbreath)* Express herself!

(They laugh)

Beneatha Oh—I like George all right, Mama. I mean I like him enough to go out with him and stuff, but—

Ruth *(For devilment)* What does *and stuff* mean?

Beneatha Mind your own business.

Mama Stop picking at her now, Ruth. *(A thoughtful pause, and then a suspicious sudden look at her daughter as she turns in her chair for emphasis)* What *does* it mean?

Beneatha *(Wearily)* Oh, I just mean I couldn't ever really be serious about George. He's—he's so shallow.

Ruth Shallow—what do you mean he's shallow? He's *Rich!*

Mama Hush, Ruth.

Beneatha I know he's rich. He knows he's rich, too.

Ruth Well—what other qualities a man got to have to satisfy you, little girl?

---

raucous rough; loud

Beneatha You wouldn't even begin to understand. Anybody who married Walter could not possibly understand.

Mama *(Outraged)* What kind of way is that to talk about your brother?

Beneatha Brother is a flip—let's face it.

Mama *(To* RUTH, *helplessly)* What's a flip?

Ruth *(Glad to add kindling)* She's saying he's crazy.

Beneatha Not crazy. Brother isn't really crazy yet—he—he's an elaborate **neurotic**.

Mama Hush your mouth!

Beneatha As for George. Well. George looks good—he's got a beautiful car and he takes me to nice places and, as my sister-in-law says, he is probably the richest boy I will ever get to know and I even like him sometimes—but if the Youngers are sitting around waiting to see if their little Bennie is going to tie up the family with the Murchisons, they are wasting their time.

Ruth You mean you wouldn't marry George Murchison if he asked you someday? That pretty, rich thing? Honey, I knew you was odd—

Beneatha No I would not marry him if all I felt for him was what I feel now. Besides, George's family wouldn't really like it.

Mama Why not?

Beneatha Oh, Mama—The Murchisons are honest-to-God-real-*live*-rich colored people, and the only people in the world who are more **snobbish** than rich white people are rich colored people. I thought everybody knew that. I've met Mrs. Murchison. She's a scene!

Mama You must not dislike people 'cause they well off, honey.

Beneatha Why not? It makes just as much sense as disliking people 'cause they are poor, and lots of people do that.

> Notice that the conflicts faced by the Youngers aren't simply between the races. They also struggle against differences of class and income.

neurotic a person with disturbed feelings and thoughts

snobbish stuck-up

Ruth *(A wisdom-of-the-ages manner. To* MAMA*)* Well, she'll get over some of this—

Beneatha Get over it? What are you talking about, Ruth? Listen, I'm going to be a doctor. I'm not worried about who I'm going to marry yet—if I ever get married.

Mama and Ruth *If!*

Mama Now, Bennie—

Beneatha Oh, I probably will . . . but first I'm going to be a doctor, and George, for one, still thinks that's pretty funny. I couldn't be bothered with that. I am going to be a doctor and everybody around here better understand that!

Mama *(Kindly)* 'Course you going to be a doctor, honey, God willing.

Beneatha *(Drily)* God hasn't got a thing to do with it.

Mama Beneatha—that just wasn't necessary.

Beneatha Well—neither is God. I get sick of hearing about God.

Mama Beneatha!

Beneatha I mean it! I'm just tired of hearing about God all the time. What has He got to do with anything? Does he pay **tuition**?

Mama You 'bout to get your fresh little jaw slapped!

Ruth That's just what she needs, all right!

Beneatha Why? Why can't I say what I want to around here, like everybody else?

Mama It don't sound nice for a young girl to say things like that—you wasn't brought up that way. Me and your father went to trouble to get you and Brother to church every Sunday.

Beneatha Mama, you don't understand. It's all a matter of ideas, and God is just one idea I don't accept. It's not

tuition payment for schooling

important. I am not going out and be immoral or commit crimes because I don't believe in God. I don't even think about it. It's just that I get tired of Him getting credit for all the things the human race achieves through its own stubborn effort. There simply is no blasted God—there is only man and it is he who makes miracles!

(MAMA *absorbs this speech, studies her daughter and rises slowly and crosses to* BENEATHA *and slaps her powerfully across the face. After, there is only silence and the daughter drops her eyes from her mother's face, and* MAMA *is very tall before her*)

Mama Now—you say after me, in my mother's house there is still God. (*There is a long pause and* BENEATHA *stares at the floor wordlessly.* MAMA *repeats the phrase with* **precision** *and cool emotion*) In my mother's house there is still God.

Beneatha In my mother's house there is still God.

(*A long pause*)

Mama (*Walking away from* BENEATHA, *too disturbed for triumphant posture. Stopping and turning back to her daughter*) There are some ideas we ain't going to have in this house. Not long as I am at the head of this family.

Beneatha Yes, ma'am.

(MAMA *walks out of the room*)

Ruth (*Almost gently, with* **profound** *understanding*) You think you a woman, Bennie—but you still a little girl. What you did was childish—so you got treated like a child.

Beneatha I see. (*Quietly*) I also see that everybody thinks it's all right for Mama to be a **tyrant**. But all the tyranny in the world will never put a God in the heavens!

(*She picks up her books and goes out*)

> What do we learn about Beneatha and her mother from what happened here? How are they different? Why does Mama slap Beneatha?

> What is the difference between the way Ruth thinks about this and the way Beneatha thinks about it?

---

precision correctness; exactly or sharply stated   **profound** deep   **tyrant** absolute ruler

Why does Ruth lie to Mama about Beneatha's apology? What does this say about Ruth's role in the family?

Ruth (*Goes to* MAMA's *door*) She said she was sorry.

Mama (*Coming out, going to her plant*) They frightens me, Ruth. My children.

Ruth You got good children, Lena. They just a little off sometimes—but they're good.

Mama No—there's something come down between me and them that don't let us understand each other and I don't know what it is. One done almost lost his mind thinking 'bout money all the time and the other done commence to talk about things I can't seem to understand in no form or fashion. What is it that's changing, Ruth?

Earlier, Ruth said that something had come between her and Walter. Now Mama says the same thing about her and her children. What would you say is happening to this family?

Ruth (*Soothingly, older than her years*) Now . . . you taking it all too seriously. You just got strong-willed children and it takes a strong woman like you to keep 'em in hand.

Mama (*Looking at her plant and sprinkling a little water on it*) They spirited all right, my children. Got to admit they got spirit—Bennie and Walter. Like this little old plant that ain't never had enough sunshine or nothing—and look at it . . .

(*She has her back to* RUTH, *who has had to stop ironing and lean against something and put the back of her hand to her forehead*)

Ruth (*Trying to keep* MAMA *from noticing*) You . . . sure . . . loves that little old thing, don't you? . . .

Mama Well, I always wanted me a garden like I used to see sometimes at the back of the houses down home. This plant is close as I ever got to having one. (*She looks out of the window as she replaces the plant*) Lord, ain't nothing as dreary as the view from this window on a dreary day, is there? Why ain't you singing this morning, Ruth? Sing that "No Ways Tired." That song always lifts me up so—(*She turns at last to see that* RUTH *has slipped quietly into a chair, in a state of semiconsciousness*) Ruth! Ruth honey—what's the matter with you . . . Ruth!

Curtain

Directions Choose the letter of the best answer or write the answer using complete sentences.

Comprehension: Identifying Facts

1. What is the setting (time and place) of this scene?
  A present-day Chicago
  B Chicago after World War II
  C the country after World War II
  D a present-day school

2. What does Travis do when he wakes up?
  A gets his clothes
  B gets his towel
  C goes in the bathroom
  D all of the above

3. Why does Ruth say Travis is so tired?

4. What is Travis supposed to bring to school?

5. Why does Walter want $10,000?

6. What does Beneatha want to become?

7. To whom does Beneatha say the insurance money belongs?

8. What does Ruth want Mama to do with the money?

9. Why does Mama slap Beneatha?

10. What happens to Ruth at the end of this scene?

Comprehension: Putting Ideas Together

11. What does Hansberry's description of the apartment tell you about the family?
  A They have a lot of money.
  B They have good taste.
  C They don't have much money.
  D They don't care about their home.

12. Why do Walter and Travis both ask about the check?
  A They are worried about Mama.
  B Walter has just lost his job.
  C Ruth needs money.
  D The money means a lot to them.

13. How do Ruth and Walter treat each other at breakfast?

14. Why does Walter say that his wife just doesn't understand the ways of the world?

15. Why do Walter and Beneatha quarrel?

16. How does Beneatha react when Walter accuses her of being ungrateful?

17. Why doesn't Mama want to give Walter money to invest in a liquor store?

18. What were Mama's dreams when she was young?

After Reading continued on next page

A Raisin in the Sun by Lorraine Hansberry

19. Describe Beneatha's character, based on what people in the play say to her.

20. How does Mama feel about her children at the end of the scene?

Understanding Literature: Stage Directions

Playwrights write notes about what the stage should look like and what the actors should do. These notes are called stage directions. Stage directions tell actors and directors how the playwright sees the characters and what happens to them.

Some stage directions, such as those for *A Raisin in the Sun,* also give readers important information about characters. For example, the playwright says that "disappointment has already begun to hang in her [Ruth's] face."

In real life, the meaning of people's words often comes from the way they are said. For example, the question "So, when are you going to do your homework?" can be asked in different ways. It can be asked with anger, with concern, or simply with interest.

21. How do stage directions help actors? How do they help readers?

22. What do we learn about Beneatha from the stage directions given as she enters the scene?

23. As Ruth reacts to the news Walter reads from the paper, the stage directions say she is to affect (put on, or pretend) "tea-party interest." How does the playwright want the words to be said?

24. Based on the stage directions given, describe the way Walter behaves at the breakfast table.

25. What do we learn about Mama from the stage directions describing her?

Critical Thinking

26. What is different about how Walter and Ruth look at the world? About how they think about the future?

27. How are Walter's, Beneatha's, and Mama's dreams alike? How are they different?

28. List three conflicts faced by characters in this scene. Which do you think will turn out to be the most important in the play? Why?

Thinking Creatively

29. How do you think this play will end?

30. Why do you think Lorraine Hansberry called her play "A Raisin in the Sun"?

Grammar Check

Adjectives are words that describe nouns, providing readers with a more complete picture of the people, places, and things they read about. These adjectives could be used to describe the Younger living room:

shabby	dark
threadbare	dignified
crowded	clean
tattered	

Use the Semantic Line described in Appendix A to arrange these words in an order that goes from most to least positive. At the top of the arrow list the adjective that is the best or most complimentary. Continue listing the adjectives until you finish with the one that is the worst or most negative. Use a thesaurus or dictionary to add four other adjectives to this chart.

 Writing on Your Own

Study the poem by Langston Hughes about a dream "deferred" or delayed. How does it relate to the events in this scene of *A Raisin in the Sun*? Think about the characters' dreams, which dreams have been deferred, and why. Write two paragraphs that explain the connection between the poem and the play.

 Speaking and Listening

Think-alouds are times when readers pause and tell a group about their thoughts about what they are reading. In small groups, take turns reading small parts of the play aloud. Stop reading when you have a reaction to what you are reading and explain that to the group. For example, you might mention how the characters or setting remind you of people you know. You could also ask a question about something you do not understand. Allow all members of the group to have a chance to think aloud. Listen carefully to what others say. How do their thoughts compare with yours? What can you add that might help other readers in the group?

 Viewing

Arrange to attend a performance of *A Raisin in the Sun* or watch a video presentation of the play. How does the Act I, Scene One that you "saw" in your mind as you read compare with the actual performance?

Writer's Realm   *by Anne Jarrell-France*

**Anne Jarrell-France
1948–**

Objectives

- To read and appreciate a comedy script
- To define and give examples of humor and puns

script the written text of a play, used in a production or performance

About the Author

Anne Jarrell-France has been a television writer, producer, and director. When she writes, especially when she writes for students, she tries to use humor to communicate information. One of her projects, "Reading Between the Lines," focuses on learning to be a better reader. Another, "Starfinder," follows the Hubble Space Telescope's development and journey. Jarrell-France is now writing and producing videos for the Social Security Administration.

About the Selection

This **script** was written for "Writer's Realm," a series that appeared on public television. A script is the written text of a play. *Realm* means field or specialty in this title. The series was developed to help students learn how to write more effectively. In this script, Anne Jarrell-France imagines that Mary Shelley, author of the science-fiction novel *Frankenstein*, is discussing her story with her husband, Percy Shelley, and their friend, Lord Byron. Percy Shelley and Lord Byron were both famous English poets in the 1800s.

In fact, that's the way Shelley's novel *Frankenstein* began. She and her friends were telling horror stories to each other one night. From these stories grew the tale of Victor Frankenstein, a curious student and scientist who discovers a way to create life from body parts found in graveyards.

Terms to Know

Here are terms that the production team needs to know as they record this scene. As you read the script, they are in the left column, which is called the *video column*. The right column is called the *audio column*.

ANGLE the person or object the camera should view

CUT to move quickly from one angle to another

TWO SHOT the camera shows two people at the same time

MCU (Medium Close Up) the camera shows a person from the shoulders up

CU (Close Up) the camera shows only the person's face

Literary Terms "Writer's Realm" presents its ideas using **comedy**. Comedies generally have the same story elements as tragedies. However, in comedies, the endings are usually happy or funny. In this comedy, Jarrell-France relies on comic devices such as **puns**. Puns are jokes based on words that have several meanings, or on words that sound alike but have different meanings. For example, in the selection, Mary says that using lightning to bring the monster to life "'sparks' the imagination."

Reading on Your Own Reading a script is different from reading a play, simply because the script format is different from the play format. A script for a television program usually is divided into two columns. The right column contains the words the actors will say. The left column contains the instructions and lists the people who will appear on camera. It also contains stage directions for the actors. As you read this script, remember that the right column contains the words you will hear and the left column describes the pictures you will see.

Writing on Your Own Write a brief description of an amusing event in your life in such a way that your readers will find it funny as well.

Vocabulary Focus In this script, the author uses some terms that describe how viewers will see this play. For example, *transition* means to move from one location to another. In this script, it means that viewers will see the host and then see the dreary room. Then, the camera *tilts down*. This means that the viewers see a picture that moves from the candelabra at the top of the room to a seated Mary Shelley. Later, the author says the shot *widens* or shows more of the room.

Think Before You Read Knowing this script is a comedy, predict how it will be different from a tragedy like *Romeo and Juliet*.

Writer's Realm

Notice the two-column format of this script. The left column tells what the audience will see. The right column shows the words the characters will say.

Morgan is the host of "Writer's Realm."

As you read, notice how the author creates humor in this comedy.

ANGLE ON HOST.	**MORGAN** Writers have been using responses from their friends and family for centuries. In fact, they say that's how Mary Shelley wrote her best known story, *Frankenstein*. It's about a Dr. Frankenstein who creates a monster. At least, that's how the final draft turned out . . .
TRANSITION TO A **MULTIPLE CANDELABRA** IN AN OLD DARK DREARY ROOM. IT'S THE KIND OF ROOM THAT IS **CONDUCIVE** TO SPOOKY STORIES. THE CAMERA TILTS DOWN AND WE SEE MARY SHELLEY READING A FIRST DRAFT OF HER NEW NOVEL.	**MARY** " . . . And, so, the monster that Dr. Quimbly-Smythe created out of plaster and hay was crushed to powder beneath the feet of the townspeople."
SHE LOOKS TO HER AUDIENCE.	Well, what do you think, honestly?
CUT TO PERCY SHELLEY **MUSING**.	**PERCY** Mary, I must admit, it gave me quite a shiver.

transition change or shift

multiple candelabra a many-branched candlestick

conducive helpful or useful

musing thinking

CUT TO GEORGE GORDON, LORD BYRON.	**GEORGE** Rather! I especially liked the laboratory part. The assistant—what was his name?
ANGLE ON MARY. SHE RISES TO GO OVER TO THE TEA SERVICE AND POURS A CUP OF TEA.	**MARY** Bertie?
CUT TO GEORGE. MARY ENTERS THE FRAME AND HANDS HIM A CUP OF TEA.	**GEORGE** Yes, that's the one—nasty fellow, what?
TWO SHOT OF MARY AND GEORGE.	**MARY** I wanted him to be different.
SHOT OF PERCY.	**PERCY** I think you succeeded there. Why the name, Bertie?
MARY.	**MARY** Short for Bertrum . . .
PERCY ON CAMERA.	**PERCY** Quite. Is he English?
MARY. SHOT WIDENS AS SHE WALKS OVER TO THE TABLE AGAIN.	**MARY** No, actually, foreign. Maybe I should give him a more **exotic** name . . . Igor—what about Igor?
SHOT OF GEORGE.	**GEORGE** Absolutely—oh, I do like that.
SHOT OF MARY.	**MARY** Did I tell you enough about why Dr. Quimbly-Smythe wanted to create the monster out of plaster and hay?
GEORGE.	**GEORGE** No, actually, that was to have been my next question.

Frankenstein's Monster

Why does Mary rename the laboratory assistant? Why is "Igor" a better name than "Bertrum"?

---

exotic strange; unusual

SHOT OF MARY SLOWLY WIDENS.	**MARY** Well, you see he thought he could create life out of dead things. He'd done quite a bit of research on the subject, you know.	

Mary has left some important details out of her first draft.

GEORGE JOINS MARY AT THE TABLE.	**GEORGE** No, I didn't. That wasn't in your draft, was it?
MARY IS PREPARING A TRAY OF COOKIES AS SHE THINKS ALOUD.	**MARY** Not the first, but now I'll put it in the second. (THINKING OUT LOUD.) Instead of plaster and hay, what about him thinking he can bring the dead back to life so he uses body parts to create the monster?
SHE CROSSES TO PERCY DURING HER SPEECH. SHE OFFERS A COOKIE TO PERCY.	Ladyfinger . . .?

The use of "ladyfinger" here is a pun. Ladyfingers are cookies—and Mary has just been talking about body parts.

PERCY. HE TAKES A COOKIE.	**PERCY** How terribly disgusting, Mary! Must admit, it would keep the readers' interest a bit more than plaster and hay . . . and give a new meaning to the phrase, "lend me a hand, will you?"

Why does Percy think changing the way the doctor made his monster is a good idea? What is the joke in "lend me a hand"?

GEORGE SNICKERS.	**GEORGE** Why were the townspeople so upset? You'd think that they would be proud to have such a famous scientist in their midst.
MCU MARY.	**MARY** I could elaborate more about the people being frightened by the monster. Even have him escape from the laboratory once or twice to terrorize the townspeople.

Here again, Mary decides to add more details to her story.

MCU PERCY.

PERCY
Good show! What about the
lightning being used to bring
the monster to life? Don't you
think that's a bit overdone?

MARY CU.

MARY
No, actually, I rather like
that part. "Sparks" the
imagination, what?

LIGHTNING AND THUNDER.

PERCY
Why did you choose the
name Quimbly-Smythe?

MARY
A fine family, Percy.

PERCY
Quite, but don't you think
another name would be more

MARY AGAIN CROSSES THE   appropriate . . . something
ROOM AND SETS THE TRAY   to go along with the Igor
DOWN ON THE TABLE.   character?

MARY
I know . . .
I could call him . . .
Frankenstein . . .

GRAND LIGHTNING AND
THUNDER DISPLAY, AS
MARY WHISPERS.   . . . yes . . .

Notice the pun on
the word *sparks*.

Why does
Percy suggest
changing the main
character's name?
What's wrong with
"Quimbly-Smythe"?

AFTER READING THE SELECTION

Writer's Realm   by Anne Jarrell-France

Directions Choose the letter of the best answer or write the answer using complete sentences.

Comprehension: Identifying Facts

1. What name does Mary first use for her scientist?
   A Bertie
   B Igor
   C Dr. Quimbly-Smythe
   D Percy

2. Why does Mary decide to change the assistant's name to Igor?

3. What is the monster made of in Mary's first draft?

Comprehension: Putting Ideas Together

4. Why is the setting described in the opening of the script an appropriate location for the events that follow?
   A It is dark and dreary, just like Mary and her friends.
   B It is spooky, and the characters Mary is creating are spooky.
   C It is sunny.
   D It is large.

5. Why is building a monster out of body parts more appropriate than building him out of plaster and hay?

6. Give two examples of the ways her friends helped shape Mary Shelley's novel, according to this script.

Understanding Literature: Comedy

Comedy has been an important form of drama since the time of ancient Greece. At yearly festivals, playwrights would present their best tragedies. Poets presented satyr plays—comedies that made fun of the gods and their myths. People began to see comedy as a way of looking at their own lives. We still see this kind of comedy on television.

If tragedy causes pity and fear in an audience, comedy brings feelings of safety and relief. Comedies make people laugh. They often feature characters or actions that are exaggerated and outrageous.

7. What are some of the comic elements that you saw in the "Writer's Realm" script?

8. How would you define comedy? Think about what makes you laugh as a way of finding your own definition.

Critical Thinking

9. Why is Mary Shelley's first choice of names for the characters in her novel humorous?

Thinking Creatively

10. What other comic elements might you add to this script?

Grammar Check

In this script, the author used *ellipses*, a series of three evenly-spaced dots, at certain points in the drama. These punctuation marks can be used in several ways. They can show that some information was left out in a sentence. They can also be used to show a pause in the conversation. Review the script to find these punctuation marks. Why did the author use them when she did?

 ### Writing on Your Own

Use the Internet to look for other teleplays (plays written for television) or screenplays (scripts written for motion pictures). Compare their formats with the two-column format used in "Writer's Realm." Use any format you find to write a short, funny scene about what happens at your house during breakfast.

 ### Speaking

In groups of five, perform a part of this script as if you were presenting it on the radio. Four people could take on the roles of the actors, and one person could be in charge of recording the performance and adding sound effects. After you feel comfortable in your roles, record your presentation.

 ### Listening

Ask a good reader to record two versions of this script for you. In the first version, the reader should use no expression. The second version should be read with expression, as if the conversation is actually happening. Listen to both versions of the script. Which one helps you see more clearly the story in your mind? Why?

 ### Media and Technology

A *storyboard* is a series of simple drawings used in television production to show how the audience will see a certain script. Use the Internet or a print resource to find a sample of a storyboard. Create a storyboard series showing what the audience will see during this script. You can use the directions included in the video column or your own vision of what is happening to guide your work.

Subject and Theme in Drama

Dramas can be written for the stage, the movies, or television. These dramas are similar to other forms of narrative literature, such as short stories, myths, and legends. They follow some of the same rules and patterns. Like a short story, a play tells a story about a main character. There is a plot that explores a certain problem the main character faces. The story takes place in a specific setting.

Drama also has a subject and one or more themes. The subject is its main topic—what the play is about. The theme, or main idea, is what the author says about the topic through the action of the play. For example, the subject of *Romeo and Juliet* is what happens to two unlucky young lovers. Shakespeare includes several themes in the play. One theme is the way people are often pushed around by the conditions of their lives, in spite of trying to do their best. Another theme is the way violence leads to violence, and how people let old quarrels shape their lives. As with most good plays, *Romeo and Juliet* does not announce its themes. The audience gradually realizes what the themes are as they become involved in the drama.

Review

1. What is the difference between the subject of a play and its theme?

2. What is the subject of Act I, Scene One, of *A Raisin in the Sun*?

3. What is one theme of Hansberry's play, based on this scene?

4. What is the subject of "Writer's Realm"?

5. What is one theme of *Romeo and Juliet*?

Writing on Your Own

Choose a subject you would like to write about. What kinds of themes might come from that subject? Write a two-paragraph description of your subject and themes.

Unit 8   SUMMARY

Drama as we know it today dates from ancient Greece. Writers of plays, called playwrights, tell their stories by means of the words—dialogue—and actions of characters. Plays are meant to be performed by actors on a stage. Because of this, plays rely on the special connection formed between the play and its audience.

Drama is often divided into two groups of plays, based on plot. In tragedies, the main character suffers or dies by the end of the play. Tragedies concern serious subjects, such as the meaning of life or the importance of human relationships. Comedies have happy endings and are meant to amuse people. Characters in tragedies tend to be noble, or at least important in their communities. Characters in comedies are usually ordinary people.

Plays are organized into acts. Acts may be divided into scenes, each taking place in one setting. Shakespeare wrote five-act plays; today's plays tend to be two or three acts. Many plays are only one act.

Today, plays are written not just for stage performance, but for television and movies. Playwrights write stage directions to help actors, directors, and readers understand such things as setting, lighting, and the way characters speak and move. Writers of television and movie scripts give directions about camera angles and sound effects.

All drama is a form of storytelling that depends on the words and actions of characters. From ancient times to the present, readers and audiences have enjoyed the special power of drama to reveal human character.

Selections

- *Romeo and Juliet,* Act V, by William Shakespeare, is the tragedy of two young lovers destroyed by family hatreds and their own unlucky fates.

- *A Raisin in the Sun,* Act I, Scene One, by Lorraine Hansberry, presents the realistic drama of an African American family in Chicago. They struggle to keep their dreams alive in the face of money problems, social unfairness, and personal conflicts.

- "Writer's Realm," a script written for television, explores the writing process by imagining Mary Shelley asking her husband and their friend for advice as she writes *Frankenstein.*

Directions Choose the letter of the best answer or write the answer using complete sentences.

Comprehension: Identifying Facts

1. Who are the two warring families in *Romeo and Juliet*?

  A Paris and Balthasar

  B The Montagues and the Capulets

  C The Prince and the Nurse

  D The Mantuas and the Veronas

2. What do Romeo and Juliet do that their families do not know about?

3. What piece of mail are the Youngers waiting for?

4. Why does Mama slap Beneatha?

5. Who is the author who is writing a novel in the script from "Writer's Realm"?

Comprehension: Putting Ideas Together

6. Why does Romeo go out of his way to avoid a fight with Paris?

  A He is afraid of Paris.

  B Paris is stronger than he is.

  C He only wants to kill himself— not others.

  D He knows Juliet loved Paris.

7. What does the friar say he did to prevent Juliet from marrying Paris?

8. How much information do readers get from the stage directions in *Romeo and Juliet*, compared with the stage directions in *A Raisin in the Sun*?

9. How is Mama's dream to own a house like a dried-up raisin?

10. Whose dream in *A Raisin in the Sun* was the most selfless? Explain.

Understanding Literature: Dialogue and Monologue

Dialogue is the conversation two or more actors share. A *monologue* is a speech by one person. Dialogue and monologue are used by playwrights to tell their stories. Playwrights cannot explain precisely what is happening in the story. Instead, they have to let the characters speak for themselves. Only through monologues can playwrights reveal some of the internal conflicts their characters face.

11. How is a monologue different from dialogue?

12. What does a character usually talk about in a monologue?

13. Give an example of a monologue from Act V of *Romeo and Juliet*.

14. What might Ruth have said if Hansberry had written a monologue for her?

15. Give an example of a monologue you might have seen on television or in a play or film.

Critical Thinking

16. What is the key event in the last act of *Romeo and Juliet* that could have changed the way the play ended? Explain your opinion.

17. Describe the character of Mama as she appears in the first scene of *A Raisin in the Sun*.

18. Compare the way *A Raisin in the Sun* begins with the way the "Writer's Realm" episode begins. In your opinion, which is the more effective opening? Explain your choice.

Thinking Creatively

19. If you could pick the character from this unit you would most like to play on the stage or screen, who would it be? Why?

20. Which play in this unit would you most like to see performed? Explain your choice.

Speak and Listen

Create a tableau based on a scene from one of the plays in this unit.

In a tableau, people pose as the characters in a scene, but they do not move. Allow other members of the class to approach the tableau and gently touch one of the characters. When characters are touched, they have to answer questions about the scene.

Writing on Your Own

Dialogue involves two or more characters speaking to each other in a play. In a monologue, an actor who is alone on the stage talks about his or her thoughts. Write a monologue for Walter Younger, telling the way he feels and what he is thinking about. Complete a first draft of the monologue and edit it, using tips for writing found in Appendix C. Create a final draft that is free from errors.

Beyond Words

Find or create a picture, sculpture, or model that could serve as a symbol for the fate of Romeo and Juliet.

Test-Taking Tip

When you read over your written answer to a question, imagine that you are someone reading it for the first time. Ask yourself if the ideas and information make sense. Revise and rewrite to make the answer as clear as you can.

Appendix A: Graphic Organizers

Graphic organizers are like maps. They help guide you through literature. They can also help you plan or "map out" your own stories, research, or presentations.

1. Character Analysis Guide

This graphic organizer helps you learn more about a character in a selection.

To use: Choose a character. List four traits of that character. Write down an event from the selection that shows each character trait.

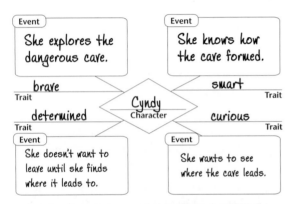

2. Story Map

This graphic organizer helps you summarize a story that you have read or plan your own story.

To use: List the title, setting, and characters. Describe the main problem of the story and the events that explain the problem. Then write how the problem is solved.

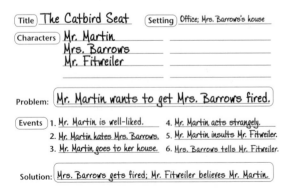

3. Main Idea Graphic (Umbrella)

This graphic organizer helps you determine the main idea of a selection or of a paragraph in the selection.

To use: List the main idea of a selection. Then, write the details that show or support the main idea of the story.

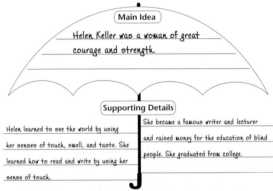

4. Main Idea Graphic (Table)

This graphic organizer is another way to determine the main idea of a selection or of a paragraph in the selection. Just like a table is held up by four strong legs, a main idea is held up or supported by many details.

To use: Write the main idea of a selection or paragraph on the tabletop. Then, write the details that show or support the main idea of the selection or paragraph on the table legs.

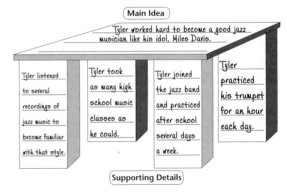

5. Main Idea Graphic (Details)

This graphic organizer is also a way to determine the main idea of a selection or of a paragraph in the selection. If the main idea of a selection or paragraph is not clear, add the details together to find it.

To use: First, list the supporting details of the selection or paragraph. Then, write one sentence that summarizes all the events. That is the main idea of the story.

Details
- The dog sleeps on the fresh hay in the manger.
- The cattle want to eat the hay.
- The dog wakes up—he doesn't want the cows to eat the hay.
- The cows think the dog is selfish.
- The farmer chases the dog away from the hay.

Main Idea
Don't prevent others from enjoying something you can't enjoy.

6. Venn Diagram

This graphic organizer can help you compare and contrast two stories, characters, events, or topics.

To use: List the things that are common to both stories, events, characters, and so on in the "similarities" area between the circles. List the differences on the parts that do not overlap.

What is being compared? _____

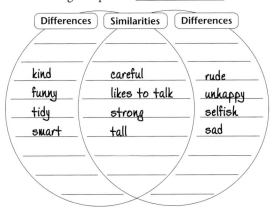

Differences	Similarities	Differences
kind	careful	rude
funny	likes to talk	unhappy
tidy	strong	selfish
smart	tall	sad

7. Sequence Chain

This graphic organizer outlines a series of events in the order in which they happen. This is helpful when summarizing the plot of a story. This graphic organizer may also help you plan your own story.

To use: Fill in the box at the top with the title of the story. Then, in the boxes below, record the events in the order in which they happen in the story. Write a short sentence in each box and only include the major events of the story.

Sequence Chain for: _Cinderella_

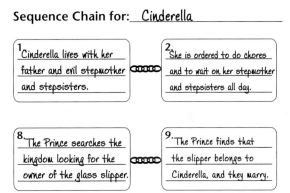

1. Cinderella lives with her father and evil stepmother and stepsisters.

2. She is ordered to do chores and to wait on her stepmother and stepsisters all day.

8. The Prince searches the kingdom looking for the owner of the glass slipper.

9. The Prince finds that the slipper belongs to Cinderella, and they marry.

8. Concept Map

This graphic organizer helps you to organize supporting details for a story or research topic.

To use: Write the topic in the center of the graphic organizer. List ideas that support the topic on the lines. Group similar ideas and details together.

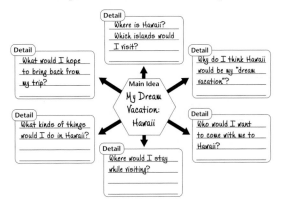

Detail
Where is Hawaii? Which islands would I visit?

Detail
What would I hope to bring back from my trip?

Detail
Why do I think Hawaii would be my "dream vacation"?

Main Idea
My Dream Vacation: Hawaii

Detail
What kinds of things would I do in Hawaii?

Detail
Who would I want to come with me to Hawaii?

Detail
Where would I stay while visiting?

9. Plot Mountain

This graphic organizer helps you organize the events of a story or plot. There are five parts in a story's plot: the exposition, the rising action, the climax, the falling action, and the resolution (or denouement). These parts represent the beginning, middle, and end of the selection.

To use:

- Write the exposition, or how the selection starts, at the left base of the mountain. What is the setting? Who are the characters?
- Then, write the rising action, or the events that lead to the climax, on the left side of the mountain. Start at the base and list the events in time order going up the left side.
- At the top of the mountain, write the climax, or the highest point of interest or suspense. All events in the rising action lead up to this one main event or turning point.
- Write the events that happen after the climax, or falling action, on the right side of the mountain. Start at the top of the mountain, or climax, and put the events in time order going down the right-hand side.
- Finally, write the resolution, or denouement, at the right base of the mountain. The resolution explains how the problem, or conflict, in the story is solved or how the story ends.

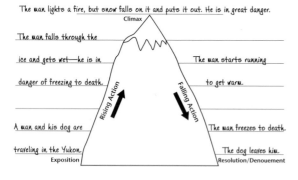

The man lights a fire, but snow falls on it and puts it out. He is in great danger.

Climax

The man falls through the ice and gets wet—he is in danger of freezing to death.

Rising Action

A man and his dog are traveling in the Yukon.

Exposition

The man starts running to get warm.

Falling Action

The man freezes to death.

The dog leaves him.

Resolution/Denouement

10. Structured Overview

This graphic organizer shows you how a main idea branches out in a selection.

To use: Write the main idea of a selection in the top box. Then, branch out and list events and details that support the main idea. Continue to branch off more boxes as needed to fill in the details of the story.

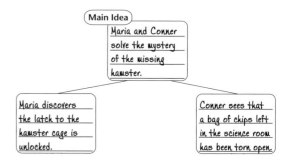

Main Idea

Maria and Conner solve the mystery of the missing hamster.

Maria discovers the latch to the hamster cage is unlocked.

Conner sees that a bag of chips left in the science room has been torn open.

11. Semantic Table

This graphic organizer can help you understand the differences among words that have similar meanings.

To use: Choose a topic. List nouns for that topic in the top row. Put adjectives that describe your topic in the first column. Then, fill in the rest of the grid by checking those adjectives that are appropriate for the nouns. That way, in your writing, you can use words that make sense for your story.

Topic: _____ Homes

Adjectives Nouns→	apartment	4-bedroom home	cabin
large	—	✓	—
expensive	—	✓	—
quiet	—	✓	✓

12. Prediction Guide

This graphic organizer can be used to predict, or try to figure out, how a selection might end. Before finishing a selection, fill in this guide.

To use: List the time, place, and characters in the selection. Write what the problem, or conflict, is in the story. Then, try to predict possible endings or solutions. Compare your predictions with others.

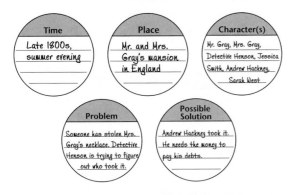

13. Semantic Line

This graphic organizer can help you think of synonyms for words that are used too often in writing.

To use: At the end of each line, write two overused words that mean the opposite. Then, fill in the lines with words of similar meaning. In the example below, the opposite words are *beautiful* and *ugly*. Words that are closer in meaning to beautiful are at the top. Words that are closer in meaning to ugly are at the bottom. The word *plain* falls in the middle.

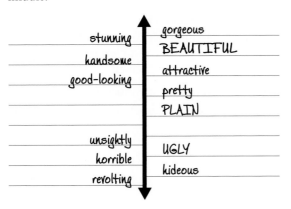

14. KWL Chart

This graphic organizer can help you learn about a topic before you start reading a selection or conducting research.

To use: Before you start reading a selection or conducting research, fill in the organizer. Write the topic on the line. In the first column, write what you already *know* (K) about your topic. Next, list what you *want* (W) to know about your topic in the next column. Then, as you start reading a selection or conducting research, write down what you *learn* (L) in the last column.

Topic: __Mount Everest__

K What I Know	W What I Want to Know	L What I Have Learned
It's a tall mountain in Asia. People may have tried to climb it. It's part of a larger mountain chain. It's one of the most famous mountains in the world.	How tall is it? Is it the tallest? What mountain chain is it part of?	It is the tallest in the world. It is part of the Himalayas. People have climbed it before. Some people have died trying.

Appendix B: Grammar

Parts of Speech

Adjectives

- Adjectives describe nouns and pronouns. They answer *What kind? Which one? How many?* or *How much?* Example: The *new* book costs *five* dollars.

- Comparative adjectives compare two nouns and usually end in *–er*. Example: *newer*

- Superlative adjectives compare three or more nouns and usually end in *–est*. Example: *newest*

Adverbs

- Adverbs modify verbs, adjectives, and other adverbs. They answer *When? How? How often?* and *How long?* Many adverbs end in *–ly*. Example: She laughed *loudly*.

Conjunctions

- Conjunctions connect parts of a sentence.

- Coordinating conjunctions connect two equal parts of a sentence using words like *and, but, nor, or, for, yet, so,* and *as well as.* Example: Do you want milk *or* water?

- Correlative conjunctions are used in pairs and connect equal parts of a sentence. Correlative conjunctions are *both/and, neither/nor, either/or, but/also.* Example: The teenagers had *neither* the time *nor* the money.

- Subordinating conjunctions connect two unequal parts of a sentence using words like *after, although, before, because, since, if, unless, while.* Example: *Since* you are arriving late, we will eat dinner at 7 p.m.

Interjections

- Interjections are words or phrases that show strong feeling, often followed by exclamation points. Examples: Wow! Ouch! Oops!

Nouns

- A noun names a person, place, thing, or idea.

- Proper nouns are names that are capitalized. Examples: Susan, New York

Prepositions

- Prepositions relate nouns and pronouns to other words in a sentence. Examples: above, from, with

Pronouns

- Pronouns replace nouns. Antecedents are the nouns that the pronouns replace. Example: Jorge takes karate lessons, and *he* practices every week.

- Demonstrative pronouns identify particular nouns: *this* hat, *those* shoes

- Indefinite pronouns do not refer to particular nouns. Examples: all, everyone, none

- Interrogative pronouns begin questions. Examples: who, which, what

- Personal pronouns refer to people or things. Examples: I, me, you, it, he, she, we, us, they, him, her, them

- Possessive pronouns show ownership. Examples: my, mine, his, hers, its, our, yours, their, ours, theirs

- Reflexive pronouns follow a verb or preposition and refer to the noun or pronoun that comes before. Examples: myself, themselves, himself, herself

- Relative pronouns introduce a subordinate clause. Examples: who, whom, whose, which, that, what

Verbs

- Verbs show action or express states of being.

- If the verbs are *transitive*, they link the action to something or someone. Example: John *hit* the ball. Action verbs that are *intransitive* do not link the action to something or someone. Example: The ball *flew.*

- Linking verbs connect a subject with a word or words that describe it. Some linking verbs are *am, are, was, were, is,* and *be.* Example: Susan *is* student council president.

Grammar Glossary

Active and Passive Voice

- Active voice is when the subject is *doing* the action. A sentence written in active voice is often shorter and easier to understand. Example: Jane drove the car to school.

- Passive voice is when the subject *receives* the action. A sentence written in passive voice can be awkward. Use a passive sentence only when the doer is unknown or unnecessary. Example: The car was driven by Jane.

Antecedent

- An antecedent is the noun or pronoun that a pronoun refers to in a sentence. Example: *Kevin* ran for Student Council so that *he* could help improve the school. *Kevin* is the antecedent for the pronoun *he.*

Appositives

- An appositive is a noun or pronoun that follows another noun or pronoun. An appositive renames or adds detail about the word. Example: Mr. Smith, *our principal*, is a great leader.

Clauses

- A clause is a group of words that contains a subject and a verb. There are independent and dependent clauses.

- An independent clause can stand alone because it expresses a complete thought. Example: Our dog eats twice a day. She also walks two miles a day. Two independent clauses can also be joined to form one sentence by using a comma and a coordinating conjunction, such as *and, but, nor, or, for, yet, so,* and *as well as.* Example: Our dog eats twice a day, *and* she walks two miles a day.

- A dependent clause cannot stand alone because it does not express a complete thought. Example: Because exercise is good for pets. This is a fragment or incomplete sentence. To fix this, combine a dependent clause with an independent clause. Example: Our dog walks two miles a day because exercise is good for pets.

Complements

- A complement completes the meaning of a verb. There are three types of complements: direct objects, indirect objects, and subject complements.

- A direct object is a word or group of words that receives the action of the verb. Example: Jane set the table. (*The table* is the complement or direct object of the verb *set.*)

- An indirect object is a word or group of words that follow the verb and tell for whom or what the action is done. An indirect object always comes before a direct object in a sentence. Example: Setting the table saved her mother some time. (*Her mother* is the complement or indirect object of the verb *saved.*)

- A subject complement is a word or group of words that further identify the subject of a sentence. A subject complement always follows a linking verb. Example: Buddy is the best dog. (The word *dog* is the complement of the subject *Buddy.*)

Contractions

- A contraction is two words made into one by replacing one or more letters with an apostrophe. Examples: *didn't* (did not), *you're* (you are)

Double Negatives

- A double negative is the use of two negative words, such as *no* or *not*, in a sentence. To fix a double negative, make one word positive. Incorrect: She *did not* get *no* dessert after dinner. Correct: She did not get *any* dessert after dinner.

Fragments

- A fragment is not a complete sentence. It may have a subject and verb, but it does not express a complete thought. Incorrect: The leaves that fell in the yard. Correct: The leaves that fell in the yard needed to be raked.

Gerunds

- A gerund is a verb with an *–ing* ending. It is used as a noun. Example: *Golfing* is fun! Here, *golfing* is a noun and the subject of the sentence.

Infinitives

- An infinitive is the word *to* plus the present tense of a verb. An infinitive can be a noun, adjective, or adverb in a sentence. Example: *To write* was her dream job. Here, *To write* is the infinitive, and it serves as a noun.

Modifiers

- A modifier is a word or group of words that change the meanings of other words in the sentence. Adjectives and adverbs are modifiers.

- A dangling or misplaced modifier is a group of descriptive words that is not near the word it modifies. This confuses the reader. Incorrect: Tucked up in the closet, Sarah found her grandma's photographs. *Tucked up in the closet* modifies Sarah. However, the photographs, not Sarah, are tucked up in the closet! Correct: Sarah found her grandma's photographs tucked up in the closet.

Parallel Structure

- Parallel structure is the use of words to balance ideas that are equally important. Incorrect: In the winter, I love to skate, snowmen, and to ski. Correct: In the winter, I love *to skate*, *to make* snowmen, and *to ski.*

Phrases

- A phrase is a group of words that does not have both a subject and a verb. Types of phrases include gerund phrases, infinitive phrases, and participial phrases.

- A gerund phrase has a gerund plus any modifiers and complements. The entire phrase serves as a noun. Example: Playing basketball with his friends was Trevor's favorite pastime. *Playing basketball with his friends* is the gerund phrase.

- An infinitive phrase has an infinitive plus any modifiers and complements. The entire phrase serves as a noun, adjective, or adverb in a sentence. Example: My mother liked to bake cookies on the weekend. *To bake cookies on the weekend* is the infinitive phrase.

- A participial phrase has a participle (a verb in its present form [*–ing*] or past form [*–ed* or *–en*]) plus all of its modifiers and complements. The entire phrase serves as an adjective in a sentence. Example: Wearing the robes of a king, Luis read his lines perfectly during play tryouts. *Wearing the robes of a king* is the participial phrase, and it modifies or describes the subject, Luis.

Plural Nouns

- A plural shows more than one of a particular noun. Use the following rules to create the plural form. Remember that there are exceptions to many spelling rules that you must simply memorize.

- Add –s to most singular nouns. Example: table/tables

- Add –es to a noun if it ends in –ch, –sh, –s, –x, and –z. Example: chur<u>ch</u>/churches

- If a noun ends with a vowel and a –y, add an –s to make the plural. Example: don<u>key</u>/donkeys

- If a noun ends with a consonant and a –y, drop the –y and add an –ies to make the plural. Example: pup<u>py</u>/puppies

- If a noun ends in an –f or –fe, change the –f or –fe to a v and add –es. Example: kni<u>fe</u>/knives

- If a noun ends in an –o, sometimes you add –es and sometimes you add –s. Look in a dictionary to find out. Examples: pota<u>to</u>/potatoes, radi<u>o</u>/radios

Possessives

- A possessive noun shows ownership of an object, action, or idea. A possessive noun ends in 's. Example: Susan's book

- A possessive pronoun also shows ownership of an object, action, or idea. Example: his glove

Pronoun–Antecedent Agreement

- Pronoun-antecedent agreement occurs when the pronoun matches the antecedent (the word it refers to) in gender and number.

- To agree in gender:
  – Replace the name of a male person with a masculine pronoun. Example: *Jake* ran down the field, and *he* scored.

  – Replace the name of a female person with a feminine pronoun. Example: *Ana* read "The Most Dangerous Game," and *she* loved it.

  – Replace singular names with *it* or *its*. Example: The *kitten* ran through the room, and *it* pounced on the ball.

  – Replace plural names with *they, them,* or *their.* Example: The *tenth graders* came into the gym, and *they* played volleyball.

- To agree in number:

  – Make the pronoun singular if its antecedent is singular. Example: *Michael* told *himself* that he did the right thing.

  – Make the pronoun plural if its antecedent is plural. Example: The hungry *teenagers* ordered sandwiches for *themselves.*

Run-on Sentences

- A run-on sentence is the combination of two or more sentences without proper punctuation.

- To correct a run-on sentence, you can break it into two or more sentences by using capital letters and periods. Incorrect: The house was built in 1960 it needs new windows. Correct: The house was built in 1960. It needs new windows.

- You can also correct a run-on sentence by adding a comma and a coordinating conjunction to separate the sentences. Correct: The house was built in 1960, *so* it needs new windows.

- Another way to correct a run-on sentence is by adding a semicolon between the sentences. A semicolon should stand alone and should not have a coordinating conjunction after it. Correct: The house was built in 1960; it needs new windows.

Sentence Construction

- A simple sentence has one independent clause that includes a subject and a predicate. Example: The afternoon was warm and sunny.

- A compound sentence has two or more independent clauses joined by a comma and a coordinating conjunction or joined by a semicolon. Example: The afternoon was warm and sunny, so we decided to drive to the beach.

- A complex sentence has one independent clause and one or more dependent clauses. Example: We are going to the beach if you want to come along.

- A compound–complex sentence has two or more independent clauses joined by a comma and a coordinating conjunction. It has at least one dependent clause. Example: Although the morning was cold and damp, the afternoon was warm and sunny, so we decided to drive to the beach.

Sentence Types

- You can use a declarative sentence, an exclamatory sentence, an imperative sentence, or an interrogative sentence in writing.

- A declarative sentence tells us something about a person, place, or thing. This type of sentence ends with a period. Example: Martin Luther King Jr. fought for civil rights.

- An exclamatory sentence shows strong feeling or surprise. This type of sentence ends with an exclamation point. Example: I can't believe the price of gasoline!

- An imperative sentence gives commands. This type of sentence ends with a period. (Note: The subject of an imperative sentence is the implied "you.") Example: Please read chapter two by next Monday.

- An interrogative sentence asks a question. This type of sentence ends with a question mark. Example: Will you join us for dinner?

Subjects and Predicates

- The subject of a sentence names the person or thing doing the action. The subject contains a noun or a pronoun. Example: The students created posters and brochures. The subject of this sentence is *The students*. The predicate of this sentence (see definition below) is *created posters and brochures*.

- The predicate of a sentence tells what the person or thing is doing. The predicate contains a verb. Example: The fans waited for the hockey game to begin. The predicate of this sentence is *waited for the hockey game to begin*. The subject of this sentence is *The fans*.

Punctuation Guidelines

Apostrophe

- Shows ownership (possessive nouns): Kelly's backpack

- Shows plural possessive nouns: The five students' success was due to hard work.

- Shows missing letters in contractions: that's (that is)

Colon

- Introduces a list after a complete sentence: We learned about planets: Mars, Venus, and Jupiter.

- Adds or explains more about a complete sentence: Lunch was one option: pizza.

- Follows the salutation in a formal letter or in a business letter: Dear Mr. Jackson:

- Separates the hour and the minute: 2:15

- Introduces a long quotation: Lincoln wrote: "Four score and seven years ago . . ."

Comma

- Separates three or more items in a series: We planted corn, squash, and tomatoes.

- Joins two independent clauses when used with a coordinating conjunction: Sam and Raul did their homework, and then they left.

- Separates a city and state: Los Angeles, California

- Separates a day and year: October 15, 2006

- Follows the salutation and closing in a friendly letter: Dear Shanice, Love always,

- Follows the closing in a business letter: Sincerely,

- Sets off a restrictive phrase clause: Angela, the youngest runner, won the race.

- Sets off an introductory phrase or clause: Before he started the experiment, Jason put on safety glasses.

Dash

- Sets off an explanation in a sentence: The three poets—Langston Hughes, Robert Frost, and William Carlos Williams—are modernist poets.

- Shows a pause or break in thought: After years away, I returned—and found lots had changed.

Ellipses

- Show that words have been left out of a text: Our dog dove into the lake . . . and swam to shore.

Exclamation Point

- Shows emotion: Our team won!

Hyphen

- Divides a word at the end of a line: We enjoyed the beaches.

- Separates a compound adjective before a noun to make its meaning clearer: much-loved book

- Separates a compound number: thirty-three.

- Separates a fraction when used as an adjective: two-thirds full

Period

- Marks the end of a statement or command: July is the warmest month.

- Follows most abbreviations: Mrs., Dr., Inc., Jr.

Question Mark

- Marks the end of a question: How many eggs are left?

Quotation Marks

- Enclose the exact words of a speaker: He said, "I'll buy that book."

- Enclose the titles of short works: "Dover Beach," "America the Beautiful"

Semicolon

- Separates items in a series when commas are within the items: We went to Sioux Falls, South Dakota; Des Moines, Iowa; and Kansas City, Kansas.

- Joins two independent clauses that are closely related: We went to the movie; they came with us.

Capitalization Guidelines

Capitalize:

- the first word of a sentence: The teacher asked her students to read.
- the first word and any important words in a title: *To Kill a Mockingbird*
- all proper nouns: Marlon Smith, Atlanta, March
- the pronoun *I*
- languages: English, French
- abbreviations: Mrs., Sgt., FDR, EST

Commonly Confused Words

accept, except

- *Accept* (verb) means "to receive." Example: The children will *accept* ice cream.
- *Except* (preposition) means "leaving out." Example: The children enjoyed all flavors *except* strawberry.

affect, effect

- *Affect* (verb) means "to have an effect on." Example: This storm will *affect* our town.
- *Effect* (noun) means "a result or an outcome." Example: The *effect* was a struggling local economy.

its, it's

- *Its* (adjective) is the possessive form of "it." Example: Our hamster liked to run on the wheel inside *its* cage.
- *It's* is a contraction for "it is." Example: *It's* a long time before lunch.

lie, lay

- *Lie* (verb) means "to rest." Example: Jenny had a headache, so she needed to *lie* down.
- *Lay* (verb) means "to place." Example: Jamal went to *lay* his baseball glove on the bench.

lose, loose

- *Lose* (verb) means "to misplace or not find something." Example: I always *lose* my sunglasses when I go to the beach.
- *Loose* (adjective) means "free or without limits." Example: Someone let Sparky *loose* from his leash.

than, then

- *Than* (conjunction) shows a comparison. Example: You are older *than* I am.
- *Then* (adverb) means "at that time." Example: Will turned the doorknob and *then* slowly opened the door.

their, there, they're

- *Their* (pronoun) shows possession. Example: This is *their* house.
- *There* (adverb) means "place." Example: Sit over *there*.
- *They're* is a contraction for "they are." Example: *They're* coming over for dinner.

to, too, two

- *To* (preposition) shows purpose, movement, or connection. Example: We drove *to* the store.
- *Too* (adverb) means "also or more than wanted." Example: I, *too*, felt it was *too* hot to go outside.
- *Two* is a number. Example: Ava has *two* more years of high school.

your, you're

- *Your* (adjective) shows possession and means "belonging to you." Example: Take off *your* hat, please.
- *You're* is a contraction for "you are." Example: *You're* the best artist in the school.

Appendix C: Writing

Types of Writing

Before you can begin the writing process, you need to understand the types, purposes, and formats of different types of writing.

Descriptive Writing

Descriptive writing covers all writing genres. Description can be used to tell a story, to analyze and explain research, or to persuade. Descriptive writing uses images and colorful details to "paint a picture" for the reader.

Five Senses in Descriptive Writing

Consider the five senses in your descriptive writing: sight, smell, touch, sound, and taste. Using your senses to help describe an object, place, or person makes your writing more interesting. Before you begin, ask yourself the following:

- How does something look? Describe the color, size, and/or shape. What is it like?

- What smell or smells are present? Describe any pleasant or unpleasant smells. Compare the smells to other smells you know.

- How does something feel? Think about textures. Also think about emotions or feelings that result from the touching.

- What sounds do you hear? Describe the volume and the pitch. Are the sounds loud and shrill, or quiet and peaceful? What do the sounds remind you of?

- What does something taste like? Compare it to a taste you know, good or bad.

Expository Writing

Expository writing explains and informs through essays, articles, reports, and instructions. Like descriptive writing, it covers all writing genres. The purpose of this type of writing is to give more information about a subject. This can be done in many ways. The two most common formats in the study of literature are the compare and contrast paper and the cause and effect paper.

- Compare and Contrast Paper—This paper shows the similarities and differences of two or more characters, objects, settings, situations, writing styles, problems, or ideas.

- Cause and Effect Paper—This paper explains why certain things happen or how specific actions led to a result. A cause and effect paper can be set up by writing about the result (effect) first, followed by the events that led up to it (causes). Or, the paper can trace the events (causes), in order, that lead up to the result (effect).

Narrative Writing

Narrative writing tells a story. The story can be true (nonfiction) or made up (fiction). Narratives entertain or inform readers about a series of events. Poetry, stories, diaries, letters, biographies, and autobiographies are all types of narrative writing.

Key Elements in Narrative Writing

Think about the type of narrative you want to write and these key elements of your story:

- Characters: Who are the major and minor characters in the story? What do they look like? How do they act?

- Dialogue: What conversations take place among the characters? How does the dialogue show the reader something about the personalities of the characters?

- Setting: Where and when do the events take place? How does the setting affect the plot?

- Plot: What events happen in the story? In what order do the events occur? What is the problem that the main character is struggling with? How is the problem solved?

There are two common ways to set up your narrative paper. You can start at the beginning and tell your story in chronological order, or in the order in which the events happened. Or, you can start at the ending of your story and, through a flashback, tell what events led up to the present time.

Persuasive Writing

Persuasive writing is used when you want to convince your reader that your opinion on a topic is the right one. The goal of this paper is to have your reader agree with what you say. To do this, you need to know your topic well, and you need to give lots of reasons and supporting details. Editorials (opinion writing) in the newspaper, advertisements, and book reviews are all types of persuasive writing.

Key Elements of Persuasive Writing

Choosing a topic that you know well and that you feel strongly about is important for persuasive writing. The feelings or emotions that you have about the topic will come through in your paper and make a stronger argument. Also, be sure that you have a good balance between appealing to the reader's mind (using facts, statistics, experts, and so on) and appealing to the reader's heart (using words that make them feel angry, sad, and so on). Think about these key elements:

- Topic: Is your topic a good one for your audience? Do you know a lot about your topic? Is your topic narrow enough so that you can cover it in a paper?

- Opinion: Is your opinion clear? Do you know enough about the opposite side of your opinion to get rid of those arguments in your paper?

- Reasons: Do you have at least three reasons that explain why you feel the way you do? Are these reasons logical?

- Supporting details or evidence: Do you have facts, statistics, experts, or personal experience that can support each reason?

- Opposing arguments: Can you address the opposite side and get rid of their arguments?

- Conclusion: Can you offer a solution or recommendation to the reader?

- Word choice: Can you find words that set the tone for your opinion? Will these words affect your readers emotionally?

There are two common ways to set up this paper. The first format is a six-paragraph paper: one paragraph for your introduction, three paragraphs for each of your three reasons, one paragraph for the opposing arguments and your responses to them, and one paragraph for your conclusion. Or you can write a five-paragraph paper where you place the opposing arguments and responses to each of your three reasons within the same paragraphs.

Research Report

A research report is an in-depth study of a topic. This type of writing has many uses in all subjects. It involves digging for information in many sources, including books, magazines, newspapers, the Internet, almanacs, encyclopedias, and other places of data. There are many key elements in writing a research report. Choosing a thesis statement, finding support or evidence for that thesis, and citing where you found your information are all important.

There are several uses of a research report in literature. You can explore a writer's life, a particular writing movement, or a certain writer's style. You could also write about a selection.

Business Writing

Business writing has many forms: memos, meeting minutes, brochures, manuals, reports, job applications, contracts, college essays. No matter what the format, the goal of business writing is clear communication. Keep the following key elements in mind when you are doing business writing:

- Format: What type of writing are you doing?

- Purpose: What is the purpose of your writing? Is the purpose clear in your introduction?

- Audience: Are your words and ideas appropriate for your audience?

- Organization: Are your ideas well-organized and easy to follow?

- Style: Are your ideas clearly written and to the point?

The Writing Process

The writing process is a little different for each writer and for each writing assignment. However, the goals of writing never change: Writers want to:

- have a purpose for their writing

- get their readers' attention and keep it

- present their ideas clearly

- choose their words carefully

To meet these goals, writers need to move through a writing process. This process allows them to explore, organize, write, revise, and share their ideas. There are five steps to this writing process: prewriting; drafting; revising; editing and proofreading; and publishing and evaluating.

⬇ *Use the following steps for any writing assignment:*

Step 1: Prewriting

Prewriting is where you explore ideas and decide what to write about. Here are some approaches.

Brainstorming

Brainstorming is fast, fun, and full of ideas. Start by stating a topic. Then write down everything you can think of about that topic. Ask questions about the topic. If you are in a group, have one person write everything down. Think of as many words and ideas as you can in a short time. Don't worry about neatness, spelling, or grammar. When you are finished, group words that are similar. These groups may become your supporting ideas.

Graphic Organizers

Graphic organizers are maps that can lead you through your prewriting. They provide pictures or charts that you fill in. Read the descriptions of these organizers in Appendix A, and choose the ones that will help you organize your ideas.

Outline

An outline can help you organize your information. Write your main ideas next to each Roman numeral. Write your supporting details next to the letters under each Roman numeral. Keep your ideas brief and to the point. Here's an example to follow:

Topic for persuasive paper: Lincoln High School should have a swimming pool.

I. Health benefits for students

    A. Weight control

    B. Good exercise

II. Water safety benefits for students

    A. Learn-to-swim programs

    B. Water safety measures to help others

III. School benefits

    A. Swim team

    B. Added rotation for gym class

IV. Community benefits

    A. More physically fit community members

    B. More jobs for community members

Narrowing Your Topic

Narrowing your topic means to focus your ideas on a specific area. You may be interested in writing about Edgar Allan Poe, but that is a broad topic. What about Poe interests you? Think about your purpose for writing. Is your goal to persuade, to explain, or to compare? Narrowing your scope and knowing your purpose will keep you focused.

Note-Taking and Research

Refer to the "How to Use This Book" section at the beginning of this textbook and Appendix D for help with note-taking and research skills.

Planning Your Voice

Your voice is your special way of using language in your writing. Readers can get to know your personality and thoughts by your sentence structure, word choice, and tone. How will your writing tell what you want to say in your own way? How will it be different from the way others write?

Step 2: Drafting

In the drafting step, you will write your paper. Use your brainstorming notes, outline, and graphic organizers from your prewriting stage as your guide. Your paper will need to include an introduction, a body, and a conclusion.

Introduction

The introduction states your topic and purpose. It includes a *thesis statement*, which is a sentence that tells the main idea of your entire paper. The last line of your introduction is a good place for your thesis statement. That way, your reader has a clear idea of the purpose of your paper before starting to read your points.

Your introduction should make people want to read more. Think about what your audience might like. Try one of these methods:

- asking a question
- sharing a brief story
- describing something
- giving a surprising fact
- using an important quotation

When you begin drafting, just write your introduction. Do not try to make it perfect the first time. You can always change it later.

Body

The body of your paper is made up of several paragraphs. Each paragraph also has a topic sentence, supporting details, and a concluding statement or summary. Remember, too, that each paragraph needs to support your thesis statement in your introduction.

- The topic sentence is usually the first sentence of a paragraph. It lets the reader know what your paragraph is going to be about.

- The supporting details of a paragraph are the sentences that support or tell more about your topic sentence. They can include facts, explanations, examples, statistics, and/or experts' ideas.

- The last sentence of your paragraph is a concluding statement or summary. A concluding statement is a judgment. It is based on the facts that you presented in your paragraph. A summary briefly repeats the main ideas of your paragraph. It repeats your idea or ideas in slightly different words. It does not add new information.

Conclusion

The conclusion ties together the main ideas of the paper. If you asked a question in your introduction, the conclusion answers it. If you outlined a problem, your conclusion offers solutions. The conclusion should not simply restate your thesis and supporting points.

Title of the Paper

Make sure to title your paper. Use a title that is interesting, but relates well to your topic.

Step 3: Revising

Now that you've explored ideas and put them into a draft, it's time to revise. During this step, you will rewrite parts or sections of your paper. All good writing goes through many drafts. To help you make the necessary changes, use the checklists below to review your paper.

Overall Paper

☑ Do I have an interesting title that draws readers in?

☑ Does the title tell my audience what my paper is about?

☑ Do I have an introduction, body, and conclusion?

☑ Is my paper the correct length?

Introduction

☑ Have I used a method to interest my readers?

☑ Do I have a thesis statement that tells the main idea of my paper?

☑ Is my thesis statement clearly stated?

Body

- ☑ Do I start every paragraph on a new line?

- ☑ Is the first line of every paragraph indented?

- ☑ Does the first sentence (topic sentence) in every paragraph explain the main idea of the paragraph? Does it attract my readers' attention?

- ☑ Do I include facts, explanations, examples, statistics, and/or experts' ideas that support the topic sentence?

- ☑ Do I need to take out any sentences that do not relate to the topic sentence?

- ☑ Do the paragraphs flow in a logical order? Does each point build on the last one?

- ☑ Do good transition words lead readers from one paragraph to the next?

Conclusion

- ☑ Does the conclusion tie together the main ideas of my paper?

- ☑ Does it offer a solution, make a suggestion, or answer any questions that the readers might have?

Writing Style

- ☑ Do I use words and concepts that my audience understands?

- ☑ Is the tone too formal or informal for my audience?

- ☑ Are my sentences the right length for my audience?

- ☑ Do I have good sentence variety and word choice?

Step 4: Editing and Proofreading

During the editing and proofreading step, check your paper or another student's paper for errors in grammar, punctuation, capitalization, and spelling. Use the following checklists to help guide you. Read and focus on one sentence at a time. Cover up everything but the sentence you are reading. Reading from the end of the paper backward also works for some students. Note changes using the proofreader marks shown on the following page. Check a dictionary or style manual when you're not sure about something.

Grammar

- ☑ Is there a subject and a verb in every sentence?

- ☑ Do the subject and verb agree in every sentence?

- ☑ Is the verb tense logical in every sentence?

- ☑ Is the verb tense consistent in every sentence?

- ☑ Have you used interesting, lively verbs?

- ☑ Do all pronouns have clear antecedents?

- ☑ Can repeated or unnecessary words be left out?

- ☑ Are there any run-on sentences that need to be corrected?

- ☑ Does sentence length vary with long and short sentences?

Punctuation

☑ Does every sentence end with the correct punctuation mark?

☑ Are all direct quotations punctuated correctly?

☑ Do commas separate words in a series?

☑ Is there a comma and a coordinating conjunction separating each compound sentence?

☑ Is there a comma after an introductory phrase or clause?

☑ Are apostrophes used correctly in contractions and possessive nouns?

Capitalization

☑ Is the first word of every sentence capitalized?

☑ Are all proper nouns and adjectives capitalized?

☑ Are the important words in the title of the paper capitalized?

Spelling

☑ Are words that sound alike spelled correctly (such as *to*, *too*, and *two*)?

☑ Is every plural noun spelled correctly?

☑ Are words with *ie* or *ei* spelled correctly?

☑ Is the silent *e* dropped before adding an ending that starts with a vowel?

☑ Is the consonant doubling rule used correctly?

If the paper was typed, make any necessary changes and run the spell-check and grammar-check programs one more time.

Proofreading Marks

Below are some common proofreading marks. Print out your paper and use these marks to correct errors.

Symbol	Meaning
¶	Start new paragraph
⌣	Close up
#	Add a space
⋃	Switch words or letters
=	Capitalize this letter
/	Lowercase this letter
ℒ	Omit space, letter, mark, or word
∧	Insert space, mark, or word
⊙	Insert a period
⌄	Insert a comma
sp	Spell out
stet	Leave as is (write dots under words)

Step 5: Publishing and Evaluating

Once you have made the final text changes, make sure that the overall format of your paper is correct. Follow the guidelines that were set up by your teacher. Here are some general guidelines that are commonly used.

Readability

■ Double space all text.

■ Use an easy-to-read font such as Times Roman, Comic Sans, Ariel, or New York.

■ Use a 12-point type size.

■ Make sure that you have met any word, paragraph, or page count guidelines.

Format

- Make at least a one-inch margin around each page.

- Place the title of the paper, your name, your class period, and the date according to your teacher's guidelines. If you need a title page, make sure that you have a separate page with this information. If you do not need a title page, place your name, class period, and date in the upper right-hand corner of the first page. Center the title below that.

- Check to see if your pages need to be numbered. If so, number them in the upper right-hand corner or according to your teacher's guidelines.

- Label any charts and graphics as needed.

- Check that your title and any subheads are in boldface print.

- Check that your paragraphs are indented.

Citations

- Cite direct quotations, paraphrases, and summaries properly. Refer to the Modern Language Association (MLA) or American Psychological Association (APA) rules.

- Punctuate all citations properly. Refer to MLA or APA rules.

Bibliographies

- Include a list of books and other materials you reviewed during your research. This is a reference list only. Below are examples of how you would list a book, magazine article, and Web site using MLA style:

Book:
Author's Last Name, Author's First Name. *Book Title*. Publisher's City: Publisher's Name, Year.

London, Jack. *The Call of the Wild*. New York: Scholastic, 2001.

Magazine:
Author's Last Name, Author's First Name. "Article Title." *Magazine Title*. Volume Date: Page numbers.

Young, Diane. "At the High End of the River." *Southern Living*. June 2000: 126–131.

Web Site:
Article Title. Date accessed. URL

Circle of Stories. 25 Jan. 2006. <http://www.pbs.org/circleofstories/>

Appendix D: Research

Planning and Writing a Research Report

⬇️ *Use the following steps to guide you in writing a research report.*

Step 1: Planning the Report

Choose a subject. Then narrow your topic. You may be interested in the poetry of Robert Frost, but that subject is too broad. Narrow your focus. The graphic organizers in Appendix A may help you narrow your topic and identify supporting details.

Step 2: Finding Useful Information

Go to the library and browse the card catalog for books. Check almanacs, encyclopedias, atlases, and other sources in the reference section. Also review *The Reader's Guide to Periodical Literature* for magazines.

Draw from primary sources. Primary sources are first-hand accounts of information, such as speeches, observations, research results, and interviews. Secondary sources interpret and analyze primary sources.

Use the Internet to further explore your topic. Be careful; some Internet sources are not reliable. Avoid chat rooms, news groups, and personal Web sites. Check the credibility of sites by reviewing the site name and sponsor. Web sites whose URL ends with .org, .gov, and .edu are typically good sources.

Step 3: Logging Information

Use index cards to take notes. Include this information for each source:

- name of author or editor
- title of book or title of article and magazine
- page numbers
- volume numbers
- date of publication
- name of publishing company
- Web site information for Internet sources
- relevant information or direct quotations

Step 4: Getting Organized

Group your cards by similar details and organize them into categories. Find a system that works for you in organizing your cards. You can color-code them, use different-colored index cards for different sections, label them, and so on. Do not use any note cards that do not fit the categories that you have set up. Make conclusions about your research. Write a final topic outline.

Step 5: Writing Your Report

Follow the writing process in Appendix C to write your report. Use your own words to write the ideas you found in your sources (paraphrase). Do not plagiarize—steal and pass off another's words as your own. Write an author's exact words for direct quotations, and name the author or source.

Step 6: Preparing a Bibliography or Works Cited Page

Use the information on your note cards to write a bibliography or works cited page. If you are writing a bibliography, put your note cards in alphabetical order by *title*. If you are writing a works cited page, put your note cards in alphabetical order by *author*.

See *Bibliographies* in Appendix C.

Research Tools

Almanac
An annual publication containing data and tables on politics, religion, education, sports, and more

American Psychological Association (APA) Style
A guide to proper citation to avoid plagiarism in research papers for the social sciences

Atlas
A bound collection of maps of cities, states, regions, and countries including statistics and illustrations

Audio Recording
Recordings of speeches, debates, public proceedings, interviews, etc.

The Chicago Manual of Style
Writing, editing, proofreading, and revising guidelines for the publishing industry

Database
A large collection of data stored electronically and able to be searched

Dictionary
A reference book of words, spellings, pronunciations, meanings, parts of speech, and word origins

Experiment
A series of tests to prove or disprove something

Field Study
Observation, data collection, and interpretation done outside of a laboratory

Glossary
A collection of terms and their meanings

Government Publications
A report of a government action, bill, handbook, or census data usually provided by the Government Printing Office

Grammar Reference
Explanation and examples of parts of speech, sentence structure, and word usage

History
A chronological record that explains past events

Information Services
A stored collection of information organized for easy searching

Internet/World Wide Web
A worldwide network of connected computers that share information

Interview
A dialogue between a subject and a reporter or investigator to gather information

Journal
A type of magazine offering current information on certain subjects such as medicine, the economy, and current events

Microfiche
Historical, printed materials saved to small, thin sheets of film for organization, storage, and use

Modern Language Association (MLA) Handbook
A guide to proper citation to avoid plagiarism in research papers for the humanities

News Source
A newspaper or a radio, television, satellite, or World Wide Web sending of current events and issues presented in a timely manner

Periodical
A magazine, newspaper, or journal

The Reader's Guide to Periodical Literature
A searchable, organized database of magazines, newspapers, and journals used for research

Speech
A public address to inform and to explain

Technical Document
A proposal, instruction manual, training manual, report, chart, table, or other document that provides information

Thesaurus
A book of words and their synonyms, or words that have almost the same meanings

Vertical File
A storage file of original documents or copies of original documents

Appendix E: Speaking

Types of Public Speaking

Public speaking offers a way to inform, to explain, and to entertain. Here are some common types of public speaking:

Debate

A debate is a formal event where two or more people share opposing arguments in response to questions. Often, someone wins by answering questions with solid information.

Descriptive Speech

A descriptive speech uses the five senses of sight, smell, touch, taste, and sound to give vivid details.

Entertaining Speech

An entertaining speech relies on humor through jokes, stories, wit, or making fun of oneself. The humor must be appropriate for the audience and purpose of the speech.

Expository Speech

An expository speech provides more detailed information about a subject. This can be done through classification, analysis, definition, cause and effect, or compare and contrast.

Group Discussion

A group discussion allows the sharing of ideas among three or more people. A group discussion may be impromptu (without being planned) or may include a set topic and list of questions.

Impromptu Speech

An impromptu speech happens at a moment's notice without being planned. The speaker is given a random topic to discuss within a given time period.

Interview

An interview is a dialogue between a subject and a reporter or investigator. An interview draws out information using a question-and-answer format.

Literature Recitation

A literature recitation is the act of presenting a memorized speech, poem, story, or scene in its entire form or with chosen excerpts.

Literature Response

A literature response can serve many purposes. A speaker can compare and contrast plots or characters. An analysis of the work of one author can be presented. Writing style, genre, or period can also be shared.

Narrative

A narrative is a fiction or nonfiction story told with descriptive detail. The speaker also must use voice variation if acting out character dialogue.

Reflective Speech

A reflective speech provides thoughtful analysis of ideas, current events, and processes.

Role Playing

Role playing is when two or more people act out roles to show an idea or practice a character in a story. Role playing can be an effective tool for learning.

Preparing Your Speech

⬇ *Use the following steps to prepare your speech:*

Step 1: Defining Your Purpose

Ask yourself:

- Do I want to inform?

- Do I want to explain something?

- Do I want to entertain?

- Do I want to involve the audience through group discussion, role playing, or debate?

- Do I want to get the audience to act on a subject or an issue?

Step 2: Knowing Your Audience

Ask yourself:

- What information does my audience already know about the topic?

- What questions, concerns, or opinions do they have about the topic?

- How formal or informal does my presentation need to be?

- What words are familiar to my audience? What needs explanation?

- How does my audience prefer to get information? Do they like visuals, audience participation, or lecture?

Step 3: Knowing Your Setting

Ask yourself:

- Who is my audience?

- Is the room large enough to need a microphone and a projector?

- How is the room set up? Am I on stage with a podium or can I interact with the audience?

- Will other noises or activity distract the audience?

Step 4: Narrowing Your Topic

Ask yourself:

- What topic is right for the event? Is it timely? Will it match the mood of the event?

- Is there enough time to share it?

- What topic is right for me to present? Is it something I know and enjoy? Is it something people want to hear from me?

Step 5: Prewriting

Ask yourself:

- What examples, statistics, stories, or descriptions will help me get across my point?

- If telling a story, do I have a sequence of events that includes a beginning, middle, and end?

Step 6: Drafting Your Speech

Your speech will include an introduction, a body, and a conclusion.

The introduction states your topic and purpose. It includes a thesis statement that tells your position. Your introduction should also establish your credibility. Share why you are the right person to give that speech based on your experiences. Lastly, your introduction needs to get people's attention so they want to listen. At the top of the next page are some possible ways to start your speech.

- Ask a question.
- Share a story.
- Describe something.
- Give a surprising fact.
- Share a meaningful quotation.
- Make a memorable, purposeful entrance.

The body of your speech tells more about your main idea and tries to prevent listener misunderstandings. It should include any of the following supporting evidence:

- facts
- details
- explanations
- reasons
- examples
- personal stories or experiences
- experts
- literary devices and images

The conclusion of your speech ties your speech together. If you asked a question in your introduction, the conclusion answers it. If you outlined a problem, your conclusion offers solutions. If you told a story, revisit that story. You may even want to ask your audience to get involved, take action, or become more informed on your topic.

Step 7: Selecting Visuals

Ask yourself:

- Is a visual aid needed for the audience to better understand my topic?
- What visual aids work best for my topic?
- Do I have access to the right technology?

The size of your audience and the setting for your speech will also impact what you select. Remember that a projection screen and overhead speakers are necessary for large groups. If you plan on giving handouts to audience members, have handouts ready for pickup by the entrance of the room. A slide show or a video presentation will need a darkened room. Be sure that you have someone available to help you with the lights.

Practicing and Delivering Your Speech

Giving a speech is about more than simply talking. You want to look comfortable and confident.

Practice how you move, how you sound, and how you work with visuals and the audience.

Know Your Script

Every speaker is afraid of forgetting his or her speech. Each handles this fear in a different way. Choose the device that works for you.

- Memorization: Know your speech by heart. Say it often so you sound natural.
- Word-for-word scripts: Highlight key phrases to keep you on track. Keep the script on a podium, so you are not waving sheets of paper around as you talk. Be careful not to read from your script. The audience wants to see your eyes.
- Outlines: Write a sentence outline of your main points and supporting details that you want to say in a specific way. Transitions and other words can be spoken impromptu (without being planned).

- Key words: Write down key words that will remind you what to say, like "Tell story about the dog."

- Put your entire speech, outline, or key words on note cards to stay on track. They are small and not as obvious as paper. Number them in case they get out of order.

Know Yourself

Your voice and appearance are the two most powerful things you bring to a speech. Practice the following, so you are comfortable, confident, and convincing:

- Body language: Stand tall. Keep your feet shoulder-width apart. Don't cross your arms or bury your hands in your pockets. Use gestures to make a point. For example, hold up two fingers when you say, "My second point is . . ." Try to relax; that way, you will be in better control of your body.

- Eye contact: Look at your audience. Spend a minute or two looking at every side of the room and not just the front row. The audience will feel as if you are talking to them.

- Voice strategies: Clearly pronounce your words. Speak at a comfortable rate and loud enough for everyone to hear you. Vary your volume, rate, and pitch when you are trying to emphasize something. For example, you could say, "I have a secret. . . ." Then, you could lean toward the audience and speak in a loud, clear whisper as if you are telling them a secret. This adds dramatic effect and engages the audience.

- Repetition of key phrases or words: Repetition is one way to help people remember your point. If something is important, say it twice. Use transitions such as, "This is so important it is worth repeating" or "As I said before, we must act now."

Appendix F: Listening

Listening Strategy Checklist

Here are some ways you can ensure that you are a good listener.

Be an Active Listener

- ☑ Complete reading assignments that are due prior to the presentation.
- ☑ Focus on what is being said.
- ☑ Ask for definitions of unfamiliar terms.
- ☑ Ask questions to clarify what you heard.
- ☑ Ask the speaker to recommend other readings or resources.

Be a Critical Listener

- ☑ Identify the thesis or main idea of the speech.
- ☑ Try to predict what the speaker is going to say based on what you already know.
- ☑ Determine the speaker's purpose of the speech.
- ☑ Note supporting facts, statistics, examples, and other details.
- ☑ Determine if supporting detail is relevant, factual, and appropriate.
- ☑ Form your conclusions about the presentation.

Be an Appreciative Listener

- ☑ Relax.
- ☑ Enjoy the listening experience.
- ☑ Welcome the opportunity to laugh and learn.

Be a Thoughtful and Feeling Listener

- ☑ Understand the experiences of the speaker.
- ☑ Value the emotion he or she brings to the subject.
- ☑ Summarize or paraphrase what you believe the speaker just said.
- ☑ Tell the speaker that you understand his or her feelings.

Be an Alert Listener

- ☑ Sit up straight.
- ☑ Sit near the speaker and face the speaker directly.
- ☑ Make eye contact and nod to show you are listening.
- ☑ Open your arms so you are open to receiving information.

Analyze the Speaker

- ☑ Does the speaker have the experiences and knowledge to speak on the topic?
- ☑ Is the speaker prepared?
- ☑ Does the speaker appear confident?
- ☑ Is the speaker's body language appropriate?
- ☑ What do the speaker's tone, volume, and word choices show?

Identify the Details

- ☑ Listen for the tendency of the speaker to favor or oppose something without real cause.
- ☑ Be aware of propaganda—someone forcing an opinion on you.
- ☑ Don't be swayed by the clever way the speaker presents something.
- ☑ After the speech ask about words that you don't know.

Identify Fallacies of Logic

A fallacy is a false idea intended to trick someone. Here are some common fallacies:

- *Ad hominem*: This type of fallacy attacks a person's character, lifestyle, or beliefs. Example: Joe should not be on the school board because he skipped classes in college.

- False causality: This type of fallacy gives a cause–effect relationship that is not logical. This fallacy assumes that something caused something else only because it came before the consequence. Example: Ever since that new family moved into the neighborhood, our kids are getting into trouble.

- Red herring: This type of fallacy uses distractions to take attention away from the main issue. Example: Since more than half of our nation's people are overweight, we should not open a fast-food restaurant in our town.

- Overgeneralization: This type of fallacy uses words such as *every*, *always*, or *never*. Claims do not allow for exceptions to be made. Example: People who make more than a million dollars a year never pay their fair share of taxes.

- Bandwagon effect: This type of fallacy appeals to one's desire to be a part of the crowd. It is based on popular opinion and not on evidence. Example: Anyone who believes that our town is a great place to live should vote for the local tax increase.

Take Notes

- Write down key messages and phrases, not everything that is said.

- Abbreviate words.

- Listen for cues that identify important details, like "Here's an example" or "To illustrate what I mean."

- Draw graphs, charts, and diagrams for future reference.

- Draw arrows, stars, and circles to highlight information or group information.

- Highlight or circle anything that needs to be clarified or explained.

- Use the note-taking strategies explained in "How to Use This Book" at the beginning of this textbook.

Appendix G: Viewing

Visual aids can help communicate information and ideas. The following checklist gives pointers for viewing and interpreting visual aids.

Design Elements

Colors

☑ What colors stand out?

☑ What feelings do they make you think of?

☑ What do they symbolize or represent?

☑ Are colors used realistically or for emphasis?

Shapes

☑ What shapes are created by space or enclosed in lines?

☑ What is important about the shapes? What are they meant to symbolize or represent?

Lines

☑ What direction do the lines lead you?

☑ Which objects are you meant to focus on?

☑ What is the importance of the lines?

☑ Do lines divide or segment areas? Why do you think this is?

Textures

☑ What textures are used?

☑ What emotions or moods are they meant to affect?

Point of View

Point of view shows the artist's feelings toward the subject. Analyze this point of view:

☑ What point of view is the artist taking?

☑ Do you agree with this point of view?

☑ Is the artist successful in communicating this point of view?

Graphics

Line Graphs

Line graphs show changes in numbers over time.

☑ What numbers and time frame are represented?

☑ Does the information represent appropriate changes?

Pie Graphs

Pie graphs represent parts of a whole.

☑ What total number does the pie represent?

☑ Do the numbers represent an appropriate-sized sample?

Bar Graphs

Bar graphs compare amounts.

☑ What amounts are represented?

☑ Are the amounts appropriate?

Charts and Tables

Charts and tables organize information for easy comparison.

☑ What is being presented?

☑ Do columns and rows give equal data to compare and contrast?

Maps

☑ What land formations are shown?

☑ What boundaries are shown?

☑ Are there any keys or symbols on the map? What do they mean?

Appendix H: Media and Technology

Forms of Media

Television, movies, and music are some common forms of media that you know a lot about. Here are some others.

Advertisement

An advertisement selling a product or a service can be placed in a newspaper or magazine, on the Internet, or on television or radio.

Broadcast News

Broadcast news is offered on a 24-hour cycle through nightly newscasts, all-day news channels, and the Internet.

Documentary

A documentary shares information about people's lives, historic events, objects, or places. It is based on facts and evidence.

Internet and World Wide Web

This worldwide computer network offers audio and video clips, news, reference materials, research, and graphics.

Journal

A journal records experiences, current research, or ideas about a topic for a target audience.

Magazine

A magazine includes articles, stories, photos, and graphics of general interest.

Newspaper

A newspaper most often is printed daily or weekly.

Photography

Traditionally, photography has been the art or process of producing images on a film surface using light. Today, digital images are often used.

The Media and You

The media's role is to entertain, to inform, and to advertise. Media can help raise people's awareness about current issues. Media also can give clues about the needs and beliefs of the people.

Use a critical eye and ear to sort through the thousands of messages presented to you daily. Be aware of the media's use of oversimplified ideas about people, decent and acceptable language, and appropriate messages. Consider these questions:

- Who is being shown and why?
- What is being said? Is it based on fact?
- How do I feel about what and how it is said?

Technology and You

Technology can improve communication. Consider the following when selecting technology for research or presentations:

Audio/Sound

Speeches, music, sound effects, and other elements can set a mood or reinforce an idea.

Computers

- Desktop publishing programs offer tools for making newsletters and posters.
- Software programs are available for designing publications, Web sites, databases, and more.
- Word processing programs feature dictionaries, grammar-check and spell-check programs, and templates for memos, reports, letters, and more.

Multimedia

Slide shows, movies, and other electronic media can help the learning process.

Visual Aids

Charts, tables, maps, props, drawings, and graphs provide visual representation of information.

Handbook of Literary Terms

A

Act (akt) a major unit of action in a play (p. 440)

Alliteration (ə lit e rā′ shən) repeating sounds by using words whose beginning sounds are the same (p. 392)

Allusion (ə lü′ zhən) a reference to characters or themes in another piece of literature (p. 466)

Analogy (ə nal′ ə jē) a comparison between two otherwise different objects that share some of the same characteristics (p. 346)

Anecdote (an′ ik dōt) a short account of an interesting event in someone's life (p. 116)

Antagonist (an tag′ ə nist) the person or thing in the story struggling against the main character (p. 192)

Anthology (an thol′ ə jē) a collection of stories, plays, or poems written by different authors collected in one book (p. 48)

Archetype (är′ kə tīp) a universal plot, character element, or theme (p. 232)

Assonance (as′ n əns) repeating sounds by using words with the same vowel sounds (p. 392)

Author's purpose (ó′ thərs pėr′ pəs) the reason(s) for which the author writes (pp. 13, 176)

Autobiography (ó tə bī og′ rə fē) the story of a person's life, written by that person (pp. 116, 337)

B

Ballad (bal′ əd) a form of poetry that tells a story, passed from person to person, often as a simple song with rhyming words and a refrain (pp. 110, 383)

Biographical essay (bī ə graf′ ə kəl es′ ā) a written work about true events in a person's life (p. 325)

Biography (bī og′ rə fē) the story of a person's life, written by someone other than the person (p. 325)

C

Caricature (kar′ ə kə chür) a character description that is exaggerated—overstated—to make people laugh (p. 145)

Character (kar′ ik tər) a person or animal in a story, poem, or play (pp. 5, 48)

Characterization (kar ik tər ə zā′ shən) the way a writer develops characters' qualities and personality traits (p. 101)

Character trait (kar′ ik tər trāt) a character's way of thinking, behaving, or speaking (pp. 101, 466)

Chronological (kron ə loj′ ə kəl) arranged in the order in which things happened (p. 299)

Climax (klī′ maks) the high point of interest or suspense in a story or play (pp. 217, 440)

Comedy (kom′ ə dē) a play with a happy ending, intended to amuse its audience (p. 499)

Conflict (kon′ flikt) the struggle of the main character against himself or herself, another person, or nature (pp. 192, 353, 466)

Creation myth (krē ā′ shən mith) a myth that tells the story of the beginning of the world (p. 48)

a	hat	e	let	ī	ice	ô	order	ů	put	sh	she		a	in about
ā	age	ē	equal	o	hot	oi	oil	ü	rule	th	thin		e	in taken
ä	far	ėr	term	ō	open	ou	out	ch	child	₮H	then	ə	i	in pencil
â	care	i	it	ȯ	saw	u	cup	ng	long	zh	measure		o	in lemon
													u	in circus

D

Denouement (dā nü män´) the final outcome of the story (p. 248)

Dialect (dī´ ə lekt) the speech of a particular part of a country, or of a certain group of people (pp. 19, 87)

Dialogue (dī´ ə lȯg) the conversation among characters in a story or play (pp. 145, 440)

Diary (dī´ ə rē) a daily record of events and feelings (p. 353)

Diction (dik´ shən) the proper choice of words; saying each word so that it is clearly understood (p. 365)

Drama (drä´ mə) a story told through the words and actions of characters, written to be performed as well as read; a play (p. 439)

Dramatic irony (drə mat´ ik ī´ rə nē) when the audience or reader knows more than the characters know (p. 440)

E

Epilogue (ep´ ə lȯg) a section coming after the story's end (p. 201)

Epiphany (i pif´ ə nē) the moment in a story when a character recognizes an important truth (p. 176)

Essay (es´ ā) a short nonfiction work on any subject (p. 311)

Exaggeration (eg zaj ə rā´ shən) in literature, making something seem more than it is; stretching the truth (p. 87)

Excerpt (ek´ sėrpt) a short passage from a longer piece of writing (pp. 101, 299)

Exposition (ek spə zish´ ən) the part of short stories that introduces setting, characters, and the situation (p. 217)

F

Fable (fā´ bəl) a story that teaches a lesson about life, called a moral, often with animals who act like humans (p. 4)

Falling action (fȯl´ ing ak´ shən) the parts of the story that follow the climax (p. 248)

Fiction (fik´ shən) writing in which the author creates the events and characters (p. 145)

Figurative language (fig´ yər ə tiv lang´ gwij) language that uses word pictures to compare or describe, and that is not meant to be taken as the truth (p. 404)

First person (fėrst pėr´ sən) a point of view where the narrator is also a character, using the pronouns *I* and *we* (p. 159)

Flashback (flash´ bak) a look into the past at some point in a story (pp. 176, 267)

Flat character (flat kar´ ik tər) a character that is based on a single trait or quality and is not well developed (p. 5)

Folklore (fōk´ lôr) stories and customs that are saved and passed along by people in an area or group (p. 87)

Foreshadowing (fôr shad´ ō ing) clues or hints that a writer gives about something that has not yet happened (pp. 129, 232, 440)

G

Genre (zhän´ rə) a specific type or kind of literature (pp. 19, 37)

H

Haiku (hī´ kü) a form of Japanese poetry having three lines with five syllables in the first, seven in the second, and five in the third (p. 404)

Hero (hir´ ō) the leading character in a story, novel, play, or film (pp. 13, 37)

Humor (hyü´ mər) writing intended to amuse (pp. 87, 338)

Humorist (hyü´ mər ist) someone who writes funny works (p. 145)

Hyperbole (hī pėr´ bə lē) an overstatement to show something is important (p. 416)

I

Idiom (id´ ē əm) a phrase that has a different meaning than its words really mean (p. 5)

Image (im´ ij) a picture in the readers' mind created by words (pp. 176, 267)

Imagery (im′ ij rē) a picture in the reader's mind created by words (pp. 311, 403)

Irony (ī′ rə nē) the difference between what is expected to happen in a story and what does happen (pp. 13, 232, 353)

L

Legend (lej′ ənd) a story from folklore that features characters who actually lived, or real events or places (p. 109)

Limerick (lim′ ər ik) a five-line poem in which the first, second, and fifth lines, and the third and fourth lines, rhyme (p. 392)

M

Metaphor (met′ ə fôr) a figure of speech that says one thing *is* another (p. 404)

Monologue (mon′ l ȯg) a speech by one person (p. 440)

Mood (müd) the feeling created by a piece of writing (pp. 129, 201, 416)

Moral (môr′ əl) a lesson or message about life told in a story (p. 5)

Myth (mith) an important story, often part of a culture's religion, that explains how the world came to be or why natural events happen, usually including gods, goddesses, or powerful human beings (p. 37)

N

Narrative (nar′ ə tiv) a story, usually told in the order that it happened (p. 299)

Narrator (nar′ ā tər) one who tells a story (p. 61)

Nonfiction (non fik′ shən) prose writing about real people and true experiences (p. 299)

Novel (nov′ əl) fiction that is book-length and has more plot and details than a short story (p. 144)

O

Onomatopoeia (on ə mat ə pē′ ə) using words that sound like their meanings (p. 392)

Oral literature (ôr′ əl lit′ ər ə chŭr) stories that were first told, rather than being written down (p. 48)

P

Pamphlet (pam′ flit) a short printed story or paper with no cover, or with a paper cover (p. 116)

Pen name (pen nām) a false name used for writing (p. 144)

Personal account (pėr′ sə nəl ə kount′) a true story about an experience, told by a person who lived through it (p. 353)

Personification (pər son ə fə kā′ shən) giving characters such as animals or objects the characteristics or qualities of humans (pp. 5, 416)

Persuasive speech (pər swā′ siv spēch) a spoken work designed to make people act a certain way or believe one thing (p. 365)

Playwright (plā′ rīt) a writer of plays (p. 466)

Plot (plot) the series of events in a story (pp. 5, 37)

Poetry (pō′ i trē) literature in verse form that usually has rhythm and paints powerful or beautiful impressions with words (p. 383)

Point of view (point ov vyü) the relationship of the narrator to the story (p. 159)

Problem (prob′ ləm) the focus, or main concern, of the plot of a story (p. 54)

Prose (prōz) all writing that is not poetry (p. 145)

Protagonist (prō tag′ ə nist) the main character, also called the hero (p. 192)

Pun (pun) a joke formed by a play on words (p. 499)

a	hat	e	let	ī	ice	ȯ	order	u̇	put	sh	she		ə {	a	in about
ā	age	ē	equal	o	hot	oi	oil	ü	rule	th	thin			e	in taken
ä	far	ėr	term	ō	open	ou	out	ch	child	ᴛH	then			i	in pencil
â	care	i	it	ȯ	saw	u	cup	ng	long	zh	measure			o	in lemon
														u	in circus

Purpose (pėr´ pəs) a nonfiction writer's main idea or goal (p. 311)

R

Realistic drama (rē´ ə lis´ tik drä´ ma) a play that tells a story just as it might happen in real life (p. 466)

Reflective essay (ri flek´ tiv es´ ā) a personal essay exploring an author's feelings (p. 311)

Refrain (ri frān´) repeated line in a poem or song that creates a mood or gives importance to something (pp. 110, 383)

Repetition (rep ə tish´ ən) using a word, phrase, or image more than once, for emphasis (pp. 311, 383)

Rhyme (rīm) words that end with the same sounds (p. 383)

Rhythm (riŦH´ əm) a pattern created by the stressed and unstressed syllables in a line of poetry (p. 383)

Rising action (rīz´ ing ak´ shən) the events of the plot that add to the conflict (pp. 192, 217)

S

Satire (sat´ īr) humorous writing that makes fun of foolishness or evil (p. 217)

Scene (sēn) a unit of action in a play that takes place in one setting (p. 440)

Script (skript) the written text of a play, used in a production or performance (p. 498)

Sequence (sē´ kwəns) the order of events (p. 299)

Setting (set´ ing) a story's time and place (pp. 19, 48)

Short story (shôrt stôr´ ē) a brief work of prose fiction that includes, plot, setting, characters, point of view, and theme (p. 145)

Simile (sim´ ə lē) a figure of speech in which two things are compared using a phrase that includes the word *like* or *as* (pp. 37, 404)

Stage directions (stāj də rek´ shəns) notes by the writer of a play describing such things as setting, lighting, sound effects, and how the actors are to look, behave, move, and speak (p. 466)

Stanza (stan´ zə) a group of lines that forms a unit in a poem (pp. 110, 383)

Story-within-a-story (stôr´ ē wiŦH in´ a stôr´ ē) a second story told within another story (pp. 61, 145)

Style (stīl) an author's way of writing (p. 365)

Suspense (sə spens´) a quality in a story that makes the reader uncertain or nervous about what will happen next (pp. 217, 353)

Symbol (sim´ bəl) something that represents something else (pp. 5, 159, 325)

T

Tall tale (tȯl tāl) a story from the past that features larger-than-life characters who have unreal adventures (p. 86)

Tanka (täng´ kə) a form of Japanese poetry having five lines with five syllables in the first, seven in the second, five in the third, and seven in the fourth and fifth (p. 404)

Theme (thēm) the main idea of a story or play (p. 159)

Tone (tōn) the attitude an author takes toward a subject (pp. 201, 338, 416)

Tragedy (traj´ ə dē) a play that ends with the suffering or death of one or more of the main characters (p. 439)

Trickster (trik´ stər) a character that uses his cleverness and quick thinking to outsmart enemies, sometimes by playing tricks on them (p. 54)

U

Unreliable narrator (un ri lī´ ə bəl nar´ ā tər) a first-person narrator whose views cannot be depended on to be completely true (p. 267)

V

Voice (vois) the way a writer expresses ideas through style, form, content, and purpose (p. 415)

Glossary

A

Abhorred (ab hôrd') hated (p. 451)

Abrupt (ə brupt') said or done suddenly, without much explanation (p. 181)

Abruptly (ə brupt' lē) suddenly; without warning (pp. 359, 472)

Accessible (ak ses' ə bəl) reachable (p. 66)

Accommodated (ə kom' ə dāt ed) supplied someone's needs; helped (p. 123)

Accommodating (ə kom' ə dā ting) making up for (p. 276)

Accumulated (ə kyü' myə lāt ed) collected (p. 277); piled up (p. 327)

Acknowledged (ak nol' ijd) admitted; recognized (p. 67)

Actual (ak' chü əl) true, real (p. 203)

Administering (ad min' ə stə ring) managing; directing (p. 221)

Admittance (ad mit' ns) entrance (p. 223)

Adorned (ə dôrnd') decorated (p. 356)

Advisers (ad vī' zərs) people who give advice (p. 70)

Aesthetic (es thet' ik) artistic (p. 223)

Affinity (ə fin' ə tē) a liking for something (p. 68)

Afflicted (ə flikt' ed) troublesome (p. 154)

Aggravated (ag' rə vāt ed) angry; upset (p. 95)

Aggressiveness (ə gres' iv nəs) forceful energy (p. 474)

Aghast (ə gast') shocked (p. 259)

Agony (ag' ə nē) great pain (p. 226)

Alcoholic (al kə hò' lik) a problem drinker (p. 274)

Alcove (al' kōv) a small, set-in section of a room (p. 167)

Aloft (ə lòft') up in the air (p. 57)

Aloof (ə lüf') apart (p. 447)

Ambient (am' bē ənt) present on all sides (p. 354)

Ambiguities (am bə gyü' ə tēz) mysteries (p. 458)

Ambitious (am bish' əs) determined (p. 348)

Ambushed (am' büsht) attacked by surprise (p. 119)

Amiable (ā' mē ə bəl) friendly, good-natured (p. 272)

Amiably (ā' mē ə blē) kindly (pp. 249, 305)

Amid (ə mid') within; between (p. 424)

Ample (am' pəl) more than enough (p. 304)

Analyzed (an' l īzd) studied in detail (p. 318)

Anguish (ang' gwish) great pain (pp. 318, 477)

Anguished (ang' gwisht) very great pain or grief (p. 227)

Animate (an' ə mit) living, conscious (p. 312)

Animated (an' ə mā tid) made lively, happy (p. 419)

Anticipated (an tis' ə pāt ed) looked forward to (p. 178)

Apathetically (ap ə thet' ik lē) with little feeling (p. 261)

Apathy (ap' ə thē) a lack of feeling (p. 258)

a	hat	e	let	ī	ice	ò	order	ù	put	sh	she	ə	a	in about
ā	age	ē	equal	o	hot	oi	oil	ü	rule	th	thin		e	in taken
ä	far	ėr	term	ō	open	ou	out	ch	child	ŦH	then		i	in pencil
â	care	i	it	ò	saw	u	cup	ng	long	zh	measure		o	in lemon
													u	in circus

Apologizing (ə pol' ə jīz ing) saying you are sorry (p. 24)

Appalling (ə po' ling) dreadful (p. 359)

Apparel (ə par' əl) clothing (p. 256)

Apparition (ap ə rish' ən) a vision or appearance (p. 73)

Apprehend (ap ri hend') to catch; to arrest (p. 449)

Apprehension (ap ri hen' shən) fear; dread (p. 356)

Approximately (ə prok' sə mit lē) nearly (p. 354)

Ardor (är' dər) deep feeling (p. 222)

Aromas (ə rō' məs) pleasant smells (p. 316)

Aspiring (ə spīr' ing) seeking (p. 224)

Assassin (ə sas' n) a killer (p. 121)

Assent (ə sent') agreement (p. 257)

Asserted (ə sėrt' ed) put oneself or one's ideas forward (p. 219)

Assess (ə ses') to determine the value of (p. 329)

Associate (ə sō' shē āt) to accompany (p. 446)

Assurance (ə shùr' əns) a promise (p. 257)

Atrophied (at' rə fēd) wasted away (p. 278)

Attribute (ə trib' yüt) to credit something to (p. 255)

Audacity (ò das' ə tē) boldness (p. 369)

Audible (ò' də bəl) loud enough to be heard (p. 261)

Audition (ò dish' ən) a tryout (p. 342)

Authentic (ò then' tik) genuine, real (p. 313)

Avaricious (av ə rish' əs) greedy (p. 255)

Averted (ə vėrt' ed) turned away (p. 257)

B

Ballad (bal' əd) a simple song (p. 21)

Balmy (bä' mē) mild (p. 395)

Baptism (bap' tiz əm) a Christian ceremony for naming and for coming into the faith (p. 270)

Barbaric (bär bar' ik) uncivilized, savage (p. 218)

Barbecue (bär' bə kyü) to grill food outdoors (p. 426)

Barnacles (bär' nə kəlz) small sea animals that attach themselves to rock or objects (p. 62)

Barometers (bə rom' ə tərs) instruments for measuring air pressure (p. 104)

Barren (bar' ən) without life (p. 405)

Barrier (bār' ē ər) something that blocks the way (p. 283)

Bated (bā' tid) kept low and shallow (p. 68)

Beget (bi get') to produce (p. 422)

Beseech (bi sēch') to beg (p. 443)

Betrothed (bi trōͰHd') promised in marriage; engaged (p. 459)

Biographers (bī og' rə fərs) people who write life stories of other persons (p. 426)

Biology (bī ol' ə jē) the science of living things (p. 479)

Bland (bland) dull, unexciting (p. 218)

Bleak (blēk) gloomy (p. 326)

Bliss (blis) great happiness (p. 453)

Blockaded (blo kād' ed) prevented escape (p. 147)

Blunt (blunt) to soften (p. 409)

Boisterous (boi' stər əs) noisy; wild (p. 233)

Borne (bôrn) carried (p. 120)

Bosom (bùz' əm) a breast; a heart (pp. 397, 454)

Bracket (brak' it) shelf (p. 259)

Brawling (bról' ing) fighting (p. 424)

Brazen (brā' zn) made of brass; bold (p. 396)

Bristling (bris' tling) standing up or out from the body (p. 67)

Brittle (brit′ l) stiff (p. 183)

Broach (brōch) to begin a topic (p. 257)

Brutal (brü′ tl) cruel (p. 424)

Brute (brüt) an animal (p. 398)

Buttress (but′ ris) part of a mountain that sticks out (p. 357)

C

Cantankerous (kan tang′ kər əs) hard to deal with (p. 95)

Captivating (kap′ tə vāt ing) charming (p. 40)

Cascade (ka skād′) waterfall (p. 306)

Caterers (kā′ tər ərs) people who supply prepared food (p. 330)

Cavalry (kav′ əl rē) soldiers on horseback (p. 122)

Champagne (sham pān′) a sparkling wine (p. 330)

Chariot (char′ ē ət) a two-wheeled cart (pp. 39, 40)

Chasm (kaz′ əm) a large opening (p. 40)

Chaste (chāst) pure (p. 422)

Chauffeur (shō fər′) a hired driver (p. 477)

Cipher (sī′ fər) to use arithmetic (p. 149)

Circumstance (sėr′ kəm stans) details (p. 456)

Circumstances (sėr′ kəm stans es) conditions (p. 150)

Civic (siv′ ik) community (p. 234)

Clinically (klin′ ə kəl lē) as a scientist would (p. 479)

Coffin (kȯ′ fən) a box that holds a dead body (p. 385)

Coincidence (kō in′ sə dəns) chance (p. 255)

Collateral (kə lat′ ər əl) property as protection for payment (p. 331)

Compels (kəm pels′) makes happen (p. 397)

Compensation (kom pən sā′ shən) a payment for damages (p. 258)

Compete (kəm pēt′) to try hard to gain something (p. 326)

Competent (kom′ pə tənt) able to do something (p. 222)

Compliance (kəm plī′ əns) the act of doing what is asked (p. 146)

Compressed (kəm prest′) compact, under pressure (p. 354)

Compromise (kom′ prə mīz) an agreement that tries to satisfy both sides (p. 41)

Compulsively (kəm pul′ siv lē) unable to stop (p. 357)

Condoling (kən dōl′ ing) expressing sorrow (p. 250)

Conductive (kən dü′ siv) helpful or useful (p. 500)

Conferred (kən fėrd′) supplied (p. 354)

Confidant (kon′ fə dant) someone trusted with your secrets (p. 327)

Confirmation (kon fər mā′ shən) proof (p. 257)

Confirmed (kən fėrmd′) made certain (p. 56)

Confront (kən frunt′) to meet face to face (p. 329)

Confronted (kən frunt′ ed) met face to face (p. 161)

Conjectured (kən jek′ chərd) guessed or supposed (p. 146)

Consequence (kon′ sə kwens) a result or effect (p. 93)

a	hat	e	let	ī	ice	ȯ	order	u̇	put	sh	she		a	in about
ā	age	ē	equal	o	hot	oi	oil	ü	rule	th	thin	ə	e	in taken
ä	far	ėr	term	ō	open	ou	out	ch	child	ᴛʜ	then		i	in pencil
â	care	i	it	ȯ	saw	u	cup	ng	long	zh	measure		o	in lemon
													u	in circus

Consequences (kon′ sə kwens es) results or effects (pp. 23, 253)

Conservative (kən sėr′ və tiv) usual, typical (p. 326)

Conspicuously (kən spik′ yü əs lē) obviously (p. 473)

Conspires (kən spīrs′) plots against (p. 458)

Consumption (kən sump′ shən) tuberculosis, a lung disease easily spread from person to person (p. 269)

Contagion (kən tā′ jən) a spreading disease (p. 454)

Contemplate (kon′ təm plāt) to study or think about (p. 71)

Contemplation (kon təm plā′ shən) study; deep thought (p. 63)

Contemporary (kən təm′ pa rer ē) modern (p. 313)

Contempt (kən tempt′) scorn (p. 445)

Contradict (kon trə dikt′) to deny (p. 454)

Convey (kən vā′) to pass along (p. 258)

Convicts (kon′ vikts) people in prison (p. 409)

Coordinate (kō ôrd′ n āt) to move or act smoothly with someone else (p. 178)

Cordial (kôr′ jəl) life-giving liquid (p. 445)

Cosmic (koz′ mik) relating to the universe (p. 314)

Countenance (koun′ tə nəns) face, appearance (p. 147)

Courtship (kôrt′ ship) the period before marriage (p. 277)

Covet (kuv′ it) to want (p. 286)

Coveted (kuv′ it ed) wanted (p. 355)

Cowering (kou′ ər ing) hiding, as if in fear (p. 165)

Creases (krēs′ es) folds, wrinkles (pp. 278, 313)

Creation (krē ā′ shən) the world (p. 312)

Credulity (krə dü′ lə tē) willingness to believe (p. 254)

Crimson (krim′ zən) red (p. 451)

Culling (kul′ ing) collecting or sorting (p. 443)

Cultural (kul′ chər əl) relating to the beliefs and customs of a group (p. 312)

Cynicism (sin′ ə siz əm) doubting (p. 369)

D

Daunting (dȯnt′ ing) frightening (p. 355)

Decipher (di sī′ fər) to make clear; to explain (p. 417)

Decorum (di kôr′ əm) proper behavior (p. 340)

Defensively (di fen′ siv lē) protecting oneself (p. 479)

Deferred (di fėrd′) put off (p. 467)

Defiance (di fī′ əns) to boldly disobey (p. 474)

Defiantly (di fī′ ənt lē) with bold resistance (p. 242)

Deliberate (di lib′ ər it) carefully saying and meaning every word (p. 152)

Deliberately (di lib′ ər it lē) knowing exactly what one is doing (p. 163)

Deliberation (di lib ə rā′ shən) careful thought (p. 227)

Departed (di pärt′ id) went away; left (p. 154)

Dependence (di pen′ dəns) something that is necessary (p. 150)

Depressed (di prest′) fell (p. 339)

Depressing (di pres′ sing) saddening (p. 254)

Desirous (di zī′ rəs) wishing (p. 249)

Despite (di spīt′) in spite of (p. 271)

Destiny (des′ tə nē) what becomes of someone or something (p. 425)

Detachment (di tach′ mənt) separation from (p. 358)

Deteriorating (di tir′ ē ə rāt ing) getting worse (p. 130)

Detestable (di tes′ tə bəl) hateful (p. 449)

Devious (dē′ vē əs) crooked; sly (pp. 226, 348)

Devise (di vīz′) to think up; to invent (pp. 57, 66); to think up (p. 459)

Diagnosed (dī əg nōst′) named the disease of someone (p. 204); determined the medical condition of someone (p. 274)

Dicey (dī′ sē) risky (p. 360)

Dignitaries (dig′ nə ter ēz) important people (p. 22)

Dilapidated (də lap′ ə dā tid) rundown, falling apart (pp. 132, 146); rundown, in poor condition (p. 186)

Diluted (də lüt′ ed) watered down; made weak (p. 342)

Dingy (din′ jē) dirty, discolored (p. 162)

Dire (dīr) severe, terrible (pp. 220, 459)

Disapproval (dis ə prü′ vəl) dislike (p. 277)

Disarray (dis ə rā′) confusion, disorder (p. 23)

Discarded (dis kärd′ ed) thrown away or cast off (pp. 62, 235)

Discern (də sèrn′) to recognize; to make out (p. 453)

Discharged (dis chärjd′) let out (p. 444)

Disciple (də sī′ pəl) a follower (p. 269)

Disciplinarian (dis ə plə ner′ ē ən) one who punishes (p. 183)

Disconsolately (dis kon′ sə lit lē) impossible to comfort (p. 73)

Discords (dis′ kôrds) quarrels (p. 460)

Discreet (dis krēt′) careful, showing good judgment (p. 180)

Disengaged (dis en gājd′) pulled away from (p. 238); withdrawn (p. 355)

Disheveled (də shev′ əld) not neat (p. 469)

Disown (dis ōn′) to refuse to recognize as your own (p. 255)

Dispatch (dis pach′) to kill (p. 445)

Dispatched (dis pacht′) sent (p. 331)

Dispatches (dis pach′ es) messages (p. 121)

Dispensable (dis pen′ sə bəl) easily done without (p. 277)

Disperse (dis pèrs′) to scatter (p. 444)

Dispersed (dis pèrst′) scattered (p. 65)

Disregarded (dis ri gärd′ ed) paid no attention to (p. 57)

Dissected (di sekt′ ed) cut up and examined (p. 479)

Distraught (dis trȯt′) terribly upset (p. 185)

Diverged (də vèrjd′) branched off (p. 418)

Diversity (də vèr′ sə tē) variety (p. 367)

Doctrines (dok′ trəns) beliefs or teachings (p. 166)

Doggedly (dȯ′ gid lē) stubbornly (pp. 252, 482)

Doleful (dōl′ fəl) sad; mournful (p. 220)

Doughty (dou′ tē) brave (p. 250)

Doused (doust) put out (p. 272)

Drastic (dras′ tik) very forceful (p. 103)

Drily (drī′ lē) in a sharp, bitter way (p. 471)

Droning (drōn′ ing) buzzing sound (p. 410)

Dubiously (dü′ bē əs lē) with doubt; suspiciously (p. 253)

a	hat	e	let	ī	ice	ô	order	u̇	put	sh	she		a	in about
ā	age	ē	equal	o	hot	oi	oil	ü	rule	th	thin	ə	e	in taken
ä	far	èr	term	ō	open	ou	out	ch	child	ᵺ	then		i	in pencil
â	care	i	it	ȯ	saw	u	cup	ng	long	zh	measure		o	in lemon
													u	in circus

Ebb (eb) to flow away (p. 73)

Ebbs (ebs) slows down; gets lower (p. 397)

Eerie (ir′ ē) spooky (p. 66)

Elated (i lā′ tid) delighted, thrilled (p. 327)

Elation (i lā′ shən) great happiness
(pp. 184, 356)

Eloquence (el′ ə kwəns) ability to speak with
great feeling and expression (p. 332)

Emanated (em′ ə nāt ed) came forth (p. 219)

Embarrassment (em bar′ əs mənt) an uneasy
feeling (p. 347)

Embedded (em bed′ ded) fixed or enclosed in
something (p. 39)

Embrace (em brās′) to hug (p. 473)

Embracing (em brās′ ing) hugging
(pp. 161, 284)

Emigrated (em′ ə grāt ed) left one's homeland
(p. 117)

Emissaries (em′ ə ser ēs) people who are sent
on a mission (p. 14)

Emotion (i mō′ shən) a feeling (p. 133)

Emphasis (em′ fə sis) importance (p. 471)

Encircling (en sėr′ kling) going around in a
circle (p. 306)

Encounter (en koun′ tər) meet or come upon
(p. 118)

Encounters (en koun′ tərs) meets or comes
upon (p. 313)

Endeavor (en dev′ ər) attempt; effort (p. 396)

Endowed (en doud′) provided (p. 367)

Energetic (en ər jet′ ik) lively (p. 268)

Engrossing (en grōs′ ing) taking in everything
(p. 452)

Enmity (en′ mə tē) hatred (p. 461)

Enterprising (en′ tər prī zing) marked by a
readiness to act (p. 154)

Enthralled (en thrȯld′) charmed (pp. 182, 393);
very interested (p. 253)

Entranced (en transt′) filled with joy or delight
(p. 67)

Entreated (en trēt′ ed) begged (p. 459)

Enveloped (en vel′ əpt) completely covered
(p. 162)

Epidemics (ep ə dem′ iks) widespread diseases
(p. 313)

Equilibrium (ē kwə lib′ rē əm) balance (p. 341)

Erratic (ə rat′ ik) not ordinary; unexpected
(p. 469)

Erupted (i rupt′ ed) rose up (p. 164)

Escalated (es′ kə lāt ed) got stronger (p. 357)

Esteem (e stēm′) honor (p. 316)

Eternity (i tėr′ nə tē) forever (p. 39)

Euphony (yü′ fə nē) a pleasing sound (p. 396)

Exasperated (eg zas′ pə rāt id) annoyed or
bothered (p. 472)

Exception (ek sep′ shən) something that is left
out (p. 121)

Exceptionally (ek sep′ shə nəl lē) more than
usual (p. 468)

Exhilarated (eg zil′ ə rā tid) excited (p. 330)

Exhorter (eg zȯrt′ er) one who strongly urges
another to do or believe something (p. 149)

Exile (eg′ zīl) separation from homeland
(p. 458)

Exotic (eg zot′ ik) strange; unusual (p. 501)

Expanse (ek spans′) something vast, spread out
(p. 356)

Expansion (ek span′ shən) growth (p. 330)

Expectancy (ek spek′ tən sē) looking forward to
something (p. 482)

Expectant (ek spek′ tənt) waiting for something
to happen (p. 260)

Expectantly (ek spek′ tənt lē) as if looking forward to something (p. 62)

Expectation (ek spek tā′ shən) looking forward to (p. 258)

Expectations (ek spek tā′ shəns) what is expected or looked forward to (p. 317)

Expediency (ek spē′ dē ən sē) self-interest (p. 327)

Expired (ek spīrd′) went out (p. 260)

Expostulation (ek spos chə lā′ shən) objection; complaint (p. 396)

Exposure (ek spō′ zhər) how something is placed so it is not sheltered from weather (p. 102)

Exquisitely (ek′ skwi zit lē) perfectly (p. 148)

External (ek stėr′ nl) outside (p. 355)

Extinguished (ek sting′ gwisht) put out (pp. 39, 356)

Extremities (ek strem′ ə tēz) hands or feet (p. 341)

Extricate (ek′ strə kāt) to untangle (p. 342)

Exuberant (eg zü′ bər ənt) high-spirited (p. 218)

F

Fabric (fab′ rik) cloth (p. 277)

Faltered (fȯl′ tərd) spoken weakly (p. 260)

Famine (fam′ ən) hunger (p. 445)

Fathomless (faᵺ′ əm lis) without bottom (p. 423)

Felon (fel′ ən) a person who has committed a crime (p. 450)

Fervent (fėr′ vənt) having strong feelings (p. 222)

Fervid (fėr′ vid) full of strong feeling (p. 223)

Fester (fes′ tər) get infected (p. 467)

Fiendish (fēn′ dish) unpleasant; bad (p. 102)

Fife (fīf) a small flute (p. 385)

Flattering (flat′ ər ing) pleasing or soothing to oneself (p. 442)

Flimsy (flim′ zē) thin, not strongly made (p. 130)

Florid (flôr′ id) healthy (p. 218)

Fording (fôrd′ ing) crossing a body of water (p. 117)

Foretells (fôr telz′) tells the future (p. 395)

Fractured (frak′ chərd) broken (p. 202)

Fragments (frag′ mənts) small pieces (p. 57)

Frenzy (fren′ zē) a state of near madness (p. 15)

Frivolous (friv′ ə ləs) playful (p. 255)

Frustration (fru strā′ shən) anger at defeat (p. 473)

Fundamental (fun də men′ tl) basic (p. 368)

Furlough (fėr′ lō) a leave of absence (p. 204)

Furtive (fėr′ tiv) secret, sly (p. 164)

Furtively (fėr′ tiv lē) secretly, as if ashamed (pp. 256, 486)

Futile (fyü′ tl) useless (pp. 280, 487)

Futility (fyü til′ ə tē) uselessness (p. 326)

Futurity (fyü chùr′ ə tē) a future event (p. 227)

G

Gamblers (gam′ blərs) people who play games for money (p. 385)

Gambling (gam′ bling) betting money on; risking (p. 484)

Garrulous (gar′ ə ləs) talkative (p. 146)

Gauge (gāj) a tool for measuring (p. 358)

a	hat	e	let	ī	ice	ȯ	order	ù	put	sh	she		a	in about
ā	age	ē	equal	o	hot	oi	oil	ü	rule	th	thin	ə	e	in taken
ä	far	ėr	term	ō	open	ou	out	ch	child	ᵺ	then		i	in pencil
â	care	i	it	ȯ	saw	u	cup	ng	long	zh	measure		o	in lemon
													u	in circus

Genial (jē′ nyəl) friendly (p. 218)

Glazed (glāzd) glassy; smooth and shiny (p. 408)

Glints (glints) gleams (p. 409)

Gloats (glōts) delights in (p. 395)

Graft (graft) getting money in a way that is against the law (p. 476)

Graphically (graf′ ə kəl lē) in a visual way (p. 476)

Grimace (grim′ is) an expression of disgust (p. 251)

Grotesque (grō tesk′) very ugly (p. 304)

Grudgingly (gruj′ ing lē) unwillingly (p. 472)

Guidance (gīd′ ns) direction; instruction (p. 220)

H

Hallucination (hə lü sn ā′ shən) a vision that is not real (p. 133)

Harmony (här′ mə nē) melody (p. 395)

Haste (hāst) speed (pp. 122, 250)

Haughty (hȯ′ tē) feeling superior to others (p. 449)

Heaved (hēvd) lifted up and out (p. 68)

Heaving (hēv′ ing) moving up and down (p. 183)

Hence (hens) in the future (p. 418); away (p. 446)

Heritage (her′ ə tij) what is handed down from one generation to the next (p. 171); background of a person's family (p. 367)

Hierarchy (hī′ ə rär kē) a list in order of importance (p. 177)

Hilarious (hə lâr′ ē əs) very funny (p. 221)

Hindrance (hin′ drəns) something that gets in the way (p. 102)

Hospitable (hos′ pi tə bəl) welcoming (p. 250)

Humanity (hyü man′ ə tē) human beings (p. 316)

Humiliating (hyü mil′ ē āt ing) embarrassing deeply (p. 178)

Humiliation (hyü mil ē ā′ shən) shame (p. 185)

Hypnotic (hip not′ ik) causing a dreamlike state (p. 300)

Hysterical (hi ster′ ə kəl) not able to stop crying (p. 182)

Hysterically (hi ster′ ə klē) in wild excitement (p. 259)

I

Idealism (ī dē′ ə liz əm) a belief in the highest standards (p. 219)

Illumination (il lü mə nā′ shən) a light (p. 301)

Illusion (i lü′ zhən) an unreal vision (p. 67); something that appears different from what it is (p. 329)

Illustrate (il′ ə strāt) to show; to picture (p. 318)

Illustrated (il′ ə strāt ed) made clear (p. 347)

Immaculate (i mak′ yə lit) very clean (p. 329)

Immortal (i môr′ tl) living forever; free from death (p. 39); free from death (p. 443)

Impart (im pärt′) to tell; to make known (p. 349)

Impartial (im pär′ shəl) fair (p. 219)

Impeach (im pēch′) to accuse (p. 458)

Imperious (im pir′ ē əs) bossy (p. 222)

Imperturbable (im pər tėr′ bə bəl) calm, steady, not easily excited (p. 23)

Implored (im plôrd′) begged (p. 284)

Impostor (im pos′ tər) one who pretends to be someone else (p. 22)

Impresario (im prə sär′ ē ō) someone who manages or directs a show (p. 341)

Impressive (im pres′ iv) able to fix firmly in the mind (p. 148); grand (p. 251)

Improbable (im prob′ ə bəl) not likely to happen (p. 367)

Inadequate (in ad′ ə kwit) unable to do what is required (p. 332)

Inanimate (in an′ ə mit) nonliving, unmoving (p. 312)

Inaudible (in ȯ′ də bəl) not loud enough to be heard (p. 258)

Inauspicious (in ȯ spish′ əs) unlucky (p. 451)

Incorruptible (in kə rup′ tə bəl) honorable (p. 219)

Incredible (in kred′ ə bəl) hard to believe (p. 314)

Incredibly (in kred′ ə blē) unbelievably (p. 304)

Incredulous (in krej′ ə ləs) not believing (p. 341)

Indebted (in det′ id) owing a favor (p. 329)

Indictment (in dīt′ mənt) finding fault (p. 469)

Indifference (in dif′ ər əns) a lack of concern (p. 470)

Indifferent (in dif′ ər ənt) uncaring, uninterested (p. 151)

Inert (in ėrt′) unmoving (p. 304)

Inertia (in ėr′ shə) not able to move (p. 359)

Inevitable (in ev′ ə tə bəl) impossible to avoid (p. 219)

Inexorable (in ek′ sər ə bəl) unable to be changed (p. 449)

Infamous (in′ fə məs) well known because of bad or disagreeable things (p. 146)

Infatuated (in fach′ ü ā tid) foolishly in love (p. 181)

Infectious (in fek′ shəs) catching (p. 446)

Inferior (in fir′ ē ər) second-rate (p. 274)

Infernal (in fėr′ nl) tiresome, unpleasant (p. 146)

Infirm (in fėrm′) not solid or stable (p. 357)

Inflection (in flek′ shən) pronunciation (p. 478)

Infuriated (in fyu̇r′ ē āt ed) very angry (p. 306)

Initiative (i nish′ ə tiv) drive; energy (p. 359)

Inquiries (in kwī′ rēs) requests for information (p. 147)

Inquisitive (in kwiz′ ə tiv) curious (p. 300)

Insignificant (in sig nif′ ə kənt) unimportant (p. 304)

Insistence (in sis′ təns) demand (p. 368)

Inspiration (in spə rā′ shən) encouragement (p. 488)

Installment (in stȯl′ mənt) one part (p. 253)

Institution (in stə tü′ shən) an important custom (p. 221)

Insulated (in′ sə lāt ed) protected from (p. 355)

Insurance (in shu̇r′ əns) coverage against loss (p. 481)

Intact (in takt′) whole, together (p. 203)

Intellectual (in tə lek′ chü əl) brainy (p. 478)

Intensity (in ten′ sə tē) strength (p. 224)

Intention (in ten′ shən) a plan (p. 185)

Intercept (in tər sept′) to catch (p. 250)

Intercepted (in tər sept′ ed) caught, blocked, cut off (p. 272)

Interminable (in tėr′ mə nə bəl) endless (p. 148)

Interminably (in tėr′ mə nə blē) without end (p. 236)

a	hat	e	let	ī	ice	ȯ	order	u̇	put	sh	she		a	in about
ā	age	ē	equal	o	hot	oi	oil	ü	rule	th	thin	ə	e	in taken
ä	far	ėr	term	ō	open	ou	out	ch	child	ᴛʜ	then		i	in pencil
â	care	i	it	ȯ	saw	u	cup	ng	long	zh	measure		o	in lemon
													u	in circus

Intermittently (in tər mit′ nt lē) off and on (p. 358)

Internal (in tėr′ nl) inside; unspoken (p. 318)

Intersect (in tər sekt′) meet (p. 177)

Invest (in vest′) to put money in something, hoping for a profit (pp. 327, 481)

Investment (in vest′ mənt) money put into something, in hopes of a profit (p. 476)

Ironically (ī ron′ ik lē) unlike what one would expect (pp. 276, 331)

Irregular (i reg′ yə lər) uneven (pp. 160, 300)

Irreverent (i rev′ ər ənt) not offering the proper respect (p. 331)

Irritably (ir′ ə tə blē) in an annoyed way (p. 483)

J

Jazz (jaz) popular dance music with strong rhythms (pp. 340, 409)

Jeered (jird) made fun of (p. 15)

Jovial (jō′ vē əl) happy; friendly (p. 234)

Jubilant (jü′ bə lənt) joyful (p. 41)

K

Kindred (kin′ drid) relatives (p. 443)

Kinky (king′ kē) tightly curled (p. 164)

Kinsman (kinz′ mən) a relative (p. 450)

Knells (nels) rings for a death, funeral, or disaster (p. 398)

L

Lamentable (la mən′ tə bəl) causing sorrow (p. 454)

Landmarks (land′ märks) objects that show location (pp. 275, 357)

Lapse (laps) to end (p. 236)

Latter (lat′ ər) toward the end (p. 123)

Lavish (lav′ ish) very free in giving (p. 277)

Lavished (lav′ isht) given a great deal of (p. 38)

Leased (lēst) rented (p. 275)

Ledger (lej′ ər) an account book (p. 485)

Lessened (les′ nd) taken away (p. 316)

Lethal (lē′ thəl) deadly (p. 72)

Liability (lī ə bil′ ə tē) responsibility (p. 258)

Likeness (līk′ nis) a copy or picture (p. 65)

Lilting (lilt′ ing) musical (p. 182)

Limber (lim′ bər) moving easily (p. 149)

Limousine (lim′ ə zēn) a large, fancy car (p. 161)

Linger (ling′ ger) stay (p. 181)

Liquor (lik′ ər) drinks containing alcohol (p. 481)

Literally (lit′ ər ə lē) actually, really (p. 179)

Loathsome (lōŦH′ səm) hateful (p. 445)

Lobes (lōbs) rounded parts that stick out or down (p. 39)

Logic (loj′ ik) reasoning (p. 185)

Lottery (lot′ ər ē) a game of chance (p. 233)

Lullaby (lul′ ə bī) a bedtime song (p. 268)

Luminous (lü′ mə nəs) filled with light (p. 349)

Lure (lůr) to attract (p. 301)

Luring (lůr′ ing) attracting (p. 424)

Lye (lī) a strong solution used in making soap (p. 164)

M

Maligned (mə līnd′) unfairly accused (p. 253)

Maneuvering (mə nü′ vər ing) planning a movement to gain you something (p. 180)

Marshal (mär′ shəl) to gather (p. 358)

Martyrs (mär′ tərs) people who die for a cause or a religious belief (p. 177)

Masculine (mas′ kyə lin) male (p. 473)

Material (mə tir′ ē əl) physical, real (p. 317)

Maximum (mak′ sə məm) the most (p. 470)

Mazes (māz′ es) webs, puzzles (p. 226)

Meager (mē′ gər) thin (p. 443)

Meandered (mē an′ dərd) followed a winding course (p. 357)

Melancholy (mel′ ən kol ē) sad (pp. 40, 397)

Mere (mir) nothing more than (p. 39)

Merited (mer′ it ed) deserved (p. 220)

Millionaires (mil yə nârz′) very rich people (p. 330)

Millmen (mil′ men) people who work in a mill where wood is cut (p. 88)

Mimicking (mim′ ik ing) imitating (p. 474)

Miraculously (mə rak′ yə las lē) magically (p. 342)

Miscalculated (mis kal′ kyə lāt ed) judged or figured out incorrectly (p. 71)

Misery (miz′ ər ē) suffering (pp. 262, 444)

Moiety (mȯi′ ə tē) half (p. 223)

Molested (mə lest′ ed) bothered (p. 121)

Molten (mōlt′ n) heated until liquid (p. 395)

Monotone (mon′ ə tōn) sameness; on one note (p. 398)

Monotonous (mə not′n əs) boring, unchanging (p. 147)

Monstrosities (mon stros′ ə tēs) things that are huge and ugly (p. 186)

Morality (mə ral′ ə tē) a system of good behavior (p. 181)

Morsel (môr′ səl) a small piece (pp. 283, 449)

Multiple candelabra (mul′ tə pəl kan dl ä′ brə) a many-branched candlestick (p. 500)

Multitude (mul′ tə tüd) crowd (p. 226)

Muscular (mus′ kyə lər) strongly built (p. 183)

Musing (myüz′ ing) thinking (p. 500)

Muted (myüt′ ed) quieted, softened (p. 177)

Mutilated (myü′ tl āt ed) damaged, destroyed (p. 260)

Mutual (myü′ chü əl) shared (p. 474)

N

Narrative (nar′ ə tiv) a story (p. 147)

Negotiating (ni gō′ shē āt ing) managing (p. 357)

Neurotic (nu̇ rot′ ik) a person with disturbed feelings and thoughts (p. 491)

Nocturnal (nok tėr′ nl) nighttime (p. 301)

Nonexistent (non ig zis′ tənt) not there (p. 339)

Notorious (nō tôr′ ē əs) well known, especially for something bad (pp. 121, 274)

Nuns (nuns) women belonging to a religious order (p. 454)

Nurturing (nėr′ chər ing) feeding or caring for (p. 312)

O

Obligations (ob lə gā′ shəns) feelings of gratitude (p. 147)

Obscure (əb skyu̇r′) unclear (p. 301)

Obstacles (ob′ stə kəls) things that get in the way (p. 118)

Occurrences (ə kėr′ əns es) happenings or events (p. 117)

Ogres (o′ gərz) monsters (p. 55)

a	hat	e	let	ī	ice	ȯ	order	u̇	put	sh	she	ə	a	in about
ā	age	ē	equal	o	hot	oi	oil	ü	rule	th	thin		e	in taken
ä	far	ėr	term	ō	open	ou	out	ch	child	ᴙ	then		i	in pencil
â	care	i	it	ȯ	saw	u	cup	ng	long	zh	measure		o	in lemon
													u	in circus

Oppress (ə pres′) to wrong someone; to abuse one's power over someone (p. 165)

Oppression (ə presh′ ən) unjust or cruel (p. 445); unjust treatment (p. 473)

Oppressive (ə pres′ iv) heavy (p. 261)

Optimism (op′ tə miz əm) hopefulness (p. 369)

Ordeal (ôr dēl′) a terrible experience (pp. 43, 202)

Oriented (ôr′ ē ent id) turned toward (p. 469)

Overcame (ō vər kām′) won against or got the better of (p. 118)

Overcome (ō vər kum′) to win or get the better of (p. 316); to make weak or helpless (p. 328)

Overpopulated (ō′ vər pop′ yə lāt ed) very crowded (p. 180)

Overwhelming (ō vər hwel′ ming) taking over one's thoughts or feelings (p. 277); too much (p. 356)

Owlet (ou′ lit) a baby owl (p. 268)

P

Pall (pȯl) a cloth that covers a coffin (p. 385)

Palpitating (pal′ pə tāt ing) beating rapidly and strongly (p. 397)

Pang (pang) a sharp pain (p. 63)

Paralyzed (par′ ə līzd) unable to move (p. 205)

Paraphernalia (par ə fər nā′ lyə) equipment (p. 234)

Parasites (par′ ə sīts) animals that depend on others for their life, giving nothing in return (p. 303)

Parched (pärcht) dried out (p. 269)

Paring (pâr ing) peeling (p. 271)

Partially (pär′ shə lē) partly (p. 339)

Participant (pär tis′ ə pənt) one who takes part in (p. 315)

Passion (pash′ ən) strong feeling (p. 182); very strong feelings (p. 226)

Passionately (pash′ ə nit lē) with great feeling (p. 477)

Penury (pen′ yər ē) poverty (p. 444)

Perceived (pər sēvd′) understood (p. 224)

Perception (pər sep′ shən) an understanding (p. 224)

Perfunctory (pər fungk′ tər ē) done merely out of duty (p. 236)

Permeate (pėr′ mē āt) to enter; to soak into (p. 314)

Permeated (pėr′ mē āt ed) entered (p. 478)

Perseverance (pėr sə vir′ əns) sticking to a purpose (p. 366)

Persisted (pər sist′ ed) continued (p. 251)

Peruse (pə rüz′) to look at (p. 450)

Pestilence (pes′ tl əns) disease (p. 446)

Petulantly (pech′ ə lənt lē) in a grouchy, grumpy way (p. 239)

Phenomenal (fə nom′ ə nəl) amazing (p. 331)

Pigmentation (pig mən tā′ shən) color (p. 282)

Piteous (pit′ ē əs) miserable; sad (p. 456)

Pitiful (pit′ i fəl) something to be sorry for (p. 456)

Pitifully (pit′ i fəl lē) causing sorrow (p. 72)

Placid (plas′ id) calm; peaceful (pp. 306, 349)

Placidly (plas′ id lē) calmly (p. 249)

Plagues (plāgs) diseases (p. 250)

Poised (poizd) held without moving (p. 249)

Pomegranate (pom′ ə gran it) a reddish-gold fruit with many seeds (p. 40)

Ponderous (pon′ dər əs) heavy (p. 354)

Portals (pôr′ tls) doors (p. 223)

Possibility (pos ə bil′ ə tē) chance (p. 204)

Potion (pō′ shən) a drink with special powers (p. 459)

Preceded (prē sēd' ed) came before
(pp. 221, 235)

Precise (pri sīs') correct; exact (p. 482)

Precisely (pri sīs' lē) correctly (p. 240)

Precision (pri sizh' ən) correctness; exactly or
sharply stated (p. 493)

Predicament (pri dik' ə mənt) a problem
(p. 342)

Preoccupied (prē ok' yə pīd) thinking of
something else (p. 256)

Prescribed (pri skrībd') a rule to be followed
(p. 316)

Presumptuous (pri zump' chü əs) too bold
(p. 251)

Probable (prob' ə bəl) likely (p. 223)

Procured (prə kyûrd') gotten or obtained
(p. 220)

Profound (prə found') deep (pp. 177, 493)

Profoundly (prə found' lē) strongly (p. 419)

Profusely (prə fyüs' lē) generously; in large
amounts (p. 233)

Progressiveness (prə gres' iv nəs) the state of
being advanced, or accepting of new ideas
(p. 218)

Prolific (prə lif' ik) producing many young
(p. 64)

Propelling (prə pel' ling) pushing forward
(p. 276)

Prophetic (prə fet' ik) able to tell the future
(p. 339)

Prophets (prof' its) people who see the future
(p. 481)

Proposition (prop ə zish' ən) a plan (p. 476)

Prosaic (prō zā' ik) everyday (p. 255)

Provocative (prə vok' ə tiv) intended to stir up,
anger, or excite (p. 22)

Provoke (prə vōk') to cause someone to take
action (p. 450)

Provoked (prə vōkt') caused someone to take
action (p. 249)

Prudence (prüd' ns) wisdom; common sense
(p. 331)

Pry (prī) to snoop; to spy (p. 448)

Punctuating (pungk' chü āt ing) marking
regularly (p. 280)

Pungent (pun' jənt) sharp (p. 317)

Purge (pėrj) to free from blame (p. 458)

Pursue (pər sü') seek (p. 368)

Pursued (pər süd') chased (pp. 122, 253)

Pursuit (pər süt') the act of seeking (p. 367)

Q

Quaking (kwāk' ing) shaking, trembling
(p. 259)

Quarantine (kwôr' ən tēn) to keep separate
(p. 275)

Quell (kwel) to quiet down or stop (p. 119)

Quest (kwest) a search for something (p. 42)

R

Radiance (rā' dē əns) glowing light (p. 67)

Radiant (rā' dē ənt) glowing (p. 224)

Radical (rad' ə kəl) extreme (p. 249)

Rampant (ram' pənt) widespread (p. 274)

Rapture (rap' chər) great happiness (p. 396)

Rapturous (rap' chər əs) extremely happy
(p. 226)

a	hat	e	let	ī	ice	ô	order	ù	put	sh	she		a	in about
ā	age	ē	equal	o	hot	oi	oil	ü	rule	th	thin	ə	e	in taken
ä	far	ėr	term	ō	open	ou	out	ch	child	ᴛʜ	then		i	in pencil
â	care	i	it	ȯ	saw	u	cup	ng	long	zh	measure		o	in lemon
													u	in circus

Rarity (rârʹ ə tē) something not usually seen (p. 71)

Raucous (rȯʹ kəs) rough; loud (p. 490)

Reaction (rē akʹ shən) a response (pp. 132, 185)

Recalled (ri kȯldʹ) remembered (p. 57)

Recital (ri sīʹ tl) a performance of music (p. 236)

Recoiled (ri koildʹ) drew back in horror (p. 359)

Recollect (rek ə lektʹ) to remember (pp. 93, 148)

Recompose (rē kəm pōsʹ) restore calmness (p. 164)

Refrain (ri frānʹ) repeated words (pp. 178, 475)

Refreshing (ri freshʹ ing) giving back strength or life (p. 67)

Reign (rān) rule (p. 446)

Rejection (ri jekʹ shən) a refusal to accept or hear (p. 181)

Relentless (ri lentʹ lis) without pity (p. 222)

Relentlessly (ri lentʹ lis lē) without softening or letting up (p. 74)

Reluctantly (ri lukʹ tənt lē) without wanting to (pp. 41, 234)

Remembrances (ri memʹ brəns es) memories (p. 426)

Reminiscence (rem ə nisʹ ns) something remembered, memory (p. 146)

Remnants (remʹ nənts) traces (p. 444)

Repetition (rep ə tishʹ ən) repeating (p. 477)

Replenish (ri plenʹ ish) to build up again (p. 327)

Repository (ri pozʹ ə tôr ē) place for safekeeping (p. 327)

Reprimands (repʹ rə mands) scoldings (p. 233)

Residences (rezʹ ə dəns es) places to live in (p. 185)

Resignation (rez ig nāʹ shən) accepting with grace (p. 41)

Resinous (rezʹ n əs) relating to sticky matter that flows from some trees (p. 347)

Resolute (rezʹ ə lüt) determined, firm (p. 396)

Respectable (ri spekʹ tə bəl) decent; proper; fit to be seen (p. 92); decent; proper (p. 485)

Restraint (ri strāntʹ) control (p. 187)

Retain (riʹ tān) keep (p. 320)

Retribution (ret rə byüʹ shən) revenge; return for wrongdoing (p. 221); return for wrongdoing (p. 368)

Revealed (ri vēldʹ) showed (p. 301)

Reverberated (ri vėrʹ bə rāt ed) echoed (p. 262)

Reverie (revʹ ər ē) a daydream (p. 320)

Revival (ri vīʹ vəl) a renewed interest in (p. 319)

Rhapsodies (rapʹ sə dēs) joyful songs (p. 219)

Righteous (rīʹ chəs) good; right (p. 452)

Rigor (rigʹ ər) strictness (p. 460)

Riots (rīʹ əts) public disorder (p. 409)

Rite (rīt) a ceremony (p. 448)

Ritual (richʹ ü əl) the way a thing is regularly done (p. 235)

Rivalry (rīʹ vəl rē) a struggle to win (p. 300)

S

Sanatorium (san ə tôrʹ ē əm) a hospital for treating certain illnesses (p. 274)

Satchel (sachʹ əl) a small suitcase (p. 332)

Savor (sāʹ vər) special flavor or smell (p. 488)

Scalding (skȯldʹ ing) burning (p. 164)

Scavenged (skavʹ ənjd) searched (p. 286)

Scoured (skourd) searched thoroughly (p. 40)

Scourge (skėrj) a punishment (p. 460)

Scriptures (skripʹ chərz) Bible verses (p. 488)

Security (si kyu̇rʹ ə tē) safety (p. 360)

Self-righteously (self rīʹ chəs lē) convinced of one's own goodness (p. 485)

Sensitivity (sen sə tiv′ ə tē) able to be easily hurt (p. 312)

Serenely (sə rēn′ lē) calmly; not at all upset (p. 148)

Sheath (shēth) a cover or case (p. 455)

Sheathed (shēᴛʜd) covered with something that protects (p. 422)

Shriveled (shriv′ əld) dried into wrinkles (p. 284)

Shun (shun) to avoid (p. 394)

Siege (sēj) a serious attack (p. 459)

Singed (sinjd) burned (p. 268)

Sinister (sin′ ə stər) evil (p. 257)

Skirmishes (skėr′ mish es) small battles (p. 119)

Slurring (slėr′ ring) leaving out or blurring sounds (p. 359); sliding together (p. 478)

Smudged (smujd) smeared (p. 186)

Snobbish (snob′ ish) stuck-up (p. 491)

Solace (sol′ is) comfort (p. 187)

Solicitation (sə lis i tā′ shən) an invitation (p. 124)

Solicitude (sə lis′ ə tüd) concern (p. 342)

Somber (som′ bər) grave, serious (p. 342)

Soughing (sou′ ing) sighing (p. 348)

Sovereign (sov′ rən) a king (p. 457)

Squabbles (skwäb′ əls) arguments or quarrels (p. 65)

Stealthy (stel′ thē) secretive (p. 261)

Steeple (stē′ pəl) a church tower (p. 397)

Sternum (stėr′ nəm) the breastbone (p. 340)

Stimuli (stim′ yə lī) something that makes you active (p. 355)

Stipulated (stip′ yə lāt ed) demanded as a condition of agreement (p. 55)

Strangled (strang′ gəld) choked (p. 269)

Strew (strü) to scatter widely (p. 448)

Stronghold (strȯng′ hōld) a protected place, safe from enemies (p. 55)

Stupendously (stü pen′ dəs lē) amazingly (p. 355)

Stupor (stü′ pər) a daze (p. 469)

Subdued (səb düd′) muffled (p. 259)

Subordinate (sə bôrd′ n it) lower class (p. 221)

Substantial (səb stan′ shəl) important (p. 369)

Suede (swād) leather with a soft, velvety surface (p. 195)

Suffocation (suf ə kā′ shən) not being able to breathe (p. 358)

Sullen (sul′ ən) bad-tempered (p. 473)

Sultry (sul′ trē) sexy (p. 340)

Supplemental (sup lə men′ tl) additional, extra (p. 358)

Surge (sėrj) a rush or flow (p. 356)

Survive (sər vīv′) to go on living (pp. 38, 43, 313, 420)

Suspicion (sə spish′ ən) hint, trace (p. 148); mistrust; doubt (p. 456)

Swathed (swäᴛʜd) wrapped (p. 423)

Swerved (swėrvd) turned sharply (p. 71)

Symmetry (sim′ ə trē) balance (p. 281)

Symptoms (simp′ təms) signs of disease (p. 204)

a	hat	e	let	ī	ice	ȯ	order	u̇	put	sh	she		a	in about
ā	age	ē	equal	o	hot	oi	oil	ü	rule	th	thin	ə {	e	in taken
ä	far	ėr	term	ō	open	ou	out	ch	child	ᴛʜ	then		i	in pencil
â	care	i	it	ȯ	saw	u	cup	ng	long	zh	measure		o	in lemon
													u	in circus

T

Tact (takt) skill and grace in dealing with others (p. 349)

Tedious (tē′ dē əs) tiring; boring (p. 458)

Tempest (tem′ pist) a bad storm (p. 358)

Temptation (temp tā′ shən) an urge to do something (pp. 163, 179)

Tenement (ten′ ə mənt) a city apartment for poor families that is usually unclean, unsafe, uncomfortable (p. 177)

Tentatively (ten′ tə tiv lē) unsurely (p. 486)

Terse (tėrs) using few words (p. 274)

Thwarted (thwârt′ ed) blocked or stopped (p. 454)

Tiered (tird) arranged in rows, one above the other (p. 406)

Tolerant (tol′ ər ənt) willing to let people do what they wish (p. 367)

Torrent (tôr′ ənt) a flood (p. 249)

Tradition (trə dish′ ən) a custom (p. 235)

Tragedies (traj′ ə dēz) misfortunes, suffering (p. 313)

Tragic (traj′ ik) sad, unfortunate (p. 315)

Trance (trans) a condition in which one can't seem to move (p. 187)

Tranquil (trang′ kwəl) calm, peaceful (p. 147)

Transcendent (tran sen′ dənt) far beyond the usual (p. 148)

Transformation (tran sfər mā′ shən) a change (p. 315)

Transformed (tran sfôrmd′) greatly changed (pp. 306, 478)

Transition (tran zish′ ən) to change or shift (p. 500)

Transmitted (tran smit′ ted) sent (p. 224)

Tribunal (trī byü′ nl) a court of justice (p. 221)

Trilled (trild) sang (p. 347)

Tuition (tü ish′ ən) payment for schooling (p. 492)

Tycoon (tī kün′) a rich business person (p. 328)

Typhoon (tī fün′) a powerful storm (p. 332)

Tyrant (tī′ rənt) an absolute ruler (p. 493)

U

Unalienable (un ā′ lyə nə bəl) cannot be taken away (p. 367)

Unhallowed (un hal′ ōd) unholy (p. 449)

Unison (yü′ nə sən) all together (p. 479)

Unpredictability (un pri dik tə bil′ ə tē) impossible to tell in advance (p. 286)

Unsavory (un sā′ vər ē) unpleasant; bad-tasting (p. 452)

Unsubstantial (un səb stan′ shəl) not physical, of the spirit (p. 451)

Unsurpassed (un sər past′) best; highest (p. 222)

Untimely (un tīm′ lē) before it should happen (p. 458)

Untrammeled (un tram′ əld) not bound; free (p. 218)

Unwarranted (un wôr′ ən tid) uncalled-for (p. 354)

Utter (ut′ ər) total; complete (pp. 185, 477)

Uttered (ut′ ərd) said (p. 285)

V

Vagabond (vag′ ə bond) wandering (p. 154)

Venerable (ven′ ər ə bəl) aged; respected (p. 316)

Vengeance (ven′ jəns) harm done in return for a wrong (p. 449); force (p. 478)

Venison (ven′ ə sən) deer meat (p. 330)

Verify (ver′ ə fī) to prove that something is true (p. 330)

Veritable (ver′ ə tə bəl) true (p. 303)

Version (vėr′ zhən) a form or type (pp. 68, 187)

Vigilant (vij′ ə lənt) watchful (p. 181)

Vigorously (vig′ ər əs lē) with energy (p. 477)

Vindicated (vin′ də kāt id) forgiven (p. 473)

Violent (vī′ ə lənt) furious (p. 475)

Violently (vī′ ə lənt lē) done with strong, rough force (pp. 183, 444)

Viragoes (vi rä′ gos) loud, harsh-sounding women (p. 177)

Virtue (vėr′ chü) goodness (p. 181)

Virtues (vėr′ chüs) good qualities (p. 255)

Voluminously (və lü′ mə nəs lē) hugely (p. 396)

W

Wanes (wānz) fades (p. 319)

Wanton (wän′ tən) without mercy (p. 424)

Warped (wôrpt) curved; out of focus (p. 186)

Wary (wâr ē′) careful or cautious (p. 275)

Waver (wā′ vər) to back down (p. 222)

Wavering (wā′ vər ing) fluttering (p. 301)

Welts (welts) lumps (p. 315)

Wended (wend′ ed) traveled (p. 220)

Whinnied (win′ ēd) the sound a horse makes (p. 57)

Wielded (wēld′ ed) held, used (p. 280)

Wistful (wist′ fəl) sad (p. 65)

Wistfully (wist′ fəl lē) sadly (p. 257)

Wretch (rech) a miserable creature (p. 444)

Writhing (riŦH′ ing) wiggling (p. 42)

Y

Yoke (yōk) a wooden bar or frame that joins two oxen (p. 88)

a	hat	e	let	ī	ice	ȯ	order	u̇	put	sh	she	ə	a in about
ā	age	ē	equal	o	hot	oi	oil	ü	rule	th	thin		e in taken
ä	far	ėr	term	ō	open	ou	out	ch	child	ŦH	then		i in pencil
â	care	i	it	ȯ	saw	u	cup	ng	long	zh	measure		o in lemon
													u in circus

Index of Authors and Titles

Index of Fine Art

Index

Acknowledgments

Pages 20–24: "The Singing Turtle" from *The Singing Turtle and Other Tales from Haiti* by Philippe Thoby-Marcelin and Pierre Marcelin, translated by Eva Thoby-Marcelin, pictures by George Ford. Translation copyright © 1971 by Farrar, Straus & Giroux, Inc. Reprinted by permission of Farrar, Straus and Giroux, LLC.

Pages 49–50: "The Beginning and the End of the World" from *Indian Legends of the Pacific Northwest* by Ella E. Clark. Copyright 1953 by University of California Press. Reproduced with permission of University of California Press in the format Textbook via Copyright Clearance Center.

Pages 55–57: "Loki and the Master Builder" adapted from *The Prose Edda of Snorri Sturluson: Tales from Norse Mythology* (Paper) by Snorri Sturluson/Jean I. Youngs. Copyright 1964 by University of California Press. Reproduced with permission of University of California Press in the format Textbook via Copyright Clearance Center.

Pages 62–74: "The Moon Spirit and Coyote Woman" (Why coyotes howl at the moon) by Clive Grace. Reprinted by permission.

Pages 88–96: "Babe, the Blue Ox" excerpt from *Paul Bunyan,* copyright 1924 and renewed 1952 by Esther Shephard, reprinted by permission of Harcourt, Inc.

Pages 102–106: from "Feboldson, Western Scientist" from *Tall Tale America* by Walter Blair. Reprinted by permission of The University of Chicago Press.

Pages 130–133: "The Phantom Hitchhiker" from *The Headless Roommate and Other Tales of Terror* by Daniel Cohen. Copyright © 1980 by Daniel Cohen. Reprinted by permission of the author and Henry Morrison, Inc., his agents.

Pages 160–171: "Everyday Use" from *In Love & Trouble: Stories of Black Women,* copyright © 1973 by Alice Walker, reprinted by permission of Harcourt, Inc.

Pages 177–187: American History" from *The Latin Deli: Prose and Poetry* by Judith Ortiz-Cofer, 1972. Reprinted by permission of The University of Georgia Press.

Pages 193–197: "Thank You, M'am" from *Short Stories* by Langston Hughes. Copyright © 1996 by Ramona Bass and Arnold Rampersad. Reprinted by permission of Hill and Wang, a division of Farrar, Straus and Giroux, LLC.

Pages 202–205: "Unfinished Message" from *The Chauvinist and Other Stories* by Toshio Mori, 1979. Reprinted by permission of the Asian American Studies Center, UCLA.

Pages 233–243: "The Lottery" from *The Lottery* by Shirley Jackson. Copyright © 1948, 1949 by Shirley Jackson. Copyright renewed 1976, 1977 by Laurence Hyman, Barry Hyman, Mrs. Sarah Webster and Mrs. Joanne Schnurer. Reprinted by permission of Farrar, Straus and Giroux, LLC.

Pages 268–286: "Red Moccasins" from *The Grass Dancer,* by Susan Power, copyright © 1994 by Susan Power. Used by permission of G. P. Putman's Sons, a division of Penguin Group (USA) Inc.

Pages 300–306: from *Kon-Tiki* by Thor Heyerdahl, translated by F. H. Lyon.

Pages 312–320: from "A Celebration of Grandfathers" by Rudolfo A. Anaya. Copyright © 1983 by Rulolfo Anaya. First published in *New Mexico Magazine,* March 1983. Reprinted by permission of Susan Bergholz Literary Agency, New York. All rights reserved.

Pages 326–333: "Of Dry Goods and Black Bow Ties" by Yoshiko Uchida. Courtesy of the Bancroft Library, University of California, Berkeley.

Pages 339–342: from *Gather Together in My Name* by Maya Angelou. Copyright © 1974 by Maya Angelou. Reproduced by permission of The Helen Brann Agency, Inc.

Pages 354–360: from *Into Thin Air* by Jon Krakauer, copyright © 1997 by Jon Krakauer. Used by permission of Villard Books, a division of Random House, Inc. and John A. Ware Literary Agency, agent for the author.

Pages 366–369: from Keynote Address by Barack Obama to the Democratic Convention on July 27, 2004 from *Dreams from My Father* by Barack Obama, copyright © 1995, 2004 by Barack Obama. Used by permission of Three Rivers Press, a division of Random House, Inc.

Page 386: "Ballad of Birmingham" by Dudley Randall from *Poem Counter Poem.* Represented by permission of the Dudley Randall Estate.

Page 393: "Blesséd Lord, what it is to be young" from *One Day at a Time* by David McCord. Copyright © 1965, 1966 by David McCord. By permission of Little, Brown and Co., Inc. All rights reserved. To purchase this book, please call 1.800.759.0190.

Page 393: "We Real Cool" from *The World of Gwendolyn Brooks* by Gwendolyn Brooks, 1959. Reprinted by consent of Brooks Permissions.

Page 405: "Dreams" from *The Collected Poems of Langston Hughes* by Langston Hughes, copyright © 1994 by The Estate of Langston Hughes. Used by permission of Alfred A. Knopf, a division of Random House, Inc.

Pages 406–407: "Oranges" from *New and Selected Poems* by Gary Soto. © 1995 by Gary Soto. Used with permission of Chronicle Books LLC, San Francisco. Visit ChronicleBooks.com.

Page 408: "flock" by Lance Henson. Copyright by Lance Henson. Used by permission of Lance Henson.

Page 408: "The Red Wheelbarrow" by William Carlos Williams, from *Collected Poems: 1909-1939, Volume I,* copyright © 1938 by New Directions Publishing Corp. Reprinted by permission of New Directions Publishing Corp.

Page 409: "Haiku" by Etheridge Knight from *Poems from Prison,* 1969. Reprinted by permission of Broadside Press.

Page 410: "Gathering" copyright 2000 by Natasha Trethewey. Reprinted from *Domestic Work* with the permission of Graywolf Press, Saint Paul, Minnesota.

Page 417: "The Poet" from *The Lives of the Heart* by Jane Hirshfield. Copyright © 1997 by Jane Hirshfield. Reprinted by permission of HarperCollins Publishers.

Page 419: "In a Farmhouse" by Luis Omar Salinas from *From the Barrio: A Chicano Anthology* by Luis Omar Salinas and Lillian Faderman, 1973. Reprinted by permission of the author.

Page 420: Lucille Clifton, "this morning" from *Good Woman: Poems and a Memoir 1969–1980.* Copyright © 1987 by Lucille Clifton. Used with permission of BOA Editions, www.BOAEditions.org.

Page 421: "My Life Story" by Lan Nguyen.

Pages 422–423: "A Headstrong Boy" by Gu Cheng, translated by Donald Finkel from *A Splintered Mirror: Chinese Poetry from the Democracy Movement* translated by Donald Finkel. Translation copyright © 1991 by Donald Finkel. Reprinted by permission of North Point Press, a division of Farrar, Straus and Giroux, LLC.

Pages 424–425: "Chicago" from *Chicago Poems* by Carl Sandburg, copyright 1916 by Holt, Rinehart and Winston and renewed 1944 by Carl Sandburg, reprinted by permission of Harcourt, Inc.

Page 426: "Nikki-Rosa" from *Black Feeling, Black Talk, Black Judgment* by Nikki Giovanni. Copyright © 1968, 1970 by Nikki Giovanni. Reprinted by permission of HarperCollins Publishers, William Morrow.

Page 467: from "Dreams Deferred" from *The Collected Poems of Langston Hughes* by Langston Hughes, copyright © 1994 by The Estate of Langston Hughes. Used by permission of Alfred A. Knopf, a division of Random House, Inc.

Pages 467–494: from *A Raisin in the Sun* by Lorraine Hansberry, copyright © 1958 by Robert Nemiroff, as an unpublished work. Copyright © 1959, 1966, 1984 by Robert Nemiroff. Used by permission of Random House, Inc.

Pages 500–503: "Writer's Realm" by Anne Jarrell-France. Reprinted by permission of the author.

Photo Credits

Cover, © PunchStock; page viii middle, © Andres Rodriguez/Shutterstock; bottom, © Anna Chelnokova/Shutterstock; page xvi top, © PhotoDisc Volumes Education 2 41307 © Copyright 1999 PhotoDisc, Inc.; bottom, © Blend Images, LLC, AR052605400; page xviii, © Images.com/Corbis; page 3, © Bettmann/Corbis; page 4, Judy King; page 6, © Diana Ong/SuperStock; page 7, ©Newberry Library/SuperStock; page 8, © Images.com/Corbis; page 9, © Christie's Images/SuperStock © D. R. Rufino Tamayo/Herederos/México/2006, Fundación Olga y Rufino Tamayo, A. C.; page 12, The Granger Collection, New York; pages 14 and 15, Inese Jansons; page 18, courtesy of Farrar, Straus & Giroux; pages 21 and 24, George Crespo; pages 32 and 35, The Granger Collection, New York; page 36, Judy King; page 39, © Gianni Dagli Orti/Corbis; page 41, Tate Gallery, London/Art Resource, NY; page 42, Scala/Art Resource, NY; page 47, Judy King; page 50, © Christie's Images/SuperStock; pages 53 and 55, Judy King; pages 56, Shana Greger; page 60, courtesy of Clive Grace; pages 64, 69, and 74, George Crespo; page 82, Dave Fisher, John Edwards Illustration; page 85, The Granger Collection, New York; page 86, San Jose State University, Special Collections; pages 89, 92–93, and 95, Teresa Flavin; page 100, © Patricia Evans, courtesy University of Chicago; pages 104–105, Hilber Nelson; page 109, © Corbis; page 112, Mike Benny; page 115, © Lake County Museum/Corbis; pages 118 and 120, © Bettmann/Corbis; pages 122 and 123, The Granger Collection, New York; page 128, © Jin Justin/Corbis/Sygma; page 131, © Macduff Everton/Corbis; page 140, © T. F. Chen Cultural Center/SuperStock; page 143, The Granger Collection, New York; page 144, © Corbis; pages 147 and 153, Jeff Spackman; page 158, © Roger Ressmeyer/Corbis; page 160, The Granger Collection, New York; page 168, © Roman Soumar/Corbis; page 170, Paper Collage Artwork by Mary C. Bertoli, SNJM; page 175, © Sortino—used by permission of Judith Ortiz-Cofer; page 180, © Brooklyn Museum of Art/Corbis; page 183, © Lawrence Manning/Corbis; page 191, © Corbis; page 196, Joel Iskowitz; page 200, photo by Steven Y. Mori—used by permission; page 204, © The Mariners' Museum/Corbis; pages 212 and 215, The Granger Collection, New York; page 216, Culver Pictures; pages 220 and 225, Kees de Kiefte; page 231, © Clemens Kalischer; page 236, © Diana Ong/SuperStock; page 240, © The Barnes Foundation, Merion Station,Pennsylvania/Corbis; page 247, © Bettmann/Corbis; pages 252, 256, and 262, Jeff Spackman; page 266, © Bassouls Sophie/Corbis/Sygma; pages 269, 273, 281, and 285, Carole Katchen; page 294, © Images.com/Corbis; page 297, The Granger Collection, New York; page 298, © Bettmann/Corbis; page 302, © Brown Brothers, Sterling, PA; page 305, The Granger Collection, New York; page 310, © Miriam Berkley; pages 315 and 319, Pamela Johnson; page 324, courtesy of The Bancroft Library, University of California, Berkeley;

pages 328 and 330, National Japanese American Historical Society, used by permission; page 333, © Tina Rencelj, Shutterstock; page 337, © Jim Stratford/Black Star; page 341, © age footstock/SuperStock; page 345, © Brown Brothers, Sterling, PA; pages 347 and 349, The Granger Collection, New York; page 352, © amygdale imagery, Shutterstock; page 354, © Robert Holmes/Corbis; page 355, © Galen Rowell/Corbis; page 356, The Granger Collection, New York; page 358, © PunchStock/Corbis; page 360, © Warren Morgan/Corbis; page 364, © Nancy Kaszerman/Zuma/Corbis; page 367, © Gary Hershorn/Reuters/Corbis; page 369, © Brooks Kraft/Corbis; page 376, © Arte & Immagini srl/Corbis; page 379, © Brooklyn Museum of Art/Corbis; page 382 top, © Bettmann/Corbis; page 382 bottom, by permission of Broadside Press; page 384, © Fine Art Photographic Library/Corbis; page 385, © age footstock/SuperStock; page 386, © Bettmann/Corbis; page 390 top, courtesy of Little, Brown & Company; page 390 bottom, The Granger Collection, New York; page 391 top, © Bettmann/Corbis; page 391 bottom, © SuperStock, Inc./SuperStock; page 393, © Gabe Palmer/Corbis; page 394, The Granger Collection, New York; page 395 top, © Tony Mathews, Shutterstock; page 395 bottom, © OlgaLis, Shutterstock; page 396, © Wendy Kaveney Photography, Shutterstock; page 398, © Sharon Harding, Shutterstock; page 402 top, The Granger Collection, New York; page 402 bottom, © Corbis; page 403 top, © Oscar White/Corbis; page 403 middle, by permission of Broadside Press; page 403 lower left, used by permission; page 403 lower middle, courtesy, West End Press; page 403 lower right, © Jeff Etheridge/Graywolf Press; page 405, © Tony Campbell, Shutterstock; page 406, © Natalia Bratslavsky, Shutterstock; page 407, © Jim Jurica, Shutterstock; page 408, © Joy Fera, Shutterstock; page 410, Royalty-Free/Corbis; page 414 top, © Jerry Bauer, courtesy HarperCollins Publishers; pages 414 bottom and 415 top, © Bettmann/Corbis; page 415 middle, photograph by Jan Cobb—courtesy, HarperCollins Publishers; page 415 lower left, photo of Luis Omar Salinas is reprinted with permission from the publisher (Houston: Arte Publico Press—University of Houston) APP Archive Files; page 415 lower right, © Christopher Felver/Corbis; page 417, © Stapleton Collection/Corbis; page 418, © Geoff Delderfield, Shutterstock; pages 419 and 420, Yoshi Miyake; page 421, © Chris Lisle/Corbis; page 422, © Jack Hollingsworth/Corbis; page 425, Robert Masheris; page 426, Royalty-Free/Corbis; page 434, © Patti Mollica/SuperStock; page 437, © Bridgeman Art Library, London/SuperStock; page 438, © Bettmann/Corbis; pages 441, 452, and 455, © Paramount/Photofest; page 465, © Bettmann/Corbis; page 475, © Columbia Pictures/Photofest; page 480, 485, and 493, courtesy of The Everett Collection, Inc.; page 498, courtesy, Anne Jarrell-France; page 501, © Images.com/Corbis; page 503, © Royalty-Free/Corbis